Long Shall You Live

" Never forget, Never again! "

Mayor H...

Reviews for Long Shall You Live

A compelling account, based on fact, of a Dutch World War II prisoner of war hero, Resistance fighter, and concentration camp survivor. The author has written a colorful page-turner that will keep you engaged in this amazing journey. This story brings hope to all that have endured the sacrifices of war and have survived and flourished. This is a story for the ages and tells of the suffering, his family, and the fulfillment of his dream of immigrating with his family to the United States.

Jim Tuor, Sun City West, Arizona

This is one family's story of faith, hope, and love. Using keepsakes, familiar family stories, and her own research, the author begins by tenderly telling the story of her father's arrest and interment in the Nazi's concentration camp at Buchenwald. After five years, nearly dead from hunger and deprivation, he was present when the US soldiers liberated the camp. It was this encounter with the US soldiers that would eventually inspire Mr. van Lith to leave his Dutch homeland and move his young family to the United States.

It was hard to read about the cruelty endured by the prisoners in Buchenwald. Prior to reading this book, I could only imagine what it must have been like for them. *Long Shall You Live* brought that all to life for me. It did happen to a real person, to real people, and the survivors surely carried the effects of their imprisonment for their entire lives.

This is also an immigrant family's story. I marvel at how much the van Liths had to give up to come to America and wonder at their willingness to start all over in a strange and distant land. I ask myself if I would be willing to risk so much. This is a beautifully written story and I highly recommend it.

Michele Towne, Richland, Washington

Long Shall You Live is an inspirational story of hope and perseverance. The author gives light to often overlooked hardships of immigrants as well as gives a voice to the tragedy of the Holocaust. With a warmly welcomed realness, the author makes history personal and gives the reader insight into the lives of courageous individuals.

Shonna Hines, Richland, Washington

The Dutch have a saying: "Every house has its own cross to bear." No one grows up unscathed. What enabled our Dad to survive was also exampled for us. Our lives were built on the foundation laid down by our parents and grandparents, and interwoven with all they experienced in the old country. What was ordinary for us, looking back now, was anything but normal. A heartwarming, good read. I came away from this book with a deeper appreciation of my family roots.

Gert Helvey (author's sister), Sweet Home, Oregon

Dedication

Part One is dedicated to Ineke, Gerrie (Gert), Suuske (Sue), Treesje (Traci), and Dominicus (Dom). We navigated through so much of this extraordinary heritage together. Though it may be difficult to relive some of the sorrows, we can be proud of the triumphs Mienus and Suze achieved, and for the beautiful parents they were to each of us. Cheers to Dad and Mom!

Lang zal ze leven, lang zal ze leven, lang zal ze leven in de Gloria, in de Gloria, in de Gloria. Hieperdepiep, hoera!

Forward

Births. Deaths. Love. Loss. Illness. Recovery. It seems all of human experience is found in this book. As a first-time author, Marja Henderson shines. Her authentic voice delights as she explains the foibles of youth. It draws indignation as she reveals betrayal. It pulls us forward into her family, and before you know it, you feel as though you are one of them. The van Liths and Bruggemans become a part of our own personal stories, and I, for one, have been honored to accept them into my life. I feel as though Mienus and Suze are my friends now, waiting for me to pass over to the other side before we continue our conversation.

There are so many stories about the Holocaust that it sometimes seems as though there can't be any left to tell. And yet Marja has found a way to introduce the continuing story of our shared humanity in a new way.

Like millions of others, Marja's parents suffered during World War II. Their faith in God stands out as a beacon of light through sorrow and uncertainty. A commitment to stay true to the faith drove them toward a better life and gave them strength to endure. A willingness to submit to God's will above their own allowed them to withstand the buffetings of evil and decay.

Marja's perspective as a second generation survivor picks up where many historians leave off. Driven by curiosity and compelled by the Holy Spirit, she spent many years gathering details from her parents before they passed away. These details complement historical facts as she provides a rich backdrop for the story of a family. Her family. But in a way, she tells the story of all families.

When I first met Marja, I thought that she was one of the most beautiful women I had ever met. Her eyes sparkle with a youthful energy, and yet somehow also an ageless wisdom that sees through you. As we discussed her intentions for this book, she consistently expressed a sense of sacredness. She knew that the book was driven by a higher cause, a heavenly cause.

Her dedication to this work has inspired me to document my own family immigration story. I watched her parents meet, marry, have children, and venture into their future. Then I watched as she did the same. I discovered patterns that echo my own experiences, and those of my ancestors. Marja manages to display universal truths through her writing in an almost effortless way. This was an enormous sacrifice for her, taking up years of her life. It has been a privilege to join with her in making sure the story of her parents and family is honored the way it deserves.

Long shall you live, my friend!

Heidi Scott, editor

wordengineer@gmail.com

Table of Contents

Prologue

This story is very difficult for me to write due to the subject matter. Much of what I write contains information I acquired after a lifetime of conversations with both my parents. I asked them to tell me their story and I listened to them intently as they relived their memories. I learned so much and I retained it all these years.

At the end of many of these personal reflections my Dad would say, "Never forget this. We should never forget!" Then he would stand up and walk about the house a bit, letting me know without words, "It's enough for today." This seemed to help him refocus on the present and cut himself off from the past once again.

The material is vivid in my mind. I write what I was told. My focus was to be as accurate as possible. I specifically needed to learn more about the early events related to the Resistance Movement in Vlaardingen, Holland, during the first part of the Occupation at the beginning of World War II, as well as the Holocaust in general.

In addition to what I learned from my parents, I gathered information through Internet searches of wartime documents and from a couple of gruesome books hidden away for years in my parent's closet. I was seven or eight when I first found them while snooping around as a child. There was also a treasure trove of personal reflections written independently by both of my parents, and videos that were made of them candidly speaking about their lives and events surrounding the war in Holland. These items were stored away and later found in a black bag in a closet in their home.

During my research, I discovered a very important, in-depth article that required me to back away from my computer because of the waves of emotions that inundated me. It was surreal to read accounts written by someone I did not know about the wartime events surrounding the life of my father. It felt as though Dad had written this piece, and he was right there with me again. It was Dad's story, and I could hear him talking to me just as he had so many times before.

An overwhelming feeling of purpose came over me, and I could hear Papa saying, "See Marja, everything I told you happened just as it was! You are on the right track! Tell them, and never forget!"

The words I use when I quote my Father throughout the book depict the way he spoke and are drawn together from what my Dad shared over our numerous conversations. He was straightforward, didn't use eloquent words, and merely said what he saw, what he knew, and what he had done. If it appears to the reader that other words could have been used to describe things more eloquently and effectively, trust me, I know. But it is my father's voice that I hear, and my father's words that I use, so I remain as true to his story as I can.

A multitude of World War Two (WWII) books, as well as many televised programs and major motion pictures have been made over the decades, providing greater insights into the mind and the workings of Adolf Hitler and his Nazis. This book will not attempt to add new information, but rather to share intimate events that happened during that time and place.

I am forever grateful to my sister, Gert van Lith-Helvey, who wrote her own book for the extended family and friends over a three-year period of research and writing. Her book, "The Continuing Family History of Dominicus van Lith and Suzanna Bruggeman-van Lith," is full of useful genealogy, history, interviews, personal letters, and family pictures. And to some family members and friends in Holland who provided me with even more information during trips back to the Netherlands, I thank you. All these references helped to fill in the many details surrounding the lives of Mienus (Dominicus) and Suze before, during, and after the war.

A Quick Explanation about Holland

"What is the difference between Holland and the Netherlands?

The Netherlands consists of twelve provinces but many people use 'Holland' when talking about the Netherlands.

Between 1588 and 1795, the area currently representing the Netherlands was the Republic of Seven United Netherlands. The republic was conquered by French troops in 1795 and became the Batavian Republic. Napoleon appointed his brother Louis as king in 1806, turning the country into a kingdom. The Netherlands remained a kingdom after Napoleon's defeat. At that time, the area called 'Holland' made the biggest contribution to the entire nation's economy and wealth. As such it became the commonly used name to indicate the entire country."

(Holland.com)

Disclaimer: While all the people mentioned in this book are real, some names have been changed to protect the privacy of certain individuals.

Part One:
First Generation Survivor

Chapter 1

"Collaborating was not an option!"

Mienus didn't listen to the many warnings of his parents. "My parents told all of us kids to keep our noses clean. In other words, stay out of trouble!" But by the time his parents had this conversation with him, their nineteen-year-old son was already deeply involved in the Resistance.

*

In February 1941, Mienus and a handful of others in the underground began gathering tools and procuring a large quantity of dynamite to carry out their next major offensive. It would be their most daring undertaking, and if carried out successfully, would create the most damage against the occupiers yet.

*

With just enough dynamite smuggled in to do the job, the Resistance was just starting to prepare the explosives when several armed SS German soldiers stormed in to apprehend them. The SS had been watching for these men to arrive, and waited until they were all together before the arrest.

*

Soldiers stood behind each prisoner, rifles pointing at the back of their heads. One by one the name of each condemned man was read, a shot was heard, and a body fell forward.

*

Mienus managed to survive the first day, and the next, and the next. But he wondered how long he could hold out? How long would this last? He just had to figure it out how to survive in this brutal camp called Buchenwald. He would turn 21 years old in five weeks, on May 14, 1941. The most important objective now was to stay alive.

*

After a short pause in our conversation, he went on to say, "So we sat on the ground by the barracks and watched the young and very frightened SS soldiers who were left in charge while they placed dynamite, wires, and detonators throughout the camp. Then we watched as they placed explosives along the outside of the fencing. It didn't take us long to figure out what it all meant, and what was about to happen. We were just waiting for the end."

*

He said to his friend, "Come, and sit here with me. I have something for you. You know there is a good chance that we will die here in the camp. But whether we live or die, by God, we will not die with an empty stomach!" Mienus reach into a pocket of his thin overcoat and pulled out a chunk of small, stale, four-day-old bread that he had been saving for just the right moment. This was that moment.

Mienus

Dad was born in Leerdam, the Netherlands, on May 14, 1920. He was the fourth child born into a growing family that would eventually number nine children. His name was Dominicus Marinus van Lith, but he would be called Mienus (pronounced **Meen**-us), with the accent on the first syllable.

Most of the children in Holland were given names that were handed down from generation to generation. It was customary and expected to continue with this tradition. The new child would be given part or all of the name of a parent, grandparent, or special relative. Dad's father's first name was Marinus.

Because of the larger family sizes of that era, it was common to have many cousins with very similar names. Names would be interchangeable, made either feminine or masculine, when it was time to reuse it again. Johannus would become Johanna, Theodorus would become Theodora, Marinus would become Maria, and Antonius became Antonia. You get the idea.

Names could be used more than once in a family. Over many generations, if a child was born alive and given a name, and then died before the next sibling was born, that exact name could well be given to the next child, helping to ensure the continuation of names. Sadly, some babies that died just after birth or were stillborn could likely receive a number instead of a name.

Dad grew up no different from any of the other children of his time. He had the normal education of the day, completing the equivalent of 8th grade before going on to trade school. After a few years of trade school, he completed his studies, having learned the basics of mechanical engineering, precision cutting as a machinist, a broad knowledge of metallurgy, and skills in welding. These newly acquired skills would have enormous significance for him in the years that would soon follow.

At some point during his youth, the entire family moved to a town called Vlaardingen where my Opa (grandfather), Marinus van Lith, worked for the railroad in Vlaardingen for many years. One of Opa's tasks was to pull track levers near the railroad station to regulate the direction of the tracks, enabling the trains to move on the appropriate lines day and night. Because of his round-the-clock schedule, the family ended up living just yards from the railroad tracks in a very humble house.

Like many families of this time period, the van Lith's lived rather poorly. They raised chickens and grew much of their own food on the property. It was just part of life, and was necessary to feed themselves, and others in need.

Mienus, adapting to the ever-growing family, knew all about helping out. His ability to work hard and take care of others while taking care of himself was an admirable quality, and would be life-saving during his early adult years.

I listened to many interesting stories about Dad while I was growing up. From these accounts I understood that even at a young age, he was already very outgoing, and loved to be with people and was very loyal to his family. While developing in his teens, he grew tall and lean and was very good looking, with black, wavy hair, something he was very proud of. Dad was athletic and loved to ice skate on the frozen rivers and canals in the winter, and play a good game of soccer any time of the year. He became very good friends with the boys in the Bruggeman family nearby. My mother was a part of that family.

Dad really enjoyed life and could be quite entertaining. He thrived on the attention he received, showing his friends and family a good time. He was not shy, and always displayed confidence. His many attributes would serve him well throughout his entire life.

My grandparents passed on their Catholic faith to all of their children. Sunday Mass was never missed, and rosaries would wear out after years of daily use. Dad's loyalty and devotion, not just to his faith and family, but to his country and countrymen, was a direct result of the strict upbringing by his father and the tender loving care of his mother.

As Mienus matured into early manhood, he developed a greater love for his faith, his family, and his country. The skills and qualities he possessed would be of significant importance to many of the Dutch people. He would be tested in ways that no one could foresee.

In just a few months, that "just normal" life Mienus had would change drastically. Very dark and dangerous times would soon overtake this peaceful and very proud little country, Holland. His life would never be the same, and all that he would desire was to feel "normal" again.

Suze

Mom was born in Wageningen, the Netherlands, on June 20, 1925. She was the youngest child with five older siblings, four brothers and one sister. Much like my father's family, her family carried on the practice of reusing the names of previous generations. Her name was Suzanna Maria Elizabeth Bruggeman, but she was commonly known as Suze, (pronounced **Soo**-za), with the accent on the first syllable. While not every girl had the name Maria in her formal name, many in the Catholic community did.

Suze's parents resettled their family in a town called Vlaardingen when she was just six weeks old. The family of eight lived in a small, three-story building located in a shopping district in the heart of the town. Her father and mother ran a bakery out of their home.

The main entrance to the bakery was at street level. The store was in the front and the actual working bakery in the back, with a very small living and working area in the middle. The second and third levels included a small sitting room and sleeping quarters for the family of eight. The third level was an attic.

When Suze was old enough, she and her sister, Mia, shared a bed in the small attic room where no heating or cooling was available. Hot water bottles to warm the bed were necessary in the freezing cold temperatures of winter, but only provided warmth for the short time it took for the bottles to cool down again.

In those days, Holland frequently had long periods of Arctic cold weather blow through that would freeze over numerous canals and waterways. Many of the Dutch people took advantage of the frozen water to enjoy ice skating, one of many things that the Netherlands is well known for.

Suze was a quiet child who would have loved more attention from her parents. Her father and mother worked long and hard for many hours each day, leaving little time to devote to the childhood needs of their youngest. The four older brothers were left to fend for the younger two sisters. Mom was especially fond of her youngest brother, Wilhelm. He provided her with loving attention and security. He was her favorite sibling.

In the winter of 1933-34, Wilhelm, known as Wim, contracted tuberculosis and was sent to a sanatorium for treatment. He succumbed to the illness and died on May 9, 1934. The trauma of losing her brother was very painful to Suze. Years later, when she spoke to me about those early years living in Holland, I could still see the sadness in her eyes when she shared the events surrounding her brother's death and the impact it had on her entire family. Losing her favorite brother stripped her of the one person in her life that made her feel loved and important. Those early years were very unhappy times for Mom.

During this period in Holland's history, every city and town had several Christian churches for worshipers, along with a number of synagogues for those of the Jewish faith. The Catholic presence was evident in most towns. The entire country was dotted with old, gothic-style churches and cathedrals and they were filled with parishioners each week. Outside of Christianity and Judaism, there were very few other religions in Holland.

Suze's biggest consolation after Wim died was the peace she felt when she went to church on Sundays and any other day when she was able to attend Mass. At nine years of age, Suze was already a very devoted Catholic. She would spend hours just sitting in the church praying and thinking about heavenly things. This dedication to her faith and love for her Savior would continue to be her greatest gift throughout her whole life. She derived great strength from her faith, and relied on it as a source of guidance through every major decision and every difficult road she was force to travel.

As Suze matured, she developed more independence and explored new interests. Dance gymnastics was a favorite activity of hers. I remember seeing pictures in the old photo albums of her posing with several other adolescent girls, each of them holding basketball size rubber balls and wearing the current trend of athletic clothing of her time. She said that sports activities with vigorous exercise and belonging to a club with dance gymnastics gave her a measure of happiness and strength. It helped her, not only physically, but mentally as well. She had friends there who liked her.

Making friends was not too difficult for Mother. She could be shy and reserved at first, but became more outgoing once she got to know someone. Compared to my father, she would always be a little more restrained, more demure, and never wanted to draw too much attention to herself. She carried that trait into her advancing years.

During her eight years of formal education, Suze kept busy in the bakery when she was not in school. After completing the required years of learning, she spent the next two years pursuing her dream of becoming a fashion designer at a private school. She excelled in her new environment and mastered the art of sewing. She delighted in creating fashion and making her own patterns.

Not only was she able to design and create beautiful clothes for both men and women; she had a keen understanding of how to use many different types of fabrics. Coats, suits, and furs were no challenge. Neither was creating lingerie and underwear. It would simply be a matter of time, she thought, before she would be able to open her very own design shop and start her own line of clothing. That was her dream, and that was what she planned for.

Almost Forgotten Childhood Moments

A lifetime of stories told by both my parents about relatives who lived long ago and who were so removed from my life was always fascinating and important to me. Dad and Mom never turned away my curious questions as a child. As I got older, those same stories took on more details and more meaning each time they were retold. Things they wouldn't tell me as a child were later more easily opened to me.

"Mom, I remember you telling me that you didn't think much of Dad when you first met him. You said he was your brother Johan's best friend, and he wasn't coming over to see you. Besides, you were just a young girl of twelve, and Dad was five years older. I get it. But I still want to know, did you think that Dad was good looking back then?" I asked.

Mom thought for a moment and then said, "Well I guess so. I never really thought about it much. He was not unpleasant to look at. But I thought he was kind of conceited, always messing with his black hair and spending way too much time looking at himself in the mirror, as if his hair was a trophy of some kind."

Mom would rarely complement anyone's good looks. Not because they weren't attractive, but she thought that too many complements would prevent a person from staying humble. And yet when she spoke of those very early years, especially about Dad, she sounded as though she may not be sharing all of the details of how she sized up this young man. She was careful not to say anything that would contradict her impressions of Mienus, the guy that was only interested in her brother. As Mom spoke, I could tell that these were good memories, and I needed to dig a little deeper.

Dad, on the other hand, always thought Mom was pretty. Suze was pretty when she was 12 years old, and even prettier every year thereafter. It's true that Mienus was best friends with Jo and would hang out at the bakery often, but even if Jo was not home or was not available, Mienus would still manage to find things to do to keep himself in the company of Suze. Mom used the term "naïve" when it came to Dad's flirting and courting. She just thought he was waiting for her brothers.

Dad Makes a Move

On May 7, 1939, a big celebration was planned for Dad's parents. They would be celebrating their 25th wedding anniversary. All of Dad's brothers and sisters helped in arranging the day. Aunts, uncles, and other family members were in attendance, including Dad's grandfather, Johannus van Lith. There were upwards of 35 people in attendance.

By this time, Mienus had grown very fond of Suze. She was just shy of fourteen years, and Mienus would be nineteen in a week. The day of the party, Dad went to the bakery to invite Mom to come to his family's house. Mom knew some of Dad's family, but only as acquaintances, not really as friends.

Suze said no to Mienus the first time he asked. He would have to do some quick thinking to get her to change her mind.

Back in 1939, not too many people in Holland owned a car. Lucky for Mienus, his uncle did, and drove it to the family event. Mom had never been in a car before and Dad knew that, so he quickly invited her to come along with him and sit in his uncle's car. To that invitation, she said yes. She still wasn't sure why he asked her and not her brother, Jo.

He took her by the hand, walked to the party, went to the car, opened the door for Suze, and got in the back seat with her. "Gee, what was he thinking, Mom?" I said sarcastically. "Did he kiss you?" I quickly added.

"Maybe," she said blushingly. I smiled at that answer, knowing that Dad made the first move on her that day. I am not naïve!

Shortly after the back seat smooch, the photographer arrived for a rare family photo. Everyone in the picture that day was related, except for 14-year-old Suze. She can be seen standing on the top row just a couple of feet from her future husband. Every time she told that story, she would smile and recall how unprepared she was for what happened that day. "How in the world did I end up at the van Lith family's celebration, end up in their family picture, and let your Dad get me in the back seat of my first car ever?" she questioned herself, not mentioning their first kiss. Not surprisingly.

After this episode, I'm pretty sure she figured out that this young man, Mienus, liked her. He continued to show up at the bakery to see her and the brothers. They even got permission to go to the movies together a few times.

Mom was comfortable around her brothers' friend, now her friend too, and she loved going to the movies to watch all the movie stars of that era. This was the first time her parents let her go to the movies with a boy. What she didn't expect to see was both of her parents sitting just a few rows behind them. They slipped into the movie theater just after the teens had. Some things never change.

After their shared first kiss in the back seat of that car, they continued to see each other off and on for a year or so. I'm not sure Mom ever really thought of him as her boyfriend during that time. Though Dad's intentions were pretty clear, Mom still didn't think of him that way. She did enjoy going out and doing fun things with him, but she also enjoyed group activities with lots of friends too. Sadly, fun things would end very soon, and Mienus and Suze's time together would end abruptly.

Chapter 2

Option C

May 10, 1940, Germany invades Holland. Like the other occupied countries that had recently fallen against the strong German aggression, Holland was no match for Hitler's soldiers and war machines. In six short days, the freedom that the Dutch people enjoyed came to a brutal end. Hitler was in power and, according to Germans, the war was over. Though the Germans tried to say their actions were justified and announced themselves as "Liberators to the Dutch people," everyone in this small, peaceful country of patriots knew better. They were now under occupation by an invading enemy and everyone knew it.

In the aftermath of their defeat, the Dutch people had to make a quick but important decision between three choices. Their options were: A) go about their business and try to live as normally as possibly during this occupation, B) collaborate with the enemy and live more comfortably, or C) resist!

Most people chose to stay out of trouble and remain as anonymous as possible, Option A. Unfortunately, a portion of the population chose to openly embrace the presence of the German soldiers for any number of reasons, Option B. And then there was a small but growing number of patriots involving themselves in, what Dad would refer to as, "the underground movement," Option C.

Suze Bruggeman's family, like most, did their best to live as normally as possible. The bakery stayed open to provide a living for the family, to feed themselves and others. Schools were still open at that time. Most of the people were able to move about still, eager to spend time in church to pray that somehow this war would be over soon. It would only be a few short years before living conditions became very difficult, destructive, and severe.

For the most part, the van Lith family carried on much like the Bruggeman's, living so as not to draw attention to themselves and their family. As Dad would say, "My parents told all of us kids to keep our noses clean." In other words, stay out of trouble! Unfortunately, Dad didn't listen to his parents' warnings. By the time his parents had this conversation with their children, nineteen-year-old Mienus was already involved in Option C.

The Geuzen Resistance in Vlaardingen

Rotterdam was just a short train ride from Vlaardingen, where Mienus lived. He worked as an apprentice machinist in the shipyards of Rotterdam, one of the largest seaports in the world.

After the Germans invaded Holland, Mienus became one angry, young Dutchman! Within days of occupation, he started considering different pathways to win back his country from the enemy occupiers. He could not, and would not, just sit by and do nothing. Dad was a patriot, and would soon become a freedom fighter.

On May 14, 1940, just four days after the invasion began, Mienus turned 20 years old. Coincidentally, that was also the day the Germans began the aerial bombing of Rotterdam. When Dad talked about the bombings, he was quick to add in his heavy Dutch accent, "That didn't sit so well with me."

The very next day, May 15, the first communication from those who began the resistance surfaced. The message was to other young patriots and was sent in the form of a chain letter. This message came from a man named Bernardus IJzerdraat, who lived in Rotterdam and was a teacher in Vlaardingen. This first letter did not circulate very far, so a second letter went out on May 18 that included dire warnings, and as a result was shared more successfully.

The letter said that before too long, Holland would be without food, clothing, work, and resources, and that coupon rationing would soon follow. Bernardus said that, "Our young men will be forced into labor for the conqueror." The readers of this memo were left with the impression that the new resistance was already growing in other parts of the country, though that was not true. The intent of this message was to stir up the hearts and minds of the people reading it, with the hope that others would join and fight together in the underground movement.

They would call themselves "*De Geuzen,*" which translates to "The Beggars." The underground resistance took its name from the first *Geuzen,* who were a collaboration of armed groups that fought the Spanish Occupation of the Netherlands in the 16th Century, during the Dutch Revolt. The initial group of freedom fighters against the Nazis would be the very first resistance group in Holland since then, and began forming just five days after the German invasion.

An ally to Bernardus IJzerdraat was Jan Kijne, a patriot from Vlaardingen. Within a few days, a small and determined group of freedom fighters agreed that the course of action against the Germans so early in the war, would consist of spying on the activities of the enemy, passing on all information to England, and sabotaging the plans and actions of the Germans wherever possible.

Within that small but growing group of men and women, was a young and strong 20-year-old loyalist, already known by others in the movement, Dominicus M. van Lith, (Mienus).

Each of the members took the *Geuzen* (Beggars) Oath:

> *I vow to be a proper Dutch Geus [Beggar] in these serious times, and will totally and unconditionally keep to the Geuzen law and the commander's rules. I declare and approve that, if my oath is compromised in any way, all my rights and properties will be passed on to and for the benefit of the Geuzen army, or if this is dissolved in anyway, to and for the benefit of the Dutch people.*

(Schlebaum)

Mienus pledged his allegiance with the Oath, and the foundation was laid. Having sworn his loyalty to the *Geuzen,* he would live for, work for, and suffer for the cause of freedom. The work of espionage and sabotage began.

Espionage and Reporting

From the beginning of the *Geuzen* resistance, Dad was heavily involved. He would say that he was a part of the "first wave of the underground movement."

In one of my conversations with him, he explained the simple structure of the underground resistance that developed after the first month or two. He said:

> *As more and more patriots committed and pledged their loyalty to the Geuzen, it soon became obvious that, to protect the identity of the growing resistance army, large gatherings were impossible. Smaller groups needed to form within each town. It was necessary to be actively involved with only five or six members in a group (cell). One person from that cell would know a member of another cell, while the rest of the group only knew of each other. This pattern continued, not just from cell to cell, but from town to town, with only one, or maybe two actively involved with another town's group. They would all take orders through the messages that were sent in the chain letters that were smuggled in from the leadership.*

This system of involvement worked for several months. Hypothetically, if anyone was caught by the Germans, that individual, when interrogated, would only be able to divulge the names of a handful of others.

A *Geuzen* cell would gather information surrounding the occupiers' activities within each of the municipalities involved with the resistance. The data would include troop locations and size, ammunition types, size and numbers, enemy headquarters, and ship traffic in and out of the harbor in Rotterdam. This very important information was then relayed to the resistance headquarters in Vlaardingen and Rotterdam, and then smuggled into England.

In addition to this vital information passed on to England, the resistance began to create lists of the Dutch collaborators with the Germans, including the Dutch women who had relations with the enemy, and were known as "moffenmeiden," a derogatory term. It was extremely important to know who your enemy was, and who you could and could not trust.

It was vital to get this information out to England for many reasons. Immediately after the German invasion, the entire Dutch government escaped to England, as did the Queen of Holland and her family. In addition, the English government was equally invested in this information obtained from the underground. The information would be useful for the collaborative effort with the Dutch and British allies in developing strategies for an eventual future counter attack. The hope was to defeat Hitler and his army and win back the freedom that was taken from the Netherlands, and to prevent Great Britain from the same fate as the rest of Europe.

Dangerous Activities

One of the written dialogues I found was of a 1993 interview between a reporter and both of my parents. Unfortunately, the name of the reporter has been lost to time.

When Dad was asked about his decision to join the resistance so quickly after Holland was overrun as part of the Western Europe German advance, he answered:

> *So in four days they captured our country, Belgium, [Denmark,] Norway, and then they started in France. So when the Germans were in our country, they were setting the rules. At that particular time, I was an apprentice machinist in the shipyards near Rotterdam. Having to work for the Germans did not come [go] over too well with me. Because they were our enemies, we sabotaged as much as we could. We were in direct contact with our government. Our government had fled to London in 1940, but we were in direct contact. So here's where the resistance started, by sabotaging and working against the Germans as much as we could. We did them a lot of damage. About three or four months after we got captured [occupied] by the Germans, we became a little more free [courageous] and the Germans got a little madder and suspicious about us.*

Espionage and reporting were ongoing activities of the underground. But that wasn't enough for those small *Geuzen* cells. They were ready and wanting to hurt the German occupiers.

One of the first acts of sabotage was to strategically cut important telephone lines. These particular lines were the ones linked to the searchlight systems and the anti-aircraft guns in Vlaardingen. The lines were restored and destroyed seven times in 1940.

Other incidents of sabotage occurred sporadically. The resistance knew how outnumbered they were against the German army. Weapons were hard to come by and it took time to plan, gather munitions, and execute tasks. Initially, their actions did more to disrupt the German occupiers than destroy them.

By September of 1940, just four months after the German invasion, Hitler's army began to take a stand against the *Geuzen* Resistance. A stern warning was placed in the local newspapers and on large posters strewn throughout Vlaardingen and surrounding areas.

"The German Wehrmacht will employ the toughest measures to the city of Vlaardingen and its inhabitants," it read. Most of the people understood its meaning. When a saboteur was caught red-handed, they would likely be fired upon immediately. After this newspaper warning, the Resistance decided to lay low for a while.

The espionage continued for a couple of months. The communication with London was still intact. Mienus continued his work at the shipyards and cautiously observed the German occupiers as they began transforming the large shipyard industry into what he would later refer to as, "their war machine."

In November of 1940, a serious breach occurred within the underground Resistance. The first arrests of the freedom fighters would soon follow.

Chapter 3

First Arrests

Vlaardingen, Schiedam, and Rotterdam are three towns situated along the inland waterway known as the *Nieuwe Waterweg* (New Waterway). Traveling west on the river, the waterway takes travelers through the *Hoek van Holland* (Hook from Holland), and into the North Sea. Before World War II, much of the economy of that area was directly linked to the huge shipyards of Rotterdam and the fishing industry. The waterway was so important to the way of life for the Dutch people, especially during their occupation.

The inexperience of the *Geuzen* Resistance was no match for the Germans very early in the war. Not all of the men and women carefully followed the system of smaller cells.

A young man named Daan van Striep, living in Schiedam and working in the shipyards of Rotterdam, was carelessly handed a copy of "De Geuz van 1940" (The Beggar from 1940). This resistance communiqué, was given to him by a coworker, Johannes Smit, who was already involved in the underground movement.

While bragging a bit to some of his friends, Daan was overheard by a group leader of the *National Socialist Movement* (NSM), saying that he knew a group of the *Geuzen* in Vlaardingen, where Mienus was an active participant. The NSM was a political group that was sympathetic to the Germans. They were no friends of the Resistance. This NSM leader quickly reported the conversation to the German security police, and a chain of events unfolded.

A trial was held that led to the arrest of van Striep in Schiedam on November 19, 1940. Smit was also arrested within days. The evidence found in Johannes Smit's house, which included the *Geuzen* newsletter, as well as other incriminating evidence, was not enough to divulge the whereabouts of others in the Resistance. It was only after intense interrogations (torture), did he finally give up the information necessary to begin the first arrests of the *Geuzen* Resistance.

The enemy was able to round many of the patriots up very quickly. Mienus was not one of those arrested in November. Somehow, he did not show up on the list of men to be arrested, and his smaller group was left intact, most likely due to those who did follow the secrecy and the structure of the smaller cells. He did, however, know many of those who were arrested. Those left behind were still very committed to the fight. The work of espionage and sabotage would continue.

The arrested men were initially taken to the basement of the courthouse, which also housed the police station in Vlaardingen. They were quickly transferred to the prison in Scheveningen known as the *Oranjehotel*. This hotel, named for the Dutch monarchy of The House of Orange, was turned into a notorious prison by the German army.

For decades prior to this, the *Oranjehotel* had been a destination of choice for the wealthier families in the Netherlands. It was located very close to the Atlantic Ocean, had many rooms, and provided excellent service and accommodations. The surroundings included beautiful rolling green lawns and meticulous landscaping.

Very early in the Occupation, it was taken over by the Nazis and converted into a prison. The Germans needed an existing facility for incarcerating arrested influential Dutch citizens and those involved in the Resistance.

Ironically, in 1945 after the Germans surrendered, the *Oranjehotel* was used to imprison many of the same soldiers who had been the perpetrators of the confinement, torture, and death of so many Dutch men and women during the Occupation. It also incarcerated many of the Dutch who chose Option B, those who collaborated with the Germans.

The old prison is now a war memorial and museum. There are events held every year to commemorate all those who suffered and died there during WWII.

A number of the men who were arrested in November were interrogated and tortured. Those who died of the wounds inflicted by the enemy became the first Resistance martyrs who gave their lives for the freedom of the Dutch people. They would be followed by many others who fought against the Occupation throughout WWII.

A trial for those men who survived the interrogations was scheduled to begin sometime in late February 1941. The Germans publicized the trial in the newspapers throughout Holland. In addition, they had collaborators distribute posters throughout the streets of Vlaardingen and other towns. Along with the announcement of the trial, a threat of dire consequences was added. The declaration read, "So that anyone who plans to offer help to England or cause the German Wehrmacht harm, know that he is playing with his life." The meaning was clear to the townspeople, and they would have to wait to hear what would happen as a result of this trial.

During this first winter of occupation, the German army tried to ingratiate themselves with the Dutch. Most of the citizens remained in Option A, and did their best living within the confines of the new circumstances they were forced into.

Unfortunately, there were too many other citizens wanting to live comfortably out in the open, and without fear. Shifting their loyalties, they now moved out of Option A to Option B, and began collaborating with the occupiers. The danger to those in the Resistance was even greater now, having to keep their eyes and ears out for traitors.

All the information regarding the arrests and trial was transmitted in code to the British and the Dutch government in exile. Those left in the Resistance were ordered to continue with their espionage but to curtail the sabotage, for now. This provided some time to seek out and recruit others patriots who would be willing to take up the fight for Holland.

As one of the original *Geuzen*, and as a consequence of the arrests, Mienus began to take a greater leadership role within the Resistance. Because the Resistance had suffered a great loss, the remaining patriots followed orders to discontinue further sabotage, at least for a few months.

During this time, the German occupiers began to make modifications to the shipyards in Rotterdam where Mienus worked. These changes were designed to benefit Adolf Hitler and his plans for domination. Hitler's intention was to occupy all of Europe and beyond, and to build a new civilization dominated by an Aryan race. His biggest challenge was to conquer and occupy the people of Great Britain. Taking control of the shipyards and the waterways of Holland enabled Germany to get even closer to Hitler's desired goal.

Espionage continued and all the information was relayed to England. News of the modifications at the Rotterdam shipyards caused great concern to the allies and the Dutch government. Sabotage to disrupt the enemy was again sanctioned, and in the minds of the Resistance, could not have come soon enough.

Mienus knew how to plan and execute attacks. "We did them a lot of damage," Dad proudly said to me in conversation. The Resistance had already blown up a few bridges and carried out several other acts of sabotage against the enemy. By the middle of February, Mienus and a handful of others close to him in the underground began gathering tools and procuring a large quantity of dynamite to carrying out their next major offensive. It would be their most daring undertaking, and if carried out successfully, would create the most damage against the enemy thus far.

Even though they all knew the odds to ever overthrow their occupiers were extremely low, and despite the dire warnings from the Germans, the Resistance would not be intimidated or deterred. When everything was ready, the exiled government in England would give the *Geuzen* the green light to strike.

Sadly, during the planning of this attack, another breech in the underground occurred. A Resistance member, or possibly multiple members, were captured and interrogated. Even when people take oaths and intend to keep them, torture has a way of breaking them. The seal of anonymity to what was left of the *Geuzen of Vlaardingen* after the first arrests months before, was broken again. More arrests by the Germans would be forthcoming.

February 24, 1941

Dad was 20 years old and still lived at home with his parents and younger siblings. Young adults lived with their families until they got married or had to move away for work. He was expected to contribute financially to the family household. There was never any question about these living arrangements and conditions. That's the way things were done.

On Monday, February 24, 1941, Mienus got up early, just like every other workday. Respectfully, he said goodbye to his parents and planned to see them later in the evening. From this normal morning routine, it looked as if their son was ready for another full day working with his hands in the shipyards of Rotterdam.

Mienus never told anyone in his family, especially his parents, about his involvement in the *Geuzen* Resistance. He knew full well how his father felt about any of his children getting too involved with fighting the German occupiers. "Keep your nose clean," his father had warned. Mienus understood that his parents were just trying to protect their children during perilous times.

It was difficult for him to keep such a big secret from his loved ones. But to protect his family from danger, and to prevent any of his siblings from getting involved with him, he simply had to. This way, in the event he was arrested, like the others in the Resistance already in prison, none of them would have any knowledge of the workings of the underground, or know any of the other Dutch patriots who were involved.

Mienus arrived at the shipyards, passed through the normal entrance now managed by the Germans, and punched the time clock to begin work. A handful of others from the Resistance entered their workstations with him. Outwardly, they performed normal activities as they began their day. However, this day was anything but normal. Today, they would sabotage the enemy in a big way. Finally!

One by one they entered the back room where the smuggled explosives where hidden. Before any of them had a chance to begin setting their explosives, several armed SS German soldiers stormed in to apprehend them. They had been watching for these men to arrive, and waited until they were all together before they moved in to arrest them. All the careful training and planning from the previous attacks were not enough to protect them this time. The interrogation of the fellow Resistance fighter(s) had exposed the plans.

Not only were Mienus and his cohorts captured on this day, so were the rest of the known Resistance fighters in Vlaardingen. They were arrested in their homes or work places. Dad was never exactly sure about the number taken on that day, but my research indicated that there were 42 men captured, including him.

The information obtained through the torture of one of their own just a few days earlier, resulted in the second largest arrest of what was left of the original group of *Geuzen*. The first wave of the Dutch underground was defeated.

The men in detention were labeled as political prisoners for being members of the Resistance. Dad was caught attempting to blow up the shipyards of Rotterdam with the illegal dynamite, to destroy the very place where he worked. He would rather demolish what he could of the shipyards and be out of work than to cooperate in any way with the enemies of Holland. "Collaborating with the occupiers was not an option!" he had said to me.

Dinner would not be shared with his parents and siblings that evening. He would not see his family and friends again for a very long time.

Give Me More

As a young child, I had the propensity to ask a lot of questions about a lot of things. I am still that way today. It's part of my character, and how I've always learned. When I'd asked my folks about our family history, they would share just enough to satisfy my curiosity, while sheltering me from too much information all at once.

As I matured, they were more comfortable providing greater details about their lives in Holland, and the hell they lived through during the war. In a way, it reminds me of a baby being fed breast milk, then moving on to mushy food, and finally being able to eat solid food. I was more than ready for a good diet of detailed information, and Dad and Mom provided. I wanted the whole story, and didn't want anything important left out. As their story unfolded, I knew that when the time in my life allowed, I would have the opportunity to retell it.

There were a number of times during conversations with Dad when he would pause and take a big breath, especially when he spoke about the events surrounding his arrest. He looked deep in thought as he stared out into the room. He needed that moment for himself before returning to our conversation.

Dad's voice softened and his face looked sad when he talked about those *Geuzen* captured just days before his own arrest. He knew they had been tortured and forced to divulge the names and activities of the underground. There was no anger or bitterness in his voice towards his fellow patriots. He showed sorrow, forgiveness, and a measure of understanding for the extreme gravity of their situation and the pain they endured at the hands of their captors.

I don't think that he ever did find out who the man or men were, or what happened to them. It didn't really matter. He was just grateful that he was not one of them. Dad simply said, "Can we really know how we would react under such extreme suffering? I'm just grateful it wasn't me."

Prisoner

Mienus was initially taken and locked up in the police station in Vlaardingen, just like the first *Geuzen* who were arrested in November. After the last of the men were detained and stripped of their rights, they were forced at gunpoint up the stairs of the jail and taken outside into the town square.

Word got out quickly around Vlaardingen that many men had been rounded up again. Many of their families came to the police station looking for their loved ones. They anxiously wanted to see what would happen. Their fear was warranted, since most remembered the warnings of September 1940, after the Resistance repeatedly sabotaged the telephone lines. "The German Wehrmacht will employ the toughest measures to the city of Vlaardingen and its inhabitants." All the families were sent home empty handed.

The prisoners were loaded into trucks and sent to the *Oranjehotel*, roughly 22 miles away. Each was led into an individual cell, approximately 6 ½ feet long and 6 feet wide. The doors locked behind them, and armed enemy soldiers stood guard throughout the building. Mienus was alone, in shock, and afraid. There would be no sleep for any of these men that first night, perhaps even longer.

Dad didn't talk very much about his time in the *Oranjehotel*. None of the prisoners really knew how long they would be there. They assumed they would stay there until the war was over. The hours turned into days, and the days into weeks. He did not see his family during this time, but I believe there had been some communications. They at least knew where he was.

The trial for the first men who were arrested in November 1940, had already begun when this second group was apprehended on February 24, 1941. Those newly arrested men were simply included with the first group of *Geuzen* on trial.

I hesitate using the word "trial" when writing about these imprisoned men. A trial should establish a sense of justice. This was just something resembling a trial, strictly for propaganda. The guilty verdict was predetermined. The only thing in question was the punishment to be handed down. Those in charge were seeking a harsh penalty for these men to bolster the threats given to the Dutch people.

On March 5, 1941, a letter was written by Arthur Seyss-Inquart, the German *Rijkscommissaris* in the Netherlands with an appeal to Hans Lammers, the German *Rijksminister* in Berlin. He requested permission to carry out a punishment for all these men. "Heil Hitler," ended the requisition just before his signature.

On March 13, 1941, a reply was delivered and included immediate orders to proceed with the sentencing that Seyss-Inquart sought.

A guilty verdict was announced, not just for those originally arrested, but for the entire group, including Mienus. Eighteen of these patriots were sentenced to death. Those included among the condemned were the three original organizers, Bernardus IJzerdraat, Jan Kijne, and a man named Ary Kop, the first leader of the Geuzen in Vlaardingen.

Three of these eighteen men were underage, so their penalty was commuted to life in prison. Three other men arrested sometime in February 1941, while instigating a large strike in Amsterdam, were found guilty of being Communists and condemned to death in their place. The total to be killed would remain 18. They would stand as, "an example to the Dutch people." The other prisoners would soon learn of their fate.

Martyrs in March

In the late afternoon of March 13, Mienus heard a loud commotion outside his cell. Orders were shouted out in German and a loud shuffling of men could be heard as prisoners were forced from their cells. The uproar grew louder, and suddenly his cell door opened up and he was given the order. "*Schnell, schnell, raus, raus!*" shouted the German soldiers as he and the others were push out the prison doors. "Hurry, hurry, get out, get out!" Not all the captured *Geuzen* were included. Dad said, "There were around 40 of us."

Spontaneous singing erupted, while these prisoners were being led away. The men remaining within their cells could also be heard singing in solidarity. The song was very recognizable. It was the Dutch national anthem, *Het Wilhemus*, sung loudly for all to hear. Some of the prisoners knew their fate. Mienus and the rest did not.

These two stanzas of this very old anthem captures the essence of the song.

Translated in English they read:

> *William of Nassau, I am of Dutch Blood.*
>
> *Loyal to the Fatherland, I will remain until I die.*

A Prince of Orange, I am free and fearless.

To the King of Spain, I have always always honored.

My shield and reliance are you, oh God my Lord.

It is you on whom I want to rely, never leave me again.

Grant that I may remain brave, your servant for always,

And may defeat the tyranny which pierces my heart.

The eighteen men condemned to death were loaded into trucks and hauled away to a place called *Waalsdorpervlakte*, just three miles from the prison. The other men were also transported by trucks to witnesses the execution, and to assist in the cleanup. Those left alone in their prison cells, with only their thoughts and fears to keep them company, listened to the singing until the distance was too great between them.

It must have been a very cold evening, just minutes before 5:00pm on March 13. Holland can get very icy and windy in March, due to its proximity to the North Sea. However, I doubt very much that the men in those trucks were thinking about the weather. Those condemned to death probably were contemplating the sacrifice they were about to endure in defense of their homeland. I can only imagine their feelings of fear, and the sadness knowing they would never see their loved ones again. As for the others, including my father, they had no idea what was about to happen.

"*Schnell, schnell, raus, raus!*" The German soldiers would have shouted to the prisoners after reaching their destination. "Quickly, quickly, get out, get out!" How terrifying this must have sounded.

The men were separated into two groups. A contingent of armed soldiers forced them all up the hill at gunpoint. They were lined up next to the top of the ridge, just above where a mass grave had been opened in advance of their arrival, most likely prepared by other prisoners.

Standing nearly motionless, looking down into the pit, the official statement was read aloud for all to hear. All they really needed to hear was the names of those condemned to death. Eighteen prisoners heard their sentence, "Immediate death by firing squad."

Soldiers stood behind each prisoner, their rifles pointing at the back of the head. One by one, the name of each condemned man was read, a shot was heard, and a body would fall forward. This happened until the last of the eighteen were executed. It was finished in a matter of minutes. The sentence was carried out at 1700 hours (5:00pm), per orders.

Dad described his experience in this way:

> *We didn't know what was going to happen. We were taken away from the prison in a hurry. It was a short ride. After we got out of the trucks, the soldiers forced all of us up a hill at gunpoint. The German commandant summoned several of the men to step forward. I knew enough of the language to know that "guilty" and "death"' was spoken. We saw several of the men being pushed close to the edge, and then the killing started. The men on either side of me were shot. It seemed like every other man in the group was called out and shot in the head. It all happened so fast. It was terrible. I will never forget it!*

Dad was spared, but sadly eighteen others were martyred that day.

To cover up the atrocity, Mienus and the other prisoners were ordered to fill in the mass grave, and quickly returned to the *Oranjehotel*. Soon after returning, these men shared the frightening story of what they had witnessed, and what the others had suffered. Every prisoner, and soon the rest of the Dutch people, would know of the bravery of these men in the face of death.

The Geuzen Remembered

This was the first mass execution in the Netherlands, occurring just ten months after the Occupation. Those eighteen *Geuzen* Resistance fighters at Waalsdorpervlakte would not be forgotten.

As the story of the *Geuzen* was told throughout Holland, it inspired many men and women to take up their cause and resist the enemy. The second wave of Resistance would soon organize and take the place of the men who were in the first wave. These patriots increased in number throughout the remainder of the war and would sadly produce many more martyrs, both men and women alike, for the cause of freedom.

I found a red and black book in the black bag mentioned earlier, the one that had my parents' written memoirs. It turned out to be of great importance to me in my research. The book was call "*De Geuzen,*" by Harry Paape, copyright 1965.

Leafing through this Dutch book, I was mesmerized by the pictures, the letters, and the newspaper clippings strategically placed within the written words of the book. I took my time sounding out the Dutch words and began translating them into English in my head. It was a difficult task for me. I speak Dutch well enough, but reading was difficult, and writing in Dutch was nearly impossible for me.

I was drawn to an article near the end of the book that I knew I was supposed to find. I needed to figure out exactly what was written. Thank God we have Internet translator sites. It was invaluable to me, as I was otherwise unable to complete it on my own.

This article was written for an underground paper distributed on April 9, 1941, and it quickly began to circulate throughout Holland. It was written by Pieter Hoen who wrote about the executions of March 13, 1941, just four weeks earlier.

He wrote:

> *Your reaction to this message of the executions must have been like mine. First there was indignation, then impotent rage erupting, then feelings of admiration and gratitude for these "unknown soldiers," and shame on us for what we must be lacking.*

> *We call upon each of us to: Proclaim the principles that patriots have done hundreds of times before us: I will remain faithful, even to death, for the Fatherland.*

> *What a noble example set by these heroes. They risked their lives without any desire for honor, fame, or profit, and with a high probability of execution if ever caught by the hands of our enemies, the destroyers of our country, our culture and our people's freedoms. These men did whatever they could to thwart the enemy even at the cost of their own lives. What an example for us, both young and old, who tend not to support the needs of the Fatherland.*

> *Hitler will not prevail! Nazism is not the destination of our Christian civilization. The lie, the betrayal, the brutal violence, the assimilation of minds, the dictatorship, these are the forces of evil. The more they become monsters, the more they will encounter even stronger resistance.*

> *These men, who fell in battle, are the evidence. They will always be a shining example. The best part of our nation shows us that no sacrifice is too great for the struggle for freedom. Through their example, their struggle is pierced into each of us.*

> *(Paape, 1965)*

Inspired by these words was a man named Jan Campert. He wrote a poem in memory of those who died. Jan would himself be sent to a concentration camp and die there in 1943. After the war, another man from Vlaardingen would turn the poem into a musical piece. I did my best to translate the poem from Dutch to English. I believe I was able to maintain the poem's integrity.

Het lied de Achttien Dodden (The Song of the Eighteen Dead)

A cell two meters long for me

But not two meters wide,

That plot of earth still smaller yet

Whose whereabouts they hide.

But there unknown I'll take my rest,

My comrades with me slain.

Eighteen strong men saw morning break,

They'll see no dawn again.

O loveliness of the air and land

In the freedom of Holland's shores.

Once overpowered by the enemy

I had no hour of rest more.

What can a man who is sincere and loyal

Do in a time like this?

Inside he fights the battle within him

And in his mind, his child and his wife he will kiss.

I knew the job that I began

A heavy duty in times of suffering.

But I could not let my heart be swayed,

Never mind the danger.

I know how once this country

Honored its freedom

Before these tensions at hand.

All other desires must yield.

They break down rights and promises.

Those absent documents truly existed.

They occupied the Dutch country

And then ransomed her ground.

Then they claimed honor,

And with such Germanic ease.

The country was forced under their control

And plundered us like thieves.

The Pied Piper of Berlin

Now plays his song.

For I will soon be dead,

And will no longer break the bread,

Neither shall I sleep with her,

Forsaking all that I provided and gave,

To the cunning fowl outsider.

Remember whoever reads these words

My companions in distress

And those who stood tall with them

In their peril most dangerous.

Just as we also have believed

There comes a day after every night,

Traveling along every sky.

See how the first morning light falls through the high window.

My God, be my dying light.

And yet I have failed.

Yet each failure can be

Your gift of grace to me.

So I can go like a man

As I stand in front of the end.

Jan Campert, 1943

Chapter 4

The Concentration Camp

He had no choice but to accept his lack of freedom and the small prison cell. What else could Mienus do?

It was particularly hard alone, without his family, and the girl he used to see at the bakery. What would become of her now? An occasional small note was all he was permitted to send to his parents. He would then anxiously await a return letter. There was no privacy at all with the correspondence. All of the mail was censored and some of it would get blacked out.

Mienus had plenty of time to think about his arrest and the emotional trauma he endured witnessing the executions. Why was *he* spared? He suffered physically under interrogations and beatings, but the mental anguish was more difficult to heal.

The *Geuzen* who were left in their cells assumed their sentence was to stay in this prison for the remainder of the war. That would change on April 9, 1941. They would soon realize that the punishment would be much harsher than what they were already enduring, and nothing could prepare them for what they were about to experience.

Papers had been sent from German headquarters to the commander of the *Oranjehotel* with immediate orders to relocate the captured political prisoners, along with other identified inmates. None of the prisoners had any knowledge that they would serve out their punishment for their acts of sabotage far away from Holland. These orders were sending them to a labor camp in Germany. Trucks were brought to the prison to transport the men to the train station.

Dad said:

> They didn't say anything. I didn't know what was happening. We thought that we would stay in Holland as prisoners. They loaded us into trucks and we were all afraid we might be killed now. I remembered another truck ride just weeks before, and that didn't work out so good.
>
> They took us to the train station and loaded us into empty rail cars like animals. There was only a small amount of water to drink, and a piss bucket for all of us to use.
>
> Many people got sick without fresh air. The only time we got fresh air was when the train stopped along the way to pick up other prisoners in other towns. They would open up the sliding door and force us to make more room for the others. Each time that happened we would empty the piss bucket and quickly fill our lungs with the open air. The smoke from the train and the dust from the tracks didn't make it much better though. The train ride was horrible.
>
> We ended up many hours later in a camp called Buchenwald, just eight miles from a town called Weimar in Germany. We didn't even know what a concentration camp was. No one had even heard of those kinds of places, so early in the war.
>
> We arrived on April 9, in the late afternoon, and were quickly unloaded from the train. The prisoners were separated into groups. Those of us in the Resistance were kept together in a group. I think there were about 160 of us altogether.
>
> The SS soldiers would shout orders to us in German, and in the confusion, we just followed the person in front of us, hoping they were going in the right direction.
>
> Looking around the place, it didn't take too long for us to figure out what kind of place this was. When we saw these zebra-striped uniforms, more like pajamas, worn by the prisoners, and

saw how thin and dirty they all were, I began to understand that this place was a hard labor camp.

With all the shouting, the brute force, and the machine guns surrounding Mienus and the others, nothing more was needed to control the newly arrived prisoners.

During 1939-41, hundreds of thousands of people were being arrested throughout Europe simply for being considered inferior by Hitler and his leadership. The Nazis desired to create a superior Arian race, and they did not fit the profile, and were therefore expendable.

At this early stage of the war, only those men that could be used for slave labor were allowed to live and work. Women were not sent to Buchenwald during this time. They were not capable of doing the heavy type of labor needed in the factories that were being built there. Most of the women were sent to "women only" camps, and they would be forced into various work the SS soldiers found necessary to support the Nazi causes, including sex slavery.

The new arrivals were forced into a large building designated for processing. Their identification papers were inspected and confiscated. Each prisoner was given a long number that he would be required to memorize. This number would be called out during daily roll call in the mornings and evenings. Names would not be used.

After identifying and processing each new arrival, Mienus and the others were ordered to take off all their clothes. They would keep nothing of their belongings.

Some of the prisoners already in the camp were assigned the job of assisting these new prisoners through the disinfection process. Without exception, each of the men had all the hair removed from their entire body, "from my head to my feet," as Dad would say. This was a humiliation and an assault on the dignity if each person. Scissors and razorblades were used from one man to another until the blades could no longer cut.

Dad could remember every detail when he was naked and debased in this way. Not only was he naked, he was now bald, and cut in many places, and as he would say, "the worst cuts were in those places between your legs where hair grows too."

If that humiliation was not enough, the men were moved into smaller groups and forced outside and into the cold completely naked. In a single file, they were paraded in front of other prisoners to another building, one that was used for disinfection.

One by one they were ordered to submerge their body completely into a large barrel filled with a very strong lye disinfectant. "It hurt like hell in my eyes and ears and all the places that they had cut me," Dad would say. This entire ordeal was done to prevent the spread of body lice, and whatever else the disinfectant could kill. After a quick, cold water hosing, the only thing left to do was to put on the thin, zebra-striped pajama uniform that was handed to each of the new arrivals. Welcome to Camp Buchenwald!

Prisoners were sent to Buchenwald for many reasons, and the German SS soldiers needed a way to identify them for their supposed crime that led to their incarceration. This was done by sewing badges onto the uniforms of each inmate. These badges bore insignias that distinguished one crime from another. These symbols were used not only in Buchenwald, but also in the majority of the concentration camps throughout occupied Europe.

Mienus had an inverted red triangle with a black N in the middle to identify the country of origin, Netherlands. All political prisoners wore the same red badge that included the first letter of their homeland. There were political prisoners from many occupied countries forced to labor in Buchenwald.

Gypsies, blacks, nonconformists, vagrants, and those who were considered too lazy to work, wore brown or black triangles. Homosexuals wore pink. Jehovah's Witnesses were singled out because of their conscientious objections to fighting and refusal to salute Hitler. They were thought of as weak, not fit for the Arian race. They wore purple triangles along with prisoners of other religions.

The Jews were arrested in great number because the Nazis believed them to be racially impure and were forced to wear a yellow star to mock the Star of David symbol. This yellow star was required to be worn not only for the Jewish prisoners, but for all Jews living throughout the occupied countries in Europe.

The next order was to eat something for the first time that day. Each prisoner was given, "a chunk of bread and a small bowl of, what they called, soup. It was more like hot water with a few chunks of vegetable and little, if any, meat," Dad explained.

Lastly, they were all taken to the barracks and assigned a bunk that resembled nothing of what they had slept in when they were free men. There were no mattresses. You were lucky to get a bunk with some straw and leaves.

Thank God he knew several of the men in the barracks from the Resistance movement. While Mienus was in the *Oranjehotel*, he had very little contact with his fellow *Geuzen*. There were rare opportunities when the prisoners were able to talk to one another in a group. The only daily communication would be with the men in the cells on either side of him. Aside from the train, this was the first time in several weeks that Mienus was able to talk with his fellow *Geuzen*.

The shock and pain stayed with Mienus throughout the first night in the camp. It was impossible to sleep. Many of the new inmates could be heard crying without shame.

Within the same barrack were other prisoners who had arrived earlier in the war. They would shout obscenities to the new inmates and tell them to be quiet. It was difficult for the inmates to share what little room they had with even more men in an already overcrowded building.

All the men were given orders to double up in their bunks, and they resented these new prisoners. In the beginning, Mienus was forced to share his bunk with one other person. That would change over time.

During the hours of that first night, Mienus would begin the process of learning who he could trust in this new environment. By daybreak, he would learn very quickly the ways of life, the ways of death, and how to survive it.

Within the last 24 hours, Mienus endure a train ride from Hell. Now he was a prisoner more than three hundred miles from everyone he loved, an inmate in a growing labor force, in the notorious Camp Buchenwald. His head, once covered with the black wavy hair he was so proud of, was now completely bald, and he struggled with the pain in the many cut places of his body. His identity was replaced by a number and a badge. The feelings of wet, cold, hunger, and fear would take a long time to get used to. Just a young man, he would turn 21 years old in five weeks, on May 14, 1941. The most important objective now was to stay alive, "I was too young to die!"

A 24-Hour Day in Buchenwald

When the first light of dawn rose, the SS soldiers securing the barracks would shout out orders, "Steh auf, steh auf, schnell, schnell!" (Get up, get up, quickly, quickly!)

This time of the year, the workday would begin sometime between 0400 and 0500. The men were ordered to stand in a single line and proceed to the latrine. The latrines were located adjacent to the barracks and consisted of several very long (>30ft), wooden or concrete rails just high enough to sit on.

There would be as many inmates as possible sitting on the rail at the same time, each of them relieving themselves into a very large trough.

It was very important to be quick with your business as there were several hundred men per barrack waiting in line for the same purpose. You could be beaten for being too slow. Your business would consist of both urination and defecation. Once you were at your workstation, you could be beaten for having to take time out to use the latrine. So after a few days, Mienus had learned to regulate his digestive system to accommodate the new schedule or risk severe punishment. If you were timely, you could then move quickly to the sanitary facility to spend a couple of minutes washing up. That was not something most of the prisoners would have time to do.

With a small bag and tin plate in hand, you would move quickly through the breakfast line to pick up approximately 10 ounces of bread and some coffee. Dad would say, "They called it coffee, but it had no taste really, but I had to drink it anyway. On a very rare occasion, if you were at the right place at the right time, you might get a small piece of margarine or a small piece of sausage with your bread. That was a welcomed addition. Sometimes I would eat the bread right away, and other times I would save it for mid-day or for the evening meal."

The next order of business was roll call. There were tens of thousands of men already imprisoned in the ever-growing camp, and roll call was long and brutal. All the prisoners had to stand at attention in the center of the camp. You were required to stand with the men from your barrack in straight rows of ten. The roll call had to include those who died during the night.

He explained:

> This roll call would last more than two hours each morning, and many times even longer. If any of the prisoners died during the night, we would have to carry the dead bodies to the front of the line. These bodies would have to be counted before they were hauled away to the crematorium to be burned up into smoke. If any mistakes were made in the count, the count would start all over again. It was so cold in the mornings. Our striped uniforms did nothing to protect us from the weather. We had to stand up straight in the rain, or snow, or wind. It didn't matter to the SS. Some prisoners would get sick during the roll call and be dead the next morning, and then the process would begin all over again. Roll call was horrible, just horrible.

> I knew a few words in German, but not enough to fully understand the orders shouted by the SS guards. We were all expected to know what they were saying from the beginning. I learned very quickly what they were ordering, thanks to the help of others in my group who understood better. If you did not do what they said right away, they would beat you again. We were also made to sing at the end of the roll call each day. They had a song a couple of prisoners with music and poetry skills were forced to create called "Camp Buchenwald." We were forced to learn the song and sing it loudly for the camp commandant and his wife to hear. It was very humiliating for us to have to do. Many times, the SS would make us sing it over and over again until we sang it as if we really loved it. They would laugh and mock us terribly. Oh, the things we had to do to prevent another beating.

I found a couple of translations of this song. It took me some time to piece together the song's intended meaning. I first used the computer translators to help me translate the German copy that Dad had in his belongings in that black bag. Then I searched for English versions in the Buchenwald websites. The more I worked to combine each of the translations, the clearer the nuances of each line became.

This song was a constant, and very painful reminder to the prisoners of all that they had given up and lost by fighting against the desires of Hitler and the Nazi regime. The Nazis had taken over their countries, their freedoms, and their way of life. Reading it can put me to tears, thinking about the tens of thousands of men having to sing this song with enthusiasm. What a cruel and twisted joke on these men. Read for yourself!

The Buchenwald Song

When the day awakes, and the sun begins to shine,

The columns of the day display into the dawning morning.

The forest is black and the sky is red

We carry a bag for a piece of bread

In the heart, in the heart we fear.

*

Chorus:

Oh Buchenwald, I cannot forget you, because you are my fate.

Who of us here can measure how wonderful freedom is?

O Buchenwald, we do not whine and complain.

Not knowing of our destiny we never the less want to say yes to life,

Because the day will come when we will be free!

*

The night is short and the day so long, again a song is heard,

Which sang of home and it cannot rob us of our courage!

Embrace change companions and do not lose determination.

We carry the will to live in the blood of our hearts, believe in the heart.

(Chorus)

The blood is hot and my girl is away, and the wind sings softly.

Yet I will be happy it is true, if you will remain faithful to me!

The stones are hard, but allow our passageway.

We have with us the picks and spades

And the heart, the heart of love.

(Chorus)

(Song of Buchenwald, Translated by Marja Henderson)

Buchenwald opened in July of 1937, when the first prisoners arrived. Many of the first inmates were captured German patriots who opposed Hitler and the Nazi party. Prisoners were coming from all the occupied countries in Europe, and since the camp was not very large in the beginning, it constantly grew throughout the war. In the end, it would end up being the largest of the labor camps in Germany.

The morning after arriving, Mienus and the others were immediately forced into hard manual labor. Land had to be cleared for the new buildings and factories to be built. There was a sense of urgency on the part of the German *commandant* who was in charge of the camp. The prisoners were forced to work quickly on the new constructions. Hitler needed more airplanes, more munitions, more of everything.

The prisoners assigned to the rock quarries were forced to run to the site where they carried out the heavy work of lifting and hauling rocks. Running was also expected of the prisoners assigned to the forest to start the long day of cutting and hauling large logs.

Mienus was a compassionate man and had respect for his fellow prisoners. He could see the toll this kind of labor was having on the men who had been in the camp before he arrived. He would do what he could to help them when their burden was too much, even though it could lead to a beating from the SS just for assisting.

Listening to the SS guards yelling, and watching the many beatings was enough to convince the inmates to toil well past their normal abilities. Groups of men would need to work together to keep the pace of the work brutally enforced by the Nazi SS just to survive another day of painful labor.

There were times when helping another prisoner was forbidden, primarily when the SS wanted someone to die. Those close to death were forced to do the impossible work, and if you assisted in any way, it could prolong their life, and that was not permitted.

Having taken the oath of the Resistance, Dad retained the heart of the *Geuzen*. His nature was to be loyal. Whenever possible, it was his duty and challenge to find ways to undermine the work he was forced to do. That gave him purpose in the camps, and he would be loyal to the men around him who were suffering for the same causes. Dad would not collaborate, but he was wise enough to cooperate and do what was needed in order to live.

Dad disclosed to me:

> *Prisoners were controlled through beatings. They used that to get us to work harder and faster. Beatings would become a routine occurrence. If you were sick, they would beat you; if you were too slow, they would beat you; if you talked, they would beat you; if they were suspicious of you, they would beat you; if they wanted to beat you just to do so, they would beat you.*
>
> *They used other methods, like withholding of food and water, or they would mock you or tie you up and give 25 lashes to your backside. They would threaten to kill you with even harder labor. These SS soldiers were the most sadistic people ever created, more like animals. They were specially trained to be as mean and torturous to anyone they considered an enemy. You could see it in their eyes. There was no soul, and they did not see us as human beings. They only showed hate, or even worse, indifference.*

He was still looking in my eyes when he finished speaking. He had endured his own beatings in the camp, and detested these inhumane men. In order to stay alive, he forced himself to control his emotions. This controlling action would alter his personality in many ways for the rest of his life.

A whistle would blow in the middle of the day for a short break to rest, drink water, and eat the bread if they still had it. When it was available, a cup of "soup" just like the one from the night before might be provided. Some would need to urinate, but quite often it was not necessary due to the severe sweating and the lack of fluids during the day. Dehydration was a daily occurrence. A whistle would blow again, and the short break was over.

After a 12-14 hour day, the whistle would sound again. Every prisoner would be expected to run back to the camp and line up again for evening roll call. Several of the men would be forced to carry the bodies of those who had died of their labor, or of a beating they received during the day. Once again, the bodies were placed at the front of the rows to be included in the count.

The evening roll call was longer and more difficult than the morning one. All the prisoners were beyond exhausted, yet they were forced to stand at attention throughout the ordeal. The end of the day roll call had an added dimension to it as well. This was the time that the SS would use for administering punishments.

At the end of the roll, once all the prisoners' numbers were called, the entire assembly would be forced to wait and see if their number might be called out again. Yours could be called for a punishment for something that happened during the day whether or not you were involved. If another prisoner didn't like you, they may have falsely accused you to an SS guard of something done during the day. It was quite possible for you and the accuser to be singled out.

Sometimes, the ruthless guards would randomly select a number to punish, merely to set an example for the other prisoners. All the prisoners knew that if your number was shouted out, you would be required to step outside of your line and be escorted away.

The prisoner would be taken away for: a beating, lashes, loss of food and water, a hanging, or worse yet, sent to the medical experimental building. The punishment was immediate.

Condemned men would be taken to the place of hanging in the camp. After they were roped and hung without covering the head, all the prisoners were forced to march past the gallows, and look at these men as a warning of what could happen to them.

Hangings did not occur every evening, but several times per week. The dead bodies would stay on the gallows until the next executions, even if it took several days for the next hanging. Then the bodies would be taken down by the prisoners and taken to the crematorium.

After work and the roll call were complete for the day, it was finally time for some food. The men would be required to run to the food line for a bowl of "soup" just like the one from lunch, and like the one from the night before. Within days, Mienus began to look more like all the others, much weaker and much thinner from these daily rations.

The end of every day could not come soon enough. A quick trip to the latrine and off to the barrack. Once in the barrack, you were not allowed to leave. As mentioned before, the prisoner would sleep two to a bunk. This was difficult. It was nearly impossible to roll over and change positions without waking the other man. Over time, sheer exhaustion would help to prevent any movement in the bunks once both fell asleep.

Mienus managed to survive the first day, and the next, and the next. But he wondered how long he could hold out? How long would this last? When would his number be called a second time? He just had to figure it out, and figure out how to obey the rules with the people that ran this brutal camp called Buchenwald. He would have to learn to speak German immediately. No other language was permitted.

Dad missed his family very much, and tried hard not to think of the young girl he had feelings for. He had but one primary objective in his life right now, and that was to live. He would control his emotions, and do whatever else he had to do in order to endure. And Dad would pray more than ever before.

Chapter 5

Mother's Own Words

The black bag offered up another treasure for me to include in this memoir. It held a handwritten, detailed story that my mother had written. The pages were filled with memories of some of the events that she witnessed and survived during the war. I changed very little of what she wrote, and did so only to help the reader better understand the way she spoke, and how she wrote. Mother had written it sometime in the late 1980's or early 1990's.

During this time, Mom and Dad had been invited to speak to some high school and middle school students about their experiences living under occupation during WWII, as well as Dad's ordeal in Buchenwald Concentration Camp.

They both worked on their own presentations. Mother, not one to draw attention to herself, found it difficult to do any extemporaneous public speaking. To make it a bit easier on herself, she chose to deliver her story by reading aloud what she had written. I was excited to find this document.

Here is Suze's own story in her own words:

When the war broke out in 1940, I was nearly 15 years old. We woke up very early in the morning of May 10, because of the noise of so many planes flying low overhead. I watched through the attic window along with my brothers and sister. Suddenly some of my brothers climbed onto the roof to get a better view. We found out quickly what the planes were doing. They were dropping bombs and explosives, and what looked like fire. They were also dropping parachute troops out of the planes. Mother turned the radio on and found out what was happening. The Germans were invading Holland. She quickly got my brothers off the roof!

The German Air Force succeeded in destroying most of the Dutch military planes in the first day. It was much like what happened in Pearl Harbor. The airfields around The Hague, where the Dutch government was located, were destroyed. The airfields of Rotterdam were destroyed and enemy airborne troops took over the fields. By May 14, 1940, the situation became hopeless, when the Germans started bombing the center of the city of Rotterdam and destroyed it. A thousand people were killed, 80,000 were made homeless, and many businesses were destroyed. I had to see it for myself and when I did, it was indescribable.

The next day, the capitulation was signed by the Dutch government. That started the beginning of five years of occupation by the Germans over us."

Everyone had to carry an identification card, including your picture and fingerprints at all times. Whenever a German soldier asked for it, you had to show it. Restrictions would soon follow. There was food rationing, as well as clothing and shoes rationed.

On the radio, only German music was played. Dancing was forbidden. In the movie theaters, only German movies and propaganda were shown. TV did not exist yet. Then came the day when everyone had to turn in their radios to the authorities. They were not allowed anymore.

We kept one radio in the house, so once in a while we could listen to the English broadcast. I remember how worried I was when that radio was on. I had heard that the Germans had a way of listening to the inside of your house.

Then came the time when all the gold had to be handed in, then copper, then any other metals, and so on. In the winter, we had to hand over our warm clothing, which would be used for the Germans fighting in the Russian front.

Every night, for hours and hours, the planes would fly over. The Germans were flying over us to bomb England. The allies would fly over us heading to Germany to bomb there. We could see the searchlights trying to spot one of the planes, and if they did find one, the other searchlights would join in and they would shoot that plane down. Quite often, these shot down planes would be loaded with bombs and would do a lot of damage wherever it crashed. There was a house across the street from us that was destroyed and two people were killed and it did damage to our home and bakery shop.

There was a nervous and restless atmosphere we all experienced in Vlaardingen. During the day, you never knew what the German soldiers would do and at night you would worry about the planes and the bombs. Later in the war, you worried about the V1 or V2 bombs on their way to England going astray and falling somewhere in Holland! We had buckets with sand ready in the attic to douse firebombs, in case they hit our house.

Starting in February 1941, the conflict intensified between the Germans and the Dutch people. The German soldiers began, what was referred to as the Razias. The meaning of the word Razia [the round-up or gathering], referred to the provocations against the Jews. All Jews were forced to wear a star on their clothes. The soldiers would knock on the front doors of each home to see if there were Jews living there. If there were Jews in the house, they were all likely taken away.

A strike broke out in Amsterdam in response to the anti-Jewish action of the N.S.B [National Socialist Party] and the Germans.

Mother then writes "Explain!" She explained how most of the people in Holland witnessed the collaboration between the N.S.B and the German occupiers. The N.S.B encouraged the persecution of the Jews, and publicly declared that the Jews were the main reason for Holland's problems and that the Germans were only interested in helping the Dutch people. Of course this was a fabrication. Propaganda over time made it easier for the Socialists to justify the injustices to the Jewish people. She went on to write,

The German police took many hostages [leaders in government, churches, etc.], to be held responsible in the event of any resistance or sabotage.

Neighbors started to hide Jews. Many were saved that way. Quite often, Jewish children would be brought to farmers who would hide them. But when the Germans would find one, they'd kill the ones who hid them.

From the beginning to the end of the war, there was resistance. For instance, at the shipyard in Rotterdam, they found dynamite to blow the place up rather than work for the Germans' war effort. A friend of my brother [now my husband] was arrested with about 160 other people. Many more prominent people were arrested as hostages when the Resistance was found. They would kill several.

For instance, they went so far as to take away all of the men of the town of Putton. The Resistance attacked an army truck, killing one German officer. Of the 590 men who were taken away from that town, 540 were killed.

In April 1943, a nationwide strike broke out because entire age groups were called up to work in Germany for the war. All the men between 17-40 years of age were to be picked up outside their houses. Thousands went into hiding. Extensive resistance sprang up to support the people in hiding. My two married brothers and their families came to live with us. My brother spent the last two years of the war hiding in the house. It was an extremely stressful time.

When I asked Mom how they were able to hide her brothers for so long, she told me about the secret room in the attic above the living quarters and the bakery. More accurately, this hiding place was not much larger than a closet. A bookcase/storage unit was built as a front for this part of the attic. When German soldiers or Dutch collaborators came to the store, her two married brothers quickly fled behind this false front of the hiding room in the attic. She said they never left the bakery in those two years, and they always lived in fear.

When I was an adolescent studying this period in history, *Anne Frank: The Diary of a Young Girl* was required reading. I asked Mom what she thought of the story of Anne Frank. She said:

> *It was difficult for all of us. Many people had hiding rooms in their homes and saved many lives. What was different about Anne Frank was that she was a young girl who ended up in the camps and died there, and she also kept a detailed diary that was found. It was a heartbreaking story, and important to tell. All of our stories are a witness to these atrocities.*

> *During this time of the war, April of 1943, it seemed apparent that the Germans were starting to lose the war. It became very noticeable in their attitude and behavior toward the Dutch people. Gradually, the age of the soldiers became younger and younger as they lost more and more soldiers fighting in other places, like the Russian Front.*

> *By then, the electricity was being rationed and the gas and the water too. More and more time during the day was taken up finding food. Lines were everywhere! Most shops were empty by then because they were not resupplied.*

> *Burglaries were a regular thing in our shop and bakery, even though there was nothing there anymore. Sometimes German soldiers would drop off flour and ask my father, "How many loaves can you make from this sack?"*

> *My father would quote 50, but you can be sure he could get 55 for instance, and we then had bread to eat.*

> *Then there were "soup kitchens," for which you stood in line for hours in freezing weather to get your soup.*

> *Curfew had already been established for a long time. No one was allowed on the street after 7:00pm. If you were seen in front of your window after that, you could be shot!*

> *Most schools continued to be open during the war. But then all the schools closed in September of 1944. At that time there was a rumor that the war was over. Belgium was freed and much of the southern part of Holland was also liberated. People believed the rumors. They began to gather outside singing and dancing, and many proudly hung their Dutch flags out the second story windows. Then suddenly there was shooting at the crowds by these young teenage German soldiers! Many people were killed and the rumor turned out to be false.*

I remember when mother first told me about this incident. It was horrible for her to have been so excited, thinking the war was over, only to witness the carnage happening around her. She could never forget the yelling and screaming of the crowd as fellow countrymen were being killed around her. She had never before witnessed such bloodshed. The fear and disappointment were nearly unbearable. To make matters worse, the greatest hardship was still ahead for Holland.

Near the end of 1944, the exiled Dutch government living in England ordered a general railroad strike throughout Holland. They did so thinking that the collapse of the German occupiers was imminent. In response to this strike, the Germans cut off all food and fuel shipments to the western territories, where 4.5 million people lived, including my mother.

She went on to write:

After that horrible day, we still had to go through the worst. We had to suffer through the awful hunger winter of 1944-1945. We were not only starving and out of food, we were out of gas and electricity too. There were contagious diseases and epidemics of polio and tuberculosis, and we were out of other things like soap and medicines. We were hungry and in need for those things as well. This was all happening in the northern and western parts of Holland.

I remember during those days that we got a package from the Red Cross of Sweden. It contained bread and butter, enough to give ½ loaf for each family member. My mother gave each of us their own portion. It was interesting to see how each one of us handled their rations. I chose to eat mine very slowly.

Then we saw the famous "Food Drop" from the allies and I still remember the crackers. We were very grateful! The hardest part was not knowing how long this situation would last. Why don't they come and help us? That's what all of us were thinking.

Finally, on May 4, the Germans gave permission for the Red Cross to enter with their famine teams into the Dutch territories still occupied. They came to give aid to the victims of the forced starvation.

During the "Hunger Winter" of 1944-45, roughly 30,000 Dutch citizens lost their lives. Of those who died, 18,000 were of starvation, the rest died in the cold weather from diseases or exhaustion.

Once the Germans began to retreat from the occupied territories, Hitler had ordered what was known as the Scorched Earth policy. Large industrial facilities were destroyed, as well as the entire transportation system in Holland. Vast parts of the land in Holland were inundated with the sea water after many of the dikes were destroyed.

In the morning of May 5, 1945, at 0800, the surrender of the German troops in Holland went into effect. Finally, after five long years of occupation, Holland was free, and totally empty of everything. But we were free, thank God!

My account of the war does not contain all the atrocities that happened! Near the end of the war, 400,000 Dutchmen were still in forced labor camps in Germany. My future husband was one of them.

I do know this; the Resistance never gave up! The first thing they did when they came out of hiding was to arrest all members of the NSB, the National Socialist Party. Holland suffered immensely from this war and from all those people who supported the German occupiers.

Since all of the police and government systems had not been restored yet, Vlaardingen was in serious need of stability. The Dutch Resistance temporarily stepped in to maintain law and order throughout Holland, providing the necessary security.

Many of the liberated townspeople suffered so very much and could no longer contain their contempt for any of the Dutch traitors. Not only did they arrest the collaborators of the NSP, they also arrested many of the women who were sexually involved with the German soldiers.

Everyone could identify these women when they were release from jail. Their heads were shaved bald, and they were paraded down the crowded streets in ignominy. In their humiliation, many of these women and their small children were forced out into the countryside to beg for mercy from anyone who would show compassion.

What would we have done, and how would we have reacted to these women? Some of the women freely chose Option B, and were traitors from the beginning. Still others, had held onto Option A as long as they could, until there was no other way to provide for themselves and their children during the extreme conditions created by the Nazi command. Now with this bit of information, how should we react? I hope we never have to answer questions like these. It's difficult enough to write about such matters.

The punishment for collaborating with the enemy was varied. Many were lynched without a trial. Many of the men who freely chose to fight with the Germans were sent away to clear minefields, and suffered losses accordingly. Those who survived this type of punishment would spend time in concentration camps or prisons, trading places with the patriots they had wronged.

Other traitors were tried for treason in the courts and received various sentences. Sadly, because of the rush to judgment, some were wrongly arrested and were later cleared of charges after having spent long periods of time behind bars.

Mother ended her written story when she wrote, "The truth is that this war was hell for all of us who lived through it!"

Throughout Suze's ordeal, she hung on to the hope that life would return to normal someday. Sadly, the life she lived before the war could never be restored. Too much had happened, and too much was witnessed. Whatever she had planned for her future now seemed impossible. Life was altered, and would never really be the same again.

Suze Bruggeman was 14 when the war came to Holland. She would lose five precious years of her youth that should have been spent developing normally. These teenage years should have been spent growing securely in herself and in relationships with others. There was no way to date, or to figure out what kind of man she might want to marry someday. The boys her age and older were either gone or were staying out of sight.

Mom never had that opportunity to create her own line of clothing and open up her shop like she had intended. She mentioned to me again that it would have been called, "The House of Suze."

What the war did not take from her was her love of God and her devotion to her faith. Suze would trust in the Good Lord to help her figure out what life had in store for her now. It would not be long before she would confront new choices that would lead her on a new path. This faith and hope of hers would help her to choose the new direction in her life.

The few of us lucky to call her "Mom," are very proud of her for taking the time to write parts of her own story about the war. I always knew that both Dad and Mom lived incredible lives. They hid it from the general public for many years, and even when they did disclose bits and pieces, they held back so much more.

They were survivors!

Mienus and Suze lived, loved, and had a family, and they are so much more than just a wartime story. To my siblings and me, they were our parents who gave up so much to make our lives better. Now they live on through us! *Lang zal ze leven*!

Chapter 6

Times to Talk

Dad kept his secrets from his family during our childhood years to protect us. Throughout my 20's and 30's, there were many times Mark and I took the family to Salem to stay with my folks for a few days. When we were older, they were more comfortable sharing greater details about their lives in Holland, our relatives, WWII, and our emigration. I could listen to Dad and Mom reminiscing for hours. When talk of the war came up, Dad would either begin or end the conversation with, "It was Hell!"

The majority of our visits included the traditional afternoon tea and chocolates. Teatime provided the perfect opportunity to talk about all kinds of things, and could easily last an hour or two. After finishing at least two cups of tea, and likely two pieces of chocolate, Dad would look at the clock and announce, "Suze, its 4 o'clock," and then head to the old stereo cabinet that held the Black Velvet whiskey, and other spirits to indulge in. It was from my dear Dad that I learned to enjoy a cold drink of BV and Seven. I still think of *Papa* when I have one.

As I mentioned earlier, I am known within my extended family as the "inquisitor." I can envision the heads of my siblings bobbing up and down as they read this part, saying to themselves, "Yep, that's Marja! She's the questioner, the cross-examiner, interviewer, and the investigator." I've heard them all, and I wear that hat with care.

I never shied away from asking detailed questions involving their time in the war. Dad would answer almost anything I asked of him, but then navigate the conversation to what he was willing, and wanting, to share with me.

Perhaps I was asking the wrong questions, or more likely, Dad wasn't eager to talk too much about certain parts of his story. He steered me into his accounts the way he wanted to tell them. This was his life to disclose, his memories to share, his journey walked, and his cross to bear, and only when he was ready to relive it again would he share the details.

Labor, Pain, and Cruelty

For the first couple of years in Buchenwald, the physical labor required of Mienus was the hardest of his imprisonment. During that period of continued toil, Mienus would lose many of his friends from the Resistance. Not only was the physical nature of the work life threatening, so was the crushing emotional toll. He must have thought, "How many more friends will die in front of me? How much longer before I can't do this anymore?"

He shared:

> The camp was situated on a hill and surrounded by forests and rocks. Sometimes I worked in the rock quarries and other times in the forest and lumber mill. We didn't have any heavy equipment to work with; we only had picks and shovels to use. There were no trucks or flatbeds for us either, only wooden carts to load and haul the rocks and wood with. Day after day we pulled stones and gravel up the hill. We had ropes on the carts we used to tug with. It would take many men to load, pull, and push tons of rock at a time up that hill. We did this even as our bodies were getting weaker from little food and rest. There would be lots of shouting and whipping going on to make us hurry and work even harder. We lost a lot of men over time. They just could not do it anymore.
>
> When I worked in the forest cutting down trees, we had to push the trees up the hill using only prisoners and no equipment. Several times the SS soldiers, just to be mean, would wait till the heavy logs were at the top of the hill, and then force the prisoners to move away so they

could push the log down the hill again. Then, of course, we were forced to start all over to push it up the hill once more. They did this many times. They would laugh and really enjoy making us suffer. Finally the camp commandant got word of what the SS guards were doing to us, and this treatment stopped. It did not stop because we were being made to suffer, but because it was taking longer to finish building the factories and the rest of the camp.

Staying alive in Buchenwald during those first two years was nearly impossible. Many prisoners had already died in the camp, and many others had been relocated to one of the numerous other concentration camps in Germany, including those that were designed for mass exterminations. Mienus would see many of his fellow inmates getting weaker and weaker because they were older to begin with, or always sick. When the infirmary was full, the SS guards would load the very sick into trains that would transport them to the killing camps.

I must have been about eight or nine years old when I found a couple of books hidden away on the floor of Mom and Dad's bedroom closet. I can't even remember why I was in their closet. What I do remember was the shock I felt just looking at the covers of these books. One of the books gave me nightmares for years. It was published in 1960, and was called, *"Medical Block Buchenwald,"* by Walter Poller. The author was himself a prisoner in Buchenwald and was forced to participate as the secretary to the camp doctor. With his assignment in the camp, he was in a unique position to be a witness to some of the most unspeakable atrocities in history. He was also able to gather important evidence that was later helpful in the war trials that followed.

Leafing quickly through the book, I got to the middle pages containing several pictures. This was the beginning of my journey to learn and comprehend what my father had been through during the war. I didn't tell Dad about finding the book until I was married. The fact that it was placed in the closet the way it was, was his way of sheltering this horror from us.

When I told him that I had found the books, he wasn't too surprised. I had so many questions to ask him about his experiences. I don't remember when I finally had the nerve to ask him the very important question that was on my mind for many years. "Dad, did they do any experiments on you in the camp?"

He thought for a minute, preparing his reply in just the right way. "Yes, I was used for something. Several of us were sent to the infirmary and given several injections. We did not know what was in those syringes. It didn't take long before I got very sick and broke out in hives all over my body. I was kept in the medical block for a day or two. Then, when I didn't die, I was sent back to the barracks. That was the only time."

Later, from my own research, I learned with greater detail the inhumane experiments that killed most of those who were forced to endure them. Even now, after so many decades, it overwhelms my mind how humans can treat others with such brutality. Thankfully, my father was spared those experiments. The SS spared him because they knew that he would be needed in the machine shops when the factories were operational.

I will not provide the names of those involved in such horrible crimes against humanity. There is enough written about them already. I do not wish to give them any other attention. Let them rot in Hell! That may seem harsh, but I'm leaving it in.

On another occasion, I asked Dad, "How did you survive when so many others didn't?" The following was his response:

That's a good question. I watched many of the prisoners kill themselves. Many men would last a couple of years, like I had, and then something would make them think about their spouse or children, and they would begin to worry and talk about them, and what might be going on back home. That would be the end of them. Within two weeks or so, we would find these prisoners clinging to the electric barbed wire fences, having grabbed them to end their suffering. Thank God, I didn't do that. I was young and single. I had a trade that was useful, and my faith in God was strong. I forced myself not to think too much. I just needed to survive another day.

That is how he survived! It sounds simple, but I know how hard he fought to stay alive. He fought for my siblings and me, and all his descendants. He just didn't express it that way.

Mienus was much thinner from his lack of food and the labor moving rocks and turning trees into lumber. At 5 feet 11 inches, a man this size should comfortably weigh 170-175 pounds. Mienus was much closer to 125-130 pounds, and still losing. His training as a machinist, and his knowledge in metallurgy would soon be utilized, and that would help to save him. The two years of hard labor in the outside elements changed to long and hard hours inside the factories, fabricating "stuff" in the machine shops.

Large amounts of raw materials and factory machine equipment was transported to the camp to be used to manufacture ammunition, spare parts, weapons, and many other products used by the Nazis fighting the Russians and the Allied forces. Mienus would spend the better part of the rest of the war in these factories. The Germans were keeping him alive to work seven long days per week.

I remember asking Dad if he ever sabotaged any of his fabrications. He looked at me and said, as a matter-of-fact, "Of course! Whenever an opportunity came about, I would try to change a small part of the machines or cause a defect in the products we were manufacturing. They would be very small but could still make a difference. The SS soldiers did not have the knowledge I did about these things. What was most important to them was making their quota. I knew it was risky, and I was very careful not to get caught. I just hoped that my small efforts made it more difficult on the Germans." I remember looking at Dad with pride when he finished speaking. He was looking out into space remembering.

A Trusted Leader

Mienus had figured out how to stay alive and navigate prison life in this horrible place. He survived a few years already, and his reputation within the barracks had grown. Among the other prisoners in his barrack, they knew he was someone they could trust, and someone to rely on. New arrivals in shock after entering the camp would be steered toward Mienus for assistance. He would take them under his wings and be brutally honest, and tell them what to do to survive in Buchenwald. He was a trusted leader.

To provide an unbiased judgment of Mienus' character and the impact he had on the other prisoners, I quote an excerpt from a book called, "*De Schok Van Het Onbekende.*" The English translation is, "The Shock of the Unknown—Vlaardingen during the crisis occupation and liberation 1936-1947," written by Dr. Klaas Karnaat. In this book, the author writes about a letter sent by Piet van der Harst to his wife and family about his few months in Buchenwald. It states:

In March of 1945 we arrived in Buchenwald. The first night we were stripped naked, shaved of all our body hair, and forced into a Lysol disinfectant bath. I had the good fortune of being given a reasonable pair of shoes, which turned out to be a salvation to me. We ended up in Barrack #43 and in quarantine. Through the fence we could recognize others from Vlaardingen. I saw Wim van Hoogerverf and Mienus van Lith, who I went to Visserijseschool [grade school] with. I also was given a rabbit skin vest from Mienus that he had made. That was wonderful since it was extremely cold. Under these harsh conditions, Dirk van der Ende contracted pneumonia which he later died from.

(Karnaat)

When I first read this passage, my attention was drawn to the man's description of his entrance into the camp. It corroborates my father's description of his first day in Buchenwald. I then found it very interesting that Dad was still recognizable after almost four years in such horrific conditions. Finally, what kind of person makes a vest out of rabbit skin, and then gives it to a new and otherwise healthy prisoner in the coldest of conditions, while he himself was emaciated? Mienus van Lith was that kind of person, and there are six of us blessed to call him our father. I could no longer hold back the tears, feeling such loving pride.

Mienus was a leader who learned to adapt and survive in harsh conditions. Even an SS soldier developed a conscience in his presence, and made a bold move by offering to share a cigarette with his prisoner.

In the book my sister wrote for the family, "The Continuing Family History of Dominicus van Lith and Suzanna Bruggeman-van Lith," Gert shares a letter that our mother wrote in February 2005, when she was just shy of her 80th birthday. Mom normally did not watch too much television, especially programs about the war and the concentration camps. This particular evening, she felt compelled to watch one of those shows. John Paul II had just died a few days before, and there was lots of coverage about the war on the television. Mother was compelled to write one last account to her children. In the middle of it she writes (edited for clarity):

> I remember it was about 1954. We were still living in Vlaardingen. Our front door bell rang. I opened the door and saw a very nice gentleman who asked, "Is Mienus van Lith living here?"

> I invited him in. Mienus and this man recognized each other and embraced. His name was Frits van Hutton and he had been searching for Mienus for years. He gave me a box of chocolate and told me his story.

> Mienus had saved his life, and he wanted to tell me how grateful he was. The story goes, as an added punishment, food was withheld from Frits in Buchenwald, so Mienus started to share his bread with him. That kept him alive! And he was ever so grateful! Isaiah 58:10-1 comes to mind when Frits said, "Mienus shared what little he had."

Later in Mother's written account, she goes on to say,

> In conversation, some stories came out. Sometimes Mienus would try to save his bread for the evening. After the hard work of the day, he was even hungrier. He wanted to eat the bread with the "soup."

> In the camp, if a man stole a piece of bread from another, fighting broke out, and when the Nazis found out, they hung the man. As Mienus said, "You steal bread from a man, you steal his life. You're not worth living.

> Within the prison camps, order was maintained between the men living together in the barracks by following the "Golden Rule." Do unto others, as you would have them do unto you! This was the strict code that was enforced, even unto death.

I asked Dad once, "Did you ever kill anyone in the camps?" He was quick to answer, "No, I never did. But men did die at the hands of others for not following the rules, but it was the SS who took control and sometimes punished whole groups because of one man's behavior."

Mother's letter to us continued:

> Then there was another man [Piet van der Harst]. He was grateful to Mienus who gave him a vest made of rabbit skin. He said that it saved his life. Winters were extremely cold there [in the camp] and all they had to wear was that thin striped pajama. Some just died of the cold. I never heard the story how Mienus managed to get rabbit skins. I can only imagine."

During conversation with the other ex-prisoners, I noticed that they saw Mienus as an "organizer/leader." He seemed to know more of the ins and outs there because he had gotten to Buchenwald so early in the war, and he was still alive."

I recall your dad saying he was used in building up the camp. He started out carrying large stones, actually, building onto the camp.

Another thing Mienus talked about was the cruelty of Ilsa Kock, the wife of the commandant of Buchenwald. She got to pick out tattoos for new lampshades she wanted, making them from the skin of those who had tattoos she liked. That would be the end of that person. She was wicked. [Author's Note: This woman would identify these tattoos from living prisoners. If she liked what she saw, she would have the prisoner killed and skinned. Some of these lampshades and book covers can still be seen at war memorials.]

All in all, he never much shared about those years to others until the neo-Nazis started approaching young people in the area and saying those things never happened. Then he began to talk to young people in high schools and let them ask him questions.

Somehow, I felt the urge to say these things before it all get lost.

– Suzanna Bruggeman- van Lith 2005

It's not lost Momma!

Letters

The van Lith family in Vlaardingen knew what had happened to their son and brother. They knew of his arrest, his time in the *Oranjehotel*, and then his transfer to a camp in Germany called Buchenwald. No one in Holland knew what a "concentration camp" was. They only knew that it was some sort of a factory camp.

Mienus began communicating with his family a few months after he was transferred to Germany in April 1941. His parents would receive his letters at their home. New mail would arrive every other month or so, when possible. These letters were sporadic the first couple of years. The hard labor, the beatings, the punishments, and the inevitable illnesses Mienus had to endure, prevented him from corresponding for long periods of time.

Each correspondence between Mienus and his parents would first have to be read by the Nazi SS. All letters leaving and everything entering the camp had to be inspected first. The German commandant was very strict, and worried about possible leaks of information that could eventually damage the camp in some way. Buchenwald was overcrowded with prisoners, including many political prisoners from several occupied countries. The Germans suspected acts of espionage could possibly be going on within the camps. They were correct.

When Mienus' letters arrived, his parents knew right away that they had been edited. They were only permitted to read what was not blacked out. He was careful not to be careless with his words out of fear for his life and that of his family. But some important information did get through using just the right words that only a very few would understand.

Suze Bruggeman would occasionally run into one of Mienus' family member while out shopping, or see them when they came to the bakery. She would ask about their brother to find out how he was doing in Germany. She really didn't understand the gravity of his situation from the information they provided. She wanted to express concern and be polite. Suze asked them to be sure and say hello to Mienus for her. Like a lot of good intentions, that particular message did not make it into the family letters.

Nearly three years had gone by since Mienus had been arrested in the shipyards of Rotterdam. It was now the end of 1943. One of his sisters saw Suze while shopping. Like before, Suze inquired about Mienus and again asked her to, "Please say hello to him for me the next time you send him a letter!"

Mother said to me, "I didn't really know what to say anymore. I just wanted him to know that others were thinking of him too."

This time, with the help of Mienus' sister, Suze's message was added to the end of the next letter that was on its way to Buchenwald. Mienus was so surprised and very happy to have received a note from the young girl he had known for a number of years, and briefly courted before he was imprisoned. "She would be 18 years old by now," he surely must have thought, and he was 23.

Genesis of Love

Beginning in January 1944, a letter to his parents arrived which included a "P.S." at the end for Suze Bruggeman. Soon after, Suze received visitors from the van Lith family. They were excited to let her know that they had passed her message onto Mienus in their last correspondence, and to let her read what he had written to her in reply. Subsequent letters arriving from Mienus to his family continued to include a P.S. message to Suze.

Letters began arriving more frequently.

> *January 1944*
>
> *P.S.*
>
> *Dear Suze,*
>
> *Thank you for the greeting. It hurt me that it took so long to hear from you. I waited three years for this. I am glad that I am not forgotten all together yet. In these hard times, you must not forget that there will be other times after this. I have thought about you often. The good times we had I have not forgotten. Hopefully we will see each other again. I long for that. Please write me a letter of how you and your family are doing. If possible a Niestadje.*
>
> *Hearty greeting, Your Mienus.*

Suze read the first "P.S." Mienus sent to her. She was so surprised at what Mienus had written, and didn't know quite what to make of the candid affection he was revealing on paper. Some of her memories and her feelings were not quite the same as his. She was, however, very pleased to hear from him after so long. Mother would later say to me, "I was a little embarrassed knowing that everyone in your Dad's family probably already read this too!"

All the letters Mienus wrote were written in German and had to be translated. Suze would then write his messages in Dutch and keep them for herself. When she read the word "Niestadje" at the end of his note to her, she knew right away what he was wanting. Pictures were forbidden in the barracks but Suze knew that he was asking for a picture of her. "Niestadje" was a photographer in town whose name they would both recognize. This request was not picked up by those censuring the mail. But Mienus didn't know that for sure until Suze responded.

Suze only had Mienus' letters to keep. He could not save the ones he received. I could only surmise what was in the letters she sent to him. It was not long before Suze was able to respond to his first letter and it seemed even quicker for Mienus to write back again.

January 1944

P.S.

Dear Suze,

I was so happy to receive your letter but even more for the Niestadje. Special thanks for that. Also, the pudding was prima (perfect) and the Niestadje underneath the packaging was good. Suze, as long I have known you, and in the time that I have been gone, I think about you a lot. Though my longing for home and all that I love is growing stronger by the day, I am hopeful we will see each other again. I have so much to say, but I can't write it. Suze, write me regularly. I will do the same. I send many greetings to your family. Hope your mother is better.

With a kiss for you, Your Mienus

February 6, 1944

P.S.

Dear Suze,

So far I have not received anything from you. I long for your letter. All is in order here. I hope that it is the same with you. Suze, I think much about you and with that Niestadje it makes me happy. You write that you think much about me also, is that as a friend or something more? I hope, maybe, it is something more? Write to me about this. When I was there, I liked you very much. You must have known that yourself. But now we are three years older and hopefully we will see each other again. What a joy that would be.

Many greetings to you and yours, in my thoughts I kiss you. From, Mienus.

April 2, 1944

P.S.

Dear Suze,

I received your letter from March the 3rd and I am glad all goes well with you. Thank you for that Niestadje in the package. I am happy with that. Suze, what you wrote in your letter made things clear for me. You wrote you were engaged and it shocked me. I have not gone that far before. I had many girlfriends but they were not the right ones. Suze, things that happened in the past, I don't think about any more. I think about you a lot and I am happy that you think about me also. What I think most wonderful would be my returning home, to my father and mother, yes, but especially returning to you. Then we can say to each other what is really in our hearts. I long for you, Suze and I would like to tell you what I am really thinking. But I cannot tell you now. We must be patient. Suze, write a long letter back to me.

I send many greeting for all at home.

A sincere hug, from your Mienus.

It is surreal to read and write these touching letters from my father to his future wife. As children, we don't think much about our parents being young and falling in love. They've just always been there with us. They've always been, well, older. When I read these letters for the first time about how my father was longing for my mother, it led my thoughts in new directions.

My mother had always been more reserved, more private. I never dreamed of asking questions about her romance with Dad as a young child. I was married by the time this subject was brought up, by me of course. My quizzical mind just wanted to know more.

It was during one of our talks about the "Old Country, Holland" that I approach my mother about dating and marrying my father. I remember asking her about what it was like being an adolescent during the war, and how she learned about relationships with boys, especially since so many of them were gone. She was quick to say that she was very naïve about boys, and was poor to pick up on their intentions.

She talked a bit about the boy she was engaged to for a short time. Apparently, she had met this young man during one of the many visits to her favorite aunt who was living in the town of 'S-Hertogenbosch, just a short train trip away. Many of her summers were spent there. Some of her best memories of her childhood were created there.

One of her favorite things to do was to slip away by herself and walk down to the beautiful St. John's Cathedral. Suze loved the old Gothic structure that was built in the 1380's. She especially enjoyed her visits when the choir was rehearsing for the weekend Masses. She could spend hours just sitting there praying and admiring the beautiful interior. This place filled her with a peacefulness that she could not find anywhere else. And she would long to be there as often as she could.

Mother shared very little about this young man that she was apparently engaged to. She, with her cousin and this young man, spent time hanging out and doing whatever there was to do for entertainment during the German Occupation, which was very little. They would take long walks and bike rides, play games, and just enjoyed the friendships between them. It was a way to pass the time.

From what I could figure out, before Suze left to go back to Vlaardingen after one of her long visits, this young man apparently said that he wanted to marry her. She was surprised by his statement and, in her confusion, must have told him that she would. There was no ring to share, no asking her father, no timeline, just the question, "will you?" and the quick answer, "um, yes!" Now my imagination is taking over, and I share my version of what might have happened between my mother and this boy.

Mother had shared, on more than a few occasions, her naiveté when it came to relationships with boys. Her mother didn't tell her much at all about the "bird and the bees." When it was her time to move through puberty, she became frightened, and confronted her mother. What her mother told her was, "Oh, you're not going to die, that's normal. It just means you're not a girl anymore; you're becoming a woman. Just use these each time, and don't worry!" That was my mother's education in the matter. That's why she was 18 or 19 years old before she had any idea where babies came from.

Because of her innocence and purity, virtuous qualities for a teenage girl, it was difficult for her to figure out what adolescent boys and young men really were wanting. I'm pretty sure this young man who was smitten by my mother during a summer visit, was maybe looking to get really close to Suze if he brought up getting married. He was probably hoping for a "homerun," shall we say!

Before she left, Suze did tell her cousin what had transpired between the boy and herself, and it took her cousin by surprise. Her cousin was concerned for Suze. Upon returning to Vlaardingen late that summer, Suze went about her business back at home helping in the bakery, and trying her best to live as normally as possible during the middle of the Occupation.

I can safely deduce what happened next. Letters passed between the boy and Suze for a short time. Her cousin kept in touch with Suze as well. At some point, her cousin had suspicions regarding the young man's credibility, and mentioned the proposal to her mother. Her mother quickly contacted her sister, Suze's mother, in Vlaardingen. Shortly after that, Suze's mother had a frank conversation with her youngest daughter. She was told to break off this engagement. The next letter Suze sent to this young man was to break off their engagement. She was not allowed to marry him.

I asked her why her mother had her break off the engagement, and she told me, "I never really knew why. She must have known something about this boy, and didn't like him. I was upset but obeyed my mother, and called it off!"

I find it interesting that this episode in mother's life coincided with the letters that were arriving from Mienus after three years of separation. Was it a coincidence or providential? I'm pretty sure I know!

> *May 7, 1944*
>
> *P.S.*
>
> *Dear Suze,*
>
> *Your letter from March 30, I received last night plus the one from April 24. Again I thoroughly enjoy them. Suze, I am sorry I cannot write you more often. I would love to write to you. I received a package that was not from my parents. I believe it must have come from you. Then Suze, you asked that I should not forget that you are always thinking about me. I will never forget. But Suze, don't forget that I might be thinking about YOU more. I long to see you again. Maybe it will be in the spring. Nevertheless, one day the flowers will bloom for us. This is my most important thought. Then, Suze, the future will be brighter for us.*
>
> *Darling, I send a hearty greeting and hugs from your Mienus.*

The next several contacts between them were happening quite often now. The feelings expressed were growing deeper with each exchange. It makes me think that my mother's letters were the most important things for Mienus now. They were giving him an even greater reason to survive his Hell. Suze was gently embracing him with her letters and packages. He had fallen deeply in love with the young 15-year-old girl that he had strong feelings for three years ago, before his capture. She is now a woman living in his heart.

While reading his letters, I imagined Mienus growing stronger in his mind, his resolve, his faith, and his heart, even as his body was slowly fading toward an end he was fighting to avoid. He was too young to die. Even as others had taken their own lives thinking about their wives and children, Mienus would not give in to despair. "One day at a time. That is how to survive, one day at a time!"

> *June 4, 1944*
>
> *P.S.*
>
> *Dear Suze,*
>
> *Your sweet letter from April 24, I call to mind. I enjoy reading that very much. Suze, the flowers you brought to my parents for their special occasion from me was very nice of you to do. I will not forget what you did. I would have loved to have been there that day, but that was not possible. Only in my thoughts was I there. I dreamed so much about home and about you.*
>
> *I am still very pleased to have your Niestadje. Do you have another one?*
>
> *Also, thank you for your well wishes for my birthday. Days like that are very difficult for us. But that is how it is. So we must be patient. Suze, when I read your question, "What is this all good for?" I believe that will be answered someday. I think about you from our earlier times so much. But when I come home it will be even better. Day and night I think about that. I long for the day that we will see each other again. Dear Suze, I think about our future.*

Give my warm greeting to your family and then.........Dearest Suze my greeting to you from your Mienus.

July 2, 1944

P.S.

Dear Suze,

Your letter from June 1, I received with much joy. Also, that package gave me much joy. Suze, I would like to write you also what I want most but don't worry too much. What I long for, you cannot give me yet. We need to be patient with that until we see each other. Suze, you understand me, don't you? I think about that often. I would like another Niestadje. This would make me very happy. Suze, next time you go into the sun, watch out that you don't get burned again. I wish you could see my tan. Suze, think about sports, life, and love, when I am back. Hopefully it will come soon--I so long for that. I have to close this letter; it is full (too bad.) There is so much more I could write.

Give my many greetings to your family. But to you I give my love and kisses from your Mienus.

Please, write me a long letter back.

August 6, 1944

P.S.

Dear Suze,

I received your sweet letter from July 28. Suze, that is the only thing I long for. I can understand that you long for my letter also. I am alright and everything is the same here. I am happy to know that about you too. First, congratulations on your birthday. So sorry I did not remember. Hopefully the words on the end of our letter will be real. I will whisper beautiful things in your ear. Your package with the Niestadje makes me happy. When I see the love and care that you used to send it, it brings me so much closer to you in my mind. Suze thank you so much. When freedom comes, we can be happy. A beautiful future lies before us!

Suze and Mienus had no idea how much longer this seemingly never-ending war would last. And it would be getting much worse for both of them soon. Each would live under the harshest winter of their lives, and their letters would soon be disrupted.

August 10, 1944

P.S.

Dear Suze,

I received your letter from July. I thought about you a lot while you were on vacation. Suze, hopefully someday we will be on a vacation together. That would be so wonderful. So sad I don't have your Niestadje anymore. But that is not the most important thing to me, just so we are healthy. There is something that K. Bass looked after. Suze I can't write anymore. My letter is full. Have courage and patience with us. We will see each other again.

Deeply hugged and kissed, Your Mienus.

Mienus no longer had Suze's picture. It is unknown to me whether it was taken from him or whether it was destroyed. Just two months earlier, the liberation of Europe was initiated on D-Day, June 6, 1944. The American troops had invaded the beaches of Normandy, and the English, Canadians, and other Allied forces were on the move as well. There were a number of bombing raids by the Allies that had destroyed the area outside the perimeter of Buchenwald. There was some destruction in the camp with casualties.

The SS soldiers of the camp were extremely uneasy and on high alert. They likely would have ordered raids within the barracks occupied by the political prisoners, and confiscated items that were forbidden. Whatever happened to Suze's pictures will remain a mystery. Mienus no longer had them for comfort. He just wanted to survive whatever happened next, and hoped that Suze stayed healthy and alive when he returned.

There were hidden messages in this letter sent on August 10, 1944. His words communicated a sense of foreboding. The current bombings at the camp were making life more dreadful than it already was. Many prisoners were dying, while many more prisoners were arriving in trainloads. This time the trains included women and children. Mienus was hoping that whoever read his letter could provide him with some information.

Mienus was also sending a message by using the name K. Bass. Bass was a distant relative of Mienus, and was a Dutch soldier working in England in the beginning of the war. Since Suze only saved the "P.S" portion of the letter, in this letter to his parents, and before the "P.S., he could have included additional clues to the message that he was trying to pass on. K. Bass was either to be contacted in England and informed of the deteriorating conditions, or Mienus' parents should tell Bass' relatives that he was with him in the camp. Apparently, those in charge of censoring the mail did not find anything of concern. None of it was blacked out. This action shows his continuing resolve to be a faithful *Geuzen*.

Chapter 7

August 24, 1944

Allied bombings around Buchenwald were sporadic. To prevent bombing, the Germans had designed the camp to resemble other prison camps that they had built, hoping the Allies wouldn't identify it as a factory labor camp. It worked for a time.

Airborne reconnaissance did eventually identify the camp as a manufacturing plant. Many aerial photos were taken, which provided enough information to create a detailed blueprint of the camp and its surrounding structures. With good intelligence, they knew where the prison barracks were, along with the SS living quarters, the factories, the railroad, and every other structure inside and outside of the camp.

Regardless of how exhausted he was from the hard labor each day, sleep was sporadic, if at all. Many nights, Mienus would wake to the sounds of the planes flying overhead and pray that they would fly past Buchenwald. He had cause to be concerned, as previous bombing runs near the compound had caused minor damage inside the barbed wire fences. Up till now, the main factories were not grossly affected, and the daily routines of roll call, meager food, and hard labor continued for the prisoners. That was all about to change.

On August 24, 1944, a bombing raid by the American Military Forces did major damage to the main factories within the camp. It demolished the Mibau factory, where the V-2 rockets were being built, and severely damaged the Gustloff Works ammunitions factory. The SS quarters, officers' quarters, and unfortunately a portion of the prisoner barracks were critically damaged as well. Roughly 385 prisoners died that day of the injuries they sustained. Some high-ranking members of the SS, as well as some family members of the commandant, were also killed.

After the bombing, life in the camps was far worse than before. Even with all the damage, Buchenwald continued to receive trainloads of new prisoners. The camp was already overcrowded, and with the fall and winter quickly approaching, survival, for many, would be impossible.

In his first couple of years in camp, Mienus had been forced to sleep with another prisoner on a narrow wooden bunk bed that was four tiers high. Now, nearly three and a half years later, and with so many new prisoners continually entering the camp, the men were forced to sleep four or five to a bunk. Though it was extremely uncomfortable with this many men sleeping widthwise together, they would desperately need each other's warmth at night to stay alive during the bitter winter months.

In these extreme conditions, a prisoner was lucky if he was provided a thin, striped prison coat that covered the thin pajama uniform. Coats and blankets were luxuries. Prisoners would quickly remove the clothes off of the dead to prevent themselves from freezing to death. Tens of thousands of prisoners would not survive the winter of 1944-45.

After much of the working factories in the camp were destroyed, the population was much larger than was needed. Attempts were made to transport many of the prisoners to other camps, but the Germans were slowly losing the war, and the infrastructure to transport prisoners out of the camp was tenuous at best.

The limited supply of food for the current population of prisoners meant there was less and less for everyone. Mienus would soon see his weight reduce down to a mere 115-120 pounds. The daily rations before the airstrike provided just enough food to stay alive to work. Now that the camp was destroyed and the work was gone, he was getting weaker and weaker. Mienus would have to figure out other ways to stay alive, if that was even possible. In his mind, he had to survive.

Jan. 7, 1945

P.S.

Dear Suze,

Your letter of October 10, I received. That made me happy again. Suze, I think so much about you. This is all taking so long. But sweetheart, I will not lose my courage. If it is possible, send me a Niestadje. That would make me very happy. Suze, keep living as you have all this time. Hopefully we will see each other again. This is my greatest wish. Give my warm greetings to your family. In my mind I hug and kiss you.

Your Mienus

This would be Mienus' last letter from Buchenwald to his future wife. Even though I know how this story ends, I still find myself hoping that the growing love between Mienus and Suze will have a happy ending. I hope their suffering will end soon. I hope they both live to see each other again, as adults. Both have grown up under extreme conditions and are not the children they once were.

My deepest gratitude, once again, goes to my sister Gert, who took the time to have our mother translate these letters. Gert told me about the look on Mom's face after reading them again, and heard her say, "Wow, these letters are very romantic! Who is this guy?"

Holocaust

A: From the History Channel

The word "Holocaust," from the Greek words "holos" (whole) and "kaustos" (burned), was historically used to describe a sacrificial offering burned on an altar. Since 1945, the word has taken on a new and horrible meaning: the mass murder of some 6 million European Jews (as well as members of some other persecuted groups, such as Gypsies and homosexuals), by the German Nazi regime during the Second World War.

(History.com)

B. From the American Heritage Dictionary

Holocaust: 1. A great destruction resulting in the extensive loss of life, especially by fire. 2. The genocide of European Jews and others by the Nazis during World War II. 3. A massive slaughter. 4. A sacrificial offering that is consumed entirely by flames.

(Houghton Mifflin Co.)

C. From Merriam Webster Dictionary

Holocaust: a sacrifice consumed by fire, a thorough destruction involving extensive loss of life especially through fire, the mass slaughter of European civilians and especially Jews by the Nazis during World War II, a mass slaughter of people: genocide

(Merriam-Webster.com)

From the first moment Mienus arrived in Buchenwald, the stacks on the crematorium building had smoke drifting up into the air during the better part of each day. But during the fall and winter of 1944-45, three and a half years later, the smoke was continuously present, 24 hours a day, 7 days a week.

Even with the constant burning, there were more lifeless bodies than the ovens in the building could handle. The dead were piling up, layer upon layer, next to the crematorium, and at different locations around the camp. The deaths were from the effects of starvation, exposure to the extreme cold of winter, forced labor, or from the diseases propagated by extreme overcrowding conditions. Death, for most, was the result of the effects of all of the above.

The fumes of the burning flesh and the smoke and ashes hung in the air like a brown fog. When the wind blew, it would propel the heavy-scented plume toward a number of the villages just miles away. Weimar, the largest city, was only five miles from Buchenwald. The people in Weimar had been living with the smoke and human ashes for over five years already. They all knew the camp was close by, but went about their business as if nothing but work was going on in the factories there.

First they came for the Communists

And I did not speak out

Because I was not a Communist

Then they came for the Socialists

And I did not speak out

Because I was not a Socialist

Then they came for the trade unionists

And I did not speak out

Because I was not a trade unionist

Then they came for the Jews

And I did not speak out

Because I was not a Jew

Then they came for me

And there was no one left

To speak out for me

(Niemöller)

This short poem, attributed to Martin Niemöller (1892-1984), has been used and misused many times to bolster different social causes. I include these verses because the message is insightful. It poetically describes a human condition referred to as "selfish indifference." This flawed state of mind disables us from looking after the needs of others who appear to be unlike us, and of no apparent value to our lives.

From whom or what do we turn away our eyes?? Are we so different from the people of Weimar during WWII who elected not to see the suffering of so many people just a short distance away? Every generation will face human evil and the tragedy that follows it. We should ponder the consequences of looking away in selfish indifference.

"That's not my problem to worry about!" "They should take care of themselves." "Someone else will help them." "We need to protect ourselves first." "I'll just be about my own business." "But that's a personal choice." "I am personally opposed but I can't tell others to stop what they are doing." "Who am I to judge?" Whether spoken or just thoughts, these statements could be said by any one of us at some point, if we are honest with ourselves.

*

Mienus and the many other *Geuzen* Resistance fighters took up the cause of freedom for all of the Dutch people, not just a chosen few. They fought, suffered horribly, and many of them died, for all of Holland.

He had been struggling for so long to stay alive in Buchenwald. He knew that the Germans were under attack by the Allied forces and was praying that they would soon come to rescue him and everyone else in the camp. He was also afraid, knowing what the German SS were capable of doing to the prisoners and the camp when the liberators did come.

The Allied Forces deployed strategic bombing raids to neutralize as much of the enemy as possible before any forward push by the GI soldiers on the ground. This action was necessary before any town or camp could be liberated.

On February 9, 1945, the American military sent their planes back to Buchenwald to destroy any remaining targets, and to cause sufficient destruction prior to the rescue of those imprisoned. Not only was Buchenwald the target of this run, so were key areas in Weimar. That city incurred massive damage.

Of the 2,000 prisoners still able and forced to work within the severely damaged factories, 316 of them were killed in this air raid. Yet again, Mienus miraculously survived. I remember saying to him as he talked about the bombings, "You must have a really big guardian angel for protection!" He just smiled.

I wanted to know if Dad knew what was going on outside the camp by the advancing Allied Forces. I asked, "Did you know about D-Day? Did you know they were coming to liberate Europe, and that they were pushing back against Hitler and the Nazi soldiers?"

He replied, "We knew something big was happening. We somehow got a broken radio, and secretly fixed it with spare parts from the factory. We were very careful when we listened to the radio station from England, and knew that the Allies were coming. We could tell by the way the camp was being run that the SS soldiers were getting very anxious. All of this made us very worried as well. What would happen to us now? Would we be able to survive another bombing? I was getting much thinner and weaker now, too. I had to fight hard not to give up, feeling as though we were so close to our freedom!"

Even with this information, the few prisoners who were aware of the advances could not act any differently, out of fear of the SS guards. They were brutal and would kill anyone for any reason to maintain control.

Even though Buchenwald was on the verge of collapse, there was still a steady stream of new prisoners arriving daily. Men and women, young and old, and many orphaned children as young as five and six, entered the camp unaware that liberators were on their way.

The SS Exodus

In the first week of April 1945, Mienus witnessed the departure of the camp commandant and his family, along with the senior officers. A few days later, a larger group of senior SS soldiers fled shortly after giving directives to the remaining, younger German guards.

Just before the senior staff exodus, a plan to destroy what remained of the concentration camp was devised. The Germans knew that the Americans were advancing quickly and were determined to cover up their atrocities. They knew that anyone entering the site would witness their inimitable inhumane brutality. There was only one order left for the frightened and disorganized soldiers remaining in the camp.

No work was going on in the camp anymore. The last of the meager food rations were running out. So many prisoners were walking or crawling around in a daze, confused and dying. Some the most recent prisoners who had not suffered as long as the others, began to group together to devise a plan. Mienus, now weighing less than 100 pounds and too emaciated to do much of anything, banded together with a few of his friends to watch and wait.

He said, "We didn't know for sure what was happening. We didn't know what to do at this point. We had no strength left but to sit on the ground and watch everything happen around us."

After a short pause and a deep breath, he went on to say, "So we sat on the ground by the barracks and watched the young and very frightened SS soldiers who were left in charge, place dynamite, wires, and detonators throughout the camp. Then we watched as they placed explosives along the outside of the fencing. It didn't take us long to figure out what it all meant, and what was about to happen. We were just waiting for the end."

"It was around the 9 of April, and the German soldiers still had not blown up the camp. All the explosives they had set were still there. I wondered when it was going to happen. I was so very weak and came very close to giving up," he shared, reliving that moment.

Collecting his thoughts, he went on to say, "Then on April 10, a group of prisoners with the strength left to fight together began an uprising and went after the remaining guards. Several young SS soldiers attempted to control the uprising, only to run for their lives into the forest when they saw how badly they were outnumbered."

Liberation

Mienus had not eaten anything in three days. During those days, he watched so many more prisoners die. No longer did he fear the SS soldiers. They were gone or dead. He was still waiting though, not knowing if it was for death and salvation, or liberation and salvation. Either way, salvation was part of the equation. But there was one last thing he had left to do.

It is the morning of April 11, 1945. Mienus called to one of his friends from Vlaardingen. The two of them had spent too many days together in Buchenwald. They had suffered together, starved together, hoped and prayed together. They were both emaciated to the bone.

He said to his friend, "Come, and sit here with me. I have something for you. You know there is a good chance that we will die here in the camp. But whether we live or die, by God, we will not die with an empty stomach!" Mienus reach into a pocket of his thin overcoat and pulled out a chunk of small, stale, four-day-old bread that he had been saving for just the right moment. This was that moment.

I can imagine him saying a small prayer with his friend before breaking the bread and sharing it. He would have done so. He then broke the piece in two, gave half away to his friend, and ate what was left. "I tell you Marja, that piece of bread tasted like the best meal I ever had. I will never forget the look on my friend's face when I gave it to him. He was very surprised I had kept it so long," he said with a smile, remembering that incredible moment in time.

He then went on to say, "After our last meal, we helped each other stand up and slowly walked our way into the barracks. Not long after that, we heard shouting outside. We looked out the door, and saw several of the prisoners reentering the camp with some of the SS guards who fled into the forest the day before. We watched as many of these German guards were brutally beaten to death while the rest were taken as prisoners. No one tried to stop them. I stayed out of all of it. I was just too weak. Several of the men who had arrived as prisoners within the last few months were now taking control of the camp, hoping to manage and organize it until help arrived."

At 1515 (3:15pm), on Wednesday, April 11, 1945, the clock on the gatehouse of Buchenwald was stopped by someone in the uprising to indicate that the camp was finally free of the Hitler's SS. This same clock still reads 3:15 today.

Not long after on the same day, four scout soldiers of the 6th Armored Division of General Patton's US Third Army opened the front gates of Buchenwald and walked right into the camp. They were surprised to see that none of the German SS were in control. They were not expecting to see fifteen young guards as captives themselves, having been apprehended by the prisoners and brought back to the camp.

Cautiously walking up to the GI's with their hands held high and speaking broken English, a few of the prisoners asked, "Are you American?" The four young soldiers, nodding their heads, said they were. They told the prisoners to put down their hands. They were there to help them. It took some time for the prisoners to truly understand that they were no longer captives, but free patriots once again.

Word spread quickly throughout the camp. Many of the prisoners were too weak to get up from their bunks or from the ground to see for themselves that the American GI's had simply walked right into Buchenwald. Liberation came too late for many who would later die on the same day, or over the course of the next several days.

The following day, on April 12, soldiers of the 80th Infantry Division arrived in the town of Weimar. Some of the liberated prisoners could be seen roaming around in their striped prison pajamas, looking for food. The rest of Patton's 6th Armored Division continued their march to Buchenwald. When they arrived at the fence line, they were shocked. Just like the four soldiers before them, these men were not prepared for what they witnessed. Dad described what he experienced in this way:

The day after the first four soldiers came, we began to hear a rumbling noise getting louder as it slowly moved up the hill towards us. The noise was coming from the American Sherman Tanks, and several more soldiers. As they pulled up to the fence line, everything just stopped. The soldiers on foot stood silent. Those in the tank opened the hatch and looked out at the prisoners still able to walk. Then, just as quickly, those tanks drove right on through the fences and into the camp. That was such a sight to see! Our liberators had come!

There were so many [21,000] prisoners in the camp when we were liberated. When these soldiers saw the condition we were in, they were traumatized. It was too much for several of the men to comprehend what they were seeing. All the dead bodies stacked like cords of wood throughout the camp, and also seeing many of us who were near death, was too much. Many of them got so sick to their stomachs they had to turn their backs to us to vomit.

Several of the GI's went back to Weimar and into the countryside looking for anything they could bring back to feed us. They confiscated several cows and brought them back, slaughtered them, and prepared them for to us to eat. They also brought in their GI rations, their chocolate, and food from the townspeople. Whatever they could get their hands on, they brought to us.

At first I ate what they prepared, but it did not stay in me very long. I quickly threw up almost everything. What little that did manage to stay in, came right out the other end. Most of the prisoners got very sick, just like me. I even saw some of the prisoners eat themselves to death. Many died eating too much. Their bodies just could not handle the food anymore. Hundreds died from the food.

The next day, when the Red Cross came, the nurses got us on a diet of milk, bread, and tea. It was like being a baby again. We were given back other foods very slowly over several days, and began to gain weight and strength. When the nurse weighed me when they first arrived, I was about 95 lbs. Within three weeks, I gained about 15-20 pounds.

Many firsthand stories were written about the conditions in Buchenwald at the time of liberation. I will not rewrite that which is already in print. I will invite you to visit the writings of a young American GI who was one of the first liberators of Buchenwald. After finding and reading his story on the Internet, I sensed that it might be significant to my readers. I recommend "Liberations of Buchenwald," by Harry J. Herder. Jr.

Each reader should decide for themselves whether to explore the extent of the atrocities that were done to so many people in Buchenwald. I will, however, share a very famous report that is not as graphic as some others.

The famous reporter, Edward R. Murrow, arrived in Buchenwald the day after liberation and wrote his report just a few days later. Murrow broadcasted the complete report over the airways on April 15, 1945. Here is his edited (and toned down), written report.

Edward R. Murrow's Report from Buchenwald

There surged around me an evil-smelling stink, men and boys reached out to touch me. They were in rags and the remnants of uniforms. Death already had marked many of them, but they were smiling with their eyes. I looked out over the mass of men to the green fields beyond, where well-fed Germans were ploughing...

I asked to see one of the barracks. It happened to be occupied by Czechoslovaks. When I entered, men crowded around and tried, tried to lift me to their shoulders. They were too weak. Many of them could not get out of bed. I was told that this building had once stabled 80 horses. There were 1200 men in it, five to a bunk. The stink was beyond all description.

They called the doctor. We inspected his records. There were only names in the little black book -nothing more- nothing about who had been where, what he had done or hoped. Behind the names of those who had died, there was a cross. I counted them. They totaled 242 (242 out of 1200 in one month).

As we walked out into the courtyard, a man fell dead. Two others, they must have been over 60, were crawling toward the latrine. I saw it, but will not describe it.

In another part of the camp they showed me the children, hundreds of them. Some were only six years old. One rolled up his sleeves, showed me his number. It was tattooed on his arm. B-6030, it was. The others showed me their numbers. They will carry them till they die. An elderly man standing beside me said: "The children were enemies of the state!" I could see their ribs through their thin shirts....

We went to the hospital. It was full. The doctor told me that 200 had died the day before. I asked the cause of death. He shrugged and said: "tuberculosis, starvation, fatigue and there are many who have no desire to live. It is very difficult." He pulled back the blanket from a man's feet to show me how swollen they were. The man was dead. Most of the patients could not move.

I asked to see the kitchen. It was clean. The German in charge...showed me the daily ration. One piece of brown bread about as thick as your thumb, on top of it a piece of margarine as big as three sticks of chewing gum. That, and a little stew, was what they received every 24 hours. He had a chart on the wall. Very complicated it was. There were little red tabs scattered through it. He said that was to indicate each ten who died. He had to account for the rations and he added: "We're very efficient here."

We proceeded to the small courtyard. The wall adjoined what had been a stable or garage. We entered. It was floored with concrete. There were two rows of bodies stacked up like cordwood. They were thin and very white. Some of the bodies were terribly bruised; though there seemed to be little flesh to bruise. Some had been shot through the head, but they bled but a little.

I arrived at the conclusion that all that was mortal of more than 500 men and boys lay there in two neat piles. There was a German trailer, which must have contained another 50, but it wasn't possible to count them. The clothing was piled in a heap against the wall. It appeared that most of the men and boys had died of starvation; they had not been executed.

But the manner of death seemed unimportant. Murder had been done at Buchenwald. God alone knows how many men and boys have died there during the last twelve years. Thursday, I was told that there were more than 20,000 in the camp. There had been as many as 60,000. Where are they now?

I pray you to believe what I have said about Buchenwald. I reported what I saw and heard, but only part of it. For most of it, I have no words.

If I have offended you by this rather mild account of Buchenwald, I'm not in the least sorry.

(Murrow, 1945)

I picked this report to share because Mr. Murrow was a well-renowned and respected journalist of his time. As I have already stated, I have read many other accounts of what happened at Buchenwald. Many of these accounts were written several years after they happened. It took a long time for the authors to recover from the trauma. Many of them did not want to revisit repressed thoughts and emotions. Fortunately, they were printed for future generations to read. The truth about this holocaust had to be told. Sadly, there will be some who, after 70 years, may read my father's accounts through me, and refuse to accept that this ever happened.

I am, by my birth, counted among a very unique and abundant group of individuals referred to as the "Second Generation Survivors." We were raised by parents who survived dehumanizing brutality. Our fathers and mothers instilled in us to, "Never forget what happened here!" Some of us have been chosen to keep the memory alive. I have always felt that, one day, I would write the story of my family. I just waited to give myself permission.

Old Blood and Guts

Reports vary as to whether it was April 13 or 14, 1945, when General George S. Patton, Commander of the Third Army, arrived with several more of his troops to see the conditions at Buchenwald. Reports were already arriving at headquarters about the conditions in the camp. Patton had to go and see it for himself.

Dad picked up where he left off and said, "Another group of American GI's arrived a couple days later. I remember when I saw this general that we had heard so much about in the past. Old 'Blood and Guts' they called him, and for good reason. He didn't stay in the camp very long, just a couple of hours, as I can recall. He walked around the camp with his men and I could tell he was very upset. He left like he was in a hurry. I only saw him that one day, but I will never forget that he came, and that it was his men who saved my life. Never!"

Mienus had great admiration for his liberators. The word "grateful" doesn't even come close to the way he felt about General Patton, the GI soldiers, and the country that sent them to fight for his freedom, the United States of America!

General Patton, after leaving Buchenwald, drove right back to the town of Weimar. When he arrived, he immediately went to see the mayor of the town and ordered him to round up the citizens. The mayor was to escort them, on foot, to the camp the next morning. They would be witnesses to what had been happening over the last several years within walking distance from their homes. Patton did not believe that these people were innocent of any knowledge of what had taken place in the camp. How could they not have known! This is a profound example of selfish indifference. "I didn't know!"

It had only been four days since the first four GI's walked into the camp. Mienus looked on as the citizens of Weimar walked slowly through the grounds. These were the same people who shared the smoke and breathed in the ashes of the nearly 56,000 prisoners who died in Buchenwald. He watched as their faces paled and the tears flow as each scene unfolded before them. Nothing was left to the imagination.

These same citizens would come back a few days later. They would be forced to place an untold number of dead bodies gently into individual, makeshift burial boxes. Men, women, and several of the youth would be assigned two, three, or four per box to carry the dead to the large massive grave prepared for them. No more than that was necessary. The boxes weighed so little, even with the bodies inside them.

The liberators made sure that each of the bodies were respectfully lifted out of the box and placed in the ground. A mass funeral was provided for the dead. All of this was recorded as evidence for the eventual trials of Hitler and his Nazi commanders, and for the future generations to witness.

More strength returned to Mienus as his weight increased. After a little more than a week, he and a few other men were escorted out of Buchenwald to live with a German woman who kindly offered to help do whatever she could to aid in the recovery of the former prisoners. Many other families volunteered, or were asked to continue aiding the process of recovery for other former prisoners by feeding and nursing them back to health.

Days turned into weeks, and the time was getting closer when Mienus could return to Holland. Before leaving Germany, he went back to Buchenwald with a camera to take pictures of where he had suffered for more than four years of his young life. There were GI's taking pictures as well, and they were developing the pictures quickly. Copies of some of these pictures were handed out to Mienus and any other former prisoner who wanted copies. Taking these pictures was a very important thing to do. He just needed to have them. "Never forget!"

One of our conversations concerning his liberation revolved around a very popular show on TV when I was growing up. Hogan's Heroes was one of Dad's favorite shows, and ran from 1965-1971. It was a sitcom based around some novel characters imprisoned in a concentration camp during WWII. The producers of the show referred to the camp in a more sanitized version by calling it simply a POW camp.

One of the actors in the show, a Frenchman by the name of Robert Max Widerman, was a Buchenwald survivor, just like Dad. He was known in Hollywood as Robert Clary, and played the character of French Corporal Louis LeBeau on the sitcom. Dad enjoyed watching this show every week, and with only one black and white TV, the family would gather around and watch it with him. Mother had some reservations!

I asked Dad if he knew, or remembered, this man who was in the camp with him. He replied, "I can't be too sure. But I do remember an evening when we had a kind of a celebration with some of the Americans GI's before we all went our separate ways. It happened to be around my birthday too. There was a small group of liberated prisoners, including a short Frenchman, who provided some good music and entertainment for us. It sure could have been him. We all sang along to the tunes that we were familiar with. Before the party came to an end, my fellow Dutch mates sang a song of our own:

Lang zal ze leven, lang zal ze leven, lang zal ze leven in de Gloria, in de Gloria, in de Gloria. Hieperdepiep, hoera!

Mienus, and a few of his friends, had survived. Hip, Hip, Hooray!

They were all a statistic now. Mienus was one of approximately 250,000 prisoners who had endured time in Buchenwald. He was one of 21,000 liberated by the Americans that day in April. There were 56,000 individuals who died from starvation, diseases, hard labor, murder, and sadly, suicide. Where the rest of the 173,000 went is unknown. Many perished after being transferred to other concentration camps scattered throughout Germany. Still others survived and experience their own liberation. For many, the mystery will likely never fully be resolved. Statistic or not, it was now time for Mienus to take back control of his own life, but that would prove to be a difficult transition.

Now that Mienus was able to listen to the English radio without fearing for his life, he knew what was happening back home in the Netherlands. The "Hunger Winter of 1944-1945" had taken its toll in the parts of Holland were his family and Suze's family lived. Even with the Allied food drops over the winter and spring, many of the people were still not able to get enough to eat. The food lines were a daily routine. One of the first acts of his freedom was to try to do something to help his family.

"What do you mean you were able to help your family back in Holland?" I asked. He said, "I got some help from the GI's in the camp and some help in town. They gave me some packages of food, chocolate, cigarettes, and some other small things to send to my family. I found a way to transport two small packages, one for my family and one for your Mom's family."

Mienus was sending packages to Holland to try to prevent both families from further hunger. Think of that for just a moment. He mentioned this only because I was probing a little deeper. I'm glad it came up during this exchange. He never thought to volunteer that bit of information before. Dad was still the author of his story. What other seemingly uneventful information might I be missing?

Chapter 8

Back to Holland

Mienus could have left Germany to go back to Holland weeks earlier, but his family and Suze's family were still under German occupation, enduring very extreme conditions in Vlaardingen. Though he longed to go home, it was not wise for him to return until the town was free of the Germans who were still holding out for a different outcome to the war.

The Declaration of Liberation was declared for all of the Netherlands on Saturday, May 5, 1945, at 8:00 in the morning. Even though the declaration was announced, it was hard for those living in Vlaardingen to really believe it. That horrible day in the fall of 1944, when word reached their town that Holland had been liberated, was still fresh in their minds. There were still a few German soldiers that either didn't get the memo, or were afraid to leave, and the people in Vlaardingen did not want a repeat of last year's carnage.

From my research, it was evident that there were no signs of Allied activities in Vlaardingen on May 5. No British or Canadian troops were triumphantly marching in as victors, such as was playing out in many of the surrounding towns. There were no tanks, no guns, no dancing in the streets. None of this kind of fanfare was evident.

What Vlaardingen did have were two or three American airmen and a paratrooper who had been in hiding, and were being cared for by some people in the town. Now that the surrender papers had been signed by the Germans, they could come out of hiding, and they did. Not long after, these American GI's were seen driving a jeep on the streets of the town, with the American flag draped over the front hood.

Finally the citizens came to believe that their freedom was real. The townspeople began gathering in the streets. It was time to rejoice and give thanks! The bells in the churches began to ring and people began displaying their Dutch flags on their doors or out their windows. It was time to celebrate their independent sovereignty. It would take several more days before the Allied forces came marching in. It was then that the people in Vlaardingen finally reacted like so many other liberated towns, with the crowds cheering, singing, and dancing in the streets.

Mienus was 20 years old when he was captured in the shipyards of Rotterdam in April 1941. On May 14, four days before he left Buchenwald, he quietly celebrated his 25th birthday with a few friends and the American GI's still at the camp. The two most priceless birthday presents he could have ever received were: being able to give thanks to the American liberators for saving him from certain death, and finally being able to go back home to Holland.

Finally, on Friday, May 18, 1945, it was time for Mienus to leave Buchenwald. Vlaardingen was free, and he was more than ready to go home. He no longer looked like the dying prisoner he did just weeks before. His weight had increased to a whopping 125-135 pounds. Standing 5 feet 11 inches at this current weight, well let's just say, he was very thin. He would never return to Buchenwald.

He arrived in the city of Eindhoven, just 80 miles from Vlaardingen, on the same day. Eindhoven was one of the first cities the Allies had liberated eight months earlier, on September 18, 1944.

In researching this time period, I learned that a large portion of the infrastructure supporting train transportation throughout much of Europe, and especially Holland, had been destroyed and was barely operational. I am making an assumption as to what mode of transportation Mienus was provided for his trip out of Germany and back home.

The American, Canadian, and British forces were frequently on the move and provided truck convoys for displaced citizens. I also discovered evidence that there were many volunteers from several European countries, including Holland, who were willing to help with transportation. Either way, whether by train, army convoy, or volunteer trucking, he did make it back to Holland, most likely by volunteers willing to help to take the freed men back to their country.

Mienus was dropped off at an American registration and medical clearance center. The only proof of his identity was his Buchenwald discharge card given to him on April 20, 1945. After filling out temporary documentation papers, he was taken for a medical check-up.

During his medical checkup, it was discovered that he had been exposed to tuberculosis. He did not suffer from the disease, but only carried the bacteria. The examination also revealed that Mienus had lost his sense of smell. Other than his low weight, there was nothing else discovered during the quick exam, so he was medically cleared. He would later find out that his heart had increased in size due to the hard labor he had endured. With his temporary ID papers stamped, he was ready to enter the general population. The black bag in the closet that I've referred to still contains Dad's original Buchenwald provisional identification card, his reentry documentation, and his medical clearance certificate papers.

As long as I could remember, I knew that Dad couldn't smell. On a very rare occasion, he would capture a scent of Mom's perfume, but that was about it. "How did you lose your smell?" I asked. "I lost it in the camp. I don't remember when I lost it. I just remember one day I could no longer smell. I think it happened over time," he answered.

Mienus could have lost his sense of smell any number of ways. Beatings on the head, a bad fall, toxic fumes, or growth of nasal polyps are just a few ways. I believe that having lost his smell while in Buchenwald was a real blessing for him. It would be interesting to know how many of the other prisoners lost their sense of smell too.

Mienus' uncle lived in Eindhoven, and so he went to live with him for three or four weeks. Word got out quickly that he had survived the war, and was back in Holland. Even though Vlaardingen technically was liberated, he and his uncle were not quite convinced it was safe enough for him to go home just yet. Mienus was better than he had been, but under his uncle's care, he felt safe, and continued to improve and get stronger.

The few weeks with his uncle helped him to gain another 5-10 pounds. The few clothes his uncle gave him were loose on his frame, but they would have to do. It was not like he could just go into a department store and buy new things. There was nothing in the stores to buy.

I've wondered what he must have thought when he looked at himself in the mirror after his ordeal. He had once been a handsome schoolboy and a good-looking adolescent. What did he see in himself now, after all he had been through?

His skin was still very pale, and his teeth were in very bad condition. Even at his current weight, somewhere around 135-140 pounds, his naturally prominent cheekbones, and his deep-set eye sockets made his face look gaunt.

Though Mienus was 25 years old, the mirror lied and made him look older. He must have asked himself, "How will my family react when they see me? What will Suze see in me now?" Suze would be 20 in just a few weeks. Would she think Mienus was handsome?

Home to Family and Suze

The nightmare of five birthdays in captivity, and over four years of living in hell, was over. Mienus' thoughts and dreams about the people he'd prayed for, stayed alive for, and loved the most, were about to surround him once again. Just a day or two longer and only 80 miles to travel, and he would be home.

He came home the second week of June 1945. It was chilly outside when he finally arrived at his home in Vlaardingen. He was rightfully emotional walking up to the front door of the small house he had lived in during his childhood. Both of his parents were waiting for him. They had been given notice that their son was on his way home. Nothing could prevent the flow of tears.

When I close my eyes to imagine what this scene must have looked like, I picture something like this:

The door opened and his mother fell into her son's arms. His father stood stoically behind his wife, trying hard to contain his emotions. That was about to change when his wife let go of her son, and stepped aside for her husband to welcome their son back into their home.

Mienus was the only one of his nine siblings who was captured and sent away. It was no longer possible for his father to hold back the tears at the embrace of his freed son. The three of them shared this reunion together, and allowed each the freedom to be open to their true feelings. There would be no shame in crying.

His mother waited on her son with the usual afternoon tea, and shared what little, if any, treats she had in her small kitchen. Nothing was spoken of the condition in the camp, and what he had endured. Mienus did talk about his liberation and the events that transpired from that point forward. It was not the right time to elaborate on anything else. He could tell from his surroundings that they also had suffered, and were much weaker too.

They talked about family members and some of the events that had transpired in his absence. His brother Jan had a couple more kids. His sister Anne was married and was near the end of her third pregnancy. His sister, Diek, was married and just had her third child. Some of the other siblings were on their own, while the younger ones still lived at home. A lot had happened with the family while he was gone.

Word traveled quickly that Mienus was back in Vlaardingen. Suze and her family were aware that Mienus was home. Out of respect for what he and his family had been through, most friends did not come to see him that day. This first day would be set aside for his mother and father, and other members of his immediate family. The following day Mienus, unwilling to wait any longer, walked to the Bruggeman bakery to see the young girl he had been falling in love with through their letters. Suze answered the door when he arrived and paused for a moment, not knowing for sure how to react.

At that moment, both were undoubtedly wondering how the other was feeling. They had not communicated in quite some time. Suze's last letter arrived in October of 1944, and Mienus' reply was sent on January of 1945. Six months is a long time without any contact.

The awkward moment ended when others in the Bruggeman family quickly gathered to say hello to their childhood friend. Everyone got reacquainted and gave thanks that they had all survived the war.

Mienus asked Suze to walk with him. They walked back to his house where she was warmly greeted by his parents. They shared a cup of tea with his family and then went outside to be alone, just the two of them. I must admit, I wish I had more interesting details to share about what happened next, but that part of their story will remain with them forever.

Pictures were taken that second day home. Of the three pictures we have, Mienus is shown in one picture standing very stiff and awkward next to his mother and father. His parents look much older than their age, and the dark clothes the three were dressed in contribute to a more formal posture.

Both of the men were dressed in suit and ties, his mother in a black dress. This suit was one of the only things he was able to wear besides the clothes he came home wearing and a couple of articles from his uncle in Eindhoven. His other clothes had long been worn out by younger brothers while he was away. Mienus had felt so unattractive for so long that he was grateful the suit helped to hide his thin body. He wanted to look nice when family and friends came to see him for the first time.

The other two pictures reveal the growing comfort between Mienus and Suze. In the first photo, he has his arm around her shoulder, and both are just staring at the camera. She got a bit closer in the second photo as she placed the side of her forehead up against his cheek. Each have an arm around the other, and it makes them look like a couple. I can see the happiness between them. The awkward feelings were melting into a familiar comfort. They had grown up now, and were not children anymore.

It's important to remember that they were robbed of a very crucial time in their lives. The years they lost were necessary to figure out who they were as individuals. Neither of them was able to pursue the natural process of dating, which made it very difficult to develop relationships with the opposite sex. Each, in their own way, needed to guard their natural feelings to survive under difficult conditions. What most of us take for granted with our freedoms, they were denied by the circumstances surrounding war. They would need to figure many things out for themselves as they moved forward.

I remember this same period of time in my own life, trying to figure out who I was, what I wanted to be, and the kind of good-looking guy I wanted to be with. It is hard to imagine being denied the opportunity, as both my parents were, to explore adolescence in a healthy way. This topic came up in conversations more than a few times over the years. The exchange went something like this:

"So, Mom, when you saw Dad for the first time, were you excited to see him?"

"Of course I was. It had been a long time since I had seen him and it was good to see an old friend having survived such a terrible time in the camps."

"Did you see each other as a couple?"

"I didn't really think about such things in the beginning. I really didn't see him that much before he was captured. He was my brother's friend too, remember?"

"Did you guys start dating right away, or did it work like that so soon after the war?"

"Dating, what's that? There was nothing to do in Holland anymore. We were still trying to grow our own food and have enough to eat each day. There was nothing. He did come to see me many times during the next several weeks though."

"Were you in love with Dad already, or were you falling in love with him over time?"

"Well, I liked him a lot. I guess we were falling in love. I know he was, for sure!"

"Well, did you get those butterflies in your stomach when you saw him coming, you know, the kind that make you want to throw-up?"

Mom looked at me with a puzzled look on her face and said, "No... was I supposed to?"

That answer was not what I was hoping for. She was so matter-of-fact about Dad. It struck me then. I could see that she had missed out on several things, one of which was the ability to size up her own guarded emotions. She had never experienced this kind of love.

To Suze, love was an action of the will, not an emotion that makes you want to throw-up. Maybe at that young age of 20, she had a more mature insight that most are not blessed with at that age. It made perfect sense after a while. Hopefully, we all learn that true and lasting love is an act of will each day.

Dad didn't exactly come across as too romantic either. Our separate exchanges over time went something like this:

"Dad, when you came home from the camps, were you excited to see Mom?"

"Of course I was! We had been in touch the last couple of years with some letters and they helped me a lot. I always liked your mother. I liked her whole family. I always thought that your mother was pretty too. I was hoping that someday we could be together."

"So, Mom said you guys didn't really date much when you got home. She said there was no dating, just visits with both families, and long walks, and a few moments when you two could be alone together, and of course, church."

"Yes, that's true what your mother said. But I loved her and wanted to marry her. So after a couple of months I said to her, 'Suze, we can have some fun for a couple of years, or we can work hard and save up some money so we can get married in a year. What do you think?'"

"Dad, is that the way you asked Mom to marry you? That's not very romantic! Didn't you ask her parents first?"

"No, I asked them after she said, OK!"

"OK.........? Mom said.......... OK?"

"Well, something like that. We just decided to get married and start our lives together. We both wanted to. We wanted to look forward, and not think about things that happened before."

So that's the way it was. Some marriages develop out of romantic and passionate love, the kind that makes your toes curl and the pit of your stomach flutter with delight in the company of your lover. Some marriages are arranged by parents, and love grows over time. Still others are quickly decided after an "unexpected little blessing" is due to arrive in a few months. What Mienus and Suze had was a love for each other as friends first, and over time discovered that they wanted to take care of each other in marriage.

Mienus would heal his wounds in the arms of the woman he loved, while Suze would "do everything I could to make him happy," as she said. She would bypass a life of fun, dating, and exploring, for the comfort of a home of her own and children to follow.

Suze did love Mienus, but not with the passion and romance that many of us discover and experience before we walk toward the altar to marry. Instead, she decided to love this man, and it was not difficult for her at all. She made that choice freely and never looked back, and love grew strong between them.

So now there was a plan. Both continued to work and save their money. They would acquire the household belongings they would need to get started before they would marry. No date was set, just a hope for some time the next year, in 1946.

Dealing with Anger

Finding work was not easy after the war ended. The type of work Mienus was trained for was not available yet. So much infrastructure needed to be rebuilt, and the money and raw materials needed to reconstruct the Netherlands - and all of Europe for that matter - did not pour in right away. It would be a couple of years before the European Recovery Program, more notably referred to as the Marshall Plan, was implemented.

Mienus was living with his Dad and Mom again. His and Suze's parents were aware that their son and daughter were planning to wed as soon as they were able. Suze worked in the bakery and sewed for others to make some money, while Mienus did odd jobs and continued looking for full time employment.

On one of those days looking for work in Vlaardingen, Mienus came across a long line-up of men and women. This group consisted of known Dutch collaborators who had been rounded up by former Resistance members.

Arrangements were being made to send these traitors to prisons in Holland, as well as outside of the country. While waiting for the justice system to be fully functional, decisions such as these were made by the Resistance members. Traitors would be punished, and the townspeople were more than happy to have these matters taken care of by those who had risked their live secretly sabotaging the Nazis throughout the Occupation.

The men and women of the Resistance who had escaped capture in the latter half of the war were already considered leaders in the recovery efforts after liberation. They also became the enforcers of law and order for the general public. The citizens appreciated having others to look after their safety and wellbeing.

Something visceral triggered inside Mienus when he saw this lineup of traitors. There were people he had known for several years in that line. He had suffered so much for having resisted the Germans and these people had betrayed Holland. He took this very personally.

Without warning, his wrath erupted. He grabbed someone he knew in the line and began to "beat the snot out of him!" as Dad had said. Others in the line stood back in an attempt to avoid getting in the middle of this public display of outrage. Even those in charge of the line-up allowed Mienus some leeway to punish someone for their crimes. Finally, when it was apparent that he was not letting up on this man, Mienus was pulled off before it went too far.

I imagine Dad went home to his parents and told them what had happened in town. Knowing what I know about my Oma (grandmother), I envision her cradling her son after his rage, holding him while he tried to calm down. His father may have had words of warning to share. It was time to move on now, and do whatever it took to live peacefully.

When Dad shared this admission about what he had done, I became quiet and deep in thought. I was unprepared for some scary memories to rise up. I'd seen Dad like this before, and I didn't want to think of him in that state.

Unfortunately, as a child I'd witnessed a small sampling of Dad's rage on a couple of occasions. As an adolescent, I'd experienced it firsthand. So now it was my turn to take a short break. "I'll be right back Dad. I need to go to the bathroom." That's what I told him anyway.

Shortly after the first incident of uncontrolled fury, Mienus went to resolve another act of injustice. He went out to reclaim the family radio stolen from his parents during the war. As it turned out, someone he knew had it. The radio was important enough for him to go to this thief's house and take it back. He needed to right a wrong for his family.

Justice for Mienus

The recovery went something like this. Not long after his uncontrolled rage and pummeling of a traitor, Mienus marched over to the house whose occupants currently harbored the van Lith family radio. No one was home, yet somehow that did not dissuade him from entering the premises. He broke in, found the radio, put it on the front of his bike, and went home.

It would not take long for the homeowners to figure out who would have entered their house and stolen this one particular item. They went to the police station to report the break-in, and to get help in retrieving what they believed to be their radio.

The officers from the newly-formed police force followed through with this request, and went to the van Lith home to see if Mienus had entered the house without permission and stolen the disputed radio, as was suspected.

When Mienus was asked if he had stolen the radio, he didn't hesitate to say, "I didn't steal their radio. You can't steal what is yours in the first place. That radio belongs to us!" After this quick admission, the radio was retrieved and Mienus was asked to come to the police station to settle the matter.

After arriving at the station, Mienus was told to return the radio to the other household, or spend some time in jail.

The man in charge said to Mienus, "You need to do the right thing and give back the radio. We need to comply with the law and order of our town, and if you took it out of his house, you need to give it back and then settle this dispute rationally. If we let this act go unpunished, that would send a bad message to the other people counting on us to protect them from such activity. Do you understand why we are doing this?"

Mienus replied, "Yes, I understand, but you should be questioning this man for having a radio. Why were all other radios confiscated and forbidden for everyone else, yet this man had ours? This was our family radio before the war, and it will be ours again after the war!"

The radio was placed in the basket of Mienus' bike, and the police escorted him back to the house that he had entered unlawfully. Upon arriving at the residence, they were confronted by the man living in the house. Mienus was told to return the radio.

Mienus looked at the man at the door, then looked at the police, and said, "This radio was our family radio before the war, and somehow it was in your house. If we cannot have our radio back then no one will have it!" Just after saying this, he threw the radio onto the ground and smashed it into pieces. He did what he was told to do, and then applied a bit of his own justice to "settle this dispute rationally." This matter was abruptly resolved, and Mienus went home to his parents.

Called to Serve

How does a burglar become a policeman in a day? This almost sounds like the beginning of a joke.

Later that same day, Mienus was greeted at his home by a couple of the men in the Resistance who were with him at the scene of the crime. They invited him to come to the police station the next day to talk with them about something important. Mienus obliged and showed up the following morning.

When he arrived, he was greeted by a group of men. Some of them he already knew from the Resistance, and some were friends of his before the war. This meeting was quite different from the day before. There was handshaking and a polite introduction.

After the warm greeting, one of the men in charge said, "I know this may sound surprising to you, but we see something in you, Mienus, that we admire. We know of your patriotism and your courage during the war, and we respect that very much. Though you were wrong to enter that man's house without permission, we understand why you did it. The war is over now, and we need men like you to become a part of the new police force in Vlaardingen. We are all in this process of rebuilding again, but law and order is very important, especially now. Our country has a lot of people out of work and lots of homeless citizens too. We need to provide safety and security once again. Would you consider joining us as a policeman?"

Dad told me how very surprised he was to be asked to join the police force. He just assumed he would return to his previous occupation as a machinist. But since Holland was not powered up yet for this kind of work, the offer sounded pretty good at the time. It didn't take long for him to agree to this opportunity. Mienus also knew that this meant he was another step closer to marrying his Suze.

Mienus likely said, "Thank you for this offer. I think I will take you up on it and join you as a policeman. Let's get to work!"

He enjoyed telling this story. It was always a source of amusement to him that he was offered a police position after stealing back the family radio. This is how Mienus served the Dutch people during the rest of the recovery phase after the war.

Making money was very important, and his intention was to live at home and save as much of his money as he could before he got married. And the more he saved, the sooner the wedding date.

Unfortunately, this is not what happened.

Not 19 Anymore

The transition from surviving Buchenwald and coming home to live with his parents was not an easy one. The newness and excitement of his return slowly faded to a more normal return to family life.

Mienus was 25 years old, and found it difficult living at home with his parents. As the oldest of the few siblings still living with their parents, he found it hard to be independent. His mother was a bit overprotective and his father was still the authoritarian in the home.

His parents were aware of their son's engagement to Suze. They knew the plan was to work hard, save money, and find a place to live before they got married. As a grown man, ready to get on with his life as quickly as possible, it was imperative to get his name on the ever-growing list of people in Vlaardingen in need of their own living accommodations. There were a number of qualifications necessary to be placed on that waiting list. Employment and marital status were the two most important factors to be eligible.

His mother was so loving toward her son, and he would not deny her the joy of having him back. But sometimes it felt like she was trying to make up for the lost years between them. It made him feel like he was a teenage boy again by the way he was being treated by both his parents.

Mienus' father thought very little about his son's plans for the near future. Once he began his employment with the new police department, he was required to hand over his income to his father for the general living expenses of the household. Mienus told his father that he was more than willing to buy his own food and clothing, but the rest of the money would be saved for his future. None of that mattered to his father. Even when he was reminded about his son's engagement to Suze, he would not bend.

There was no reasoning and no compromising between them. He grudgingly yielded to his father's demand for his paycheck out of respect, and a little fear, of his father. What else could he do? He had nothing of his own to speak of. He didn't even have clothes that he could call his own. He felt trapped, and was afraid to stand up to his father. His new-found freedom tasted bitter with the restrictions placed upon him. Mienus felt 19 all over again.

When some of his brothers and sisters found out what their father was demanding of Mienus, they became very angry with their dad. Trying to offer support, they said to Mienus, "Stand up to your father! You have your own life. You are not a teenager anymore."

Some of his siblings went to confront their father and mother about this untenable situation. They all knew that their mother would defer to their father. She was not one to get in the middle of her husband and their children. Their father would not listen to the grievances. This matter was between him and Mienus.

I can only guess why my Opa (grandfather) was so adamant about the way he managed his post-war household. Was it fear? Was his pride crushed during the Occupation? Did he lose his income because of the destroyed railroad system? Did Mienus' income make his life easier? I'm fairly sure that the answer to these questions would explain why Opa did what he did.

After another few months living with his parents, Mienus was finally convinced by his sister Anne to leave the family home. Anne said to her brother, "You are not responsible to our parents anymore. You are 25 years old, you have your own job, you are a policeman, and you are planning to get married next year! Mom and Dad will understand when you leave." To make the decision less of a burden, she said, "Jan

(Anne's husband) and I will make room for you to live with us. You can then save your money and get on that waiting list for your own place to live."

Mienus would never forget the act of kindness Anne and Jan did for him. He gathered up his courage and what little belongs he had, and moved in with his sister's family. It was not a total surprise to his parents. Within a short amount of time, he was welcomed back for a visit anytime he wanted to see them. Mienus finally felt like he could breathe again. It was time to feel free, and build the next chapter in his life.

Weeks turned into months. A new year had begun, and Mienus and Suze's names were on the list for a place of their own, and moving up quickly. He was working long hours, and changing shifts every couple of months. Except for a small amount paid to his sister for food, he was saving most of his salary, and continued to plan ahead for his future.

Suze was also doing her part. She had a growing list of people who paid for her sewing skills, and was still working at the family bakery. Every moment that the two of them were not working, the young couple would spend together getting more comfortable with each other, and looking toward their future as husband and wife.

Chapter 9

Something Borrowed and Nothing New

There were many who lost their homes, or whose homes were rendered uninhabitable during and after the war. Finding places to live for these citizens was one of the top priorities of the early recovery. In addition to that hardship, rationing the most basic of commodities continued throughout the Netherlands. Wartime coupon vouchers were still in use to allocate almost everything from fuel, food, clothing, and shoes to raw materials, transportation, and more.

A great deal of pressure was placed on all citizens who still had intact houses or apartments to share their lodging with others until more of the reconstruction was completed. As an incentive to help house the homeless, families sharing their homes were likely to get extra coupons.

Over a year had passed since the war ended, and the post-war inventory of merchandise was still only a small fraction of what the pre-war volumes were. When word got out that a shipment of this or that was arriving, long lines would develop outside store entrances. As soon as material goods were placed on the shelves, everything would immediately be purchased. It would take several more years before the long lines and the vouchers would phase out completely.

Even though they were engaged, it still took a year and a half for Mienus and Suze to reach the top of the waiting list for the next available place to live. In the fall of 1946, the young couple was told that a place was ready for them. The second floor of a two-story townhouse, owned by an elderly couple, was offered. They would live in the two bedrooms and small landing at the top of the stairs. The owners would live on the main floor, which consisted of a small living area, one bedroom, a small kitchen, and the only bathroom in the house. Both couples would share the bathroom. These arrangements would just have to do. They immediately agreed to take this assigned offer, and would make it work for them.

Preparing for a wedding in 1946 was nothing like the experience of planning a wedding now. Today, planning begins long in advance of the date set by the couple. It is common for couples to spend tens of thousands of dollars to finance the nuptial ceremony and elaborate reception. The honeymoon can set them back several more thousands. Burdensome expectations and expensive arrangements can hang like a noose around the necks of everyone involved. Much of the emphasis is placed on the production and choreography of the entire wedding weekend. It often appears that little thought is given to the sacred vows pledged between the couple, that are meant for life. Mienus and Suze's ceremony preparations paled in comparison to today's standards. To them, only their vows mattered.

Many engaged couples, with hopes of progressing quickly up the list for living quarters, would legally marry at the City Hall in the presence of an official. Since Holland was a very religious country, many of these couples would not live together until after the church wedding was performed. This wait could last anywhere from several months to a couple of years.

The practice of two marriage ceremonies still goes on in Vlaardingen. There will be the civil exchange of vows first, followed by the marriage ceremony in the church. As devout Catholics, Mienus and Suze considered themselves blessed to be able to celebrate both ceremonies on the same day, and not have to wait. They planned well, and stayed faithful to their beliefs before living together as man and wife.

With a place to move into, they had only weeks to make arrangements for the wedding. They would need to reserve the City Hall in Vlaardingen for the first part of the wedding day, and have that coincide with the availability of the Catholic Church for the second part. They found a room large enough to have a simple reception with family and a few friends. Only then they could set a date to accommodate all three venues. Based on availability, the date of the wedding was planned for Wednesday, October 2, 1946.

Suze had almost nothing she needed for her wedding day. New and fancy dresses were nonexistent, and fabrics used to design and make new dresses were not available either. Practical by nature, she would have to accept the next best thing. She would borrow!

Recently, she attended a wedding of a cousin whose twin sisters stood in as her bridesmaids. The bride had worn a lovely wedding dress, and the twins wore beautiful matching gowns. In Suze's mind, the search for a wedding dress and bridesmaid dresses was over. She would simply ask her cousins to be bridesmaids for her upcoming marriage to Mienus, and ask the bride if she would allow her to wear the wedding dress.

All three women agreed to help Suze in whatever was needed to make her wedding day special. Her cousins were glad to be her attendants, and the previous bride was happy to loan the dress for the occasion. What little alteration the dress needed was skillfully accomplished by Suze in a way that would not ruin it for the next bride to borrow.

I am pretty sure that women had worn this wedding dress before Suze and her cousin had, and more than likely, it was worn by others after Suze's wedding. I've seen the old photos of both women in their wedding gowns accompanied by the twins wearing the same bridesmaid dresses. Each bride looked happy, and Suze was beautiful.

Most women have thoughts, desires, and expectations about what their wedding day will be like. Suze was no different. Sadly, the war had dashed her original expectations. She knew that it was crucial to accept what was, and not what was lost.

Suze would not have the chance to design and create her own gown, or to wear her own beautiful wedding dress with pride. She would alter one instead. Not all of her family and friends would be there to celebrate with her. She and Mienus could only afford to accommodate a few people. Lavish gifts were out of the question. Only a few necessary and practical items and flowers were gifted. No diamonds would be included in her wedding ring. A simple gold band would do. No music would play at the reception to dance the night away. The reception would end when the food and drinks were consumed.

With the information I garnered over the years, and the photos that were taken the day of the wedding, the following is what I envision took place the day Mienus and Suze got married.

Wedding Day

On the morning of Wednesday, October 2, 1946, Suze would spend her last morning in the home with her mother and father. Her father likely sat in his easy chair, dressed in a suit, derby hat by his side, a cigar in his mouth, just waiting for the events to unfold. He would not say much to his daughter, which was his way. Though she loved her father, Suze never understood why he never spent much time with his children. She very much missed that.

Her mother would quietly assist her daughter by helping her primp for the ceremony. They would share simple thoughts with one another. The two women loved each other dearly, but it was not customary to get too intimate in conversation. And it would be left up to the young couple to figure out what the wedding night would consist of. Suze had some understanding and a vague idea of what to expect, but had very little foreknowledge of anything specific. At age 21, Suze was still very innocent.

The City Hall was within walking distance for many of the invited guests. While the wedding guests passed through familiar neighborhoods, many of the townspeople would look out their doors and windows, wave, and ask the guests, "Where are you going all dressed up on this cold day? Is someone getting married?"

People just wanted to witness life returning to some normalcy after all that they had gone through during the war. "Suze Bruggeman and Mienus van Lith are getting married today," they likely replied.

Later that morning, a covered horse and buggy arrived at the family bakery to pick up the bridal party and take them to City Hall. Another buggy picked up the groom's party at the family home and headed toward the same destination. When Suze arrived, Mienus opened the door of her buggy and greeting his bride. She accepted his outstretched arm and was assisted out of the buggy.

The groom stood tall and thin in his long, tailed, black tuxedo. He appeared even taller after placing the black top hat on his head, completing his look. A radiant smile revealed his joy. His bride would soon be his wife. His thoughts must have taken him back to those simple letters they shared back and forth while he was still in Buchenwald. The day that he longed for, the one that helped to keep him alive those last two brutal years, was finally here.

The bride looked radiant in her modestly elegant, white wedding gown. Her dark brown hair was tucked back neatly and was covered with a flowing white veil, long enough for her bridesmaids to carry. Her head was crowned, temple to temple, with a tasteful adornment of small white flowers. The large bouquet in her right hand completed the look with several long-stem, white carnations and green trim. She smiled at her groom, reached for his arm, and was escorted up the stairs and into City Hall.

The time spent there was very short. Simple vows were promised, rings exchanged, papers signed, and then back down the stairs after a few pictures were taken. Together the couple would share a buggy ride to St. John the Baptist Catholic Church, but not before some of the groom's co-workers came out of the police station in the bottom level of the City Hall building to congratulate the newly married couple. These guys could be quite a rowdy bunch when they got together to socialize after work. Like brothers, they looked out for each other, and some friendships would endure into the future and across thousands of miles. I can imagine them singing that old familiar song to congratulate Mienus and his new bride, Suze.

Lang zal ze leven, lang zal ze leven, lang zal ze leven in de Gloria, in de Gloria, in de Gloria. Hieperdepiep, hoera!

The second exchange of vows took place during the celebration of the Holy Mass. Mother's only piece of jewelry worn on her wedding day, aside from the gold band she would receive, was a small gold cross on a thin gold chain hanging around her neck.

Mass began with a processional played on an old organ. The couple walked down the aisle toward the altar where the priest was already waiting for them. Family and friends filled the first few pews of the large sanctuary.

This time the vows they exchanged were full of meaningful words that spoke of love, God, devotion, commitment, honor, children, and promises to stay together till death. This time the ring exchange was given and accepted with a more complete understanding that their marriage was now a sacramental union. They would choose to love each other, bless each other with children, support each other's hopes and dreams, and also encourage each other during the difficult times ahead.

After a simple meal at the reception and a few more pictures, the newlyweds would make their way to their modest upstairs rooms in the shared townhouse. There they would begin creating their new life together as husband and wife.

Like most couples, their vows would be tested within a few years, but not on this day! This was their first night alone, and every moment was savored. Sunrise would come soon enough.

Before heading back to work, Mienus planned to spend the next few of days fashioning a small makeshift kitchen on the upstairs landing, and Suze had some plans of her own to create a cozy sitting room in the other bedroom. It wouldn't be too long before their windows would be adorned with twelve-inch lace valances, so typical of those displayed in many Dutch homes. Similar lace curtains have been hanging in many windows throughout Holland for hundreds of years.

The first morning following their wedding, after a simple breakfast, they took a long walk back to the church to give thanks, and then headed for a store to pick up the few items they would need to make some simple changes to their living arrangements.

Just a few steps into their walk, Suze began to notice flower pedals every few steps. "Look Mienus! It looks as if someone has marked our way back to the church. I wonder how this happened. I don't remember seeing them yesterday, do you?" she said.

"I didn't really see them either, but then, I wasn't looking at the ground. I was looking at you!" Mienus replied.

These "out of the ordinary" flowers in October were meant for them, and they followed those peddles all the way back to St. John the Baptist Church. This moment between them would always be remembered.

Nightmares and Other Signs

Mienus was not your ordinary policeman. His reputation was widely known as a kind man, with an endearing love for children. The only weapon he had to keep himself and others safe from lawbreakers was a billy club, also known as a police baton. It was attached to his belt, and was visible for all to see. After witnessing so much violence at the hands of the SS guards during his captivity, he just didn't want to risk shooting anyone with a gun. When confronted with lawlessness, he'd rather threaten bad guys with a stick to let them know who was in charge.

Times were very different back then. Uniformed police officers walked around or rode their bikes in town to keep the peace. Most of the time that was all that was necessary.

The kids in town seemed to know when their favorite policeman was in their neighborhood. Mienus was known for carrying something else each day to work. You could hear their voices shouting out with excitement, and then run to greet him, knowing that his pockets contained candy that he gladly handed out to the children. He would continue his usual route only to find a small pack of children following behind him like a Pied Piper of Vlaardingen.

There was no fear or worry when Mienus and the other policemen came around. These men helped to restore order from the past chaos and gave the citizens of a sense of relief. People began to feel safe once more, giving them time to heal. The anxiety produced during the previous years of occupation was slowly fading.

Mienus looked good in his uniform. In his new work clothes, he was perceived as strong and tall by others who looked up to him. This was such a contrast from the horrible striped pajama uniform he was forced to wear by those who didn't care if he lived or died, and who treated him worse than an animal. He needed to feel good about himself again. His manhood was being restored, which helped in his slow process of healing.

Mienus had much to heal from. I know he never could fully recover from the trauma he endured during his time in Hell. How could he? That experience changed him forever.

It didn't take long before Suze was conscious of the nightmares her husband frequently suffered from. There were many times in his sleep when he would move about the bed, thrashing and moaning loudly, his body covered in sweat. He would wake up abruptly and sit up in bed as if someone had just attacked him. Crying out in fear, his tears were unremitting, and they gave him no relief.

Suze would make her presence known by gently calling out to him. "Mienus, Mienus, wake up! I'm here! You are having a bad dream!" she would say while cradling his head in her arms and rocking him like a child next to her breasts.

It would take a few minutes for him to gain his composure and quiet himself long enough to realize it was a dream. "Oh, Suze, I'm sorry I woke you. I'm so sorry. I have these nightmares. I'm sure they will go away soon," was all he would say about the incident. He could not yet talk about Buchenwald in much detail to his wife. He wanted to spare her.

As a police officer, rotating work shifts was a necessity. This made his sleep even more difficult. When his shift changed, he would work the current shift first, immediately followed by the new rotating shift before he was able to go home again.

This 16-hour double shift every two to three months was very difficult at times. Mienus would be very fatigued and become quite irritable. Suze worked very hard to keep their rooms neat and clean before her husband returned from these shifts. She would prepare his food with extra care to avoid any conflict, and be sure the rooms were very quiet so as not to disturb him.

She saw a side of Mienus that she had not experienced before, and it was not a good one. He displayed emotions that seemed out of place and extreme for many situations. She dreaded the shift changes because of the way he acted around her when he got so tired.

At some point, Suze would need to approach her husband about this behavior. But it would take some time before she had the nerve. Though she wanted to, now was definitely not the time. She needed to take good care of herself. She was going to have her first child in just a few more months.

She was more timid, and he was patriarchal and more in charge. He was very loving and caring most of the time, but could very quickly become loud and angry over the littlest mishaps. He had a very short fuse.

With things that others would simply overlook, Mienus would blow up as if it was the biggest mistake ever. Every one of us in the family had to do our best to read his moods and try not to light the fuse.

One of the worst offenses Suze could do was to forget to salt the boiling potatoes! She became visibly fearful when Mienus pointed out that she had forgotten that most important ingredient. It was not good enough to simply salt them on his plate. The pattern continued for a good portion of his life. As children, my siblings and I knew to keep our heads down until the tension subsided. There were other examples, but this example illustrates the problem. Mienus had lots to heal from.

Growing Out of Small Spaces

On July 17, 1947, Wilhelmina Suzanna Maria was born. She was given this name to fulfill the family obligation of naming their first-born daughter after her grandmother on her father's side. Apparently Mienus' father was a bit disappointed when the baby was born a girl. He had hopes for a boy so his name would have been used.

My sister did not go by her very formal name. She was called Ineke, (pronounced **E**-nah-kah). Our mother delivered her upstairs in the bedroom with the assistance of a midwife. Like many first births, this was a long labor and difficult delivery.

Suze would remain in bed for two weeks. Back then, that was the norm after giving birth. She and her new baby would be waited on by family and friends.

Within 24 hours of her birth, Mienus would take Ineke to the church to have her baptized. Suze's mother (our Oma) would bring the family baptismal dress for Ineke to wear. She would be clothed in the same gown that Suze and all her siblings wore at their baptisms. There would be a few family members in attendance to witness the event.

It was important to parents to have their children baptized soon after they were born. The mortality rate for babies of previous generations was much higher than today, so there was a sense of urgency for immediate baptism. This was a typical practice in Holland. Today, many couples wait a few months for a variety of reason, and the mother is generally present.

Suze's oldest brother, Herman, was the very first to wear this handmade dress on the occasion of his baptism. He was born on March 16, 1916, and was no doubt baptized within 24 hours. Suze was the last of her generation to wear it. My siblings and I would all wear the same dress at our baptism, and so would many of our Bruggeman cousins. We would be the second generation to wear the beautiful little white dress.

Suze and Mienus loved being parents. There was never any doubt in their minds that a baby would quickly follow after their marriage. That was so natural and almost expected. It was nine months and fifteen days after the wedding when Ineke was born, and baby would follow baby!

On August 29, 1948, Gertruida Maria Johanna was born. She was named after her maternal grandmother. Her common name would be Gerrie, (pronounced like Harry, only with a G, spoken as if you were clearing the back of the throat). Now, don't make fun. It is the Dutch accent and it becomes important to the story later on.

There were thirteen months and twelve days between Ineke and Gerrie. Suze had the same long and hard labor and the same two weeks' stay in bed, only this time with a walking one year old. The same white baptismal dress would be worn again within 24 hours of Gerrie's birth.

When Mienus worked his night shift, he would need to sleep during the day just a few feet away from the rest of his family. It was a real hardship for Suze to keep her young babies from making too much noise. She did her best to prevent Mienus from sleep deprivation, knowing how grumpy he would become.

The living arrangements were no longer suitable for the young family of four. It was equally problematic for the older couple living below them. They needed a bigger place, one with a third bedroom, and soon. Even with the reconstruction going on around Vlaardingen and the rest of Holland, there were still not enough living accommodations for the number of people needing them. There was no time to waste in applying for a single-family dwelling. Like the first time, they would have to wait for their name to reach the top of the list, and time was running out. The wait better be short. By the time Gerrie was eight months old, Suze was pregnant with her third child.

Was it luck or divine intervention? With Mienus' influence in the police department and his relationship with the mayor, a bigger home was found for Mienus, Suze, and their growing family. With the extra bedroom, a real kitchen, a bathroom, and a larger living area, this brick townhome was more than twice the space that they had before, and it was all theirs. With the time running short, they moved in quickly.

Just before the new baby was born, Mienus' father paid a visit to his son and wife in their new place. The purpose of his visit was to make sure that the two of them knew that this child was to be named after him! Even if this baby was a girl, they were to use the feminine version of his name because that was expected.

Suze was stunned that he came over to make such demand like that. She and Mienus had a heated talk after his father left. Not one to stand her ground easily against others, it took a lot for her to show her disappointment and anger. She was about to settle the naming of their children once and for all.

Marching right over to her in-law's house, Suze rang the doorbell and was greeted by her mother-in-law. "I need to talk to Opa!" Suze said. Her father-in-law was sitting in his easy chair with a surprised look on his face. Suze had never come over by herself like this before. She remembered how stubborn and demanding he was toward Mienus after he returned from the camp, and felt intimidated by him. That would soon change.

"What is it Suze? I'm surprised to see you so soon," Opa said.

Suze mustered the courage to say, "Mienus and I have kept the tradition of naming our girls after their respective grandmothers. I am sorry that you were disappointed that they were not boys. It is not for you to decide that our new baby will have your name, no matter what! Both sides of the family have a grandparent whose name was handed down, first to Ineke, and then to Gerrie. Now we have decided to break with tradition and name any future children what we want to name them. That is what I came here to tell you!"

Opa was so taken with Suze's forthright manner that he agreed with her and let her know that he would avoid any further meddling in their decisions as parents.

When Suze later shared these memories with me, I could tell that this was a big turning point in her life. It was empowering. "After that confrontation with your Opa, my relationship to both his parents was great. Your Opa saw something in me that he suddenly respected. I was no longer intimidated by him and he knew it. It was good."

Suzanna Christina Theresia joined her other two sisters on October 31, 1949. She arrived fourteen months after Gerrie was born. Suzanna was called Suuzke (**Sūz**-ka). Very few people were called by their formal name in those days.

Suze enjoyed her three little girls and took delight in sewing clothes for them. She had her hands full, for sure. She was passionate about her role as wife and mother. She would do her very best to make her husband happy and keep her children healthy. Mienus would work hard providing for their needs, and Suze would do just about everything else.

Giving birth to her three very young girls put a strain on Suze's body. She tired easily from the many months of pregnancy and nursing babies over the last two years. I remember her telling me, "I prayed to God for a year without being pregnant." Her prayer did get answered. Suuzke had her first birthday, and within a couple of weeks, Suze discovered she was expecting her fourth. With a smile on her face she said to me, "I should have asked for more time!"

Living in a single dwelling home was so much better than the first place they had shared with the elderly couple. Watching all the new construction being built around the neighborhoods of Vlaardingen, Suze brought up to her husband the subject of buying a new place of their own. She wanted enough of a backyard for the kids to include a garden and lots of flowers. Mienus was convinced, so the search was on.

They made an offer on a two-story, corner unit townhouse with a small backyard. No more sharing, no more waiting, this would be theirs for as long as they wanted. The offer was accepted and they moved in quickly. This was the nicest home either had ever lived in. She planned to stay there with her husband the rest of her life. What more could she ever ask for? Life was good.

There is always enough love for one more. Sometimes it takes nine months to get used to the idea that a new member of the family is being added. But when that new child is placed in the arms of a mother, a primal love takes over between them. She sees a familiar look in the eyes of her newborn. "Yes, Lord, you were right! I do have enough love for all my children," she may have said when looking at the face of her fourth little girl.

Just two weeks after moving into their new home, Theresia Johanna Maria made her appearance on July 25, 1951. She would be called, Treesje (pronounced **Trā**-shaw). Within 24 hours, Mienus and his three little daughters would accompany their new baby sister to St. John the Baptist Church for her baptism, wearing the long white gown each of them had worn before her. There was comfort in this tradition. Sadly, Suze was not there to witness any of these happy events.

Treesje's two oldest siblings, young as they were, would need to become Suze's "little helpers." Ineke and Gerri did what they could to help with light chores. They were trained to pick up after themselves, to play nicely with Suuzke, and to be quiet when naptime came around.

Suze continued to sew Mienus' clothes, as well as most of her children's clothes. She had been doing this for her husband even before they were married, and continued for many years after.

Mienus continued working as a policeman, but missed using his skills as a machinist. He had worked hard to learn his trade, and silently yearned for that type of work again. He enjoyed working in the shipyards before the war, and police work did not suit him well. He allowed himself to think about what he wanted in life, and what he wanted most for his family. Mienus was getting restless.

Life was more satisfying, and much less complicated, living in their new home. Store goods began arriving in larger quantities, and the long waiting lines were behind them. New businesses were opening, and people were going back to work. Living a normal life after the war was getting easier for much of Holland.

In Suze's mind, things were as they should be. In Mienus' mind, they were not. He was doing his best to suppress the memories of those horrible years in Buchenwald. He thought doing so was the right thing to do to be able to handle the emotional trauma from the torture he endured. Suppressing emotions made it difficult for him to express other feelings more appropriately. Feeling strong emotions of any kind would often be communicated in exaggerated or inappropriate ways.

"This evil war must never be forgotten. What happened to so many people, should never happen again," Mienus said many times in my life.

This exhortation was a lifetime goal of so many of those who suffered in the concentration camps, and a necessary warning for future generations. Mienus could not shake off this self-imposed mission. Trying daily to suppress his memories was the biggest challenge in his life. Telling others to remember while trying himself to forget was an impossibility.

Chapter 10

Plotting and Planning for the Future

A lot happened in the first six years after Mienus was liberated. At some point, he must have looked back at his life and saw just how far he had come since those dark years. Why wasn't he feeling more content? Unfortunately, he felt restless and far from satisfied with where he was and what he was doing with his life. He longed for relief of the conflict he was experiencing. In time, he came up with a bold solution for what troubled him, and he knew what he wanted to do.

Mienus had thought a lot about the men who had rescued him and the country that sent them to fight to free millions of people like him. "What country sends over hundreds of thousands of men and women to risk their lives fighting a war to liberate others and their country?" he would say. He got to know several of these brave men personally, and that made all the difference to him. "I owed my life to them!" he said.

A surprisingly large number of people in Holland were quietly exploring the possibility of immigrating to another country. Most were doing so with the thought of providing a better life for themselves and their family. Some were dreaming of adventure. Still others were thinking about relocating for reasons only they could explain.

Mienus was a dreamer, and had his own reasons for wanting to emigrate. He did want a better life and the adventure that went along with it. This dream kept growing and growing, and eventually became a clear vision and no longer a dream.

He began to talk privately with some of his best buddies in the police department about his growing desire to emigrate. Several of them had been having their own thoughts about the subject matter. These conversations would go on for a few more months before he had enough nerve to approach the topic with Suze.

He had a lovely wife, a good stable job, four beautiful healthy little girls, and a house of their own that worked well for them. That should have been enough. However, there were all sorts of reasons why he wanted to move his family to the US, and they outnumbered the reasons to stay. His mind was made up. He just needed to convince his wife.

Emigrate! Merriam-Webster's dictionary defincs emigrate: "to leave one's place of residence or country to live elsewhere" (Merriam-Webster), and yourdictionary.com states: "to emigrate is defined as to leave the country where you are from and move permanently to another" (YourDictionary.com).

There were many countries opening their doors to legal immigrants, especially Canada, Australia, and the United States of America, just to name a few. Mienus' choice was easy. "I wanted to be an American."

*

"Let me help you dry those dishes!" Mienus offered to his wife. "You know Suze, I've been thinking. Some of us at the station have seen friends and relatives moving out of Holland for a better life somewhere else. Several of us have been talking about doing the same, and relocating together. What do you think about that?" Mienus said to begin the conversation.

There was an awkward pause while Suze silently pondered what Mienus had just said. She took a deep breath and replied, "What do I think about that? I don't think I like it one bit. Why would we leave everything we have here to start over someplace else with your police friends?" She was friends with some of her husband's police buddies, but she had reservations about some of the others.

Mienus figured that was what his wife would say. "Well, we'll just think about it for a while then," he said while planning his next move. He finished drying the last dish and quickly slipped out of the room. Now it was clear to Suze why Mienus offered to dry the dishes. She knew he was up to something!

Sometime after Treesje's first birthday, Mienus stopped "just thinking" about emigrating. He would take matters in his own hands and do something about it, and would tell Suze later.

It was early in 1953 when he went to the emigration office and filled out the application for himself and his family to relocate to the United States. He was told that there were many people on the waiting list before him wanting to immigrate to America.

Certain qualifications needed to be addressed before being approved by the US government for entrance as a new immigrant. Mienus was willing to wait and do whatever was necessary to leave Holland with his family. He figured it would give him plenty of time to figure out how to tell his wife that someday they would be leaving Holland.

Trying hard to be patient, Mienus would wait a few months before dropping by the emigration office to check on his application. He was told that his family was slowly moving up the list, and that he would be given adequate notice to find a required sponsor in America willing to help when they arrive in the US.

"Sponsor, what do I need a sponsor for?"

The clerk standing behind the counter explained, "You are required to have a sponsor when relocating in order to help with the transition, and to assist you financially until you are able to support yourself."

This was getting a little more complicated. He would have to talk to Suze again and fill her in on what he was planning.

*

"Suze, I want to talk to you again about moving to the United States. I've thought it over and think it is best for us to do this. I know you didn't want to move when I brought it up the first time, but I want to do this, and I think it is best for our children."

"Why? Why do you think it is for the best? Our children are fine here in Holland. They have their family and their friends. We have a nice house, and you have a good job. Tell me why. I don't like anything about this!" Suze emphatically stated.

Mienus hesitated for a moment, and then turned and stood in front of his spouse. "I want to live in a country where we will be free and never suffer like we did during the war. I don't ever want our children to suffer like we had to. I am so grateful to the GI soldiers from America that liberated me, and I want to live in that country. They have much greater opportunities for us and for our children! I am just not happy here anymore."

She became quiet after he spoke. After a few uncomfortable minutes Suze said, "I will think about it, but I don't want to."

Her husband, now calm after his resolute statement, said, "Thank you!"

She had agreed to think about it, but the subject didn't come up again for months. She didn't want anyone else to know what Mienus was planning, out of fear that they might encourage him. When she was stressed and concerned about something, Suze did what she always did when life was difficult. She went to the church to pray.

"Dear Lord, you know I want to trust you in all things but I am struggling with my husband right now. You know he wants to leave Holland. Please help me to know what to do. I don't want to go. Please, if this is what you want, then let everything happen according to your will, and remove any obstacles toward that end. If it is not, please make it clear for both of us by making it impossible to leave. Mother Mary, pray for us too! Lift my prayer up to your Son, and have Him work this out for me, for us, please."

Though she wasn't telling anyone about possible plans to immigrate to the United States, Mienus was. Several of his police friends made a pact with each other to relocate to the US. There were at least two other men who had placed their families on the list before Mienus had. Others said they wanted to go too.

There was one little obstacle, besides his wife, that needed to be worked out. How would he get a sponsor willing to help his family emigrate?

Conversations among Mienus and his friends often turned to the subject of leaving Holland. One of his coworkers had recently taken his family to the United States, settling in Salt Lake City, Utah. Another friend from the force had been notified to begin planning for his departure. Mienus' name was moving up the emigration list quickly.

It took months to get all the paperwork in order. When they received notification the first time, they knew they had better be prepared for the time their name was at the top of the list.

Suze became aware of the rumor that her family was on some list to emigrate. "Mienus would never do that without talking to me first, would he?" So she thought.

It was easy for her to push back the thought that her husband wanted to leave Holland for good. Months had gone by since the last time they seriously talked about it. People were starting to ask her about their plans, and she was not ready to discuss anything with anybody just yet.

"Mienus, I have been hearing from our friends that you have been telling people that we are going to leave Holland. Why would you do that? Someone even said that we are on some list to emigrate. Is that true?"

"Well, (pause) that is true. These things take time to work through. It can take years before we would actually go, so I put our name on the list at the emigration office a year ago just to be ready when we both decide to go. Huip's family (Mienus' police friend from work) is getting their paperwork in order because they were finally notified. They will be leaving in a few months, and there are more of my friends from work who are on the list too. They signed up after I did. You said you would think about it, and I just wanted to be ready," he said, as if he did nothing wrong or unusual.

Suze found it was necessary to compose herself before asserting, "Saying I will think about it, and agreeing to it, are two different things, Mienus."

"Suze, I am not doing this because our friends from work are leaving Holland. And I surely do not want to make you angry or hurt you. But hear me out! I want to give our children a better life and keep them safe. If we do not leave when our children are still young and together, they will probably emigrate themselves and leave us when they are grown. I see many parents whose children are leaving them. I don't want that to happen to us. Don't you see Suze? It is what's best. I know it!" Mienus said, hoping to convince his wife to change her mind about leaving.

Listening to his words, Suze realized just how badly her husband wanted to go to America. She had only one place to go for her own answers. Back to St. John the Baptist Church.

After praying in church, Suze went home, with a promise in her heart. She knew that God would not give her anything she could not handle. "If this is meant to be, it will happen according to His will," she assured herself.

She would agree to leave Holland under those conditions. That was the only consolation she received. She would not fight her husband; she would follow him. She had promised to do whatever she could in her marriage to make him happy, didn't she? There was still hope, she thought. Perhaps the roadblocks will start showing up soon.

Suze would wake up often in the middle of the night just thinking about what might happen next in their lives. It was difficult to turn her thoughts off long enough to fall back asleep. Her appetite wasn't the best either. "I must be stressing too much about what may or may not even happen," she thought. Or maybe it was something else.

Treesje was just a few months' shy of her third birthday. No more diapers and good sleep cycles had long been set. Ineke was in second grade and Gerrie was in first. With just Suuzke and Treesje left at home, it was so much easier to get around for family visits or shopping.

"How would the children adjust to leaving Holland? They would all have to learn a new language and leave everyone they knew behind as well," Suze thought.

After a few more days, she began to think that her fatigue was not just from waking up at night thinking about all the possibilities. She was pretty sure she was pregnant again. So many ambivalent emotions flooded her thoughts. "If I am pregnant, surely this would be the roadblock that was meant to prevent us from leaving Holland. Mienus would certainly think that too, wouldn't he? I will wait another week or two before I share my good news!" she thought. "Thank you Lord for this new life coming into our family at just the right time."

And so it happened. Mienus took the news like every other time Suze got pregnant. He loved children, especially his own. Though it was a surprise for both of them, it didn't take too long before they were exploring names for their new little one.

Immigrating to the United States was not the biggest priority, at least not for Suze. Mienus still checked periodically at the emigration office to see where they were on the list. So many people were waiting like he was, but now he just didn't know whether it would be possible to take such a long journey with a pregnant wife. He would not risk it, even if it meant going back to the bottom of the list and starting over again.

Still, he worried about finding a sponsor in America, if and when the time came. Mienus would consult with others who had managed to find family or friends to sponsor them. Their sponsors were already in the States. He may not have spent as much time in prayer like his wife did, but in this particular matter, needed some Divine intervention.

While waiting for the new arrival, the conversation between husband and wife was more about the new baby, and very little about moving. Suze planned to have her fifth child at home like she did with the others, but this time she was planning to have a doctor help with the delivery. She had difficult labors and deliveries with the others, and now with a doctor available, she hoped it would be easier on her and the baby.

On the late evening of January 28, 1955, the doctor was notified that labor had started for Suze. They wanted to give him plenty of notice that she was in early labor. Mienus got word to Suze's friend who had helped care for their little children when she gave birth the last few times. He wanted everything to go just right for his wife. Even though he had been in this position four times already, the doctor had told him that this time, it would be different. The doctor was so very sure that, from all the signs, this baby was a boy!

Mienus loved his girls with all his heart, but the thought of finally having a son was exciting. He made sure that he was able to stay home from work to be with his family when his son was born.

Suze's friend came over early in the morning. She wanted to be there in case any of the children woke up and started wandering about. The doctor arrived shortly after.

I find it hard to imagine a doctor making such a house call and staying the entire time until after the birth of the baby. But this was a different time and a different place. I suppose there were still some doctors in the United States at that time who made house calls. Most did not.

When the children woke from their sleep, their father would leave his wife and the doctor, and explain what was going on with their mother. By now, labor was intensifying to the point that an occasional loud groaning from within the bedroom could be heard. None of the girls had any memory of Treesje's birth, but this time the three older ones would be old enough to remember this labor and delivery.

Shortly after mid-day, on Saturday, January 29, 1955, Suze finally was ready to have her baby, and Mienus to finally get his son. "Doctor, you're still thinking that this one is a boy, right?" Mienus asked cautiously.

"I am sure. From what I can tell, this one is different from the others. When I saw Suze in my office, what I could hear and feel made me think it was a boy. Even the labor is different," the doctor said with encouragement.

They planned to name this child after his father. He would be named Dominicus Marinus van Lith Jr. Mienus and Suze never did pick out a girl's name, so assured by the doctor that it was a boy.

After several hours of labor, Suze was finally ready to deliver her baby. Ineke and Gerrie stood just outside the door, very excited. Yet, they had a sense of real concern for their mother due to the loud noises coming from the room. Both were told by their dad to go outside with Suuzke and Treesje and play with them. He needed their help as the big sisters, by helping the woman who came to take care of all of them.

Mienus was at his wife's side, anxious for his son to arrive.

"Ok, Suze, this next contraction, push hard. The baby's head is right there," said the doctor.

"He's coming honey, and with lots of dark hair," Mienus spoke quietly.

Slowly and forcefully, Suze pushed. "It's almost over," she thought.

Then, after a moment of silence, their new baby cried out the first breath. Waiting for someone to say something, Mienus finally looked up to see the doctor's red face, which said it all. Dad walked over to see me and said to Mom, "It's a girl Suze, another girl."

After the initial disappointment, the important feelings of gratitude were expressed by both parents. They had another beautiful, and even more importantly, another healthy, baby girl. God had blessed them with their fifth daughter in 7½ years. "We make beautiful girls, huh Suze?" Mienus would have said, just to alleviate any concerns his wife may have had regarding his disappointment.

The doctor felt so sorry that he had predicted a boy, and apologized several times to them. "Maybe you should stick to what you do best, and not hand out predictions anymore!" Mienus said with one raised eyebrow. A moment later, Suze, Mienus, and the doctor had a good laugh, and then a round of congratulations flowed between them. I can only assume that this doctor held his predictions to himself from then on!

When it came to naming me, my parents had to do some quick thinking. Dad came up with my name by reversing his name and putting it in the feminine form. My name is Maria Dominica van Lith. Though my four older sisters had three names, I was given just two. They would call me Marja (**Mar**-ya). I was taken to St. John the Baptist Catholic Church the following day, on January 30, in the well-worn family dress for my baptism.

Sports, Trains, and Sponsors

My parents were dear friends with a woman named Bertha "Puck" (pronounced *Perk*) Brouwer. Puck was a well-known athlete in the Netherlands, and first made a name for herself in the European Championships in 1950 in Brussels, Belgium. It was there she won the silver medal in the 4x100m relay. She then went on to compete in the 1952 Summer Olympics in Helsinki Finland in the 100m, 200m sprint, and 4x100m relay. Again she won the silver medal, this time in the 200m race. In the 1954 European Championships in Bern Switzerland, Puck won another silver medal, this time in the 100m race.

Puck traveled all the way to Melbourne, Australia for the 1956 Olympics, only to be disappointed when the Netherlands pulled out of the games in protest of the Soviet Union invasion of Hungary. When the Soviets sent their players to compete, Holland, Spain, and Switzerland boycotted the Olympics in solidarity with Hungary.

Prior to the 1956 Olympics, Puck traveled to different venues in Europe for intensive training. On one of those occasions, she traveled with a young married couple, Gil and Heni, who were also good friends with Mienus and Suze.

These friends already knew of Mienus' plans to immigrate to America. They also knew that the van Lith's had been on a waiting list of families wanting to leave. Mienus asked the three of them to help him with his pursuit by writing the required character references his family would need before they could emigrate. There was still the last big hurdle left to climb over, the business of finding a sponsor. He happened to mention that to the three also.

On one particular train trip, Puck, Gil, and Heni happen to be seated in a train car with a man from the United States. Joe D.W. was traveling through Europe on business and for some sightseeing. He introduced himself and before too long, a conversation was struck between the three friends and this American businessman.

Their discussion was relaxed and casual. Travel and sports often make for good conversation amongst strangers. At some point in the exchange, Puck and Heni brought up their good friends, Mienus and Suze. Joe listened while they talked about their friends' time as a prisoner in Buchenwald, and about his liberation. He appeared very interested in what they were telling him.

The conversation quickly turned to immigration. Puck and the others wanted to know more about this American businessman. Hoping to get a good feel for Joe's overall character, the three friends carefully asked more personal questions of him. After feeling more confident that this Joe was a good guy, they felt better about asking him for a huge favor.

"Joe, we would like to ask you a very important question. As you know from our conversation, our friend and his family want to immigrate to America. They have most of their paperwork in order, but they have one more thing they have to do before they will be considered eligible to emigrate. They need someone in America to be their sponsor. Someone to help them get settled when they arrive. Would you be interested in helping the van Lith family by being their sponsor? They are a wonderful family, and Mienus has many skills for work. Could you help them?"

Joe took a moment to digest their request. Thinking as a businessman, he must have weighed the pros and cons. There was something about this family and the story he was told about Mienus that peaked his curiosity and interest. A Dutch patriot, survivor of Buchenwald, liberated by General Patton, desiring to be an American, father of five daughters, all made for a great story.

As they were closing in on their destination, Joe had enough time to give them an answer. He told his new friends from Holland that he was interested in helping the van Liths, but he would give them a definite answer before he traveled back to the US. They all exchanged contact information, gave appropriate parting remarks that included an assurance from Joe that he would be in touch soon.

Puck, Heni, and Gil were optimistic that they had found the right person to help their dear friends. Soon after they returned to Holland, they paid my parents a visit. Mienus was quite pleased to hear about their encounter with Joe D.W.

Suze, on the other hand, had real reservations. She still hoped for more roadblocks that might prevent them from even needing this man named Joe.

A letter arrived at Puck's house not long after her recent trip. It was from Joe D.W., agreeing to take on the sponsorship of their friends. Joe was already home in the United States. The van Lith's would have to trust their friends that this stranger from Salem, Oregon, would help them make the adjustments in America.

Time to Decide

It was not long after Marja was born that a notice came in the mail from the emigration office letting the family know that it was time to get their passports in order. Though they were not at the top of the list yet, it would take time to get everything in order.

When the passports finally arrived, Mienus watched as Suze quickly opened the envelopes to study them. There were just two passports, one for Mienus and the other for Suze and their five daughters. He walked close to her and said, "Suze, I know that this was completely my idea in the first place, and I know that this has been hard on you. Please honey, you know I never meant to hurt you, but I still believe we will have a better life in America. I just know it is the right thing to do for our family."

With a look of acceptance, she said:

> *I have thought a lot, and prayed a lot about your desire to become an American. Ever since I found out that you went to the emigration office and put our names on the list to go to America, I have been praying for any obstacle that God would put in our way that would make it clear to both of us that it would be a mistake to leave Holland. I thought you were happy in your job as a policeman, but you were not. You wanted to work with machines and with your hands, like you did before the war. After we got our new house, I thought that it would have been our home for many years. You did not see it that way. And then I got pregnant with Marja. I thought for sure that this would be the sign for us to stay. But here we are, a year later, and you are still planning to leave.*

> *As I watched these and many other obstacles fall down one after another, I began to pray even harder. I prayed that if this move would not be good for our children's salvation, then soften my husband's heart, and let him decide that our family should stay in Holland. If, on the other hand, going to America will be better for the salvation of our children, then soften my heart, and I will obey and leave.*

> *When I married you, Mienus, I promised to love you, and follow you for better or for worse. I just want to make you happy.*

It was Suze's heart that softened, and she had waited for the right moment to say these words to her husband. As Mienus held his wife, tears began to fall. They both understood that they shared a single goal for their family. The faith that got them both through the awful years of the war, now provided the hope for their future.

Spring warmed into summer, summer mellowed into fall, and fall cooled into winter again. At the end of January of 1956, the family was celebrating Marja's first birthday. Over three years had passed since Mienus placed the van Lith family name on the list at the emigration office. Marja's name was added soon after she was born.

Not much was different from their daily routine. Suze continued to care for her girls and sew the family's clothes. Mienus still worked his changing shifts at the police department. He continued handing out his pocketsful of candies to the children that followed him, until those pockets were empty. Ineke and Gerrie enjoyed their school and friends while the other three girls kept their momma busy.

The short dark days of winter grew longer and brighter each day, and the deep freeze of the winter thawed. Spring began to bring forth new life from the earth, nourishing new blossoms and leaves on the trees once again. But this year, the van Lith family would not be in Holland to see the tulips in full bloom.

Early in March of 1956, a letter arrived from the emigration office. It stated that the van Lith's were able to be in the next group leaving Holland for Canada and the United States of America.

The letter explained the procedures necessary to obtain a medical examination for each member of the family. There would be x-rays taken of both adults and anyone else that the doctor required, based on any medical findings.

Also included in the envelope was the necessary paperwork to be completed and ready for inspection at the same visit. It was stated that another letter would soon follow after their exams. This letter would provide information with the names of the family members that could departure to America in early April.

"Oh Mienus, it's really happening, isn't it? What do you think they mean by 'providing the names of the family members that could depart?' I don't like the way that sounds," Suze said.

"A lot of people got sick during the war and were exposed to tuberculosis. I know that when I was in the camp, I was exposed to it. Many prisoners died from that. When I left the camp, I had a physical after I arrived back in Holland and I tested positive for the virus, but I never got sick from it. I imagine they must need the x-rays to see if we have TB," Mienus replied.

"What about Suuzke and her asthma? Do you think that will keep us from going?" Suze asked. Now that she was agreeable to leaving, she worried that it might not happen at all.

Mienus encouraged her. "Let's follow the instructions, schedule the medical appointment, and get the paperwork ready. I will make sure I don't forget the references they are asking for! I would imagine all the other people who got this letter will be making their appointments right away too. I want to get it over with so we can find out, once and for all, if and when we leave."

Mienus was consoled by the change in his wife's outlook. If anything felt like an obstacle, these examinations sure did. They both must have felt like their faith was being tested. Suze would follow Mienus for a new life in America, and he would stay with her and the children in Holland if any one of the family members did not pass the exams.

Finally there was a decision that Suze and Mienus agreed on. They decided to let the Good Lord do what was best for their family. Each would freely sacrifice for the other, no matter what happened. In other words, they still didn't have a definite answer. It was all out of their hands, and always had been. Mienus and Suze gave up their own will for the good of the other, and in return created a loving and gentle peace between them.

*

I've listened to a variety of answers to this question. "What advice can you give couples for a successful marriage?" The most common reply was, "Well, it's a 50-50 proposition. It's always a compromise, and a give and take."

I no longer believe that 50% from the husband and 50% from the wife is good enough for any marriage to flourish. That advice is flawed. What I have observed and come to understand for a truly fruitful and rewarding union, each should be willing to offer 100% of themselves to the other. Married couples should do their best to give to the other what the other truly needs, even at a cost to themselves.

Nobody said marriage would be easy. On the contrary. It can be hard work. But this formula for success generates unconditional love, and a never-ending loop. It often requires great sacrifice and produces a profound union that turns two lives into one.

Mom and Dad demonstrated this principle to their children. I hope and pray that Mark and I have done the same for ours.

Chapter 11

Medical Clearances

In less than a week, all seven of us stood in line at the emigration office for our physicals. We were escorted to the medical wing of the building, where the men were separated from the women. The medical wing was filled with separate cubicles. Treesje and I stayed with our mother, while Ineke, Gerrie, and Suuzke were escorted into their individual cubicles.

The children were told to strip down to their t-shirt and underpants, and wait for the doctor or nurse to do the examination.

*

Not long ago I spent some time with Ineke and Gerrie (who now goes by Gert). I asked Ineke what it was like and how she felt during this physical examination. She said, "I hated it! I didn't understand what this was all for. I just did what I was told."

I then asked, "Did Dad and Mom prepare you for this exam and tell you why this was being done?" She said, "Heck no! They didn't tell us much of anything. We didn't communicate with our parents like that."

Gert had some thoughts of her own in the matter. "I really didn't think too much about this examination. Here I am sitting on a cold table, waiting for some exam in my undies. I just figured that Mom and Dad must think this was ok, so I didn't worry too much about it."

After interviewing Ineke and Gert, I thought it best to call Suuske and Treesje (who now go by the names Sue and Traci). They didn't really remember much of this event. They just had some very vague notions. I asked Sue if she had any memory of her exam. She said, "The only thing I really remember was the big shot in my thigh. It really hurt! I also have a vague recollection of having to stand still for a chest x-ray."

*

Suze did her best to keep all her children calm. There were several families going through the same process, which made for a lot of noise. Having all the responsibility of the children made it even more difficult.

Mienus was the first one in the family to complete his exam and x-ray. He was given permission to take care of his children so Suze could finally get her exam and x-ray completed. At the end of this ordeal, it was time to go home and wait for the next letter to arrive with more information.

Waiting was difficult. The extended families were also waiting to hear when or if their loved ones were really going to leave everybody and everything behind, and start over in America. Within days, the letter of instruction arrived with all the details they were waiting for. The families no longer had to wonder.

Two and a Half Weeks

"Mienus, the letter arrived today. We **all** leave from Rotterdam on Wednesday, April 4. That's just two and a half weeks away! We will need to move quickly, if we are really going!" Suze said.

Mienus replied, "It says that we have all the paperwork in order too. Suze, I have thought about this for such a long time. It makes it kind of hard to believe that it is really going to happen for us. The last thing left is to pay for the tickets."

"No Mienus. The last thing we have to do, when the time comes, is to say goodbye to our family and friends. That will happen after we sell and give away most of our belongings. It says that we can only take to America what fits in a 6'x6'x6' wooden crate. That sure doesn't sound like much to me. We will have to pack as much of the most important belongings to survive when we get to Salem, Oregon, as we can. I need to look on a map again to see for myself where Salem, Oregon is located before we go," Suze added.

Suze didn't use the words, "if we go," anymore. After seeing the excitement in her husband's face, and watching as the last obstacles fell away, she knew what she had to do, and would do it willingly now. "We should tell our children after dinner tonight, and then visit our parents and tell them about our news," Suze mustered the courage to say.

Word spread quickly among family and friends. Within a couple of days after the notification arrived, Mienus quit his police job. He had been saving money for quite some time in anticipation of this moment. There were many things to do before they were ready to leave. Before leaving the police force for the last time, he encouraged his best friends to follow him to America, and reminded them of the pact they made. Mienus was now the fourth policeman in the force to quit and immigrate to America.

Fortunately, Suze had already begun sewing clothes for each of the children. It made for a difficult task for her though. The challenge was not the sewing part, but sorting out the kinds of clothes the children would need for the next four seasons in their new homeland. In addition, she would have to guesstimate how much each girl would grow during that time to ensure the fit of each piece of clothing. Yet if the clothes didn't fit the older two daughters, who wore the same size, they would be handed down to the third and fourth daughter, who also shared the same size. I would be a more difficult challenge. At only fifteen months old, I was growing rapidly.

Suze took her time sorting through their belongings. Mienus left her in charge of picking out the items she felt were absolutely necessary to run the household when they reached their final destination. In addition to the practical things, she carefully packed their most prized possessions. They both decided on which of the hanging pictures, photo albums, statues, curtains, memorabilia, and religious items to take.

It was a bittersweet time for the family. The girls continued to play with their childhood friends and go about their daily lives with just a vague idea of what was about to happen. "We watched as many of our household belongings were carried out of our home. We knew that we were moving away, but Gert and I figured it couldn't be that far. I mean, we figured we would still be able to come back to visit every so often and see our grandparents and extended family, as well as our friends. Having to say goodbye didn't feel like forever!" Ineke shared.

Gert added, "Our grandparents came to see us a few more times than they usually did during the last couple of weeks. So did some of our aunts and uncles and cousins. And yet, we still didn't feel like it was such a 'Big Deal.' Other people moved away but still managed to come back once in a while, or we would go to see them. The hardest part for Ineke and I was leaving our teachers and our friends before the end of the school year."

Mienus and Suze worked hard physically getting ready for the departure. Each of them coped as best they could. The emotional toll weighed heavily between them. For the most part, these feelings were kept in check through the final days of their long and often grueling wait.

Suze would not allow herself to break down in front of her children. She would maintain a degree of normalcy, while chaos ensued around them. There was no time for her to feel sorry for herself, or to feel bitterness toward her husband. "For better or for worse, in good times and bad, for richer or poorer, in sickness and in health...I do." These were the words that she had promised to keep.

*

"Mienus, wake up! Mienus, wake up!" Suze said to her husband in the middle of the night.

Mienus was dripping in sweat and very agitated. "Oh Suze, I'm so sorry to wake you again. I had another one of those dreams," he said through his tears. As they embraced, he began to doubt himself and his plans. The days of hard work, and the frequent emotional moments he hid from Suze, had taken him back to another time and another place.

As hard as he tried, Buchenwald was never far from his mind. When it was too much to bear, his emotions would rule the night within his dreams, or burst forth in misdirected anger toward his beautiful wife and his handful of daughters. There would be little sleep the rest of this night for either of them.

It had been eleven years since his liberation. It may seem like a long enough time, but in reality, it is more accurate to write that it had only been eleven years! Hard as he tried to suppress his emotional trauma, the pattern of terror, rage, and anger continued to manifest in Mienus. His wounds were still raw.

They made it a priority to have one last family photo taken just weeks before leaving Holland. Copies of the picture were made and given to the extended family, and to their closest friends. Suze wore a simple dress adorned with a pearl necklace, and Mienus wore a dark suit, white shirt, and a tie. The four oldest daughters were dressed in identical plaid skirts and white cap-sleeved shirts, while the youngest wore a little white dress and white socks. All five girls had the same short haircut including very short bangs. The happy looks on everyone's faces would make anyone smile. It was evident to those who knew our family that Suze and Mienus took pride in their beautiful children, and made sure they always looked their best.

Time was moving fast. There was a little more than a week left before the van Lith family boarded the ship. Much of the household belongings had been sold or given to a relative or friend in need. Many of the kitchen items were to be given away as well. The bed Mienus and Suze slept in would be the only one placed in the big crate and stowed with the other cargo.

Three large leather suitcases were packed with what the family needed for traveling. In addition, a large baby buggy to transport me, my clothes, and other baby essentials was allowed.

A few items too cherished to part with were stored in the large crate, including: a large wooden chest wardrobe, two matching night stands that went with the bed, Dutch curtains, a small wooden windmill, blue Delft pottery pieces, Suze's collection of decorative tea spoons, and a small handmade anvil Mienus made for himself in Buchenwald.

There was also a large hand-painted picture that a good friend of Mienus' had painted, of St. John the Baptist Church with a scenic canal and fishing boats. This was significantly important to Mienus and Suze. Over the years, it would give them great comfort seeing it prominently displayed in our home.

Great care was taken while packing important religious mementos. These items included: a beautiful glass figurine of the Virgin Mary that was given as a gift before we left, a black slate wall-hanging of the face of Jesus crowned with thorns, a large rosary, a large Catholic Dutch Bible illustrated by the famous artist Gustave Dore, Catholic missals for church, a set of translation books, and the family Baptism dress that was given to Suze by her mother just before we left. All of these special keepsakes were strategically placed between packed clothing, linens, sheets, etc., to protect them from any damage during the long voyage.

Mienus spent as much time as possible with family and friends. Suze had been saying goodbye to her family and friends in her mind and in her heart for some time already. It was how she best handled the sadness she was feeling as she dealt with the practical things getting ready for their departure.

Voices from the Past

Mienus procured a microphone and recorder to be on hand for the last few days before our departure. Family and friends who gathered around us were given the opportunity to record their sentiments. Later on, in our new homeland 5,000 miles away, we would be able to listen and remember the voices and well wishes of the loved ones we left behind.

Today, nearly 60 years later, it is not easy listening to the spontaneous words and unguarded emotions spoken by the many relatives I never really knew in person.

Ineke is the keeper of this tape. During a visit to her home in Oregon, I asked to listen to the recording again and then borrowed it to learn more about the events that happened just before our departure. I'd only listened to it two other times in my life that I could remember. The last time was roughly 30 years prior.

The tape was still in the reel-to-reel recorder as if we had just put it away yesterday. The quality was compromised by the aging of both the tape and the machine. I later took both to a sound studio and had the double-sided recording transferred onto a master CD, speeding it up slightly, allowing me to hear the voices with clarity. After listening to the entire recording, I sat down to a very difficult task, translating Dutch into English, and telling the story as it happened so long ago.

The recording begins at a quickly-arranged gathering of friends in the middle of the afternoon on March 29, 1956, at a place called Café Central. Our closest friends came to the café for a fun visit, and of course coffee, tea, and sweets.

A few days later, on Easter Sunday, April 1, 1956, Mienus had prearranged for a friend, a professional TV and radio personality, to help record voices at an open house planned for the afternoon and evening. Everyone would have an opportunity to say a few meaningful words on the recorder, as they said their goodbyes to the family.

This second and largest goodbye event took place just three days before departure. Mienus and Suze had announced an open house days earlier, and word spread quickly. Many family members started arriving early in the afternoon.

The place felt bigger without the usual furniture, but was still quite small for such an occasion. Chairs were brought in and set up against the walls around the room for the guests to sit. The kitchen was used for the food and drinks that were either brought by guests or provided by Mienus and Suze.

There was a steady stream of aunts, uncles, and cousins. The children would play outside or upstairs in the empty rooms. There was lots of laughter, tears, and well wishes for our family. Hard as it was for most, it was good to take a moment and say what needed to be said and heard.

Mienus was the master-of-ceremony, and the handler of the microphone and recorder. His professional soundman was there to help as needed. Mienus spoke with such love and respect toward his parents and siblings. He spoke with that same affection toward Suze's parents, calling them, "Father and Mother." He assured them of his and his wife's love, and promised to take good care of his family in America.

Mienus said to his parents and family:

> *Thank you for the time we shared together in the past. Sometimes we have had troubles, but that happens. Thank you so much for the words that you spoke to us today. In a couple of days we are leaving. Know in the first place, we thank you for the wonderful Blue Delft windmill/music box, and for the silver warming plate. I will make a special shelf in our living room to place the windmill, so that every time I look at it I will think of you, my family.*

We hope to return for a visit in the years to come, but we will not be saving our money for this right away. I have to save and use our money for my wife and my five little children in the near future.

And now brothers and sisters, live good with each other and try to understand one another. Sometimes that is hard, I know.

Father and Mother, live well with each other and don't worry about the things that may happen in the future. It will make things harder for you, and please don't do that to each other. And let us all just remember, that every household has its cross.

The meaning of "its cross," had more than one meaning. He knew that life would always have its challenges, and that pain and suffering is inevitable in this life. But the cross hanging in each of their homes was there to remind them to hold fast to their faith.

Mienus wanted them all to love each other, and hoped and prayed that the family would be together in the future, in a place where there would be no more pain, and no more suffering. Someday!

The microphone was given to Suze, and she added, "Thank you so much for the warm way you have treated me when we got together, and thank you so much for the wonderful windmill, and the warming plate."

She was never the orator like Mienus was. She kept things short, simple, and to the point. Her words were loving and sincere, just like her. She was doing her best to keep it all together throughout all the packing, the caring of her children, the planning, the festivities, and now all the goodbyes.

Family and friends continued to drop in throughout the day and evening. The same sharing, well-wishes, and goodbyes were recorded. One, in particular, stands out. Mienus' nephew, who was named after him, spoke words that produced some light-heartedness. Cousin Dom said, "Goodbye Uncle Mienus and Aunt Suze and small cousins. Have a good travel, and don't forget Uncle Mienus, the cowboy outfit I asked for!"

Someday Mienus would have to make good on the promise he made to his nephew, Dom. He didn't know how or when he would find a cowboy outfit and send it to his nephew, but he would never forget the request.

As it turned out, he made good on the wish 37 years later, at the family reunion in Salem, Oregon in 1993, when Dom and his daughter, Bianca, and his brother and sister-in-law, Bert and Els, came to visit us. Dom was presented with a small cowboy doll to fulfill his childhood request.

After most of the van Lith side of the family left, the Bruggeman family started arriving in numbers. Mienus said to Suze' parents, "Father and Mother, I want you to know that before I took this step, I thought long and hard about what we are about to do. I am doing all this for my wife and my children. I promise I will take good care of them."

Trying very hard to hold back her tears, Suze said this to her parents, "Father, Mother, thank you for your kind words. I just wish that I could have heard them under different circumstances, and not when we are going away. And Mia, I never thought it would be like this!" She was speaking to her sister, who had just become a widow two weeks earlier. Suze could no longer hold back her tears, nor could anyone else during this poignant exchange. The tape recording stopped.

Not long after, it was time for my sisters to say their goodbyes, quickly followed by some of my very first spoken words that were captured on the recorder.

Many friends came over to join in the evening festivities. Most of them had stories to tell about Mienus and Suze, and how much they would be missed. Everyone hoped the family would have a safe journey, and have good fortune in our "New Fatherland."

Hearing the term, "New Fatherland," undoubtedly induced an emotional response every time someone said those words. Mienus and Suze must have had ambivalent feelings. The meaning of those words was not hard to comprehend. Our heritage would always be Dutch, having been born in Holland, but we would become American citizens someday, and call the United States our new homeland. In years to come, we would refer to Holland as, "the Old Country!"

Finally, the open house ended late in the evening. We girls would need to go to bed and get some sleep. We would only have two more days to live in the land of our birth.

On the evening of the last day, Tuesday, April 3, 1956, dear neighbors, Jan and Miep, invited the family over for a meal and dessert. They enjoyed each other's company very much. The recorder was turned on to capture, and later remember, the friendly chat among friends. Jan and Miep would deeply miss us, having been such close neighbors for the last few years. The recording finally fades out to the sounds of laughter and fellowship.

Our parents were so grateful to have had the opportunity to say goodbye to so many wonderful people. Their recording was filled with the voices of their loved ones, and would later provide them with a measure of consolation during those times when they just needed to hear the treasured words of the ones they left.

The recorder and tape would be safely tucked away in the large wooden crate that would soon be stamped with the family name and its destination. In less than two days, it would be put in storage, along with thousands of other large crates, deep in the belly of the ship that would leave Rotterdam to sale west. This tape will continue to be cherished for generations to come.

On our last full day in Holland, Suze would likely have gone to Mass at St. John the Baptist Church one more time. The Mass was still said in Latin (the vernacular change would not be initiated for several more years). She knew that Mass would look, sound, and feel exactly the same in America. That was a consolation.

There were only had a handful of friends dropping by to say goodbye on this last full day. The instructions on the letter they received from the emigration office advised against too much activity on the day prior to departing. They were also instructed to tell relatives not to try and meet up with family at the ship's dock. It would be too difficult. They should be picked up early in the morning and taken immediately to check-in, and then proceed to the gangway to embark.

Before leaving our house for the last time, we girls would have one more bath, and in the morning, dress in the clothes laid out for us the night before. We would be expected to keep our clothes clean, having to wear them for the next couple of days, at least.

The last three remaining luggage pieces were already packed and ready to be closed. It had always been so clear to him over the last eleven years, just how determined he was to make this life changing move to America. Now, Mienus struggled with doubt. You can hear in his voice on the recording when he shared these words. "These last few days I have wondered to myself if I was doing the right thing."

Suze, on the other hand, was at peace. She would continue moving forward, and would not look back, at least for the moment.

Chapter 12

April 4, 1956

The night before departure, the family slept together on the floor of our living room. Fortunately for me, I got to sleep in the buggy at the neighbor's house. Dear Miep offered to take care of me, hoping that this would help Dad and Mom have a better night's sleep.

Mom endured Dad's restless night. Saying goodbye was more difficult then he thought it would be, and having watched the large crate leave the house earlier in the day filled with what was left of the family's belongings, made it even more difficult. Dawn could not come soon enough. Thankfully, the children managed to sleep through most of the turmoil.

When daylight came, everyone got up, cleaned up, dressed up, and ate up the last of the food. Once the three pieces of luggage were closed, the only thing left was to wait for the cars to arrive to take the family to the ship.

By midmorning the vehicles came to take us to the pier in Rotterdam. Dad's police friends volunteered to transport all seven of us, plus the buggy and the luggage. The drive from Vlaardingen would take roughly 20-30 minutes. Dad went in one car with three of the girls while Mom followed in another with the other two. The buggy and the luggage were divided between them.

Not much was said as they pulled away from their home in Vlaardingen. The children were very quiet during the ride. Ineke and Gerrie still didn't understand why they were leaving, or just how far they were being taken. The children simply did what they were told, without question, staying close to their parents.

As the cars got closer to the pier, the ships and other boats came into vision. Our ship, the *Groote Beer* (Big Bear), was the largest ship at the front of the large dock. There was a hierarchy of importance to these boats, leaving no doubt which ship commanded the highest priority. It was our ship, the *Groote Beer*!

Several smaller fishing boats, tug boats, and freighters were dispersed in the harbor away from the immigrant ship. Many of them would participate as part of a flotilla to escort the *Groote Beer* out of the harbor and partway through the River Mass. It helped create a festive atmosphere for family, friends, and other spectators watching the departure.

The waterways of Rotterdam, including part of the Old River Mass and the New River Mass, create the largest shipping channel and shipping ports in all of Europe. It has been a vital part of the Dutch economy for hundreds of years. We were about to navigate these waters out to the North Sea and across the Atlantic Ocean to New York City.

I'm still not sure how Dad pulled this next feat off. Apparently, he and some of those same police buddies of his managed to make arrangements with the port authorities to allow a group of family and friends to come onto the pier and be in close contact with us as we boarded the ship. As the family was escorted to the gangway, many of them reached out one last time to say goodbye with hugs and kisses.

Finally, we were told to move up the gangway. Apparently, we were holding up the traffic of other emigrants wanting to get on board, whose family and friends were not close by.

Gerrie wrote these words in the family genealogy book. She recounts her perception during this momentous occasion:

> It was April 4, 1956. Ineke was 8¾ years old, Gerrie was 7⅔, Suuske was 6½, Treesje was 4¾, and Marja was 15 months old.

We went on board a very big ship called the Groote Beer. With a name like that, how can we children not feel frightened?

When we got on board the ship there was considerable confusion. It was difficult to find our place on the ship. The staff directed us to the female quarters, and Dad was told to go to the male quarters. This action increased the anxiety that everyone was already feeling. How can they split up our parents like that?

It was dark and dreary down in the passenger holds. We didn't feel very safe, alone with our mother, with all those strangers in the one big room. How could Mom take care of four little girls, and one baby, alone? Mom's angst, coupled with our own fear, would prove to be too much.

Dad quickly took control, and addressed the problem with someone in authority. The situation quickly got resolved. God answered Mom's prayers very quickly, and mercy was given to the family. A stateroom was provided for all seven of us to stay together the entire voyage.

The luggage was carefully placed on the bunks in the stateroom. Soon after, we went out onto the deck to wave to those who were waiting at the dock. No one seemed to be in any hurry to leave. This was a moment to savor.

In 1956, the security screening on any mass transit travel was nothing like what we are accustomed to today. No one took x-rays of the crates or looked inside the luggage. Security was so relaxed that somehow my parents were able to have Mom's sister, Mia, and her two children, Leen and Els, come aboard and stay with us on the deck until it was time to sail. Even their friends, Puck and John, were allowed onboard. That could never happen with today's security measures.

It was extremely difficult for Mom to say goodbye to her sister. It was so soon after Mia's husband, Jacob, was killed working in the shipyards of Rotterdam. A terrible industrial accident left Mia alone with her two small children. And now her only sister, Suze, was leaving her too. This made the departure much harder than it already was for both of them. They stayed together as long as possible.

The ship horn finally blew. It was time for anyone who was not a paid passenger to disembark. The time had come.

In Gert's book, "The Continuing Family History of Dominicus van Lith and Suzanna Bruggeman-van Lith," she writes:

We were all on the outer deck when the loud horn sounded, indicating it was time to set sail. People were shouting and waving while hanging over the railing. They waved and waved continuously. Who would stop waving first?

Streamers were flying everywhere. I found one all coiled up in my hand that Mom had placed there. I really wanted to keep mine, but I was encouraged to throw it too.

I asked Gert if she still had that streamer as a memento. "No. I obeyed Mom and threw it over the railing like the other passengers did," she answered.

The *Groote Beer* blew one long blast of the foghorn, and the churning of the water on the port side of the ship began. The last of the large mooring ropes was thrown back into the water for the ship's crew to pull in and ready for the next port docking. The noise of the crowd on the docks intensified as they competed with the sounds of the slow-moving ship and the swirling water now encircling her.

"A better life is waiting for them at the end of this voyage," many people on the dock and shore would have thought, hoping for a good outcome for their loved ones.

The ship's log indicated that departure occurred on April 4, 1956 at 1640 (4:40pm).

While looking down at the water, admiring the many other boats in the flotilla, shouts could be heard from the tugboat moving us away from the dock. Gert writes:

> The little tugboat next to us had some of our family and friends on her deck. Mom would later explain that Dad's policemen buddies had connections with the harbor patrol, and some special favors must have been cashed in to pull this feat off for us.

On board that tugboat were Puck and husband John, Dad's sister Diek and husband Jakop, Dad's sister Annie and husband Jan, and one of their sons, Dommy.

Shortly after Dad's liberation from Buchenwald, Annie and Jan stuck with their plan of naming their newborn son, Dominicus Marinus, (Dommy) after my Dad. Not knowing whether her imprisoned brother would survive his ordeal, Annie planned to honor him by naming the child she was pregnant with after Mienus. Dad's nephew, Dommy was just shy of eleven years old in the tugboat picture.

Dad had a soft spot in his heart for all of Annie's boys, and had lots of fun with them in their early childhood years. The fact that his namesake was waving from the tugboat made it very special for Dad. Of all the pictures taken that day from onboard the ship and from family members on the dock, this photo was one of his favorites.

Now free from the dock, the *Groote Beer* slowly worked her way toward the west. The crowds on the dock and shore waved continuously to those on board the emigrant ship until she was no longer in sight.

After the ship sailed through a long bend in the river, Vlaardingen came into view on the starboard side. There, standing on the dock, just a short walk from their home, was Dad's father and mother waving white handkerchiefs above their heads.

Though he tried not to show too much emotion, Dad could no longer hold back his tears as he returned the wave until he could no longer see them. He must have wondered and prayed to himself, "Will I ever see my parents again? I hope that I have done the right thing for my family. Dear Lord, I hope that you will guide us and protect us." Sadly, seeing his parents standing together on the dock would be the last image he would ever have of them, and the last time my Oma and Opa would see their son and his family.

The homeland Dad knew for nearly 37 years would soon be out of sight. Living in Holland was behind him now, and his memories would be tucked away and stored alongside those tortured images and recollections he wished to forget, the ones that continued to give him those horrible dreams.

The family stayed on the deck to watch the boats of the flotilla peel off of the procession one after another. Soon the ship was unaccompanied, sailing by herself.

As the evening darkness set in around the ship, many of the passengers left the decks and made their way to the cafeteria for their first meal of their journey. Everyone was exhausted physically and emotionally, but hunger had to be satisfied.

Instinctively, the van Lith children stayed very close to their parents. They had no intention of exploring their new surroundings alone. For these young and confused girls, the whole experience felt overwhelming.

After eating a small meal, a quick walk about the ship was all any of them had energy for. It was cold and dark outside, and time to head to the cabin to settle in for the night, and for the next nine days on the Atlantic Ocean.

Everyone on the ship could feel the new sensations the moment the *Groote Beer* passed through the Hoek van Holland and into the North Sea. The slow and smooth pace of the last two hours gave way to wind buffeting the ship. It did not take long for the passengers to feel the vessel sway from starboard to port, and the occasional rolling momentum from bow to stern. The movements of the ship made it hard for their first meal to stay comfortably where it belonged.

Nighttime came early that first day. The rocking and rolling of the stateroom made it abundantly clear that the wheels of the baby buggy had to come off. The buggy was meant to stay in place near the center of the small stateroom, not roll from wall to wall.

The sleeping quarters consisted of a porthole, two small sinks with mirrors, three sets of bunk beds fastened securely to the wall of the room, a very small closet, and not much else. Seven people in a room about the size of a tiny parlor, but it was home to the family for now. Small though it was, at least we were all together.

The Groote Beer

Information about the *Groote Beer* can easily be found through Internet searches. While looking for her history, I ran across a short synopsis of the ship written by Reuben Goossens, maritime historian and Cruise'n'Ship reviewer, entitled, "The Three Dutch 'Victory' Ships."

> Three Victory Class ships, SS Cranston Victory, SS Costa Rica Victory and the SS La Grande Victory, were built for the "United War Shipping Administration" as troop and cargo ships...These three ships were built toward the end of World War II, and were part of the new larger improved version of the famed "Liberty" ships. Each ship had strengthened hulls for them to go into the war zone, but by the time they were completed, the war was coming to an end.

> In 1951, they were sent in turn to the Netherlands Dry-Dock Shipyards Company in Amsterdam to be rebuilt for general passenger use. An extra deck was added and the bridge was moved on top and placed forward. Their original accommodations were gutted and cabins were fitted to accommodate up to 830 passengers.

> The Costa Rica Victory, renamed Groote Beer, made three voyages to Australia before her reconstruction. Her reconstruction commenced in November 1951. Now at her new tonnage of 9,190 tons, she commenced services in 1952.

(Goossens)

Another website, "Hugo's Groote Beer Page," includes more specific information pertinent to my story.

> In 1952 she was owned by Holland America Lijn (HAL) and used as an emigrant ship. There were three Victory ships and were renamed Zuiderkruss (Sothern Cross), Groote Beer (Big Bear), and Waterman (Water Carrier). These names represent constellations in the night sky...

> Managed by the Holland America Line, she was refurbished from a troop ship to carry 850 passengers and commenced her first Rotterdam-Halifax-New York voyage on June 18, 1952. In August 1952, she made her first Rotterdam-Quebec sailing and in August 1965, made the last of 105 round voyages when she sailed from Rotterdam for New York...

> Both the Waterman and Groote Beer were sold to John Latsis, a family-owned Shipping Company. Waterman was renamed Margareta and Groote Beer became Marianna IV.

> Marianna IV (Groote Beer) was chartered in 1966 to the Atlantic Education Program for four roundtrip voyages between Rotterdam and New York. For this purpose, she was renamed Groote Beer once again. Holland America Line acted as agent. In 1969, she was renamed Marianna IV once more, but was laid up at Piraeus. Then in 1971, she became the last of the three Dutch Victory ships to be scrapped. She was broken up in Eleusis, Greece.

(Schouten)

Life on the Ship

I was just 15 months old when we left the Netherlands, and have no firsthand memories of that journey. My two oldest sisters, Ineke and Gert, can still recall much of what they experienced during the voyage and what the conditions were like.

My desire for even more information intensified while researching the *Groote Beer*. I was fortunate to find and contact another passenger from this same voyage our family was on. His name was Peter and he grew up in Detroit, Michigan. He was eleven years old when he and his family were passengers on the ship. He was able to provide additional details of what it was like traveling across the Atlantic. From the accumulated recollections of my siblings and Peter, I have a good understanding of the journey.

According to first-hand accounts, the departure day was cold. The wind added to the chill in the air, making it imperative to wear warm coats and hats. After the bon voyage and procession of the flotilla, passengers were not aware that the conditions would change intensely in just a couple of hours.

Upon entering the North Sea, the wind increased immensely. A squall on the ocean produced an abundance of rain. The slow, steady pace enjoyed in the River Mass now gave way to the buffeting of high waves generated by the windstorm in the open international waters.

The emotional sadness and anxiety after the departure was replaced with fear and sickness from the battering of the *Groote Beer*. It seemed none of the passenger were prepared for the conditions that lay ahead.

The effects of seasickness manifested quickly in many of the passengers. Several of them could be seen rushing to the open decks and toward the railings to heave the meal they had just eaten a couple hours before. Others, inside the hallways of their staterooms or quarters, could be seen hastening into the shared bathroom facilities. They had no time to get to the open decks to vomit. Still others could not hold their stomach contents long enough to get to either place. The hallways had many stained areas, and the odor was present throughout most of the passenger decks.

Very few staterooms had their own bathrooms. That was a luxury only reserved for high-paying passengers. Like us, the majority had only one or two sinks to wash up.

The storm lasted the better part of the first four days, and most passengers spent them entirely in the cabin. Only those well enough, and hungry enough, would make their way to the cafeteria for something to eat. It was forbidden to take food up to the staterooms, but that rule was ignored by more than a few, including Dad.

People stayed close to their rooms to avoid other illnesses. Sadly, with the conditions on board at the time, sickness spread quickly. There were no fancy hand sanitizers strategically placed throughout the ship to help prevent the spread of disease. Many were forced to stay in their cabin to sick it out when stricken.

The ship's medical facility was overwhelmed with the demand. Seasickness and viral or bacterial infections took their toll. It could take several days, but eventually most would get better on their own.

Several decks, but not all, were meant for the immigrant passengers. Common areas were clearly marked, as were the forbidden ones. Though the Holland America Line promoted the ship as having "No First Class" passengers, there were places that only the "higher paying" passengers could go to, and those were obviously off limits to the general population, so to speak. The top decks were reserved for them.

Archived pictures of the *Groote Beer* show an elegant dining room for those higher paying guests to enjoy. There were also social areas with tables and chairs, and a live band for entertainment. Mom and Dad never mentioned those areas. I'm not sure they were even aware of them.

The more fortunate passengers able to stomach the storms and avoid illnesses spent their days strolling about the ship, playing games, sharing in meals with other family members, and making acquaintances.

The healthy children could actually enjoy the adventure. They could be seen kicking balls, running about, playing games, or just gazing out over the sea. They would wait for whatever sea creature might make an appearance, or observe an occasional sea bird seem to come out of nowhere. Cloud watching by day and stargazing by night (on the clear nights), delighted the imaginations of both young and old.

When the storm finally gave way to a few days of intermittent sunshine, the outer walking decks quickly filled with passengers eager to take in the sunlight and fresh air, trying to grasp the endless miles of water around them.

Many of the passengers snapped photos with their cameras that would later be placed in memory books for future generations to appreciate. These images document the stories that are still told of their ancestors, the ships, and the landmarks experienced by those who endured this journey. There must be many photo albums like ours.

Every passenger had a destination and someone waiting for them at the end of the trip. Half were on their way to Canada. The rest were bound for the United States. Some would reunite with families already settled. Others, like us, were stepping out in faith, hoping and praying that their new "Fatherland" would welcome them and help them with the huge transitions still to come.

Gert reminisced in her book:

> *Deep within the ship I recall the sleeping areas for the female passengers and for the male passenger. They were not well lit. They were on the inside of the ship with no windows. I was so relieved not to have to stay there. Our stateroom had a porthole, but it was very small, leaving dark corners in the room. Not much light could filter through. It felt like a dungeon, and created an unhomely feeling in my memory.*

> *The eating area was not a dining room. It was a utility chow hall. Alternating stools and tables were well fastened to the floor (curious, I recalled). The smell of strange food could churn a little tummy in a hurry. This often was too much to take in and keep down. A quick run to the outdoor deck made our tummies calm down. But, if we wanted to eat, we had to get to the cafeteria.*

> *There were occasions when the sea rolled, and we understood why some of the chairs were fastened to the floor. It was a funny sight to see people slide away from their plates with fork in hand when the sea was a bit rough.*

> *We never ate as a family. Someone had to stay back with one or more of the children who were very seasick. When it was time to eat, we went back down to the lower deck. The swaying and the smells would again become too much. During the second half of the trip, only Dad and Treesje were able to walk hand in hand to the cafeteria.*

> *Treesje kept Dad company, and he took good care of her. Eventually Dad would sneak in food for those of us left in our berth. Little food went down, or I should say, stayed down. I'm sure we caused a lot of worry for the folks because we soon were only able to keep down only a little water.*

On sunny days, we were all taken to the deck to get some refreshing air. Somehow that did make us feel better, even if for just a while.

Mom and Dad had good reason to worry about their children. Treesje was the only one of the kids who did not get sick. After a few days into the voyage, dehydration became a real issue. I was seen by medical personnel on board for help with my illness. "I was so worried about you, Marja. I was praying for all of us, but you were the one that was the sickest, and I wasn't sure you would survive the trip!" Mom said to me. That was a sobering revelation.

April 11, 1956

It had been a long seven days for the van Liths, and for the others onboard the immigrant ship. In the early morning of April 11, 1956, the Canadian land was visible from the decks. Passengers left their cabins to watch as the *Groote Beer* passed through the mouth of the Halifax Harbor. The weather was overcast with scattered showers and a light breeze, typical for Halifax, Nova Scotia in the spring. By mid-morning, the temperature was in the low 40s, too cold to go outside without bundling up in coats and hats.

At 1045h, the *Groote Beer* came to a standstill at the large dock just across from George Island and its landmark lighthouse. This lighthouse stood out as if to welcome the vessel and passengers to Canada. There was minimal movement of the vessel as the ship's officers quieted her diesel engines and powered down her massive propellers.

The ship bustled with activity as the crew prepared the vessel for arrival, and the disembarkation of more than half of the passengers completing their voyage. Many of the remaining wayfarers took the opportunity to sit out on the deck furniture and watch the action unfold around them. Still others took this opportunity to move about the ship for some needed exercise.

Excitement was visible on so many faces. They were about to enter their new homeland. While happy to see the Canadian immigrants complete their voyage, the rest of us still had two days left until we could experience the same energy.

The large crowd watching and waiting from the docks were there to pick up family and friends who had just arrived. Even before the ship came to rest at the dock, there were shouts and waving from land as travelers were spotted by their loved ones and sponsors.

This was a much different occasion from the one we all experienced when leaving Rotterdam. The tears shed now were no longer for goodbyes. These feelings were of gratitude and relief that the ship made it across the rough Atlantic Ocean safely, and for the warm welcomes from those awaiting their arrival.

It was now 1700h. The bullhorn blew the unmistakable sound, "all clear and ready to set sail." None of us really knew whether new passengers came aboard in Halifax. What we did recognize was that familiar sound of the huge engines powering up again, and the crew reeling in the ropes that had kept us tied to the dock. We would be sailing back into the Atlantic to our last stop, New York City.

The family enjoyed the break from the previous dreary conditions of the ship. Though the smell in the hallways was still evident, it was nothing like it had been in the beginning, when so many people were sick. Efforts had been made to clean the ship up throughout the week.

The amount of fresh air and the nice break from the ship's movements, made it possible for each of us to keep down much of the small portions of food eaten during the day. Everyone that is, except for me. I still wasn't able to eat much, and keeping me well hydrated was a continuous challenge.

The *Groote Beer* traveled in relatively calm seas the rest of her voyage. She moved SSW, heading down the Canadian coastline. After a few hours, she would approach and soon travel along the eastern seaboard coastline of the United States.

The next morning, April 12, 1956, would dawn the last full day on the ship. I can only imagine the excitement my parents and siblings were experiencing when word got out that we were traveling parallel to the US coastline

None of my sisters had knowledge of what was in store for us after we reached our destination. Only our parents knew. Once we arrived, we would still have a long way to travel to get to our journey's end. Like many parents of their time, they only told their daughters what they needed to know, and nothing else.

April 13, 1956 – Lady Liberty

On the last full day at sea, arrival instructions were provided for the remaining passengers. Mom would follow the instructions without deviation. Dad on the other hand, didn't worry about details like instructions. He was just content knowing that the moment he had planned for in his mind was about to happen in just a few more hours thanks to the sacrifices they both had made. He would simply help his wife with the packing and be responsible for the heavy lifting of the suitcases. She would be in charge of the children, and be time manager for the following day.

In the very early morning hours of April 13, 1956, the *Groote Beer* made her final navigational turn westward. The sun rose at 0620h, and so did many of her passengers. Shortly thereafter, the ship was no longer in the Atlantic Ocean. She entered New York Bay and slowly sailed toward the Hudson River to her scheduled dock in Manhattan's Passenger Terminal. Everything seemed to be moving quickly now.

My family quickly dressed and went out on the deck to see the landmarks coming into view. The morning fog was lifting and the Statue of Liberty, although miles away, suddenly appeared in the distance. She's not always visible in April. Thankfully, she was there for us to see, holding her torch for the new immigrants and hopeful future citizens.

Many of today's American citizens sadly do not know much about the Statue of Liberty, other than the fact that it is a gigantic statue with a woman holding a lamp, and is a tourist must-see landmark in New York City. If you were an immigrant passing through these waters, seeing her for the first time likely produced abundant tears from simply gazing upon her. People came to America for a better life for themselves and their families, just like most immigrants still do today.

If you have never seen the Statue of Liberty before, here is just a little information I found during my research:

The Statue of Liberty Poem

Between 1820 and 1920, approximately 34 million persons immigrated to the United States, three-fourths of them staying permanently. For many of these newcomers, their first glimpse of America was the Statue of Liberty in New York harbor.

The statue, sculpted by Frederic Auguste Bartholdi, had been conceived of as a gift of friendship from the people of France, marking the two nations' commitment to liberty. France provided $400,000 for the 151 ft. 1 in. (46.15m) statue, and a fundraiser drive in the United States netted $270,000 for the 89-ft pedestal.

The Jewish American poet Emma Lazarus saw the statue as a beacon to the world. A poem she wrote to help raise money for the pedestal, and which is carved on that pedestal, captured

what the statue came to mean to the millions who migrated to the United States seeking freedom, and who have continued to come unto this day.

The New Colossus by Emma Lazarus

Not like the brazen giant of Greek fame,

With conquering limbs astride from land to land;

Here at our sea-washed, sunset gates shall stand

A mighty woman with a torch, whose flame

Is the imprisoned lightning, and her name Mother of Exiles.

From her beacon-hand

Glows world-wide welcome; her mild eyes command

The air-bridged harbor that twin cities frame.

"Keep, ancient lands, your storied pomp!" cries she

With silent lips.

Give me your tired, your poor,

Your huddled masses yearning to breathe free,

The wretched refuse of your teeming shore.

Send these, the homeless, tempest-tost to me,

I lift my lamp beside the golden door!

(FactMonster.com)

The legendary Ellis Island was also visible that morning, as the ship got closer to the Hudson River. Used until her doors closed on November 12, 1954, this island would have been the first stop for any immigrant coming to America from the Atlantic. They would have first stepped foot on this island before being transferred to the mainland. All the processing and physicals were done on Ellis Island.

Ellis Island, in Upper New York Bay, was the gateway for millions of immigrants to the United States as the nation's busiest immigrant inspection station from 1892 until 1954. The island was greatly expanded with land reclamation between 1892 and 1934. Before that, the much smaller original island was the site of Fort Gibson and later a naval magazine. The island was made part of the Statue of Liberty National Monument in 1965, and has hosted a museum of immigration since 1990. Long considered part of New York, a 1998 United States Supreme Court decision found that most of the island is in New Jersey. The south side of the island, home to the Ellis Island Immigrant Hospital, is closed to the general public and the object of restoration efforts spearheaded by Save Ellis Island.

(Wikipedia, Ellis Island)

The Statue of Liberty and Ellis Island were photographed and placed in our family photo albums. I still admire those old pictures. It is my hope and prayer that my children, grandchildren, and those yet to be born, will cherish them too. "Long shall you live!"

Having passed through the Upper New York Bay and her famous landmarks, the *Groote Beer* continued up the Hudson River. New Jersey was on her port side and Manhattan Island on her starboard side.

New York City appeared just like the pictures Dad and Mom had viewed in books before they left Holland. This was one of those iconic moments in life they would never forget. Fortunately for my three oldest sisters, they would also have some memories of those first images so classic to the United States of America.

At 0845h, the *Groote Beer* came to rest at the Passenger Ship Terminal. Once again, the ship's crew was busy readying the ship for disembarkation. Once again, crowds had formed on the shoreline to greet the ship and her passengers as she passed by. Still others had gathered at the docks to cheer and wave when they first saw their loved ones just arriving from their long, nine-day voyage. No one was there to greet us though. We still had a long way to go to see anyone our family recognized.

We children stayed close to our mother and father. With all the pushing and shoving and bags bumping into others, it was easy for the small girls to feel frightened as they slowly worked their way off the ship and onto dry land.

The terminal employee's instructions were delivered in English. Fortunately, Mom had a good understanding of the language, and Dad knew just enough to get by. The older children hadn't learned enough in school to be of any help. When it became necessary to speak English, much of it was left to Mom. The "Dutch to English" and the "English to Dutch" books were never far from our parents' hands, ready to use.

With the loud instructions in English, and the slow-moving lines, there must have been a moment when Dad displayed signs of anxiety. This experience must have reminded him of another time and place, when he was forced to stand in long lines while someone belted out orders in a language not his own. With the care and love of his wife, Dad was able to move forward.

Arriving at the front of the line, all the immigration paperwork was checked and new papers were issued. Anyone wishing to change their first name and/or family name did so at this time.

Some immigrants had last names that could be difficult for others to master in English. Many of them wanted to immerse themselves quickly into their new surroundings, and didn't want their given names to set them apart, so they choose more American-sounding names. Still others had names that could be simplified, making it easier to pronounce as they integrated themselves into the new culture. Our family name remained van Lith, with a lower case "v." Van means "from" in Dutch. Our ancestors were from the town of Lith. Dad and Mom had no intentions of changing any names, so the luggage was stamped, and the family entered another line for medical examinations.

There was really only one hiccup during the slow process entering this new country. It happened during the medical examinations. Dad was taken away from the rest of us, which made for a few tense moments.

There was concern on the part of the doctor because the records from Holland indicated that Dad was positive for Tuberculosis mycobacteria. This was a reason to deny him from entering. After a quick review of the required x-rays he brought with him from Holland, and the fact he only tested positive for the exposure, Dad was cleared for entry after no other findings were revealed outside of what was already documented prior.

I was treated for dehydration. Each of the children had lost weight during the voyage, except Treesje. She was lucky to have remained healthy the entire time.

Everyone was hungry and thirsty, now that they were no longer seasick. Simple foods and drinks were provided to each immigrant as they worked their way through the system. But my family still had a long way to go to regain our health. The first priority was to find something more substantial for each of us to eat.

Our parents were the only ones who knew how much farther we still had to travel. After getting some food, the next thing on the agenda was a taxi ride to Grand Central Terminal. It was this famous New York station where many immigrants headed after arriving in the United States. From there, train tickets could be purchased to final destinations traveling north, south, and west throughout the United States.

> *Grand Central Terminal (GCT) is a commuter (and former intercity) railroad terminal at 42nd Street and Park Avenue, in Midtown Manhattan, in New York City, United States. Built by and named for the New York Central Railroad in the heyday of American long-distance passenger rail travel, it is the largest such facility in the world by number of platforms with 44, serving 67 tracks along them. They are on two levels, both below ground, with 41 tracks on the upper level and 26 on the lower, though the total number of tracks along platforms and in rail yards exceeds 100. The terminal covers an area of 48 acres.*

(Wikipedia, Grand Central Terminal)

With a wave of his hand, a cruise terminal porter hailed a taxi for us to take us to the trains. Gert shared the memories of this part of our journey in her book:

> *With our sea legs still a bit wobbly, we stepped into a yellow cab which took us to the train station. My first impression of New York City was not a good one. I thought these buildings were so tall, dingy, dirty, and gray. It made me feel so enclosed that I wanted to rise above it and breathe deeply, like we did on the ship. Soon, however, we arrived at the train station.*

> *We were good little kids, and cooperated even more when we didn't feel well enough to run around. We were told to sit on, what appeared to us like large wooden church pews in the railroad station.*

> *I can remember the commotion when it was time to purchase the train tickets to get to Salt Lake City. At that time, Mom spoke better English than Dad. But one of the locks on a suitcase had just broken, and much of the contents spilled out onto the floor. The tension rose.*

> *"What do we do now?" I thought.*

> *It was Mom who stayed with us while Dad got the tickets. She somehow obtained a leather strap to secure the suitcase.*

> *We felt anxious. How long would we have to wait? We felt sick. Finding food and communicating our needs was difficult. We sensed potential danger lurking.*

> *Mom had us girls well dressed, with the two oldest dressed alike, and the next two dressed similarly. People stared at us as they passed by. As children, we did not know why. One curious lady even asked Mom if she could shake our hands. Mom gave permission. We must have looked awfully cute.*

> *Evening came, and the waiting was over. With tickets in hand we boarded the train with a sigh of relief. "ALL ABOARD!" was heard loud and clear.*

> *Two of the girls sat across from the other two sisters, and a suitcase was tucked under our legs. With a blanket thrown over us, we had a make-shift bed. The predictable rocking motion of the train eventually calmed us all to sleep.*

The train travel was a bit easier, having more scenery to look at. Eating on the train was still not easy. Night time came once again, the blankets came out, and the lights dimmed. It was quiet once more. By the next day, lack of food had taken its toll.

Restlessness set in. "When will we get there," was asked more than a few times by the children. After nine days on the ship, and the beginning of the third day traveling by train, everyone had enough.

Salt Lake City, Utah

On April 16, 1956, three days into the second leg of our journey, we arrived in Salt Lake City, Utah. We were met at the train station by family friends who had undertaken the same journey just a year or two before us.

After warm greetings, our host family took us to their home for much-needed rest and recuperation. It was also quite apparent to the adults that I was still very sick and in need of a doctor.

A doctor arrived at the house the day we arrived. He treated me for severe dehydration, and left instructions to see him again within a couple of days if I did not recover quickly. The other children were examined briefly by the doctor as well. Dad and Mom were assured that each of them would bounce back to normal health after a couple of days of sleep and food that they could keep down.

After a small meal, the four older girls were quickly bathed, dressed in clean pajamas, and sent downstairs to a room with one available twin bed. Within minutes, all four were sound asleep, each laying widthwise on the bed. Sleep was what they hungered for most. They hardly moved throughout the night, and would not be bothered for several hours. No one could wake the girls until they were ready to be aroused.

To the relief of the parents, the doctor's prognosis was correct. Within a couple days all of the girls were quickly gaining weight and strength, and eager to explore their new surroundings.

The original plan was to stay for a month, but it didn't take long before Mom felt pressure mounting by the host family. They were hoping to convince Dad to stay in Salt Lake City, and not move on to Salem, Oregon.

There was a large Dutch community who had already settled in Utah, and Dad was greeted by others he already knew. These ex-patriots were comfortable hearing and speaking Dutch and eating familiar foods. Dad was tempted to stay, but Mom was adamant about moving on with their travels. Though the mountains surrounding Salt Lake City were beautiful, the landscape was nothing like Mom was familiar with or comfortable with.

She said to me, "It felt like we were living in a fishbowl, especially with the large lake there. It was too much of a change for me. I was not comfortable at all when we were in Salt Lake City. It just didn't feel right at all!"

Mom took her husband aside for a private conversation. "Mienus, we are not staying here any longer. I can see how being here has affected you, and it's not good between us. We had a plan to move to Salem, Oregon, and I think it is time to contact Joe DW and let him know we are planning to come sooner," she said.

"What do you mean? We have friends here already. They can help me get a job, and the kids seemed to be enjoying it here too!" Dad answered.

"That's part of the problem! Why did we leave Holland only to end up in a place that has lots of Dutch people with the same mindset as if they were still living in Holland? We hear the same language, eat the same food, tell the same stories, sing the same songs, and on and on. You wanted to come here for a better life for us and our children. This is not what we wanted, or we might as well go back to Holland!" Mom reminded him.

After listening to what his wife had to say, Dad had to admit, "I understand what you are saying. I even heard that some of our friends have joined another religion. They were so warmly welcomed by their sponsors, they thought it would help them by joining their church. I don't want to feel any pressure to do that. You are right. Let's follow through with our plans."

Another hurdle was crossed when Dad chose to follow Mom's lead and continue on with their original plan. It may have begun with Dad's dream, but was completed with Mother's final push. What an epiphany.

It was hard for their friends in Salt Lake City to understand why Dad and Mom felt they needed to leave so suddenly, and not stay the full four weeks as planned. They were so sure that they would have decided to stay in Salt Lake City instead.

Mom and Dad had another plan, and it did not include living in a "little Holland" in America. Neither of them shared with their friends their real reason for wanting to leave so abruptly. They did not want to hurt anyone's feelings by sharing too much of an explanation. It could easily have caused misunderstandings, and be taken personally. As it turned out, their friendship remained intact for many more years with correspondence and visits between them.

Finally, late in April, the final leg of their journey would commence, including another train ride, from Salt Lake City, to Salem, Oregon. In two days they would meet their sponsors and beginning living in the new surroundings they would soon call home.

Salem

We arrived in Salem early in May. Mr. Joe DW and his wife May (both names have been changed) were there at the train station to meet us and take us to their home. Joe was friendly and matter-of-fact. May was very sweet and caring.

Our sponsors were much older than our parents. They had children that were grown and on their own, and had recently become grandparents. Our family stayed in the empty basement of their home for a short time, but Dad and Mom were eager to move into a house of their own.

A small house in an older part of Salem, on Winter Street, became our temporary residence for a couple of months until a more permanent solution was found. There was just enough time to unpack the 6x6x6 ft. crate of belongings that had arrived at the train station on May 7, 1956. Mother kept the original freight receipt from Salem Navigation Company with the treasures I found in the black bag. The amount on the receipt was $5.15, including tax.

One of the first things Dad did after the crate had arrived was to make furniture out of the wood that the crate was made out of. Those finished pieces were used inside the house for the first few years, until they were able to purchase nicer furniture. I was eight or nine years old before I realized that the two outside patio chairs and the coffee table between them, were made from the wooden storage crate.

Within days of our arrival, we went to our new church, St. Joseph Catholic Church, for Sunday Mass. Fortunately it was in walking distance from our rental home, and had a very nice Catholic grade school and high school on the campus.

The following day, after registering the family at the church, Mom went over to the school and enrolled Ineke and Gerrie for the remainder of their second and third grade classes. Both parents wanted the girls to integrate quickly with their new surroundings before the next school year began after the summer break. There was never a question in their minds of sending the girls to public schools. Neither thought much about what it might cost for private education, as it was a non-issue in Holland. Most private education was subsidized by the government, making it more affordable.

While registering for the last month of school, the principle's front desk assistant calculated the cost. Mom had no idea that they would be asked to pay for tuition. When she found out how much they were being charged, she was stunned.

"We just arrived from the Netherlands, and we only have $75 left. My husband doesn't have a job yet, and my children have been attending Catholic School for the last few years already. Is there anything you can do to help us?" Mom said.

The assistant excused herself to invite the principle into the conversation. After she explained the van Lith's circumstances, the principal came to greet Mom and said she was sorry that she was could not help them. Mother felt helpless.

She left that day with great sadness and worry. "How can they not see our needs right now, and help us. Could they not understand how important it is to have our children educated in the Catholic school?" Mom asked Dad.

The next day, mother did what she often did when she lived in Vlaardingen. She went to the 8 o'clock morning Mass, while Dad stayed with the girls. The familiar Latin Mass helped her to feel at home. She could follow along without any confusion with the help of her prayer book and the amount of English she had already learned.

She stayed in church for several more minutes after the service ended. There was lots to pray about. So far, this journey was not working out as she had hoped. She knew it would be difficult, but there were some things she never envisioned having to sacrifice.

"Why would you send us to this country only to be denied access to a good Catholic education for our children? You led me to believe that this move would be good for our children's salvation. I am afraid for what will happen next, and wonder what we are supposed to do now." Mother prayed through her tears.

Father Vanderbeck (a good Dutch name), the pastor of the parish, recognized Mom from their introduction after Sunday Mass just a couple of days before. He had extended the invitation to come back the following day to register the family at the parish office as new members. They both assumed that would include registering the girls for school as well. He walked over to her and their encounter went much like this.

"Suze, isn't it?" Father Vanderbeck asked.

"Oh, yes Father."

"I could not help but hear you crying just now. Is there something I can help you with?" Father asked her.

She composed herself while searching for the right words to say. "Thank you Father, but I don't know exactly how to say in English what I am feeling right now. It has been a difficult time for me and my family. Everything is so different from where we came. Back in Holland, I knew what life would be like. Now I am not so sure we made the right decision in coming here."

Father listened carefully to what Mom shared privately. It's not often a parish community is given the opportunity to help a new immigrant family. He admired the sacrifices made by people like Dad and Mom, who chose to make such a change in their lives, praying for a better future for their family.

"Give it time! You trusted in God to get you through this big change. Now offer him a little more time to let Him show you why and how He works, and how much He loves you and your family. You already mean something to us as well. I saw how the parishioners looked at you and your beautiful and well behaved children at Mass on Sunday. Just being with us in church, you and your family help to remind us how important it is to welcome others, to be hospitable, and to help you settle in to your new life with us. Give it time," he encouraged her. "Has your husband found work yet, or is it too soon?"

"Our sponsor has talked to a few people about us and the kind of work my husband is very good at, but nothing else has happened yet," Mom said with disappointment.

Sensing that Mom was still struggling, Father Vanderbeck questioned her again. "Is there anything else you were praying about that I might be able to help you with?"

Mom became quiet, and was overcome with tears. Taking a deep breath to compose herself she replied, "Thank you again, Father. I was just praying for a way to send our two oldest children to St Joseph's School for the last month before the summer break. With Dad not having a job yet, and with only $75 left, we will need that money for food and our rent. I prayed that my husband, Mienus, finds work soon, and that he will make enough to be able to send our children to St. Joseph's next year."

The priest was taken aback by what Mom had just shared. It became clear to him that she must have gone to the school to register the girls for the remainder of the year and for classes when they resumed again in the fall. With resolve, Father asked her to accompany him to the school to have a chat with the principal.

"How nice to see you Father, and you too Mrs. van Lith," Sister Maria (not her real name) said to them in her office. "What can I do for you?"

Father Vanderbeck said to the principal, "The van Liths would like to have their two oldest daughters finish out the school year and then have three of their daughters enrolled in classes for next year. I would like you to make sure that they get signed up for hot lunches for the rest of this year, and for the entire upcoming school year as well. And hopefully, Mr. van Lith will be in a position the following year to begin to contribute financially toward their daughters' education. Until then, please offer them our school, and assist them when possible to ease the burden this huge transition has had on the whole family."

Sister Maria responded, "Of course, Father. I will have the registrar take care to have the children signed up for classes and hot lunches right away. Is there anything else?"

"I just thought of something else," the priest stated. "Do the girls speak any English yet?"

"They don't speak much. Ineke is only in third grade, and Gerrie in second. I'm hoping they will begin to speak the language quickly though," Mom added.

Sister Maria was quick to say, "I think it would be good for the children, and good for the other sisters who teach here at the school, to provide English lessons during the summer months for the girls. What do you think Mrs. van Lith?"

Overcome with relief, Mother looked at Father Vanderbeck and Sister Maria and said, "Sometimes God takes His time answering my prayers, and not always how I think He should. But this time, He worked very fast, and gave me more than I had asked for! Thank you very much." Even through her tears of gratitude, Mom was able to express herself well enough for Father and Sister to understand her perfectly.

While Mother and the priest walked to the corner of the school campus, he asked her to have her husband come to see him the next day. She agreed and walked the few blocks back to the rental house with a weight off her shoulders and a lightness in her steps.

This experience left a positive lasting impression on Mom when she desperately needed it. This made it much easier for her to make St. Joseph's Church her new favorite spiritual place to go to find serenity. She finally felt welcomed, and hopeful.

It was well passed 10:00am before Mom walked through the front door of the rental house. "You were gone a long time. What happened to you?" Dad asked her.

"I just had a long conversation with Father Vanderbeck. He came up to me after Mass. He saw that I was crying a little and asked me what was wrong," Mom answered.

After telling her husband all that had just transpired between the priest, the principal, and herself, they hugged each other. They had been given a wonderful gift by the parish priest. A huge burden was lifted off both of them. Today was a good day.

In her haste to share the good news, she almost forgot. "Father Vanderbeck asked me to tell you to go and see him tomorrow. He didn't say what time or what for, though."

"I wonder why he said that. I'll go see him after we get the girls off to school. Let's plan to go to 8:00 Mass first though. I think that would be a good idea after what happened with you today." Then he added, "Let's go and tell Ineke and Gerrie that they will be going to their new school tomorrow."

The two oldest siblings were escorted to their new classrooms. Both were given warm welcomes by the nuns who would be their instructors. After each was introduced to the rest of their class, they were assigned a desk.

Our parents instinctively knew it would be hard on both girls to be separated from their family so soon, but it was so important to have them get adjusted as quickly as possible. What they didn't realize at the time was how much the two sisters relied on each other to get them through such a big change in their lives. Now, they were separated by grade and in separate classrooms full of children they did not know and could not understand.

Gert writes:

Language was a problem for a while. Ineke and I were in the second and third grade at St. Joseph's School for only the last four to five weeks until the end of the school year. Summer vacation was in sight.

We did not know what was expected of us or what was being said to us, or about us. We just sat unsure and frightened, and for the first time, alone. We were treated like all the other kids in the class.

We played outside on the playground, like all kids do. During those times I always hoped to get a view of my sister on the playground during recess. Ineke knew what I felt like and I knew what she was going through. If we got lucky, we would run to each other, hold hands and then share a few moments of tears together. I always drew my strength from her. If she wasn't crying, then I could be strong too. But often I can remember not wanting to be torn away from her, and crying outside my classroom, not wanting to go back inside. God was merciful, and I recall being blessed all by myself in the hallway, with time to finish crying without anyone having to see me.

Separation anxiety lasted a while for us. Mom recalled walking us to school. Ineke and I cried because we did not want to be left at school, and our sister Suuske cried because she wanted to go to school. Then there were Mom's tears. Even though she knew it was best to take and leave her children at school, it was very hard on her too."

Mom recalled the times that we cried on her shoulders. We would ask her, "Why did we have to leave Holland anyway?" Secretly, and never uttered by our mother, our sentiments were her sentiments."

Toward the end of those first few weeks in school, it got a little bit easier. Still, it was a traumatic and sad ending of the school year in early June of 1956.

After our school was out for the summer, we received a few extra lessons in the proper pronunciation of words, and some extra help in reading from the willing teachers.

Mom missed Holland and all her family and friends very much. For the sake of her husband and her children, she withheld these feelings. She did not want anyone to know her inward struggles and worries. It was decades before Mother shared with any of her children just how difficult it was for her during the first several years in America.

Work in the New Fatherland

After taking their daughters to their respective classrooms, Dad told Mom to walk home with the three youngest girls without him. "I'll go see Father Vanderbeck and find out what he wanted to talk to me about," he said.

Conversing in English was getting a little easier for Dad, and he was ok with making mistakes. He was good humored about it, and would even take correction from his children when they became more fluent.

The conversation between Dad and Father Vanderbeck went something like this:

"Good morning, Father. My wife and I want to thank you for what you have done for us. My wife told me about it yesterday."

"You are very welcome, Mienus. Your wife mentioned that you were still looking for work. She told me that a few people are trying to help you find a job. While you are waiting, I wanted to see if you could help out with some work for the parish. We are a large parish with many members, and we have funerals almost every week. I am in need of a laborer to dig the graves for the deceased. You would be paid $25.00 for each grave. I know there are other funeral businesses that could use your help too. Is this something you would be interested in doing while you are waiting for a job?"

Dad readily agreed. "I am willing to do whatever I can to provide for my family. I am not afraid to work hard. I can do it again. When can I get started?"

"Come and see me tomorrow morning. I am preparing for a couple of funerals right now, and I will talk to the owners of the funeral businesses and let them know I have someone to dig graves if they need help. I'm sure you will be working several times per week. Do you have a phone number at home for us to call you when we need you?" Father Vanderbeck asked.

They didn't, but Dad explained that he or his wife would be walking the girls to school and could check in after Mass each day until they could afford to get a phone. They both knew it might take a while.

After their visit, Dad left the priest and walked home to tell Mom the news. He could be working as soon as tomorrow.

Mom was happy to hear about the offer, even though she knew that this wasn't what her husband really wanted to do because of the physical labor involved. However, this was an opportunity to provide the needed money to buy food and pay the next month's rent. Nothing would stand in his way from taking care of his family, not even hard labor or pride.

Dad worked as often as he could digging graves. On the days he was home, he spent time preparing to move the family to a more permanent rental house.

What were Dad thoughts, and how did he feel, digging graves? I can only imagine the flashbacks of death and dying from what he had witnessed every day for so many years in Buchenwald. This line of work must surely have triggered some moments of anxiety and memory nightmares. These flashbacks dwindled over time. But throughout his life, Dad suffered from, what is commonly referred to as, post-traumatic stress disorder (PTSD). "Never forget," was impossible for him.

Church members rallied around their new immigrant family. Wanting to reach out in kindness, new friends would pay a visit to the family and ask how they could help. Some families dropped off food items while others gave beds, drawers, a used sofa, tables and chairs, and other items.

Used clothes were also given, but mother had her own ideas about what the girls would wear. She thanked them for their kindness and then passed most of the clothing to families with even greater needs. Dad and Mom showed gratitude for everything that was being provided. She would not let anyone know just how incredibly difficult it was for her to accept their current situation, having to rely on others to help them.

Mom was not used to having things given to her. To be very clear, she was grateful, but she and Dad had worked very hard for many years in Holland, acquiring a lovely home and nice belongs that satisfied them both. When she looked at the old and worn furniture, the second-hand clothing, and other items that were given them in Salem, she would become melancholy. There was no denying she was homesick for Holland and all that they had sold or given away.

"Look at these things, Mienus. Is this what we came here for? We had it so good in Holland, and now we have old furniture to sit on, in an old and dusty house, with other people's old and used things that they no longer needed," she said through her tears. Mom was sad and angry at the same time.

We came to America with very little, and it was overwhelming and humbling.

Now, unquestionably apparent, Mother felt poor, because we were poor, she felt ashamed, because we had needs.

There was goodness in the people who wanted to help our family with their support and hospitality. But sadly, their generosity served to remind Mom of the truth of her new circumstances. It was she who would have offered to help others, and now with her role in reverse, she struggled.

It was summer. School had ended and a more permanent rental house was ready for the family. This house was also on Winter Street, but a few blocks closer to the church, school, and shopping. The new neighbors had many children similar in age to the girls, and were a huge blessing to our family.

Within weeks of arriving in Salem, the girls were speaking English with their new friends. There were no agencies providing Dutch translators to help the family. That was not a privilege provided new immigrants, like it is today. It was total and complete immersion into the new language and culture. We were melting into the American dream of our father.

It was impressed upon us to speak English everywhere outside of our home. Dutch was liberally spoken at home and continued for many years. It made me feel different, in a good way, from other families around us, and it offered me a connection to my heritage I otherwise may never have had.

My four older sisters continued to grow more comfortable with our new surroundings. The tears that were shed at school before the summer break, gave way to laughter, smiles, and fun. By the time September rolled around, the three oldest girls were ready for their new school year.

Sometime later in the year, Dad was offered a full-time job with the City of Salem. This new job enabled him to utilize his machinist's skills. He loved to work with his hands and with machines, manufacturing equipment. This was always his favorite type of work.

In addition to working in the city shops as a fabricator, he worked in the transportation department doing roadwork when work was slow in the shops. The prior months of digging graves strengthened him physically, and provided him with the stamina necessary for his new job.

From the outside, things appeared to be falling into place for the van Liths, and life was getting better. Dad and Mom, on the other hand, were concealing their true feelings concerning their new surroundings. Neither of them felt they could tell the other what was weighing heavily on their minds.

None of us girls at that time were conscious of the fact that our mother was miserable, and our father was worried about how to support his family, and whether or not he had made the right choice to leave Holland. Those revelations came out later in life. As far as the children were concerned, as long as Mom and Dad were around, we felt safe and taken care of.

Early Years in America

Letters to Holland took roughly ten to fourteen days by regular mail. Telegrams would take 24-48 hours to arrive. On very special occasions like Christmas, Easter, birthdays, special anniversaries, etc., Mom and Dad would either receive or initiate a long-distance telephone call. These calls were limited to three to five minutes, tops. It was just too expensive to make and the reception was very poor.

The family would gather around the only phone we had during one of these calls. Each of us was given a chance to say hello to whoever was at the other end of the phone. It took practice communicating between the two parties. You needed to allow a long enough pause during the conversation to let the message get to the other side of the Atlantic Ocean. If you didn't wait long enough, you could end up talking at the same time, and it was always easy to tell when that happened. The conversation from our end would sound something like, "No you go ahead! No, I'll be quiet! Its ok, you go first! Are you still there?"

*

None of the family or friends from Holland were able to visit us for the first few years, except for one. We did enjoy a visit from Mom and Dad's dearest friend, Puck Brouwer.

True to her words, Puck made the trip to see us within the first year of emigrating. The original plan was for her to visit us after competing at the 1956 Summer Olympics. As mentioned earlier, the Netherlands boycotted these Olympic Games, and brought all their athletes home. This action delayed her initial first visit.

This was to have been Puck's last Olympic Games. After her devastating disappointment, she left sports competition for good. Her way of moving forward was to keep her promise to visit our family. She arrived a few months later, in January 1957. This was her time to heal.

She was one of those individuals who lived life to the fullest, just like Dad. Both of them were charismatic, able to draw people into the moment with them.

My sisters and I enjoyed her company. Puck was so much fun to be around. She took the time to play and interact with each of us.

Having Puck in our home made us feel like we hadn't been forgotten. She came with greetings from family and friends, and a large package full of presents.

The box was filled with treats that were special to our family. Each of the items were plucked out of the box one at a time to prolong the moments of anticipation. Dad was given a box of his favorite cigars, and Mom was pleased with more of her favorite fragrances, 'Tosca, Eau De Cologne,' and deodorants. The children took delight in the candy and other food items not available in the Salem stores.

It would be years before Mom discovered the Dutch store less than 50 miles from where we lived and become a regular customer. Until then, we could count on an annual gift box of goodies at Christmas time.

The family explored a few places in Oregon with Puck. Oregon was still new to all of us, and this was a good opportunity to venture out to see the sights.

One of our first trips was to Mount Hood, where we enjoyed lots of snow time, sightseeing, and absorbed the beauty around Oregon's tallest mountain.

There was another excursion to Multnomah Falls, located roughly 30 miles east of Portland, following the Columbia River toward the Gorge. This impressive natural waterfall attracts hundreds of thousands of visitors from around the world each year. Sightseers typically hike up to the center bridge that spans the bottom of the first major drop of the waterfall. It is there, standing on the bridge, where you can get up close and witness the falls' beauty and feel the mist on your face.

Puck enjoyed the day we visited the Oregon State Capitol building and its beautiful campus in Salem. Atop the dome of the capitol building stands a very large, 8½ ton, bronze statue covered entirely in a shiny gold leaf finish. It proudly stands 22 feet in height atop a large marble pedestal and can be seen from several miles away in all directions.

The figure is of a pioneer man facing toward the West, holding a cape over his left shoulder and an axe in his right hand. He symbolically represents the pioneers who emigrated from the eastern states to settle the western territories, with their own expectations of a better life.

Walking up the stairs toward the main entrance, we stopped to admire the two impressive walls that flanked the front stairs of the Capitol. Sculpted into one of the large marble slabs is a scene depicting explorers Lewis and Clark, guided by Sacajawea. The back side shows a map of Lewis and Clark's western expedition during the early 1800's. The other sculpture shows a pioneer family with a covered wagon. The Oregon Trail is outlined on the back.

Puck wanted to fulfill a promise she made to Joe D.W. and May on the farewell tape that was made before the family emigrated. She wanted to meet May, and thank them both in person for all they had done to assist Dad, Mom, and we children.

Joe and May came to visit at our home. As soon as their car drove up, the girls rushed out to greet them, with Puck not far behind. May crouched down low with her arms wide open, waiting for the anticipated hugs the children typically greeted her with.

*

Puck's presence created a positive spirit in Dad and Mom. It was fun spending hours watching the three grownups talk about shared memories of family and friends. It was important for us to listen to these stories. The photos taken during this time captured the joy in all of us.

Before returning to Holland, Puck announced her plans to come back within a couple of years. This time, she would be coming with her husband, John, and mutual friends, Hennie and Gil. With the promise of another visit, Dad and Mom were happy to have an occasion like this to look forward to.

With cards and letters routinely arriving, and with their first visitor from Holland having come and gone, the family felt a little closer to what was going on back in Vlaardingen. Sometimes the correspondences lifted the spirits of my parents, and sometimes it would make Mom melancholy. She did her best to hide her sadness from the rest of the family, but when my sisters were in school, and I was alone with Mom, every once in a while, I could hear her cry softly, thinking I didn't notice.

Chapter 13

Freedom

The English Standard Dictionary defines "freedom" as: "the condition of being free; the power to act or speak or think without externally imposed restraints; the state of being free, of not being imprisoned or enslaved" (TheFreeDictionary.com).

I had always presumed that Dad must have felt true freedom by this point in his life. I came to understand, after examining the multiple layers of my parents' lives, that Dad had yet to enjoy the freedom he desired. He didn't experience real freedom after his liberation from Buchenwald, or after returning home to his parents in Holland. Nor did he feel free walking off the *Groote Beer* while taking his first steps on American soil. Sadly, he would be denied his freedom not long after arriving in Salem, Oregon, and would be challenged to fight for his freedom yet again.

Not an Honorable Person

I have memories of the very early years in America. They begin near the end of 1957, just before my third birthday. Some of my memories are cloudy, while others more vivid. I remember sitting in a highchair watching Dad carve the first turkey that Mother had ever prepared, and singing Dutch Christmas carols with my sisters on stage in the gym at St. Joseph's during the St. Nicolas festival (we did that a couple of years in a row). Then in 1958, I clearly remember making a Fourth of July costume and getting a blue ribbon for my Hawaiian outfit. Some of my most vivid recollections are of playing with my best childhood friend, Vija (pronounced **Vee**-ya), whose family emigrated from Latvia. They lived just a few houses down from our first rental. Our mothers had us play together when we were just toddlers. She is my longest friend, spanning over 60 years.

My memories of Joe D. W, our sponsor, were not pleasant ones. He was older than my parents, had a stern look on his face, wore suits and hats, and smelled like smoke. I stayed close to my parents or my sisters in his presence. On the other hand, his wife, May, was a sweet, soft-spoken, grandmotherly type, someone whose hugs and lap were welcoming.

Joe and May came over to visit us quite often during the first couple of years. They would take us to see things that Salem had to offer, and would introduce our family to some of Joe's acquaintances.

Joe showed a lot of interest in my sisters and me, and after a while Mom felt slightly uneasy. He would stress the importance of having the children take voice lessons and learn to play piano and other instruments. He would promote the family to others and schedule outings where he would insist that we sing for his guests. There was talk about dancing and entertainment that made Mom very uncomfortable. Dad said very little about the activities and the arrangements Joe had made for us children.

Somehow, pictures taken of us would end up in the newspaper during the first couple of years. There would be a small write up about the "Dutch girls" and their parents, referring to us as new immigrants.

Our parents never wanted our family to be in the spotlight. That was not part of their plan in the new Fatherland. Their desire was to blend into the new culture and be part of the American "melting-pot," and not stand out as different or special in any way.

Mom and Dad did not see us as special in any way. Millions of immigrants came to America like we did. Most intended to continue living with the best of their previous culture and to share the gifts they had to offer, all the while adapting and blending into their new surroundings. This is the definition of the "melting pot." Immigrants left behind the things that made them want to leave their native countries in the first place, for the pursuit of the greater opportunities and better life that America had to offer.

*

Dad's nightmares were growing more frequent again, and the fuse to his anger was much shorter. Mother knew something was troubling him. He looked downright fearful at times. When she asked what was wrong, he would deny that anything was.

Most people looked forward to the weekends. Not Dad. He approached it with more anger and frustration. Though they tried to hide it from the children, there was more tension between them. Mother couldn't figure out why, but she knew something was the matter, and noticed some odd behaviors that didn't always make sense.

Almost every Saturday morning, Dad would get on his bike and be gone from home for a couple of hours. When asked where he went, he would say he was just out for a ride. Other times he would come home with something he purchased at a store to make it look like he had an agenda for that morning. She began keeping track of this predictable routine of his.

Mother tried to explain away their quarrels to her girls. She would simply say that it was more than likely the consequence of the nightmares Dad suffered from, reliving some of the years he spent in the concentration camp. My older sisters may have had some understanding of what that meant, but I was too young to comprehend any significance. I just followed my sisters' lead as they stayed out of the way of our father when his anger got the better of him.

Wanting desperately to clear the air between them, Mom finally got the nerve to approach her husband with some of her concerns, hoping that Dad would open up to her as well. As this part of their story was shared with me, the amalgam of their conversation went something like this:

"Mienus, I am getting more and more uncomfortable with Joe D.W. and the way he is interfering with our family. The girls don't know any better, and are not complaining about being asked to sing for others, but I don't like it much. You should talk to Joe and tell him not to interfere with our children so much."

"I don't know what you are worried about. I'm sure Joe knows what he is doing. There's no harm in letting the girls sing, and the people like it, too."

"That's not the point. These are our children, not his! There's something wrong when I don't have the final say about our girls when Joe is involved. He doesn't take 'no' for an answer when he wants them to do something. That is not right. I want you to talk to Joe, and I will talk to May about it. Just explain to him that if our children sing in public, that is our choice to make, not his."

"NO! I will talk to Joe. Don't say anything to May. I don't want to make a big deal about this. Just let me talk to him, and I'll tell him to listen to you. Don't worry, I'll take care of this," Dad retorted.

For a short time the atmosphere in the home settled down. Mom assumed Dad must have followed up with the conversation with Joe, but Joe continued to be more involved with the family than she liked. But knowing her Mienus would "take care of this," made her feel better. For now.

*

Within our second year living in Salem, Dad and Mom moved the family into a nicer home for us. This was the third move in less than two years. This house was on 16th Street, just blocks from North Salem High School and a big city pool. It would become our permanent residence. I grew up in this house, and almost all my childhood memories were created there. Coincidentally, my childhood friend Vija and her family moved to 16th Street that year too, just one block away.

We rented this house from a very kind older woman whose name was Mrs. L. Miller. She lived on the other side of the block. I'm pretty sure that Joe and May knew Mrs. Miller, and were aware that her rental house was available.

Mrs. Miller showed great affection for our family. Though she had retired as a piano teacher, she agreed to provide piano lessons for each of the girls. I may be speculating here, but I'm pretty sure Joe had something to do with that.

Months had gone by without major arguments between Dad and Mom. He worked hard not to let his emotions get the better of him. But he could not control the restless, sweaty nights, when peaceful slumber never came. He could not control any of this, nor hide it from his wife. "Mienus, wake up, wake up! I'm here, wake up!" Mom whispered while shaking him awake. Many times the look on his face frightened her, but not enough to prevent her from reaching out to cradle her terrified husband.

After he had been calmed down, he would give in to the night's darkness and collapse from fatigue. Morning could not be postponed, and would arrive too soon.

The Saturday morning biking routine turned into a monthly event after a while. It was much easier for Dad not to draw attention to himself, and cause Mom to get suspicions again, so he thought. Rain or shine, it just looked like a bike ride. So he thought.

We had our first rotary phone installed in the house by now, and on a particular Saturday each month, Dad would leave on his bike soon after having received a call. He was unaware that Mom was attentive to the timing and the regularity of these phone calls, and was very skeptical that "nothing was wrong."

*

"Mienus, where do you go on your bike every so often on Saturday mornings?" Mother asked.

"What do you mean? I just ride around."

That answer was not good enough for Mom. "No Mienus! There is something else you are doing and I want to know what it is. Every time you come back from your bike ride you are upset, and want to be alone, and get angry at the smallest things with the children and me. Now, please Mienus, where do you go and what do you do?"

Dad could no longer pretend. He knew that his wife was rightly suspicious. He knew that the children were afraid of making their Dad angry. Mother worked hard to protect us, but by now we were conditioned to tread lightly around Papa on Saturdays.

Dad sat down and thought for a moment about the consequences of what he was about to say. Looking for the right way to say this, he finally revealed, "I go to see Joe D.W. after he calls me. In the beginning, he said he wanted to make sure we were adjusting to our new surroundings and wanted to know how much money I was making digging graves for the Church. I thought this was what a sponsor was supposed to do. He was just looking out for us, Suze."

"Why didn't you tell me that in the beginning? Why did you think you had to keep this to yourself? I can understand that he was trying to take care of us," she asked.

Dad went on to say, "Joe told me not to say anything about our visits. He just wanted to talk to me and not involve you. I trusted him. But after a while, he changed. He wanted to tell me what to spend my money on, and how things worked in this country. I believed him, and wanted to let him know how much we appreciated his help in bringing us to America."

"What do you mean, how things work in the country? What does that mean?"

Dad explained, "He told me that to make money in this country, you have to be smart and clever. You need to take advantage of people in order to get ahead, and he would teach me. I then began to understand that he might be doing that with us too. I was concerned and started to worry.

"So, I asked him how he made money and became rich. He told me that he made money in real estate, at least in the beginning. He would buy houses and rent them to others, and then talk them into buying them from him, knowing they couldn't afford it. He would loan them the money and then after a few years, force them to pay back what they owed him. When they could not pay back the money right away, he would force them, somehow, I'm not sure how, to lose the house and all the money they put into buying the house. He laughed at how easy it was to do. And that is just one of many ways to make money, he said."

Mom's heart was troubled by what her husband was saying. Joe, the man they thought they knew, was without honor. She began to understand what Dad had been going through. As he continued to describe his dilemma, it became clear to her that she had good reason to be uncomfortable with the way Joe had been controlling her children, and now, it seems, her husband.

Dad felt utterly trapped. Joe was trying to mentor Dad in the art of dishonest and unethical business practices. "I can't believe that is the way you become wealthy. That is not right. Did you tell him that you could never do that?" she asked.

"I was afraid to say anything. I just listened in the beginning. He told me to keep what he said between the two of us. He also said that if I didn't make it financially in the first year, he might have to send us back to Holland. So, he told me what to buy each week, and how much to save. I had to show him how much money I had each week. When I got the job at the City of Salem, and got paid once a month, I only needed to come back after paydays. I didn't know what else I could to do. I've never known anyone like him before, and he was so kind in the beginning."

The hurt and anger Mom felt toward Joe was hard to contain. Her husband's fears and anxiety had been fueled by Joe. How she wished she had known this sooner. She could have given him strength and understanding long ago. Thinking how this man may have been using their children to further some financial scheme of his made her wonder what he was really planning for the girls!

Conversations Mom had overheard between Joe and other cohorts of his now frightened her. References about the "Lennon Sisters," or the "King Family," famous musical groups during the 50's and 60's, made her think that Joe had grand ideas about creating the next famous musical family in order to make himself rich.

Joe nearly always introduced the family as the "new immigrants from Holland." He would then tell others about how Dad was a survivor of the German brutality in the Buchenwald concentration camp. Their story suddenly became Joe's story. Their lives were now his lives, and the van Liths were now a commodity to make money off of. No longer would Mom allow her husband to face this alone.

She announced, "The next time Joe calls on Saturday morning, you tell him that I am coming with you to see him. We will go together and tell him that he will not interfere with how we spend our money anymore, or teach you how to become wealthy by mistreating others. And as far as the children are concerned, they will not be used for his entertainment anymore either."

She could see the fear and anxiety build in Dad's face. "I don't know how Joe's going to handle this. He just wanted to keep this between us. Let's just think about this some more and try to figure this out before I see him next week."

"What is there to figure out? Joe is not the man we thought he was. If he is dishonest with other people, he is being dishonest and controlling of us," she returned.

Mom stood in front of him and said, "Look at you Mienus! You are afraid. Afraid of what he can do to you. You have made him your Master and not your friend. You have allowed him to control you for too long. This is not what we came here for. You survived all those years being told what to do by your captors. You had no say in whether you lived or died. You were a slave to them. Now you have become a slave once again. But you have the say in whether you are free or not. Do not give that power to Joe, or anyone else, ever again. Take back what you have given away. Don't live in fear anymore, never again!"

Though Dad was still afraid, the words his wife spoke began to convince him. The truth in what she said was giving him strength and a measure of hope. "Never again," Dad must have thought. "Never again!"

The two embraced. "I love you Mienus."

"I love you too Suze."

*

Dad answered the phone. "Hello Joe...Yes I'm coming...Oh, that is Suze...She wants to talk to you...Well, she wants to come with me this morning."

The long pause in the conversation was deafening. Mom continued to look to her husband for any kind of response. Dad remained silent as Joe continued the one-sided banter.

"What did he say? What just happened?" Mom asked after Dad put the phone down.

"Let me think for just a minute." He replied.

After collecting his thoughts, he said, "Joe said that I can't see him with you. He said not to bring 'that woman' here. He figured I must have told you something that made you want to see him, and he doesn't want any woman to interfere in his business."

Still shook up, Dad took a big breath and continued. "Joe said we will be going back to Holland very soon. He said, 'I am going to ruin you so that you will not be welcome anywhere in this town. No one controls Joe.'

"He also said that he would be calling my work and would tell lies about me to my manager, and my manager would fire me when he was through. He's going to make sure no one will hire me after that. There were a lot of other things he said, but I didn't understand some of it. He just repeated his angry words over and over again. At the end he said something about making a phone call to Puck, and the others, 'to finish what they started,'" Dad added at the end.

"What do Puck and the others have to finish?" Mom asked

"I don't know! I guess we will hear something after Joe talks to them."

The significance of what had just happened deeply troubled Dad. Mom sat silent for a few moments. While Dad's demeanor revealed feelings of defeat, Mom did what she always did when confronting difficulties in her life. She turned to her faith and felt the comfort, wisdom, and strength she needed to help carry the emotional weight her husband had fallen under.

"Honey, Joe cannot take away our faith and our hope for our future. We have come this far because God allowed it. Joe has no power over us. Let's turn to our Lord for guidance and not worry about what Joe thinks he can do to us. I, for one, am glad we will never have to see this man again. I will miss May though. I feel sorry for her too." The rest of the day they devoted to their children.

*

The following day, the family planned to attend the City of Salem's annual summer picnic. This was the first time they were invited, and it provided a good opportunity to meet others in the community.

The food consisted of the standard hamburgers and hotdogs, and a potluck dish provided by each family. Mom brought a special Dutch beet salad that she frequently made for her family during the warm summer months. Everyone at the picnic seemed to enjoy the new ethnic addition.

At some point during the picnic, Dad had intentions to talk to his boss about the conversation he had with Joe. He assumed Joe would be calling him on Monday with the lies he was preparing to tell, with the singular purpose of ruining Dad's chances of finding future success. Though he was reluctant to talk to his boss at this social gathering, he just could not wait till Monday.

Jack, Dad's foreman, was making the rounds, greeting and visiting the employees he managed. Jack liked working with Dad, so he was hoping that Jack would understand his need to tell him what had transpired the day before with Joe. This exchange went something like this:

Jack shook Dad's hand. "Mienus, it's good to see you and meet your beautiful wife and daughters."

"Thank you, Jack. It's very nice to see everyone here. My wife, Suze, and I are happy to meet so many new friends. Outside of our church friends and acquaintances, we don't get a chance to meet too many other people."

Jack replied, "It takes time to make new friends and find your place in a new community. I just want you to know that everyone in your group has nothing but good things to say about you at work. I know how hard you work and I am very glad you were finally able to get hired on at the City. I had heard about you and your family from several different sources, but I also heard that you were already working for someone else."

"I don't understand. The only job I was able to get right away was through the priest at my church. I was digging graves while my sponsor, Joe D.W., was getting my name out to others for a machinist job. I would have been here much sooner if I had been called," Dad replied, puzzled.

Jack also looked puzzled when he said, "Hmm, that is interesting. But I guess I shouldn't be too surprised."

"I don't understand. What do you mean?" Dad asked.

"Well, I got this call from Joe yesterday, and he had a lot to say about you, Mienus. It seems he doesn't much like you anymore, and had some very nasty things to say about you and your lovely wife," Jack said with a smile on his face.

Dad, stunned into silence, must have looked like a deer in the headlights, ready to be clobbered by a car and too petrified to move.

"Relax Mienus! There is nothing that Joe can say or do to change my mind about you. Everyone in town knows what kind of a man Joe is. He has had the reputation of a crooked dealer for many years. When I heard about him sponsoring a family from Holland, I thought, pity that poor family! I thanked Joe for his call, and told him that I would take his information and think about what I should do with it. What I will do is what I always do when I hear from Joe. I disregard 99% of everything he says, and give the other 1% to his wife, just to be kind to her," Jack declared, as he broadened the smile on his face.

It was hard for Dad to hold back the tears that were growing in his eyes. But he managed to do so just long enough to say, "Thank you, Jack. Thank you! I have been afraid of that man for too long. I was so sure we would be sent back to Holland. You have no idea what this means to me."

"Oh, I think I do Mienus. I knew right away what Joe was trying to do, and I would have none of it. I'm a good judge of character. I already know you are a good and decent man, Mienus, and we are lucky to have you work with us at the City of Salem. You have nothing to worry about. Now, please enjoy yourself with the others who are waiting to get acquainted with you and your family. I'll see you on Monday." Jack then turned to greet other families.

Dad couldn't wait to tell his wife about the conversation he just had with Jack. Mom hadn't been formally introduced to Dad's boss yet. When she heard what Jack had said, she could no longer wait to meet him. Joe had no power over them anymore.

As Mom reached out to shake hands with the man who just lifted the heavy load off her husband's shoulders, she said, "Mr. Jack, I am so happy to meet you. My husband and I are so very grateful for you showing such kindness to us. My husband has not had it easy these last couple of years. He..."

Mom was interrupted when Jack stepped forward, took her hand, and provided these words of comfort, "No thanks, please Mrs. van Lith. No need at all. It is I who would like to apologize for the actions of Mr. D.W. What he did to you and your family was so very wrong. Joe has a reputation in this town, and it is not a good one to most of us. Not everyone is like Joe. He is what we call 'an opportunist,' someone who is constantly looking for another way to use others for his gain, and it doesn't matter to him who gets hurt in the process."

The picnic and the encounter they shared with Jack would be remembered as a turning point for Dad and Mom. Their hopes for a better future was restored. Mom was able to open herself up to new friends that day, and Dad enjoyed a greater measure of freedom. His hope for a brighter future for his family was restored.

Difficult Losses

Sad news from Holland arrived. In the autumn of 1959 a telegram was delivered with the news that someone had died. The first to pass on was my dad's mother on November 4, 1959. Wilhelmina Maria van Lith, my Oma, had already been dead a few days by the time we got the news. A formal announcement would arrive nearly two weeks later, long after the funeral and burial, in a white square envelope with a black border.

It would be exactly thirteen months later when the identical scenario played out when Dad lost his father, Marinus Theodorus van Lith on December 4, 1960. The same type of telegram, followed by the black-bordered envelope, set in motion the grieving process once again.

As he mourned his losses, Dad must have thoughts about waving goodbye to his parents from the *Groote Beer* the day we left Holland. He was right after all. The last image of them at the waterfront in Vlaardingen was indeed the last time he saw his parents in this life.

Sadly, twelve months later another telegram arrived. I remember mother looked very anxious as she opened this message. Tears flowed slowly down her cheeks as she read the news that her dear mother, Geertuida Maria Bruggeman, had died on December 30, 1961. We knew to look for the black-bordered envelope to arrive soon.

These were extremely difficult losses for Dad and Mom, with three parents dying in just over two years. They both understood that any future visit to Holland would never be the same. The hopes they had of seeing their parents again died with each telegram. Mother would see her father, Albertus Bruggeman, twice before his death on October 16, 1975.

Our parents had to deal with another kind of unique loss during the first few years adjusting to their new life. The names they had given their children would not remain the same. Within the home, Mom and Dad continued to call us by our given names. Unfortunately it was not long before it became apparent that some of the names were problematic for the girls in their new surroundings.

The girls weren't always treated kindly by some of the school children. Their Dutch names were made fun of. Over time, as we became more American and a little less Dutch, the names our parents thought they would always hear, evolved into something more acceptable to their daughters and the other children around them.

Ineke's name was the only one that did not change in any way. Her name was easy to say and had no English translation. Perhaps the kids in her class were old enough to know better than to hurt another person by making fun of their name.

Gerrie's name was difficult to say for most people in general, but especially for her classmates. From the beginning of her first year at St. Joseph's School, the children began to call her "Jerry" and teased her for having a boy's name. She explained to them that her name in English was Gertrude, and then unilaterally changed her name to "Gert." And that was that!

Suuske's name morphed into the English version, Susan, even though her given name was Suzanna like her mother. For the majority of her life, she would be called Sue.

Treesje's name changed as well. The pronunciation of her name sounded nothing like it was spelled. She could have gone by Teresia or Theresa, the English version, but she chose to go by Traci. She liked it better, and it sounded more similar to her Dutch name.

My name, Marja, was somehow mispronounced my first year of school. When my mother introduced me to the teacher, the Dutch accent she was working hard to diminish, made the R in my name nearly silent to the listener. So, for the first 27 years of my life, my name was spelled correctly, but was pronounce Mī-ya, (long i).

I just assumed my name was said properly throughout my years in school. I just remember having to explain to people who looked at the spelling, that the R was silent.

None of us legally changed our names. Our identification papers and other important documents have our full Dutch names. It would have been a real headache otherwise.

Just after graduating from high school, I traveled back to Holland for my first return visit. After landing in the Netherlands, I heard the customs officer pronounce my name correctly for the first time. My name was not Mi-ya. He called me Mar-ya! The R wasn't silent; it is part of my name! All the relatives I met for the first time addressed me with the correct pronunciation too.

It would take me another ten years before I finally got the courage to introduce myself using the correct pronunciation. Today, when I hear someone call me Mi-ya, I know that this person has known me for a very long time. A few holdouts are set in their ways and unable to call me anything else, including my oldest sister, Ineke. I just smile when I hear them use my old pronunciation.

Not long after Dad began working at the City of Salem, he realized that co-workers had difficulty calling him Mean-us. So he began to refer to himself as Dom. Dom was his name for, pretty much, the rest of his life. The only time he was referred to as Mienus was with Mother, Dutch people who knew him, or their best friends in Salem.

My mother didn't tell us for decades how she mourned the loss of her name. We had only been living in the U.S. a short time when others decided that they would call her Sue or Suzie. At times, she was even referred to as Susan. "But that was not my name!" she said many times. Just as it was for Dad, she would hear her real name from her best friends in Salem, Dutch family and friends, and her husband. "Why was it so hard for people to call me Sooza?" Mother lamented.

I suppose other immigrants went through similar transitions, hearing themselves called by a variation of the name that was given them at birth, or something completely different. Apparently it was necessary to accommodate others unable, or unwilling, to accept something too foreign sounding. If I was in a similar situation, I would grieve the loss of the name I felt was my right to share, and my right to pronounce.

*

Just as she had promised, in April 1960, just four years after our family emigrated from the Netherlands, Puck, John, Hennie, and Gil flew over to stay with us for several days. They had plans to do more traveling within the States before they returned to Holland.

They came bearing gifts from family and friends in Vlaardingen again. There were a lot more goodies packed in this gift package. It was from within this box that I first fell in love with *hagelslagg*.

Hagelslagg (hail storm), are chocolate sprinkles that are gently scattered over a piece of bread or toast lathered in butter and usually eaten for breakfast, or any time it sounds good! If you know a Dutch person, you are probably smiling with recognition. Unless you have tried it, you don't know what you have been missing.

Hagelslagg also comes in another flavor, anise, and is sprinkled over a twice-baked piece of round, toasted bread called *beschuit* (dried biscuit). This form of *hagelslagg* is called *muisjes* (mice). It's probably called that because it looks like pink and white, or blue and white mouse droppings. I know that sounds disgusting, but it tastes so good.

My older sisters got excited when they saw the black salted licorice pieces called *dropes*. They come in either soft or hard salty pieces. I never acquired a taste for them, but the rest of the family seemed to love them.

Also the box of goodies was a package of special cookies call *speculaas*. These cookies are usually eaten at Christmastime. Though they were tasty out of the box, nothing compared to the ones Mom made from scratch.

Mom's dough would include spices of cinnamon, cloves, nutmeg, and other ingredients that produced a wonderful aroma when she baked them. She had a wooden pressboard that had four or five different windmill indentations on it. After rolling the dough, she would press the board into the dough to form the cookies into the windmill shapes. She then carefully placed these cookies onto the cookie sheet and baked them. They were awesome!

Dad would find his favorite box of cigars within the gift box, and Mother found her favorite Tosca perfume once again. Some hand-written cards and letters from family and friends were also included in the box. It felt like Christmas in the springtime.

A couple of days after arriving from the Netherlands, Puck and the others wanted to pay a visit to Joe and May. Dad and Mom were hesitant to tell them about the falling out that occurred a couple of years before, but agreed that it was important to tell them what had transpired between them.

The friends were stunned as they listened to the story about how Joe had manipulated Dad and, unwittingly, Mom. After hearing the details, the four began to recall some interesting questions Joe had posed to them when they met on the train years ago. They were required to agree to certain conditions before he was willing to sponsor the van Liths. It was now obvious that Joe had manipulated them too.

Dad asked his friends, "You know, I have been wondering for the last couple of years about something Joe had said to me the very last time we talked on the phone. Joe said something about calling each of you, and making sure you finish what you had started. What do you think he meant by that?"

The four looked at each other for a moment, and then Puck said, "Well, Mienus and Suze, we told Joe about you and your children, and the reasons for wanting to immigrate. He could tell how important it was for you to have a sponsor in America, and he seemed genuinely interested in helping your family. He asked us about our friendship too. We told him how special you are to us, and how much we would miss you after you left for America. And then, before we parted ways, he asked us just how much we valued our friendship. We told him you are the dearest of friends to us. But then he said, 'No, just how much is your friendship worth?'"

Still a bit confused, Dad asked, "I don't understand. What do you mean?"

"Joe wanted to make sure that if things did not work out for you and the family in America, we would be willing to pay for all of you to come back to Holland. He wanted us to put a price tag on our friendship," John replied.

For a moment, Mom was stunned into silence. Looking at Dad, she said, "If we had known that this man had pressured our friends into agreeing to pay for our return, we would never have agreed to those conditions! This man had a price for everything."

"We talked about what Joe was asking of us, before he would agree to be your sponsor. We were never really sure if he meant what he was saying. It all just sounded so strange. We didn't even think about saying anything to you," Puck said, with John, Hennie, and Gil agreeing with her. Dad and Mom didn't know how to respond.

"None of us ever worried about the money anyway. We knew that you would make it in America. There was never a question in our minds. Please, don't be angry with us for not telling you. We had forgotten the conversation long ago. That was five years ago already," John said.

"It's not you that we are unhappy with. I just can't believe that there are people in this world that can put a price on friendships like that. We have always appreciated everything you did for us before we emigrated. You know how we feel about that," Mom reiterated. "I guess it is done now, and we don't have to worry about Joe anymore. It is unfortunate that we have no contact with May anymore as a result. She is the sweetest lady," she added.

*

A few years later, Joe passed away. May phoned Mom not long after.

"Hello Suze, It's May. I've been missing you and your family ever since Joe parted ways with both of you," May said to open the conversation.

Mom was so happy to hear from May. "Oh May, we've missed you too. We were sorry to hear that you lost your husband. I hope you are doing ok," Mom replied.

May was conciliatory and said, "It wasn't always easy living with Joe, but I do miss him. Suze, I want to apologize for the way Joe treated you and Mienus. It was not right. I never did know exactly what happened, but I know how Joe could be with others when things did not go his way. I hope you can forgive us."

Mom always had room in her heart to forgive. "May, you and Joe were there for us in the beginning, and we will always be grateful. We would love to see you again, and I know the children would too."

Their friendship would last several more years, until May passed away.

*

The week of visitors went by quickly, and it was time for our guests to move on with their travel itinerary. Dad was not about to let them leave before he had a chance to use his new movie camera. I think this was the first times he used this new toy. It was one of those reel-to-reel camera recordings that came with a stand, and had the biggest and the brightest light bulbs ever invented, at least through my youthful eyes.

After setting up the movie camera and placing the lights in just the right spot, each of the children were required to rehearse the hugs, kisses, and the farewells before actually filming it.

Starting with Ineke, each of us took our turn walking over to the four family friends to say goodbye, and then waited for our guests to say something to us in return. Before we could leave, we were expected to give a hug and a kiss on the cheek of each of them. A couple of my sisters were quite embarrassed with the whole production, but performed anyway, just as we were supposed to.

116

Most of the siblings felt very self-conscience knowing the camera was rolling. You could hear lots of giggling around the room. After watching what my older sisters did, by the time it was my turn, I knew just what to do. My performance ran smoothly. At the very end, I turned, looked at the camera, and waved.

I think this is what triggered my ambition to want to entertain others. Each time Dad pulled out that movie camera and those painfully bright lights, I saw it as an opportunity to practice my new skills.

Congratulations Citizens

Having lived in Salem for nearly five years, Dad and Mom were now eligible to begin the process of becoming naturalized citizens. They had no second thoughts about becoming citizens, and looked forward to doing so just as quickly as possible.

Classes were being offered in the spring of 1961, and both understood what was expected of them in order to pass the naturalization test. They studied American History, Government, Civic Responsibilities, and other related subject matters. Passing this course would bring them one step closer to, what was now, their shared goal.

In addition to passing the exam at the end of the course, they had to demonstrate their proficiency in the English language. This was an important process, and expected of every immigrant before becoming an American citizen.

After completing all the requirements, they waited for the next scheduled ceremony to pledge their allegiance to the United States of American. That moment arrived just a few months later.

Dad, Mom, and 32 other immigrants from around the world, gathered together in a large room at the Court House in Salem, on July 20, 1961. They were seated in three ascending rows, our parents in the second tier. Family and guests looked on, including five wide-eyed sisters waiting for the ceremony to begin.

A few state and local governmental officials were present. A couple of these dignitaries spoke a few words of encouragement to the candidates who were soaking in the experience. When the time came for the U.S. Citizenship Oath, each candidate was asked to stand and raise their right hand.

The judge presiding over the ceremony asked the candidates to recite the Oath of Allegiance. They each had a written copy of the oath, making it less likely for anyone to miss any portion of what they were about to swear to. Prompted by the judge to begin, they said aloud:

> *I hereby declare, on oath, that I absolutely and entirely renounce and adjure all allegiance and fidelity to any foreign prince, potentate, state, or sovereignty, of whom or which I have heretofore been a subject or citizen; that I will bear true faith and allegiance to the same; that I will bear arms on behalf of the United States when required by the law, that I will perform noncombatant service in the Armed Forces of the United States when required by the law; that I will perform work of national importance under civilian direction when required by the law, and that I take this obligation freely, without any mental reservation or purpose of evasion, so help me God.*

After the pledge was completed, the judge turned to the others in the chamber and invited the children of those newly sworn in, older than thirteen years of age, to swear their allegiance as well. This act was more of an opportunity to participate than it was for legal purposes. The minors of the new citizens were automatically declared with all the rights and privileges that are provided in the Constitution of the United States.

Ineke and Gert stood up and raised their right hands, along with several other older children. Before reading the pledge aloud, the judge began by saying, "Do you swear?" And those standing replied, "I do." It was a proud moment for the girls. Dad and Mom were surprised by this unexpected gesture.

"On behalf of the United States of America, I would like to congratulate our newest citizens," the judge declared.

Everyone in the room burst into applause. Then the judge began to shake hands with each of the 34 new U.S. citizens. He was the first of many dignitaries eager to welcome those who had worked and waited so long for this milestone in their lives.

Everyone in the room had a smile on their face. Many of those who were sworn in had tears in their eyes. Though Dad would try hard not to show too much emotion, he could be spotted looking up now and then, so as to avoid any moisture from dripping down his cheeks.

Each of the new Americans had their own reasons for coming to this country. Undoubtedly, they all had their individual stories to tell, of a different life in a faraway country they left behind.

This was, and still is, the "land of opportunity," for anyone willing to work hard, be law abiding, and make the sacrifices necessary to provide for themselves and their family. The common denominator was their desire to leave a legacy of a better life for the next generation.

America is like no other country in history. It recognizes and provides the God given freedoms so poignantly described in the Declaration of Independence, and spelled out in our Constitution. Millions of people long to experience this freedom. Sadly, many of our citizens take our freedoms for granted, while others want to water them down. Even more frightening are the enemies who endeavor to take these freedoms away from us.

I pledge allegiance to the flag, of the United States of America, and to the Republic for which it stands, one Nation under God, indivisible, with Liberty and Justice for ALL.

Our parents must have felt a gamut of emotions that day. Aside from the obvious pride, I'm sure they must have pondered all that they had given up for this moment. In some ways, I think Mom made the bigger sacrifice as she freely renounced the country of her birth. But her faith in God's providence always remained.

"I'm still trusting in you, Lord! Your ways are definitely not my ways, but I'm confident you know what you are doing for my family." Mother repeated words like these many times. This prayer was quite suitable during a number of very challenging situations she was forced to endure throughout her life.

A journalist and a photographer from the Salem newspaper were present at the occasion, and the celebration that followed. Our parents were approached and asked to have a photo taken of our family for the newspaper story that would be written and published about this event. They agreed. The last time a photo of the family was posted in the paper was just a few years earlier, when they referred to us as the "new immigrants." On July 21, 1961, we were on the front page again, only now we were regarded as "new citizens."

The picture showed us lined up against a bare wall. Dad was on the left next to Mom, and we girls were lined up by age. We all had our right hands up as if we were being sworn in. The caption to the photo read, "Five Daughters 'Automatically Naturalized'." Three of our names were misspelled. We were used to that.

All of us wore identical dresses. Mother had just finished making them the week before. They were all made of gingham check fabric, and each of us had a different pastel color. Earlier in the week, we each spent time cross-stitching the flowered design that mother had sketched on the fabric on the front of our dresses.

It was a big moment and a memorable day for our family! I'm going to guess that we went out to dinner that night. We didn't go out very often, but on the day you become an American citizen, that sounds like a good day to eat out.

Pietro's Pizza, just off of Market St. and Hawthorne, would have been a great choice. We all loved pizza, and Dad was able to afford feeding his family of seven with a couple of large Hawaiian pizzas. What an exciting way to end a great day.

A celebration was scheduled for the middle of the afternoon in the backyard of our home, on Saturday, July 22, 1961. Several friends came to celebrate with us. Earlier that day, cards and letters began arriving in the mail. Elected officials from the federal, state, and local governments sent congratulations along with welcoming remarks. Most notably was the congratulatory letter sent from the then-Governor, Mark O. Hatfield. Dad and Mom were so proud to show their guests these official-looking letters with their impressive letterhead embossing.

With great delight, my folks took turns opening the presents they were given. Each of the gifts looked as though they were well thought out, something memorable for the occasion. The most inspiring gift through the eyes of this 6-year-old was the beautiful collection of tall drinking glasses inlayed with red, white, and blue flags and patriotic symbols and a silver carrying holder for the set of eight. I was awestruck; they were so beautiful. I don't ever remember using them. I was too afraid to!

After the festivities, it was time for our parents to go through the naturalization packet that was given to them after the swearing-in ceremony. In it was their certificate of naturalization, an application for new passports, voter registration cards, and instruction to update their Social Security information within ten to fourteen days. When it was all said and done, there was no doubt that our parents felt a greater sense of belonging and attachment to their new Fatherland, the United States. Dad had high hopes of assisting other family members who might have longings to come to America. He was more than willing.

Wim, Wil, Martin, and Joke

Not too long after becoming citizens, Dad got his chance to become a sponsor. During the first part of January 1962, his youngest sister and her family left Holland to join us in Salem. Willy arrived with her husband, Wim, and their son and daughter, Martin and Joke (pronounce **Yō**-ka). As children, we weren't given much information ahead of time.

Their arrival unfortunately coincided with the telegram that arrived just days before, with the news of the death of Mom's mother, our Oma. Though Mother was grieving during this time, she did not display much of it. She did what she was known for. She provided for Dad's sister and family in every way possible, and demonstrated her great virtue of hospitality. She showed her graceful strength while serving others. Mom was always like that.

My Tante (Aunt) Willy's husband, Om (Uncle) Wim, quickly landed a construction job, and within a month moved his family just a couple of doors down from us on 16th Street.

I was in first grade at St. Joseph's. Cousin Joke, less than two months younger than me, was added to my classroom shortly after they arrived. Martin was three years older and joined the fourth graders. Neither could speak English sufficiently at the time.

Joke and I became best of friends. She was energetic and a lot of fun to be with. I was called upon by Sister Cynthia, my first grade teacher, to help with translating almost everything for Joke. This was a daunting task for someone just turning seven years old. I did the best I could until Joke was able to understand and speak for herself. Amazingly, it was just a few short weeks when my skills as a translator was no longer needed.

Having to learn a new language when fully immersed worked out rather well for my cousins. When you have to learn, you just do it, like my older sisters did.

Joke and I were the tallest kids in our classes. We were also very competitive. She was always just a little taller, just a little faster, weighed just a little more, and was picked first when I was picked second each time we divided into teams at school. It only bothered me a little. I was just happy to have her in my life.

Our families spent a lot of time together. Living so close kept us in daily contact. In hindsight, perhaps we spent a little too much time together. Tante Willy never really appreciated living in the United States. She witnessed our humble life, and decided that living in America didn't seem all that different from living in Holland where she was more comfortable. She missed her family and the life she had in the Netherlands. It was Om Wim's dream to make a good living in America. He was a talented carpenter, and wanted to run his own company someday.

Sadly, the summer after my third grade ended, Wim, Willy, Martin and Joke sold much of what they had acquired over the last two and half years, and said goodbye to us in July 1964. They returned to Holland. We were alone again, and I would miss them.

Uncle George and Aunt Elsie

By now we were well integrated into our new homeland, and our relatives were thousands of miles away. Now that Dad's sister and her family were gone, I had a better understanding of just how alone we really were. It was we who were the distant relatives, not them. We left them, they didn't leave us

I never felt the void without grandparents, aunts, uncles, and cousins before then. I figure, you don't really miss something or someone you don't know that much about. I had my siblings and my parents. That was family enough for me. And we all had Uncle George and Aunt Elsie.

George and Elsie Van lived in Salem, after having lived for many years in California as dairy farmers. They also were Dutch, from an area in the Netherlands called Friesland. Friesland is a separate cultural region and has its own dialect of the Dutch language.

In retirement, George and Elsie lived in an old farmhouse on the outskirts of Salem. They raised chickens and had a few dairy cows on their acreage. They belonged to St. Joseph's Church, like we did.

Dad and Mom were introduced to George and Elsie not long after the family arrived in Salem. There was an immediate connection between both couples and they became the best of friends for the rest of their lives. It was George and Elsie who were grafted into our orphaned family, and filled any void in our lives. Though we called them Uncle George and Aunt Elsie, they were more like grandparents to us girls, and without question, the best of friends to our parents.

Every Sunday morning after 8:00am Mass, Dad drove the family to the old farmhouse on Hampden Lane so the adults could share a cup of coffee or two, and we girls would drink the red Hawaiian Punch Aunt Elsie had ready for us. We would be treated to her freshly baked coffee cake, fresh cookies, or homemade cinnamon rolls that she was famous for.

There was a routine to our visits each Sunday. It had developed over many years. My favorite thing to do was to hug Aunt Elsie as she greeted us at the door, and then scurry over to Uncle George who was sitting in his chair at the dining room table just waiting for me to climb onto his lap.

For 20 minutes or so, I would sit and watch Aunt Elsie absentmindedly swirl the sugar in the sugar bowl in front of her with a silver spoon she was holding in her hand. I would listen to the adults talk about all sorts of interesting topics. They seemed to have all the answers to so many of the world's problems.

I continued this same routine of sitting on Uncle George's lap for years, until one particular Sunday. I realized that maybe I was getting too big to sit on his aging lap. Mom and Dad had been saying this for a while already, but I wasn't ready to accept what was obvious to everyone else. Though he never refused me, I knew it was time to sit next to him, instead of on him. That was sad day for me, and probably for Uncle George as well.

Coloring books and crayons were in the top left drawer of the built-in dining room cupboards, and board games and other toys were stored behind two small doors installed in front of the unused fireplace in the living room. We knew how to entertain ourselves while the adults conversed for that hour.

Before leaving, Mother and Aunt Elsie would head to the back door, where Mom would buy two or three dozen brown eggs, and a few gallons of fresh cow's milk, not long out of the udder. No store-bought milk for our family, as long as Bessie the cow had enough to share with us. Aunt Elsie would often give us fresh seasonal fruits and vegetables too. This stuff was reliably organic.

One of the first things mother would do with the fresh milk was to ladle off the thick top layer of pure cream and store it properly in the refrigerator. She kept it to make fresh whipped cream during the week. The girls would take turns beating that cream with a handheld mixer while Mom added enough sugar to whip it to a point.

Every Fourth of July and Labor Day was spent at the farm with Uncle George and Aunt Elsie. There we celebrated the good old-fashion potluck barbeques and outdoor games that are so much a part of the American culture. Did I already tell you about Aunt Elsie's famous warm and gooey cinnamon rolls with the white frosting just dripping down the sides? They were so good I just wanted to mention them again!

I could say much more about these people, but I believe I've shared enough to show you how well we were loved. This endearing older couple filled the void of not having grandparents, and as a grandparent myself, those are big shoes to fill.

Through this paperless adoption, God blessed and provided us with the love and friendship Uncle George and Aunt Elsie Van generously offered. They embraced us as their own, and will always be missed.

Chapter 14

One for the Records

During the mid-afternoon hours of Friday, October 12, 1962, gale force winds pummeled the states of Oregon and Washington. No one living in the Northwest at that time, nor any time since, had experienced such a ferocious storm that caused such major damage. Many weather experts say that this was one of the biggest and most significant hurricanes ever recorded in the Pacific Northwest. She would be known as "The Columbus Day Storm."

Today's meteorologists gather information from weather satellites, ocean buoys, and the constant data flowing in from air, land, and sea. Plugging in all this data, computer models produce maps of the current weather conditions, and forecast scenarios. The predicting of the weather can be extremely precise from hour to hour, and be projected with reasonable accuracy for up to ten days in advance.

In the early 60's, weather forecasts were developed by using airport reports, cloud observations, barometric readings, Teletype data gathered from ships at sea, and lots of phone calls to and from other weather stations. This data was calculated and hand drawn onto maps that meteorologists would use to predict the weather for the following day. The information would be made public via TV, radio, and newspaper. Back then, forecasting the weather was more difficult and less reliable.

The weather forecast on the morning of October 12 was for wind and rain in the morning, and increasing winds in the afternoon. This was a common forecast for the Willamette Valley, where Salem is located. Much of the Pacific Northwest is known for this type of weather during the fall and winter months. Unfortunately, the information the meteorologists were using was not enough to accurately measure the changing environment that was producing just the right conditions for the perfect storm.

This weather event was rapidly developing into a strong, Category Three hurricane. The weather conditions on October 12 were so unusual, and changed so quickly, that it was difficult to know how to advise the public regarding any necessary precautions to take.

With today's technology, warnings would have gone out as much as a week in advance. Everyone would have been told to take safety measures to protect themselves and their homes from heavy rains, flooding, damaging winds, and power outages. Families would have stocked up on food, batteries, and topped off the gas tanks of their cars. Schools and work would have been cancelled, and people would have been told to stay out of harm's way. These precautions were rarely called for where I grew up, and they were only issued for the very infrequent winter snow and ice storm, or for severe flooding.

The strongest wind gust of The Columbus Day Storm was recorded at Cape Bianco, along the Oregon coast, just SW of Eugene. Reports differed, with gusts ranging somewhere between 147-179mph. Eugene had its highest gust at 86mph, Salem was 90mph, and Portland reached 115mph. This storm continued its march up the coastline and inland of Washington State, with gusts in Longview of 88mph, Olympia at 78mph, Renton at 100mph, Oak Harbor at 90mph, and Bellingham, just south of the Canadian border, at 98mph.

Dad had been working with the City of Salem for a few years already. On the day of the storm, he was assigned to work out of town at a road construction site. As the storm was developing, he was working just a few miles from the Oregon coast.

To help with the growing financial demands of the family, Mom had just taken a part time job at Meier & Frank department store in downtown Salem. She was hired to do clothing alterations and repairs for the entire store, and had only been on the job a couple of weeks.

Ineke (15) and Gert (14), now attending Sacred Heart Academy, had volleyball games on Friday evenings, and did not come home right after school. The nuns, upon hearing the growing ominous weather reports, decided to keep the girls safe in the gymnasium and were busy notifying the parents of their decision to do so. That meant my sister Sue (nearly 13) was in charge of Traci (11) and me (7) at home after school, while we waited anxiously for the others to arrive.

We were still trying to get used to that fact that our mother was not home after school like she had always been before. Sue, Traci, and I we were the first to arrive home that afternoon. We were alone and frightened as the wind began to pick up intensity. I remember feeling very anxious without having our older sisters there with us.

Mother phoned us from her work and could hear us crying. She advised us to go to our Aunt and Uncle's house. Tante Willy and her family were still living in Salem at the time. It would be another year and a half before my aunt decided that she wanted to return to Holland.

The downtown stores were all shutting down their businesses due to the worsening conditions. Management at Meier & Frank decided to keep the employees safe in the basement of the building and not let anyone go home. Apparently, the large Meier & Frank store sign on top of the roof was breaking away in the wind, and the store manager did not want to risk having any of the employees getting hurt, or worse.

While on the phone with Sue, Mother could hear how terrify her youngest three children were. Each of us was scared to tears. She calmly reassured us one by one that she would be home soon. "I will pick you up at Tante Willy's house. Try not to worry, I'll see you soon," Mother promised.

Mom had already made up her mind to sneak out of the store one way or another. She was not about to stay away from her frightened children. After the nuns had contacted her, she was much less worried about Ineke and Gert's safety. She knew they would be safe until someone could pick them up. In addition to the chaos surrounding her children, she was very worried about her husband, and what he must be going through working outside so close to the ocean.

Being alone with my two sisters, and looking out the front window at the two big walnut trees by the street in front of our house, was frightening. They were swaying and bending way over in the wind. We could hear the branches of the big old cherry tree in the front yard violently shake and snap as the wind beat them onto the roof of the house and front porch. Heaps of branches, big and small, were breaking off and falling in the front yard and onto the street.

With little warning, a large gust of wind suddenly broke the power lines to the house. We had been watching the reports on the TV of all the debris and fallen trees on houses, cars, and power lines, just before the house lights went out.

It was late in the afternoon, and very dark in our house, when Sue, Traci, and I decided to make our way through the heavy wind and deluge of rain to Tante Willy's house. It was the big walnut tree in the backyard, the one that gave us all our shade from the late afternoon sun that finally convinced us it was time to run for it.

The noise of the great gust that toppled our walnut tree was terrifying. Just before it happened, there was a pause in the storm, followed by a steady buildup of wind that climaxed with a giant gust that pull that old tree right over, slowly laying it down between our house and the neighbor's house. The tree missed both houses, but smashed the neighbor's old fence. Half of the tree roots were sticking straight up as if they were raising their arms in defeat.

In my mind, this gust was like some invisible giant who took an enormous inhale, grabbed the house between its hands, and exhaled into us with all its strength. It shook the house from top to bottom, while at the same time, killing our tree. It was a scary experience!

We prepared ourselves to make a run for it and decided to try and time the frequency of the worst gusts in an effort to avoid being injured by falling debris. Even between the gusts, the sustained winds made it impossible to stand in one place for very long without holding on to something.

I didn't even think to put my coat on. I was just going to follow whatever the three of us decided to do. Finally, after standing on the porch for a few minutes, my sisters and I made a run for it.

Just as I was about to grab the iron handrail on the front steps of my aunt's house, a forceful gust of wind sent me crashing, knee first, onto the slippery wet grass. My knee hit so hard it ripped my favorite pair of pants. I made it up the stairs, and through the front door, afraid and crying.

My tears were not for the pain from my bloody knee, but for the loss of my orange and pink flowered peddle-pushers. I had so few clothes and shoes to begin with, that losing my best pair of pants just devastated me. I would have rather stayed and taken my chances with that unseen giant at home than fall and ruin my pants in the safety of my aunt's house. I wished I had never left.

After slipping out of Meier & Frank undetected, Mom was just getting home. While making her way through the streets, she managed to dodge the debris that had fallen. We hurried back to the house, together with Tante Willy, Martin, and Joke. They decide to come to our house and stay with us until Om Wim came home. He was picking up Ineke and Gert on his way home from work. They were home not long after.

In less than an hour, the wind ceased, and the sun came out. We were all amazed at how quickly the winds died down. Looking up into the setting sunlight, we saw the clearing in the sky surrounded by big fluffy clouds. Unknown to us at the time, we were observing the eye of the storm. None us had ever experienced anything quite like this before, and did not realize that the hurricane was not over yet.

For a moment, we surveyed the damage around us. In addition to the lost tree in the backyard, we lost another walnut tree in the front. The old cherry tree still had the biggest branches left, and we still had another walnut tree in the front. There were broken branches everywhere, and many of the houses in our street had been damaged by falling trees and flying debris, but our home was intact.

Just as quickly as the wind stopped and the twilight sun broke through, the darkness once again invaded and the wind became violent. The branches of the last standing walnut tree began to move wildly. We were observing the full force of the second half of the storm. At least we had the family to band together and support each other through the rest of the hurricane. That is, all of us except Dad.

Mom tried not to show any signs of worry in front of her children, especially when we asked over and over again, "When will Daddy be home." Earlier in the day, she received a phone call from Dad's boss. He told her that the crew was packing up to leave the work site near the coast. The City of Salem office had received reports of the worsening weather conditions, and advised everyone to stop work and go home quickly. That was hours ago, and there had been no communication since then.

Salem is nearly 60 miles inland from the coastal town of Lincoln City. The work crew was ten to fifteen miles inland from Lincoln City. It should not have taken much more than 90 minutes to get home from this location, even on the old two-lane highway.

It was around dinnertime when Wim, Willy, Martin, and Joke went back to their place. Mom invited them to stay and eat something first, but they did not want to be an imposition on a day such as this. Knowing that Willy and her children were still worried about Dad, Mom assured them that she would let them know as soon as he got home.

Without electricity, most of the light came from the candles we lit in the living room and kitchen. Sandwiches were probably the only item on the menu for that evening. It was important not to open the refrigerator and freezer for more than a few seconds so as to keep the food cold as long as possible. There was no telling when the electricity would work again. We had no phone service anymore either. That had gone out after the trees fell.

Mother was trying to maintain the normal routine of the evening, and helped us to remain calm. We huddled together with her in the living room, where most of the candlelight was. At one point she walked to the kitchen, opened a drawer, and returned with the oval tin box that carried the family's seven rosaries. Each of us had our individual rosary to pray with, and Mother knew just who to give each one to. Dad was missed that evening for our customary prayer time.

This evening Mom would begin the prayer, something usually reserved for our Dad. She would recite the mysteries of each decade of beads, and each of us would recite the "Our Father" and the ten "Hail Mary's" we were responsible for. This was the practice after dinner every evening. The candlelight helped to create a prayerful setting.

Throughout the late evening, the storm continued to weaken. The wind blew softer and the rain fell lighter, but it remained very dark and dreary. Before any of us could even think about going upstairs to bed, it was important to survey the damage in our street, and check on our neighbors.

Others in the neighborhood were opening their front doors to survey the damage too. Flashlights illuminated the foreign landscape. People could be heard lamenting the debris all around them. The elderly woman next door ventured out and was frightened by the ordeal, but otherwise unhurt. We could find no one seriously injured on 16th Street.

We didn't stay out in the dark very long. There were hazards everywhere with all the fallen trees and debris. The real risk of danger was electrocution. Fallen electrical power lines were somewhere buried under the rubble.

It was way past my bedtime, and still no word about our father. Mother walked me up the narrow staircase to the second floor and into the bedroom I shared with my two oldest sisters. There was no way I was going to sleep any time soon. I wanted my dad home with us, and I was afraid to fall asleep.

"Mom, I'm afraid by myself upstairs. Can I please stay downstairs with you until the others go to bed? I'll get a blanket and lay on the couch and I won't say anything, please Momma?" I pleaded.

Mother consoled me and acknowledged the trauma we had all just experienced. "We will all stay up awhile longer and hope that Daddy comes home soon," Mom answered.

It was sometime between 10:00 and 11:00pm when Dad opened the front door and walked into the house. You could hear the excitement in the room as Mother embraced her husband. The stress and the responsibilities she bore the entire day finally gave way to tears of relief.

None of us girls were asleep, or if we did doze a bit, we quickly jumped out of bed to greet Dad. Everyone in the room wiped away tears of relief and thanksgiving. The long wait was over. Daddy was home and unharmed!

We sat together for a few minutes and let Dad rest. Curiosity replaced some of our fears when he began to share bits and pieces of what it was like passing through the belly of the worst Northwest storm on record. As he spoke, the imaginary angry giant that shook the house resurfaced in my mind.

He didn't tell us everything right away. Mother thought it best to leave some of it till morning. It was too late for any more. We already endured enough trauma for one day. "Ok, off you go upstairs! Daddy can finish the rest tomorrow. Up to bed now," Mother ordered.

Sleep was hard to come by that night. Even though the wind and the rain had subsided, there was just enough of both to keep me awake, reliving the events of the day's hurricane. Even at that young age, I understood there was a lot of work to be done to rebuild our neighborhood. It would take time to restore my sense of security as well.

The following morning, Dad finished telling us about his trip home through the storm. We were all ears. The story went something like this:

We got a call from work that morning, from my boss in Salem, that we would be experiencing a lot of wind and rain. We didn't really worry too much about it though. We just kept working.

The wind really began to get bad after lunchtime, and at about 2 o'clock, it was almost impossible to do any road work. The foreman finally stopped the work for the day after we got more information from the boss in Salem.

The traffic got pretty bad from all the people trying to get away from the beach. Everyone must have thought they would be safer inland. There were so many motorists wanting to pass the flagman trying to control the traffic at the site. Many of the waiting drivers got out of their vehicles to tell us that others behind them were getting trapped behind trees that had falling over the roads.

Nobody was traveling toward the coast, so we let the people fleeing drive on the left side of the road. We closed the road going west because of the danger.

We had a lot of equipment to gather up and secure before we could leave the site. We were already in the process of packing up when we got the call to leave from the Oregon Transportation Department guys. That's when I tried to have someone call you. I was told that you got word before that, right, Suze?

It got kind of scary when we saw the first trees falling in the forest. The wind blew so hard. Many times we just had to hold on to something or be blown over. Finally we got everything secured at the site and were ready to leave.

We knew that trees had fallen over the roadway behind us, and I worried and prayed for those people who might be trapped. By the time we were ready to leave, most of the traffic had already gone ahead. We were one of the last vehicles to pull out, followed by just a couple of cars that made it through the mountain range somehow. We left around 4:00pm

Just minutes after we left, trees began to fall closer to the road. We kept looking in all directions, especially when we felt a gust of wind build and blow, making it hard to control the car.

Watching the trees fall on the road behind the car worried me. So far we were lucky, and managed to avoid those trees. How long would it take before the trees started to fall in front of us, we all wondered.

It was so dark outside. With no other cars coming toward us to help us see the road ahead, it got kind of scary!

At one point, the wind became very violent, and we watched as a couple of trees collapsed in front of us, blocking the entire road. We had just enough time to stop safely. We had to wait for the wind to slow down before we got the equipment out to move these trees out of the way.

Within minutes, the darkness in the sky turned into bright colored light and the wind stopped. I couldn't believe it. We got out of the car and grabbed the chainsaws we always traveled with, and worked our way to the fallen trees in front of us. After several minutes we were able to remove just enough of the trees out of the way to let the truck pass through.

Once we got back in the truck, a big gust of wind nearly made us roll over. The wind, the rain, and the darkness came back, stronger than ever, and we still had a long way to go to get out of the trees.

Not long after we stopped for the first tree that blocked the road, other trees toppled over and got in our way. Somehow we were able to cut our way out each time, even in the dark, wind, and rain.

The men I was with said they had never seen anything like this before. After we saw the clearing in the sky and the light open up, and when the storm came back all over again, the guys said that we were in the middle of a hurricane.

We couldn't drive more than 20 to 25 miles per hour, sometimes even slower to avoid all the things on the road. Finally we made it back to the shop in Salem around 10 o'clock, and one of the guys offered to drive me home. I could not believe all the damage done around our house, and I'm so thankful that everyone was safe, and the house has no major damage.

Dad looked around at each of us. He knew he had said enough, maybe too much. Having just told us about his harrowing experience in the storm, Dad went on to say, "Ok everybody, that's enough for one day. We have work to do and I need everybody to help!"

Those of us with our mouths still open in amazement suddenly snapped to attention. We really did have a lot of work to do. There were no Saturday morning cartoon shows like the Jetson's, Johnny Quest, or Bugs Bunny to watch with Dad anyway. Having no electricity in the house made it a little easier for me to go outside and start picking up the smaller branches.

The Columbus Day Storm took away more than the walnut trees. It took some of my carefree innocence that we are all blessed with as young children. I worried like I never had before, even after my Dad walked through the door. The carefree feelings of security and comfort were compromised with the emotions of fear, anxiety, stress, and pain. Because of that storm, I was forced to grow up a little faster than I wanted to.

The concept of death was now a concern. "What if Dad or Mom had died? How would I be able to live without either one of them?" I thought. The consequences were pretty clear to me. It would take some time to put to rest these uneasy thoughts. Eventually, they got stored away with the other memories of my youth, until now.

The events on October 12, 1962, would be the first of a number of incidents in my life where I could recall exactly where I was and what I was doing. Other tragic dates like November 22, 1963 – the assassination of President Kennedy, July 20, 1969 – the moon landing, or January 28, 1980 – the NASA Challenger explosion, are others days I will never forget. More recently, September 11, 2001 – the worst and most costly terrorist attack on American soil, profoundly affected many of us to the point of changing the course of our lives forever.

Other storms followed in my life, but these were not weather related. These were personal challenges, and only through a rearview mirror have I been able to discover the forks in the road I had to choose between, or I was pushed onto without my consent. These forks altered my life forever as well.

"Long shall you live, long shall you live, long shall you live in the Gloria, in the Gloria, in the Gloria! Hip Hip Hooray!"

Lang zal ze leven, lang zal ze leven, lang zal ze leven in de Gloria, in de Gloria, in de Gloria. Hieperdepiep, hoera!

Mom's Big Decision

"When we got married, my hope was to make this man happy!" Mother had said. That was her vocation and commitment to her husband. She was called to be a wife, a mother, and a homemaker, with all the talents and duties that got bundled into her mission in life. After the big storm, she quit her job at Meier & Frank, making everyone in the household very happy.

Not long after the hurricane, Dad left his job working for the City of Salem. His new job at Salem Equipment and Supply was just off of D Street, roughly two miles from our house. With only one car in the household, he was able to ride his bike to work.

Not only did Dad's hourly wage increase, he was also given the opportunity for overtime pay by working half day on Saturdays to meet the growing financial demands of his family. Dad was given greater opportunities to use his skills in the machine shop, and was awarded a few bonuses for the innovative techniques he used for fabricating metals in a more effective way. Though we lived by modest means, Dad and Mom felt more secure financially. Life was good.

Mom had long settled into her routine at home. All of the children were in school, providing her ample time to pursue her in-home sewing business. This was her way to provide the extra income needed to make ends meet, or to save for the future.

Her wooden sign hung just below the address of our house. It read "DRESSMAKING AND ALTERATIONS." It was a prominent advertisement, one that helped to generate a healthy number of clientele, primarily women, who hired Mom to make them beautiful dresses, suits, and other clothing. I don't remember the house without that wooden sign.

Mom had a big heart and loved her family very much. She and Dad were happy raising us, and took great pride in their girls. Ineke turned 18 years old and graduated from high school. I turned 10 years old and was working my way through school at St. Joe's. How quickly the years had gone by.

In less than a year, our family would mark the tenth year of living in the United States, and the fifth year as US citizens. What started out as a dream 21 years ago, after Dad's liberation from Buchenwald, was now reality. It seemed like everything had fallen into place, or so we thought. Apparently not everything had. In less than a year, our family would be given a new addition.

As I mentioned, Dad loved children. In many social gatherings, he would be seen holding the babies and laughing with the young children. Even though he was no longer the policeman carrying candy in his pockets, children still seemed to gravitate to him. Maybe it was his accent. Maybe he was drawn to their innocence, something that was lost in his own life.

In one of my conversations with Mother, the subject of babies came up. "I spent some time thinking about what it would be like to have another child. You were 10 years old already Marja, and I was 40. Your Dad really did not talk much about having more children, but somehow I felt myself opening up to the idea, and imagined what it would be like after all these years, to have another baby," Mom admitted.

"So what happened to change Dad's mind?" I asked.

"Well, we really didn't talk much about these things. I simply said to him one night, 'Mienus, I know how much you love children, and I am not getting any younger. So if you want another child of your own, we better not wait too much longer, or it will be too late.' That's pretty much all I had to say to him," she said.

Dad, now likely with a big smile on his face and a raised eyebrow, didn't need much time to think about his reply. He was very much in love with his wife, and if she was willing, he was equally willing to have another child to love and nurture. He was 45.

I am still amazed at how little they discussed having another child. I mean, with today's values, the majority of couples in their 40's would be more likely looking forward to being empty nesters, not new parents again.

Mom and Dad were satisfied with the five daughters that God had already blessed them with, yet they were still open enough to bring another child into the family. They knew that if the Good Lord allowed this to happen, they would remain willing and open to participate in this creation. It was no time at all before Mother was pregnant.

*

Ineke had just graduated from Sacred Heart Academy in June. She planned to discern a vocation as a Catholic nun by entering the The Holy Name Sisters at Marylhurst Convent and College, located in Lake Oswego, Oregon. Near the end of August of 1965, she left the family to begin her first year of studies at the convent and college.

One of the convent rules for new postulants (the title given to those entering the convent), was that they could have no contact with their parents or siblings for the first three months. We had to wait until Thanksgiving for our first visit with Ineke.

When we could finally got see her, Ineke came running out to greet us in her long black habit with the big pockets, the big rosary around her waist, and her short black veil that covered all but her bangs. She was so happy to see us. Most of us were in tears, and we could tell right away that she was homesick.

The family was escorted to one of the parlors in the convent for our two-hour visit. I don't remember much of that visit. I spent most of the time thinking about what it would be like to be a nun and to wear the habit. At one point, Mom and Dad wanted to talk with their Ineke by themselves. The rest of us stayed in the parlor

When it was time to go home, the family took turns hugging Ineke. We promised to come back to see her at Christmastime, but to Ineke it must have felt like a long time to wait. She could no longer hold back the tears as we waved goodbye.

None of us said much on the trip home. I think we all were feeling the emptiness in our hearts. What made it more difficult for Ineke was that she knew the secret that the rest of us had to wait for. None of the girls knew at the time that our parents had told her that they were expecting a baby. Ineke would be alone again with her thoughts, and could hardly think of anything else but the news that a baby was on the way.

*

Mom was nearly halfway through her pregnancy when it was becoming obvious to Gert that something was going on.

School would be out for Christmas and New Year's break in another week or so. I came home from school and could tell that something was not quite right in the household. My sisters were whispering things, but Mom told me not to worry about it. I was suspicious and wanted to know what was going on. I was pretty sure that Gert had figured out a secret. I, on the other hand, wasn't aware of any secrets in the household in the first place.

"I think Mom and Dad have something important to tell us, but Mom's waiting until Dad gets home!" Gert said with a smirk on her face.

"Gert knows something," I thought to myself.

Soon after Dad got home, Mother requested that we all come and sit down in the living room. Gert still had that smile on her face, but I was pretty certain she wasn't 100% sure about what she thought she knew.

"Your Dad and I want to tell all of you something special," Mother began. "We wanted to wait as long as we could before telling you this, so as to be sure everything was going to be OK. We also didn't want you to have to wait too long before this happens. Dad and I are going to have another child, and the baby is due to arrive in April."

There was a stunned silence just before my sisters burst out, "Are you kidding?" "No, really?" "Oh my goodness, another baby?" or something to that affect.

I just sat there stunned. I remember having very ambivalent feelings. Everyone else seemed very excited, but I wasn't feeling it at the moment.

I was contemplating the fact that I would not be the youngest child in the family anymore. However, that didn't bother me as much as my next thought. The image in my brain bothered me even more.

There was a problem I had to overcome, and it had to do with something Mom had explained to me last year when I was nine. She had these little booklets stored under the sink in the bathroom, and she quickly walked me through the information within. Though she was a little vague with specific detail, I now had a pretty good idea where babies came from, and how they got there.

I could feel the disquiet in me, and I didn't like what I was thinking. I felt anger toward my father. It would take time before I would admit this, but I was mad because...wait for it..............

"Oh my Lord, you touched my mother in that way," was the immature thought of my ten-year-old mind. I just didn't want to think about those things. When my children read this, they are going to shake their heads with complete understanding!

After the initial shock wore off, I began to get excited about having a new baby brother or sister. It took me just a few more days to grow up and get over my childish concerns!

I was glad Mom and Dad had waited to tell us their news. It still seemed like a long time before our new baby sibling would arrive. Four and half months can seem like forever to a ten-year-old.

All of us helped to decorate the Christmas tree a few days later. With my new knowledge about babies, I felt comfortable enough to ask my mother this simple question. "So Mom, you kind of filled me in on how babies were made right? So then with you being pregnant with your sixth baby, you and Dad must have done it six times then, huh?" I asked without shame.

Though everyone in the room waited a few seconds before reacting to my question, it was not long before the snickering burst forth from everyone but me. I think Dad left the room at that particular moment, leaving all those with estrogen in the family to sort this one out. Their reaction showed me that apparently my supposition was incorrect.

Sweet Mother simply said, "Well not exactly, Marja, it doesn't always work that way." I decided not to ask any more questions. I just left it alone among the giggles of my older, and apparently better-informed siblings.

*

Christmas and New Year's did not feel the same this year. Everyone felt Ineke's absence. We all wanted to see her again, and she needed to see us. So we traveled to Lake Oswego to spend some of Christmas Day with her.

No gifts were exchanged at the convent. The only thing Mother could gift her daughter were Jan Hagel cookies, *boteletter*, some *speculass* cookies, and salted licorice. Only gifts that could be shared with the other nuns were allowed.

Though we didn't know at the time, Ineke had already made up her mind, weeks earlier, to leave the convent. Her decision was solidified after she was told about the baby. The older sisters at the convent convinced her to stay long enough to complete her first semester at the college. She agreed that it was the right thing to do. Ineke left the convent and came home for good sometime in early January 1966.

We watched Mom's belly grow, and felt our little sibling kick and hiccup. All of these new events, and more, taught us about the wonderful process of pregnancy and infant care. In our own ways, each of us were preparing for the new arrival. We women were going to have a baby!

Aunt Elsie and her grown daughters provided a wonderful baby shower for Mom. This was our first baby shower experience. There were lots of friends who came to celebrate with us. All the silly games and the adorable baby gifts made the whole occasion so much fun. Seeing all the baby stuff made it so real.

The baby was coming soon. With just days to go before Mom's due date, the baby crib, cloth diapers, plastic diaper pants, blankets, and lots of cute new clothes were in their places and ready to go. Everything we could prepare ahead of time was ready. There was nothing left to do but wait a little longer for baby van Lith. "Let's get this show on the road!" as Dad would say.

Mother was never one to go to the doctor unless she was very sick, or in this case, pregnant. She had good prenatal care, yet, because of her age, she was at greater risk for complications than her younger counterparts.

The added weight of the pregnancy was taking its toll on Mom. Without ultrasounds, which we take for granted now, there were fewer options available to the doctors to accurately measure the size of the baby or to look for preterm complications. Manual palpation of the belly, measuring tapes, and a stethoscope, were heavily relied on for their best educated guess. Occasional blood work or x-rays were used to detect other anomalies.

Labor started very early in the morning of April 13. The day had finally arrived to deliver baby van Lith.

This would be a new experience for Dad and Mom. She had never delivered a baby in a hospital before, and had every intention to solicit the help of the doctors and nurses in providing whatever pain management they were willing to give. At her age, she felt she deserved an easier delivery than what she had experienced with her girls.

None of us really knew what was going on during the labor and delivery. We just stayed close to the phone for someone to call and tell us that everything was all right, and if we had a baby sister or brother. The plan was to meet up with Mom and Dad at the hospital as soon as we were allowed after the birth.

Mother relived her memories with me in later years, something like this:

I remember feeling those old familiar labor pains and thought, "Oh no, I'm going to need something for the pain." I was so exhausted already. I had labored for hours, and the doctor was getting a little bit concerned. He said that he thought the baby might be a little too big to deliver naturally. The head was almost in the right place, but my body was just not getting the job done.

The nurses were told to give me some strong pain medications along with something to relax me. He thought if I could just rest and relax enough, I might find some new energy. I would need it when the time came to push the baby out.

I don't remember much after I got the medicine. I don't even remember being taken to the delivery room. Apparently, your Dad was told that he could not be in the delivery room with me. They were just starting to allow fathers in at that time, but only if the doctor allowed it.

Next thing I remember was waking up in tears. I said to the doctor that I just couldn't do this anymore. I said, "Please help me."

The doctor and nurses told me that I had the baby already, and it was a boy!

I was so surprised. I had no memory of any part of the delivery. What I do remember is how relieved I was that the whole thing was over, and very happy for Dad that he finally got his son!

Dominicus Marinus van Lith Jr. was born April 13, 1966 at 1725 (5:25pm). He was 21 inches in length, and a chunky 10½ pounds in weight. Good Lord, no wonder Mom was having trouble pushing her son out. Without question, at Mom's age, he would have been born by C-section today, and probably should have been then.

Congratulations were in abundance when family and friends found out about the birth of baby Dominic. There was lots of joking about the fact he now had five older sisters to smother him. Babysitting would not be an issue in our family.

It was more like Dommy had five more mothers, instead of five sisters when he was little. In truth, he was raised as an only child because of the years between him and his sisters. I was the closest in age, with eleven years between us. Dom only has a few memories of us living together at home.

Our brother would be raised quite differently from his older sisters. He was a boy, and that made a huge difference, especially to our father, who in many ways still held to the deep-rooted standards of the old country. Dom had older parents that, to others, looked more like his grandparents. He was little when our family experienced the political unrest and assassinations of the 60's, as well as the unrest that followed the many changes within the Catholic Church after Vatican II. And we are still suffering from the impact the "free love, rebellious hippie movement" has had on our culture. Dominic was born in a tumultuous time period.

Life would not be easy for our younger brother. But it was not easy for his siblings either. Furthermore, it also needs to be recognized that it was definitely not easy for Dad and Mom raising five adolescent daughters along with a little boy. But, throughout any and all the trials and tribulations that impacted our youth, there was never a question of our love for one another.

Dominic was meant to be a part of our family. He was born in America, and his birth was a new and profound way of anchoring our family to this country. With our brother's birth, the van Lith name could be passed on to the next generation. And it did.

I wrote the heading of this section (Mom's Big Decision) for a significant reason. Mom could have been moved years before to make the offer to her husband to accept another child into their lives. But she hadn't. She could have done so, say, six months earlier. But she held back. In addition, she should have gone for annual female visits with her doctor. But she never did.

At Mom's six-week post-partum checkup, a requirement she had never experienced after her other deliveries, she underwent her first comprehensive gynecological check-up. A few days later, her doctor called her back to his office to go over her test results.

"Thank you coming in right away, Sue. Did your husband come with you?" the doctor asked.

"No, was he supposed to?" she replied with a smile.

"I was going to have him join us if he had. I have to let you know the results of your Pap smear, and it's not good news. You have cervical cancer," he announced.

Mom sat quietly for a moment while she reflected on what her doctor had just told her. "What happens now? Am I going to die? Is there something we can do to stop it?" she asked.

The doctor quickly replied, "I believe that this cancer can be treated, but I will need to send you to a surgeon. It appears that the cancer is confined to your cervix, but you will need to have a hysterectomy to prevent its spread. I know this is not what you expected to hear, and I am sorry to be the one to tell you. However, I am confident that after your surgery you should be just fine. It will be so very important for you to continue to have six-month examinations for the next few years as a precaution."

"When should I schedule this surgery?" Mom asked, still trying to digest the information she had just be given.

"I think you should have this done right away. You know Sue, you are a lucky woman. There's no way to tell for sure how long you've had this cancer, but from the looks of it I'd say that your pregnancy may have saved your life. There's lots to be thankful for," her doctor said with encouragement.

Though Mom was not feeling lucky, she was grateful for his optimism.

The doctor left the room for just a few minutes and called the surgeon's office to make an appointment for his patient. "Here is the name and phone number of the surgeon. My nurse made an appointment for you to see him. She will give you a few other instructions before you leave my office. Please, Sue, try not to worry. Choosing to have your baby son at your age turned out to be a blessing in so many ways! Call me if you have any questions after you leave here. We'll get you all taken care of," the doctor said as he left the room.

Writing this book helped me to understand just how special my brother's birth actually was. I'm not just referring to the significance of our brother being born into our family, though that was amazing. And I'm not just thinking about how Mother and Dad's openness to life, in fact, saved my mother's life. I'm also amazed at the actual day that he was born. He was born on the date that General Patton reportedly entered the newly liberated Buchenwald Concentration Camp 21 years before, and born on the same date when we disembarked the *Groote Beer* in New York, our new Fatherland, exactly ten years earlier. April 13 is a significant date, and becomes a new thread in our story.

As a Christian, I see times, places, and events through the prism of my faith. It was God's timeline and always has been. That's why Mother didn't make that "big decision" any sooner.

"Long shall you live, in the Gloria, Momma!"

The Years that Followed

In the early summer of 1968, Mom's only sister, Mia, flew to Oregon for her first visit to the United States. The last time the two sisters saw each other was as the *Groote Beer* was leaving the port in Rotterdam. That was an emotionally draining time for her, having just lost her husband.

Tante Mia never remarried, and raised her son and daughter, Leen and Els, by herself. Working in a department store in Vlaardingen much of her adult life, she managed to make ends meet for herself and her children. It wasn't easy being a widow at such a young age (33). She did the best she could on her own, and was sustained by her family and friends.

Tante Mia had a special place within the extended Bruggeman family in Holland. With her sister so far away in America, and their mother now deceased, she became the matriarch that filled the void that had been created in their absence.

The reunion of the two sisters was mixed with tears of happiness, as well as sorrow. So much had changed for both of them. The lives they had planned for as young women were too quickly upended by the death of a spouse, and an ocean between them. Each had endured tremendous challenges in the last twelve years.

Mom wanted to be a perfect host for her sister, and Mia delighted in the attention and efforts she provided. The sisters enjoyed going shopping to pick out fabrics and patterns so Mother could sew new clothes for Mia to take back to Holland.

Aside from an occasional day of sightseeing, most of their time was spent just being together under one roof, getting reacquainted by filling in what had happened during their time apart. The sunny summer days and the longer evenings provided many opportunities for relaxed conversation.

Little Dommy had just turned two a few months before Tante Mia's arrival. She had a lot of catching up to do with her five nieces and young nephew. There was very little of her time that was not filled with attention.

Communicating was a bit of a challenge. Tante Mia only spoke Dutch. We still understood everything our parents said in Dutch, but like my sisters and little brother, our responses were nearly always in English. Sad in some ways, Dad and Mom were slowly moving in that direction as well. Having Tante Mia with us forced us to turn up the Dutch and dial back the English.

Even today, most of us still use Dutch words when referring to items and chores in the kitchen: spoons, fork, and knives (*lepels, vorken, and messen*), wash or dry (*wassen of droog*). Simple sayings might be responded to in our first language, like when we were sick: I have a headache (*Ik heb een hoofdpijn*), or good night (*lekker slapen*). Then there is one of my children's favorite, dishrag (*vadoek*).

My sisters' Dutch accents, quite obvious to hear when listening to the old tape recording, by now had all vanished. When we spoke Dutch, it was with an American accent. It was apparent to my aunt that my mother spoke Dutch with an accent. Mom tried hard to get rid of her accent, but ended up with two. Whether she spoke in Dutch or in English, she had a slight accent. That was inevitable.

Dad and Mom knew how important it was for them to go back to the Netherlands in the very near future. Before Mia flew back to Holland, they promised they would begin to save for their return trip. Twelve years was a long time apart from their family and friends.

There were many tears when Mia left, but also the reassurance that her sister and brother-in-law would see her again soon. That made the farewell a little less painful. It would still take a couple of years to save the money, but they would make the journey at their earliest opportunity.

Chapter 15

Welcome Back to Holland

During the next few years, our family went through many changes. Ineke graduated college, moved back home, and began teaching at a rural grade school. Gert was married and living with her husband at a military base in Germany. Sue was a flight attendant stationed in Los Angeles, California. Traci was working in a medical office in Salem and was planning to marry her boyfriend. I was getting ready for my junior year of high school, while four-year-old Dommy was and getting ready for preschool.

With Dommy old enough to be taken care of by his older sisters at home, it was time for Dad and Mom to plan their return trip to Holland.

Ineke was the first member of the family to make her way back to Holland. After completing her first full year of teaching, she had saved enough money for a two-week vacation in Europe. Traveling with her best friend, her first stop was the Netherlands. Her visit added to the relatives' excitement, anticipating the return trip Dad and Mom were planning.

Having been prudent with their finances, my folks were finally able to purchase airline tickets to Holland in 1970. They were scheduled to leave in July, just after Ineke's return. With Gert now living in Germany, they saw this an even greater incentive to fly to Europe.

They landed in Frankfort, Germany, at the Rhein-Main-Flughafen International Airport. Gert and her husband were there to greet them and take them to their small apartment close to the Army base.

The young couple shared a two-story brownstone building that had been converted into three separate apartments. Mom and Dad were happy to stay with Gert, and looked forward to the day trips planned for their visit.

Gert later shared her thoughts and observations of our Dad during their visit. "This was the first time since his liberation that Dad had set foot in Germany. There was a young woman living with her father just above where we lived. Dad seemed very uncomfortable with our surroundings and appeared agitated. I saw him looking at the men and women his age, or older, and wondered out loud what they were doing during the war. He had a hard time letting go of his suspicions and his fears. By the time we took Mom and Dad to the train station for their trip to Holland, Dad was more than ready to go."

I remembered a similar experience I had with Dad many years later at a family reunion in Pasco. My husband and I were introduced to a really nice couple who became part of our circle of friends. We had only been in Pasco two or three years when we met them through mutual friends. He was an immigrant from Germany, a very muscular, bodybuilding guy with an obvious German accent when he spoke, and she was a beautiful, all-American woman. We really enjoyed their company.

This particular incident occurred during our first family reunion at our place, just after we put the swimming pool in the back yard. We invited several of our friends over to meet the family, including our German friend and his wife.

Several of us were standing outside next to the keg of beer when I asked Mom and Dad to join us so I could introduce them to our friends.

Warm greetings were exchanged, but as Dad shook our German friend's hand he held it just a second or two too longer, and had a quizzical look on his face. With little warning, Dad began to ask a few probing questions. "So, how long have you been living in the States? And, how old are you now? What part of Germany are you from? I was in Germany during the war. What did your father do during the war? He would be about my age or so I think?"

Our friend replied with simple answers. I knew where Dad was going with this line of questions, and I was getting concerned for our friend, and for Dad. So, I stayed close to both of them and quickly steered the conversation in a new direction, before it got even more obvious and uncomfortable. I knew what Dad was after, and I did not want my friend to have to submit to this intrusive line of questions.

Gert and I understood that Dad was unable to resolve his deeply-held reservations about Germans in his age group. He did admit that not all of the Germans were responsible for the Holocaust he endured. He also said that he forgave those who abused him. "As Christians," Dad would say, "we are all called to forgive."

Much like citizens who lived in countries under occupation, each household in Germany had their own A, B, or C, choice to make during the war. Those who chose to resist their Nazis government suffered horribly too. Many were killed or sent to concentration camps to live or die there. But it was impossible for our father to separate his suspicions of any of the older Germans still alive. It made it difficult for him to know who he could trust, just like the countryman in Holland who had collaborated with the enemy.

It is important for me to say that Dad would never have blamed his suffering on the German people who were born after the war ended. So many of them are burdened with their own crosses to bear. There are still stories of adults in Germany who find out many years later that their parents or grandparents were active members of the Third Reich, with notorious résumés. Many of them have gone on to repair and rebuild the damage done by their ancestors.

"Never Forget" kept Dad bound to his past suffering.

*

It was good to have had three or four days in Germany to recover from their long trip and the nine-hour time change. Dad and Mom knew that once they got to Vlaardingen, they would need every ounce of energy to keep up with the itinerary they were hoping to complete on this momentous occasion.

They weren't sure what to expect, seeing their brothers and sisters and her father again. The nieces and nephews that they knew as little children were now grown up and tall. There were new brothers- or sisters-in-law to meet, and more children. It was a lot to think about on the train trip from Gert's place.

As the story goes, they neared the train station and could see the large crowd waiting for the arriving passengers. It was difficult to contain their emotions, knowing that they would reunite soon with loved ones.

Once they arrived, my folks were able to pick out their relatives and friends holding up their arms and waving, each hoping to be the first to spot their visitors from America. Some carried their small children on their shoulders to get a better look. Still others carried flowers to present to their arriving relatives. Both the van Lith and Bruggeman families were gathered together. Many of them knew each other, having lived in Vlaardingen for many years.

Dad was 50 years old and Mom was 45 when they returned to the "old country." They were about to step off the train and into the arms of so many waiting for them. Pictures in the old photo album capture the intimate portrait of this event, and provide an additional dimension to what our parents were really experiencing.

Dad, wearing one of his favorite hats, is hugging one, two, or three individuals at a time. Mom was quickly presented with flowers, but they did not prevent her from the many hugs and kisses coming her way. There were smiles and laughter on every face photographed during this warm reunion.

In addition to family members in the crowd, their dear friends, Puck, Jan, Heni, and Gil were waiting for their turn. They would not have to wait long before the hugs and kisses were shared with them.

Mom and Dad had contacted some of the relatives ahead of time to let them know what they wanted to do during their visit. Each side of the family helped to arrange some of their time and activities, so before leaving the station to go to their first relative's home, everyone seemed to know when and where they would next have a chance to spend time with Mienus and Suze.

Every day was filled with someone or some place to see, which kept them very busy.

True to Dutch formalities, most of these gatherings consisted of tea, cookies, and chocolates. However, there were a few, how shall I say………. rowdy, drinking, dancing, singing *Lang Zal Ze Leven*-type of parties too. What can I say? Our family is Dutch, and no matter what time of the day it is, there is always someone or something to celebrate.

After leaving the train station, one of the first things they did was to take a quick trip to the *Visbank* (Fish Bank), by the canal in Vlaardingen. Until 1949, this fish market, located in the center of the town, was the gathering place for those who wanted to buy one of the many fresh catches of the day. Now a landmark in Vlaardingen, it is a small, open market where you can still buy some fresh fish, a drink, and a sandwich, along with fresh cut flowers. It's a comfortable venue to sit outdoors and just rest a bit.

Dad struck a familiar pose for the camera at the Visbank. He was looking straight up toward the sky with his mouth wide open, ready to place into his mouth one of his favorite things to eat, a nice and juicy, raw herring. With him were a few of his relative, holding their herrings and posing for the camera too, so as to not be outdone by their guest.

Other places they visited include: the Bruggeman Bakery, where Mom grew up; the railroad tracks and ground where the van Lith home once stood; the Catholic Church, with all its memories; the gravesites of their parents; and the Maas Waterway in Rotterdam, where Dad worked before the war and almost blew up. They would also take pictures at the City Hall, where Dad was first jailed, where he worked as police officer, and where he and Suze had their civil marriage performed and recorded.

Mom had ambivalent feelings the day she planned for her first visit with her father. He was 80 years old now, and living in a retirement center. Upon entered her father's room, she saw him sitting in his easy chair with the expected cigar held between his fingers.

Mother told us that our Opa Bruggeman woke up in the morning, lit a cigar, and turned the light off at night when the last cigar of his day was consumed. He smoked cigars all day long.

When she was born, Suze's mother was 41 years old, and her father 36. Both of them worked hard running the bakery. As a result, the older kids were left to fend for themselves and to look after their youngest sister.

Mom's relationship with her father was strained. He was not able to provide what she needed from him in her youth: his time, his attention, and the feeling of being loved by him.

Father and daughter were opposites of each other. To more than a few people, Opa Bruggeman came across as stern, authoritarian, and somewhat cold and grumpy. Whereas, Mom was more outgoing, warm, caring, and hospitable to others. None of that seemed to matter during this visit. The man in the room was her father, and she was his daughter, coming to spend time with him after having been apart for many years, with many miles between them.

The tears began building in her eyes at the sight of her father's open arms. Was there a tear in his eye too? They embraced where he sat, and both gave in to what they were feeling. After the moment passed, each had to wipe the tears that had fallen. Mom composed herself quickly, and sat in a chair next to her father and took his hand in hers. Dad sat by her side, paying his respects with a handshake, calling him "Father."

Mother pulled out the pictures she brought with her, of their children, their home, and of vacations the family had taken. She cherished these moments, sharing them with her father. The pride she displayed was evident in the words she used to describe each picture.

Opa did not disappoint her. He likely made comments such as, "My how the children have grown. It looks like you have taken good care of your family, Mienus. And Suze, the children look beautiful and so grown up. Mienus, you finally got your boy, but I think he looks like a Bruggeman, ya Suze?" Dad likely agreed with Opa's assessments.

The conversation was lopsided, with Mom having more to talk about than what her father had to share. But that was about to change. It was time for the morning coffee or tea, with cookies and chocolates.

Just before the tea was brought into the room, Opa had invited a guest to meet his family. In came a very sweet old lady named Johanna (Jo). She walked into the room and sat next to Opa. The staff at the residence had prepared the customary midmorning goodies, and carried them into the room behind her.

Jo turned out to be a special lady in Opa's life. I'm not sure what adjective to use here, but they were "in a relationship," more than just friends.

The family knew that Opa had a special friend, but I'm not sure Mother knew they were an item in the retirement home. What mattered most was that her father seemed to be comfortable in his surroundings, and especially in Jo's company.

Jo was a lovely companion for Opa. Perhaps the warmth and tenderness he was providing his daughter was due, in part, to the loving tenderness that was shown to him by this charming "friend." Sometimes it just takes a special lady!

These moments with her father seemed to melt some of the hurt that she had felt in her youth. Looking back over the years, she came to understand, and said with clarity, "As the saying goes, with age comes wisdom. My father did the best he could with the conditions he was faced with in his life." There are good and bad changes that happen as we progress through life. I look forward to more of that wisdom!

Their return trip to Holland was physically and emotionally exhausting. Both saw that not much had changed as they walked around Vlaardingen. The town looked like they remembered, though some buildings were added, and a few torn down. But, for the most part, Vlaardingen looked the same. However, they both were aware of a change that concerned and saddened them.

Noticeable changes had happened to the people around them, and to the culture in general. The way the people talked about their lives and each other was troubling.

Frequently, conversations among family and friends were filled with complaints about the government intrusion in their lives, a lack of faith in many of the children, and a diminished interest in long-held beliefs. The changing values, morals, and ideals were often mentioned, among many other grievances. So many foreign immigrants moving into Holland from culturally diverse countries was also a hot topic. Apathy was predominate in their exchanges with one another.

There was a sense of surrendering to these changes instead of a strong will to do something about them. The sentiment, and overall conclusion among many was, "good or bad, it is what it is. Out with the old ways, and in with the new, and there's nothing we can do about it!" There was hardly a thought of the consequences that could, and would eventually ensue. "What business is it of mine? Everyone has to figure it out for themselves!" These were the types of remarks often expressed.

It is possible that these problems and attitudes had begun developing many years ago, even before our family emigrated. Perhaps they didn't recognize it at the time, being so busy with their own growing family. Whatever the case may have been, for the last fourteen years, things had changed in Holland. These changes were hard to ignore and difficult to watch.

*

A few of his closest friends from the Resistance were excited to visit Dad. They spent time together in Buchenwald, and were there when the Americans liberated them.

I can only image what went on between them. I wish I knew. It must have been good to look back over the last 25 years as free men, and find out how everyone's lives were turning out. Hopefully each of them had been able to work through the hell that they had lived through, and resolve for themselves why they survived when the vast majority did not.

Dad brought an article that had been written about the 25th Anniversary of the Liberation. The article was run on April 5, 1970 and filled half of the front page of a section of the Salem Statesman Journal Newspaper. It was titled, "Salem Man Recounts the Hell of Buchenwald."

Right in the middle of the article were two 3x5 pictures of Dad. The top picture was a current photo of him at 170+ pounds, standing with his arms behind his back at his waist, looking at the camera. Below that was a photo taken of him just days before leaving Buchenwald for the last time. His posture is the same, but he weighed 125+ pounds, having gained 25-30 pounds from the time the Red Cross found him and cared for him after liberation.

This was the first time Dad's story had been published. Though the story was well written, and certainly given adequate newspaper space, it was more of an outline of the events that began with his first involvement with the Dutch Resistance, his eventual liberation by the Americans, and his return to Holland.

The article generated real interest. A few who felt they were in some way connected to the story called the staff writer to find out how they could get in contact. These requests were passed on to Dad. Still others who recognized him were shocked to find out about this horrific ordeal he had suffered in his past. Many were moved to send him cards and letters of congratulations.

After reading the article to his friends, it was obvious to them that their Resistance brother was still working as a machinist back in Salem. "Mienus, you are still working? You didn't retire then?" one of them asked.

"Of course I am still working. I have a family to support. Don't you still work?"

"Aren't you getting your pension from Stichting 1940-1945? You know about this, don't you?" another questioned him.

"I never heard about this before. What is it that I don't know? How could I know something living so far away?" Dad continued.

"It is called the Extraordinary Pensions Act 1940-1945. We are all receiving a good pension from this Act. I will get you the information you need to get started for your pension too. It offers financial support to those of us who participated in the Resistance against the Germans any time during 1940-1945. We receive this money every month, and when we die, our wives will continue to get some of it too," they told him.

"But I am an American citizen now," Dad said, assuming it made a difference.

"That doesn't matter. You were a Dutch citizen when you were fighting and imprisoned in Buchenwald. Mienus, I am so glad for you now. There is no question in any of our minds that you will be entitled to your pension, too. None of us have to work if we don't want to anymore. We will take you to the Stichting [Foundation] 1940-1945 administration building to have you begin your application. They are the ones to talk to, who handle all the financial part of this Act," a couple of his friends offered.

This reunion quickly turned into a robust celebration. It no doubt lasted a little longer than what was originally intended. Another round of drinks has a tendency to do that. It was time to cheer! Mienus was about to undergo a big change in his life!

Dad was so excited to tell Mom what he just learned. Maybe he would be able to retire too, or at least not have to work so hard if the pension was only enough to supplement what he was currently making. In any event, he knew he had to pursue this extraordinary Pension Act 1940-1945.

This turn of events was unexpected. They both had a lot on their minds near the end of their journey. Their return trip would provide plenty of time to talk about all they had accomplished, things they would have done differently, concerns that they both had, and other topics. Much of it would have to wait until they got home. With both of them mentally spent, it would be important to give each other the time to decompress and discern what all had transpired on their first trip back to Holland.

Mom appreciated her life in America in a new way. It was apparent to her that she was spared some of the unwelcomed changes that had impacted so much of the family in Holland. "When we got back from that trip, I remember feeling like I could breathe easier again, and I was able let go of the tension I was feeling. It was so very good to see everyone, but I have to say, I was ready to come home when we finally did," she said.

Dad seemed happy to be back home too. He brought all the paperwork for his possible pension with him. He filled out the application, provided whatever verification was requested, and sent it back to the Netherlands.

Within nine months, Dad was approved and awarded a healthy pension that he was more than qualified for. This compensation was for the nearly five years that encompassed his involvement in the *Geuzen* Resistance group, including the forced labor he endured in Buchenwald Concentration Camp. The investigation concluded that Dad had suffered lasting damage to his mind and body as a direct result of his imprisonment.

The pension started arriving the following year, and was retroactive from the day of his application months earlier. The income it provided was considerably higher than the wages he made working as a machinist. He continued to work several more months until he decided that he just didn't need or want to anymore. He finally gave notice at work and retired. Dad was almost 52 years old, but added to the severe conditions he endured at the camp, his body was much older.

Retirement and Real Changes

Retirement was a blessing. Everyone was pleased for Dad. He deserved to enjoy life like never before. Mom had some adjustments to make, having her husband home during the day. She hadn't had time to think about what it would be like to have her husband home all the time. They would both need to develop a new normal routine.

Dad took down the "Dressmaking and Alteration" sign at some point. His wife would no longer have to sew for other people if she didn't want to. Maybe he just wanted her to know it wasn't necessary anymore.

They had managed their finances very well over the last fifteen years. In nine years, they managed to pay back the debt they owed to Uncle George for what they had borrowed to get a clear title to their house. There were two cars in the driveway they owned without having borrowed any money. They had no credit cards and were debt free.

Except for the house, everything they ever purchased while raising their family was with cash, and absolutely no credit. If they needed something, they saved the money to pay for it. From what I have observed in my own life, it is still quite common for first generation immigrants to manage their finances this way.

Dad devoted some of his extra time volunteering at the church and with the Knights of Columbus, a Catholic fraternal organization. The "honey-do list" got a little shorter as he completed the expected repairs or redo's around the house that didn't always get done right away.

If Dad wanted to putz around, he would putz. If he wanted to take a nap, he would indulge himself with one. If he felt like going fishing, he would pack some food and coffee and be gone for a few hours.

*

Ineke married in 1970, while Gert was still living in Germany. Sue was still flying for United Airlines, engaged and planning to marry in June 1971. Traci was still working and engaged to her high school sweetheart. They would be wed in August, just a couple months after Sue. Whew!

Dommy and I were the only siblings living at home with our parents. In the fall of 1971, I began my senior year at North Salem High School, and my brother was beginning kindergarten. Let me state the obvious. Our family was going through many changes in a very short amount of time.

We were in the midst of experiencing the normal continuum of growing up, finding our mates, moving away, and planning for the next generation to follow. Unfortunately, not all of us had the same understanding of what the "normal continuum" should look like. It wasn't easy. There was a good deal of stress in our lives, and it had the potential to disrupt our close family.

Before too long, our folks were promoted with new titles. For the rest of their lives, they would be referred to as Opa and Oma, and it gave them great pleasure. Ineke and Lloyd's son, Rick, was born in 1971, and Gert and her husband would bless them two months later with their son, Erick. I wonder if Dad and Mom thought about those wedding vows they promised each other almost 25 years before. A typical blessing given to a newly-married couple asks God to bless them with a long and happy life, where they will live to see their children's children.

Before the birth of their first child, Gert and her husband were on a train from Germany to Holland for her first visit. "This was my first time back in fifteen years. I just remember feeling pretty big with my pregnancy, sitting there in the train. I was excited to show my husband where I came from, and have him meet more of my relatives. We didn't spend too many days though, we only had so much leave we could use, and I knew we would need to take more time off after the baby was born," Gert said.

Mother flew to Germany to be with her daughter in June 1971. She planned to be there well before the due date, so no one worried about her not getting there in time to help when the baby arrived.

As it turned out, Mom had plenty of time to wait with Gert. Her baby was in no hurry to make his entrance into the world. He was quite comfortable staying where he was for another three weeks to grow even bigger.

Mother managed to slip in a quick trip to Holland to see her family for a second visit in less than a year. She knew that she would be able to return quickly if the baby decided to make his entrance, or should I say, exit. Her initial plan was to visit her family after the baby was born, before flying back to the States.

The visit in Holland was much shorter than the previous one, less than a week. But in that time she did manage to see who she wanted, and do what she wanted, all the while staying close to a phone, just in case Gert should call.

Finally, on July 21, Erick was born at the military hospital, weighing just under 11lbs. Let's just say, this was not an easy birth. From what I was told, my sister was a real trouper, and she deserves a medal for her sacrifice.

Mom spent a few more days helping Gert after Erick was born. She wanted to spend more time, but none of them could have predicted such a delay in the birth. It was time she got back to her husband,

Dommy, and me. We had been apart for nearly five weeks, and were anxious to have her home again. Gert would have to manage without her.

Three months later, on October 2, 1971, Dad and Mom celebrated their 25th wedding anniversary. Gert's little family returned to Oregon a few weeks before. Sue, now living in Portland Oregon, was but an hour's drive away. With the whole family living in such close proximity, we were all able to gather together for this important occasion.

After guests arrived, Dad and Mom renewed their wedding vows in the comfort of their own home, with Father John officiating. This was a happy time for all of us. It was a new beginning, a next phase, another chapter in the lives of our parents and their grown children.

Now retired, my folks traveled more frequently. They went to Hawaii, enjoyed time at the Oregon coast, and bought their first motorhome to spend more time enjoying the wonderful campgrounds in the Pacific Northwest. Dommy went with them for many of their trips, or stayed at home with me when they flew somewhere for several days.

I was about to experience some new adventures of my own, and make some important decision in my life, but that part of the story will have to wait for now!

Chapter 16

Some Serious Fishing

Dad was exploring a variety of activities he never had time for when he was working. Fishing seemed to be an activity he was ready to embrace. This worked nicely for Mom, since she had been encouraging him to develop his own interests outside of the home. Like most couples, navigating retirement can be an interesting challenge for both.

Dad was not an avid fisherman. You know, the kind with the boat and all the accoutrements. But don't underestimate him. He thought of himself as a serious fisherman, and that was good enough.

To those of us who observed him, Dad was more of the "I'll be down by the water to throw a lure out to see what I can catch," kind of a guy. It was a simple activity that he enjoyed taking up part of his day. Dommy would occasionally accompany him for a father/son outing.

One of his favorite places to fish was at Detroit Dam, which was located on the Santiam River, 40-some miles east of Salem. It took him just under an hour to drive there, but that never bothered him. He enjoyed the beautiful drive.

Depending on the time of year, Dad either fished above the dam or below it. On one particular fishing trip in early summer, he went to fish below the dam.

It was mid-morning when he cast his first lure out into the river. He was there just a short time when he began to feel lightheaded, a little out of breath, and sweaty. He attributed these symptoms to the slow hike to his fishing hole, and the nice warm weather he was enjoying.

Suddenly Dad began to experience severe chest pain, and an ominous feeling overpowered him. His heart began to pound and fear gripped him. His neck was sore and one of his arms began to hurt. The only thing Mienus could think to do was to sit on a rock by the river and wait to see what happen next. "Just rest and wait it out. It will stop soon," he thought.

Within the hour, the severe pain began to subside, and his heart rate slowed down some as well. He could breathe easier as long as he didn't exert himself. For a moment he felt better and even considered casting his lure into the river a second time. Still, it was hard to shake that ominous feeling that had come out of nowhere.

Coming to his senses, he decided it was time to drive home. This was not going to be a good day to fish. He was pretty sure what had happened, but thought, "Perhaps the worst is over, I'm sure I'll be ok."

"That was a short fishing trip!" Mom said when her husband came home.

"The fish weren't biting! What's for lunch?" he said deceptively.

We were always aware that Dad had an enlarged heart due to the hard labor in Buchenwald. But that was just part of his problem. He was a big fan of meat and potatoes with lots of gravy. No matter what we ate at dinnertime, he had a habit of combining or layer his food, then mound it to a peak in the center of his plate. We'd watched as he drizzled the first big helping of whatever gravy was prepared before he began to eat. It was always quite a production.

On many occasions, mother would cook Dutch meals for us. One of these meals included potatoes and carrots cooked in the same pot, and after draining the water, she would mash it all together with just enough salt and pepper to flavor. She frequently served this dish with strips of bacon on the side.

As usual, Dad would combine the bacon strips into the mashed vegetables, and build the food mountain on his plate. Since bacon only produces bacon grease, and not gravy, he was content to drizzle tablespoons of the grease right from the frying pan onto his food.

Dad's weight was never an issue, but his cholesterol level must have been through the roof. The years of smoking all those unfiltered Camel cigarettes didn't help matters either. It was never "if," but "when" he was going to have a heart attack. He was almost 54 years old when he finally suffered his first major heart attack.

"What's the matter with you, Mienus? You don't look like you feel well, and you didn't get much sun on your face either. You look a little pale," Mom said to Dad after he woke from an afternoon nap on the couch.

Thinking about what happened earlier in the day, it became obvious that he should at least tell his wife what happened that morning.

"Well, to tell you the truth, I don't feel so good. I had to stop fishing for a while and sit down on a rock. My heart was kind of hurting me, and I got a little sweaty from it beating too fast. But after about an hour or so, I felt a little better and I could breathe better too. I decided it was time to go home and rest."

"What!? That's it, Mienus. Get up, and get in the car. I'm taking you to the hospital now," Mom ordered. "And there will be no ifs, ands, or buts about it. Now get going," she added.

I loved that about Mom, taking charge of Dad when he was in the wrong. Dad did not resist her one bit that afternoon. That alone made Suze realize the urgency.

The staff of the emergency room at the Salem Hospital took Dad back to a room, and immediately hooked him up to oxygen. After his vital signs were taken, they quickly placed the twelve lead EKG on him, poked him with an IV, drew vials of blood, took a chest x-ray, and continued following the advance cardiac life support (ACLS) protocol. Meds were given to keep him alive and help him remain calm and comfortable while waiting for a definitive diagnosis.

After the findings, he was rushed into an ambulance already waiting to transport him to a large medical facility in Portland, Oregon. The hospital was notified of his condition, and the medical staff in Portland would be ready for him in their ER. It took less than two hours, from the time they left their house, to when Dad was headed to Portland. Mom would later follow him there in her own car.

That morning at the dam, Dad had suffered a major heart attack. Part of his heart was permanently damaged. The operating room staff in the Portland hospital was already setting up a sterile room for surgery, in anticipation of his arrival.

Mom was informed about her husband's condition, and was assured that he would be in the best hospital for the coronary artery by-pass surgery he needed right away. She was instructed to go home, pack a bag for herself and her husband, and plan for him to be in the coronary unit of the hospital for approximately seven to ten days. There would be someone at the hospital to assist her with housing throughout Mienus' stay.

Angioplasty with coronary stent placements were not available in 1974. That technology and procedure would not be introduced to the medical community until 1977. Dad would have to undergo coronary by-pass surgery to keep him alive.

Mother began making phone calls to alert the rest of the family of Dad's heart attack and treatment. The siblings reached out to each other for support, and then notified family friends, requesting prayers for a successful surgery, quick recovery, and strength for Mom.

The surgery lasted several hours, and included more than one artery to bypass. They harvested a section of artery from both of Dad's legs, and used them to circumvent the blocked segments of the affected arteries. The procedure was a success, but his recovery was tenuous.

The day after his surgery, Dad suffered a major setback when his heart developed a potentially fatal dysrhythmia.

Mother shared, "I was sitting next to him that morning, and everything seemed to be going well for Dad. We had just finished saying a few words to each other when he made an unexpected noise and suddenly his eye closed. Immediately those machines he was hooked up to started to beep real loud. Several of the nurses came rushing in, and then someone else came in quickly with yet another machine. I was asked to leave the room so they could help your dad. It looked bad. I sat in a chair outside of the room and someone from the hospital came to sit with me.

"I had a strange feeling when all those people rushed in to help your father. I was at peace during the whole hour or so that they worked on him. I was praying for his recovery, but also for me to accept whatever would happened to him."

Mother paused for a moment and said, "A priest had come to see your Dad just before his surgery. He came to administer the sacrament of the sick. And do you know what your father said right after he received it?"

"I bet I can guess, knowing Dad, but you tell me," I answered.

"I could tell he was very nervous before the priest arrived. But after he was anointed and forgiven, your Dad seemed to calm right down, and even joked with the priest. He said, 'Whatever happens now, it doesn't matter, because I am clean as a whistle on the inside, thanks to you!'"

As she talked about Dad's close call after the surgery, I was convinced that the sacramental intercession had a profound effect on both of them. God's grace strengthened and blessed them to surrender their fear and actually experience peace, regardless of the outcome.

Once again, it was not Dad's time to die. Not only did he survive his heart attack, he also survived the otherwise fatal heart dysrhythmia, thanks to the skilled interventions provided him in the coronary care unit.

*

A "wake-up call" or "ah-ha moment," is an experience many of us have when we, or someone we love, suffers an illness or accident that is life threatening. An event like this can amplify an awareness of our mortality, and often triggers a kind of "fight or flight" syndrome within us. You either want to run away from the reality of the event, or do something about it.

For better or for worse, a health crisis changes things. Hopefully the experience will lead us in a positive direction and turn us toward a new and better path to follow in our lives. For many, it provides opportunities that otherwise would never have been presented in any other way, and be exactly what was needed to help us find greater happiness and peace.

Most are familiar with the proverbial saying, "When life gives you lemons, make lemonade!" In other words, if life gives you something bitter, turn it to something sweet. But be prepared! It may require real sacrifices and change to figure out how to make sweet, what otherwise tastes bitter. Even so, there's a very good chance for this unpleasant experience to end up a great blessing in disguise! I love lemonade!

*

When Dad suffered his heart attack, he and Mom both experienced a wake-up call. Together, and separately, each examine their lives and chose to refocus on the things that mattered the most to them: their faith, their family, and their future.

Dad and Mom made positive changes in their physical, mental, and spiritual lives. Their young son, Dommy, was so worried that his father was going to die that he pleaded with our father to quit smoking. Dad needed no more convincing. He began the process to stop smoking those non-filtered cigarettes, the ones that stunk up the car, the home, the clothes, and everything else. It didn't take too long before he overcame his addiction.

It was not easy for Dad to quit his decades-long habit. Occasionally he would sneak a filtered cigarette and smoke it where no one could see. This was a far cry from his full addiction. When he was caught smoking in his shed, Dad's version of a man cave, he always said that it was his "last one." It would take just a wee bit longer before we stopped finding hidden cigarettes in the oddest places.

In addition to becoming a non-smoker, Dad and Mom made healthier choices with regard to their physical fitness and diet. They were willing to do what they could to improve their health which included routine doctor visits.

Once Dad had fully recovered, the two of them decided to increase their travels. They traveled on cruised ships often, sometimes three or four times per year. They got to see many interesting places around the world. In addition, they managed a few more trips to Holland as well.

Some of the relatives in the old country decided it was the right time to visit their distant relatives in Oregon and Washington. Mark and I always planned a trip down the Columbia Gorge to visit whoever made the long journey from Holland. There were a number of times that my folks brought their guests to see us in Pasco for a few days too. That was a treat.

Mom and Dad were wonderful hosts, and very generous to their family. As long as they were able, they went out of their way to show them some of the many wonderful things to see and do in the Pacific Northwest. Their generosity even included taking cruises with some of them, something their siblings would otherwise never have been able to experience.

Both pursued an even greater involvement with their faith community. Having already received many healings from God, and aided by the prayers of the faithful, they were inspired to do the same for others.

They nurtured this calling by getting involved with a healing ministry at the Shalom Center in Mt. Angel, Oregon. At this retreat center, individuals seeking physical or spiritual healing, could come for prayers. Many were blessed with one form of healing or another, and it was always Christ-centric in nature, giving God the credit for their healing through the prayers of others.

Mom was a bit more involved with this ministry, but Dad was content to support this work with his presence and prayers. Witnessing the Good Lord's healing power provided them a renewed purpose. It was evident to those who knew our parents, just how much their faith had multiplied.

In 1974, my folks purchased a two-acre piece of property in the southeast hills of Salem. It was a new development that had a beautiful vista of several of the mountains scattered across the Cascade Mountain range of Central Oregon and Washington, along with the miles of hills and farmland stretching between them. It was not long before they began planning the home that would be theirs for the rest of their retirement years.

Dad was the general contractor for the project. A draftsman drew up the blueprint that Dad had drawn by hand, and Dad was confident in his ability to make sure everything was done correctly. There was a lot of excitement during the construction, some good, and some not-so-good.

In the summer of 1975, the house on 16th Street sold. In the agreement, my folks and Dommy would be able to live in their home and pay rent until the new house was completed four months later. The old, remodeled house had been home to us for roughly 18 years. Though we were all happy for Mom and Dad, it felt strange going to visit them in a new place.

After Dad's retirement and subsequent heart attack, I really believe that our parents enjoyed the most fulfilling times during their 50's and 60's, and a bit beyond. I think my siblings would agree with me.

*

It was a bittersweet time for Mom. The joy of moving into a beautiful new house built on land with such a stunning view, was overshadowed by the death of her father, Albertus Bruggeman. He passed away quietly on October 16, 1975. He was one month shy of his 86th birthday.

There was no envelope with the black border to arrive two weeks later, like the ones delivered in the early years. That practice was phased out when international phone calls became less costly. Mom received a call from her sister Mia, with the sad news of their father's death.

As often as she was could, mother continued her practice of attending the 12:05pm Mass at St. Joe's. The day after my Opa died, I join her for the mid-day service. I could tell she was trying hard not to show too much emotion. There was a sweet smile on her face when I scooted in next to her in the pew. "Thank you for being with me. I appreciate it very much," she said.

"I happened to get off early from work today. I figured you might be here today, so I decided I would join you at Mass to pray for Opa," I explained. She didn't say anything after that until Mass was over.

Mom invited me over for lunch. Dad was not at there at the time. Several things still needed to be done at the construction site.

Our conversation was light as we ate. I waited for her to lead the conversation toward what she was more comfortable talking about. During the usual afternoon tea and chocolates, the conversation made evident the obvious grief she was feeling.

"I am so grateful that Mienus and I took Dommy to Holland earlier this year. Opa got to meet your brother, and I got to see my father for the last time," she began. She went on to refer to the childhood concerns she had about her father, while recalling her own inner healing through the prayers at the Shalom Center in Mt Angel. During the majority of her life, the bitterness and resentment she suffered, thinking she had been an unwanted child, were replaced with love and forgiveness.

"It's not worth holding onto the past like I had done for so many years. I have a better understanding of my father, and know in my heart that he did love me, and did the best he could," she reiterated. "Now that he is gone, I pray that he can rest in peace, and somehow know how much I love him."

"I hope so too, Mom, but I'm pretty sure he knows," I returned.

After a moment, I said, "Mom, I've never grieved the loss of a loved one before. Are you able to share what it is like, now that both of your parents are gone, if you can? I'm trying to image what that will be like, you know, several years from now."

"I will tell you. I have a clear understanding that I am the oldest person in my family, the one I share with your father. There is no one left for me to call Father or Mother anymore, here on Earth. It's a strange feeling, and a bit of a shock. Dad and I have only our children and grandchildren left now. I'm feeling a new sense of responsibility, being at the top of our family. I knew at some point that it would be this way, but suddenly I feel old, and I am only 50. It's probably normal to feel this way, but I do miss my Mother and Father," she shared from her heart.

I never forgot that conversation. What new responsibilities was she referring to? I knew it was something for me to hear and figure out on my own, when I am where she is now. Someday, I will be the oldest in the line I share with my husband.

*

Was Mom and Dad's marriage perfect? No. But now it was a time of new discovery for both of them. It was a time to explore new things, and it was a time to relax. It was a second chance to hold new babies, play with children, and a time to hand them back. It was a time to be tested, and a time to overcome. It was a time to think for themselves, and not be bothered. It was a time to "Hang Loose," as mother would say too often, and a time to build up those they raised. It was a time to grow even stronger in their faith, and a time to discern where God was leading them now. It was a time to look ahead and enjoy life, and to not look back too long and be troubled. And, it was a time to remember, and "Never Forget!"

Chapter 17

Keeping the Memory Alive

" 'Never again,' says survivor of Buchenwald."

That was the heading for another Salem Oregon newspaper article about Dad, written by Claire Martin, published in the Capital Journal on Thursday, April 20, 1978. This article was published a day after a four-part television documentary series called "Holocaust" had ended.

The article begins, "Dominic van Lith still has nightmares about the four years he spent as a prisoner in Buchenwald concentration camp." The picture of Dad that accompanied the article shows him sitting at the dining room table, discussing his ordeal with the author of the article. He can be seen sharing some of his old photos that were taken in the camp just after liberation.

As I quote Dad's own words from this article, I want to point out that 32 years had gone by since these events happened. He didn't always get the small details exactly right when relying on his memories alone. Slight variations in distances, dates, and other numerical facts may be found from what I discovered through my research.

Dad was telling his story through the questions asked of him, and I am confident that there were no exaggerations in the commentary. The words below were his responses to questions given by the interviewer:

> *When the Germans captured the Netherlands, they were our enemies. So we fought back. We sabotaged, used espionage, and began the underground, one of the first.*

> *I got captured at the place where I worked [as a machinist]. They caught us when we were going to blow it up. Eighteen of us were shot. That was February 1941. First I was sent to prison in Scheveningen, in the Netherlands by The Hague, from February to April 9.*

> *They didn't say anything. They [the German officers] just put us on a train, and we ended up in Buchenwald, eight miles from Weimar [Germany]. There were 160 of us, all Dutch people. They crowded us into the trains. The officers were really as cold, as in "Holocaust" [the documentary just aired on national TV]. They just took orders, didn't ask what was right or wrong. They just took orders.*

> *How can you resist with a machine gun at your throat?*

> *We didn't know we were being taken to a concentration camp. We hadn't even heard any rumors of camps, but that was at the beginning of the war. We didn't know until we came in the camp and saw people in striped uniforms. Then it was obvious.*

Dad went on to talk about life in Buchenwald. He said that for the first two years he worked in a stone quarry where he was told to carry heavy rocks, sand, and bricks to help in building the large factory and other buildings. After the factory was built, he then was forced to work the laborious hours as a machinist for the Germans.

> *It saved my life, working as a machinist. It wasn't as hard and rough as the other jobs.*

Prisoners were kept alive for the kind of work they were able to provide to the Nazi's war effort. As a skilled machinist, his life had some value. If you were unable to do your job, you would be dead in no time.

> *You got up at 4 or 5 in the morning and you got one cup of coffee - what was called coffee - what we called surrogate, fake coffee. Black junk. Nothing to eat.*

You worked until the sun set, until 6 or 8 at night. You got one piece of bread when you came home, about two inches thick, and a bowl of thin soup - if you'd call it soup. If you were lucky, you saved your bread to have with your morning coffee.

When it came to food in the camps, if a prisoner stole someone's food, he could be clubbed to death by the other prisoners. That was considered tantamount to killing the prisoner whose bread was taken.

Many people died of starvation. He went into the camp a normal weight for someone 5' 11," but weighed between 90-95lbs when he was liberated.

Many people took their own lives there. A married man could stay for three years, and when he began worrying about his children and his wife and home, that would be the end of it. He'd be gone in two weeks.

I was young - 20 when they took me - 25 when I came out. I wasn't married, so I had nobody to worry about, to take care of. I had no wife. I had the will to live. I thought I was too young to die.

This article goes on to say that Buchenwald was liberated on April 11, 1945. Of the original 160+ Dutch Resistance fighters arrested and sent to Buchenwald, "perhaps 30 survived."

Nobody can understand, unless they had been there. I tried to forget the whole thing, but no, it's wrong. You cannot close your eyes to these things. You must try to see that it never happens again.

*

To commemorate the 40th anniversary of the end of WWII, the Salem Statesman-Journal newspaper decided to run an article each day for one week under the heading, "Days of Remembrance," for the victims of the Holocaust. The article that appeared in the paper on April 17, 1985, by Gary Panetta, a writer for the newspaper, was titled, "Buchenwald survivor recalls horror and liberation."

More than 40 years had gone by since Buchenwald was liberated. The article quotes Dad saying, "I am glad to be alive. My Creator who put me on this earth simply had decided it was not my time to go."

The commentary goes on to tell the story of Dad's involvements in the underground, his arrest, and his imprisonment in Holland and Buchenwald. Like other write-ups, Dad talked about the conditions in the camp, the struggles to survive, and his eventual liberation. He shared his pictures with the newspaper writer, just like he did seven years earlier.

The story is the same as before, and it includes the family's immigration to America. But this time the picture that accompanied the article was of Mienus proudly holding up a neatly framed silver cross medal attached to a colorful striped fabric ribbon above it.

To commemorate his role in the Dutch Resistance, the queen of Holland awarded and sent Dad the Resistance Cross, given only to those who can be verified as having been involved in and sacrificed for the Resistance during WWII. His medal, along with the paperwork accompanying it, arrived on Sept, 16 1981, having finally located him residing in Salem, Oregon.

This was an incredible moment for Dad. I remember him saying that, "I was never forgotten by the Dutch people. Even now, when I am an American, I was not forgotten." This was a high honor, and he was proud to be a recipient of this award.

The stripes on the fabric attached to the cross was explained in the article. "The black symbolizes the lives lost to the Nazis, the orange is the color of the royal family, and the red white and blue are the colors of the Dutch flag. Engraved on the medal cross was a line from the sixth verse of the Dutch National Anthem: "To drive away Tyranny."

Dad displayed his medal in the living room of his house. He said that it is there, "as a reminder of the past so I will never forget what happened in the Second World War, and the terrible things that were done."

*

"Resistance Fighter Lauds Dutch"

A guest opinion written for the Statesman Journal, Salem, Oregon

By Dominicus van Lith

Date: late 1980's

I agree wholeheartedly with the Nov. 12 letter by [name withheld] of Salem, who wrote about the guest opinion by social studies teacher [name withheld].

[The teacher's] opinion said, "If the Dutch people had been like the Danes, and had had the courage to protest, Anne Frank and many others might not have died."

What an insult to the Dutch people to insinuate or even think that they allowed the Nazis to overrun their neutral little country and kill millions of Jews without resistance.

Let me tell you a little something about the Resistance. I was one of the original Resistance fighters in Holland. At the age of 19, I did everything in my power to sabotage the German efforts to turn our Dutch factories and shipyards into weapons against our innocent people.

My friends and co-conspirators were quite successful for a while, until one day the Gestapo captured one of our fighters. Torture produced names, and it was not long before there was a pounding knock on our front door. I was taken to prison, along with many of my fellow Resistance fighters. [Note: Dad was captured in the shipyards in Rotterdam. His family received the soldiers' knock on the front door, looking for him.]

I will never forget the night fifteen of my friends were allowed to say goodbye to the rest of us. The next morning they were taken to a lonely stretch of beach and executed as a notice to the Dutch people that further resistance would be useless. [Note: Eighteen men died in the dunes by the sea, and was carried out immediately after the letter from Hans Lammers, the German Rijksminister in Berlin arrived on the afternoon of 3/13/1941.]

I was sent to Buchenwald for the next four years. I was forced to labor for the Germans from dawn to dusk for little food and filthy water. One by one, my friends were hanged after being picked out of the bunch at random, or they starved and lost the will to live, or they hurled themselves against electric fences, thereby ending the nightmare quickly.

When the Americans came to liberate us, I weighed [roughly] 90 pounds. And then there were the other brave Dutch citizens who endured the German Occupation. What would [this teacher] have done had she lived in Rotterdam during those first four days? The Nazis bombed the city and the harbor for days until there was nearly nothing left. They wiped out the tiny Dutch Navy, Air Force, and Army in four days.

And where was there to run away to? One of the Dutch borders is the North Sea, another Belgium, which was occupied by the Germans as well, and the third border is Germany.

The Danish people had a great advantage in having Sweden as a neutral and still-free neighbor. How would [this teacher] have reacted if she had been among those poor hungry

Dutch people, women, and children, who ran for the food that the Americans had dropped from planes on the beach?

German soldiers who had been waiting in ambush popped up from their hiding places and mowed down these people with machine guns.

And how brave would she have felt celebrating armistice in the streets of Vlaardingen only to have several Germans who had been hiding in a neighborhood house come out with automatic weapons and start shooting until they either escaped or were killed?

[This teacher] did make one statement in her guest opinion that is true: "When good people do nothing, evil will flourish." That is why I must speak out. There are people who would have you believe that the Holocaust never happened, that millions of Jews were not murdered. These people would have history slide over this un-event and be forgotten.

That will never happen as long as I live, or as long as my children and their children live.

*

In the late 1980's and early 1990's, Dad and Mom received many invitations to speak to middle and high school youth about their extraordinary experiences during WWII. They accepted every invitation they were able to. It was very important to both of them to keep teaching the young people about the Holocaust and the Dutch Occupation. They were the living survivors that could still speak for their generation, with the hope that future generations will not make the same mistakes of the past.

I kept in storage copies of each of the newspaper articles written about Dad, or by him. The last one written by him had the biggest impact on me. I never forgot the last thing he had to say in his article, "That will never happen as long as I live, or as long as my children and their children live."

Mark and I were well into raising our four children when we were in our 30's. It was during those years that Dad and Mom began to tell their stories with details and real purpose. We traveled as often as we could to visit them in Salem, to ask the questions, to listen, learn, and remember.

The seeds were planted, they were watered well, and grew into a historic story to be handed down. I am a second generation survivor speaking to third generation survivors, and placing them on alert. Are you listening Ben, Matt, Tim, Jessica, and all you nieces and nephews? Some day you will be called to tell the story. Never Forget! Long shall you live!

What Happens in Reno

In the spring of 1993, Gert called and had me check my calendar for the weekend of June 18-20. Cousins from Holland were coming to visit the family in Salem that weekend. Our cousin Bert and his wife Els Vredenbregt, along with cousin Dom Vredenbregt (Bert's brother) and his daughter Bianca, were coming to see the family for the first time. It had been 37 years since my cousins Bert and Dom Vredenbregt waved goodbye to us from the ships dock in Rotterdam, and a lot had happened since then.

There was no question about whether we would be there, and were now even more excited knowing that we would meet new relatives. This would be another one of the many eventful trips driving through the Columbia River Gorge. We were not aware at the time just how life-changing it would be.

Father's Day and Mom's birthday fell on the same day that year, Sunday, June 20. Most of the family gathered at their house in Salem, Oregon to celebrate with them, much like we always did. We had just celebrated Mother's Day and Dad's birthday just weeks before. Ironically, these events often fell on the same day too.

Dad had a lot of fun being with his nephews, teasing them as if they were still the young boys he remembered so long ago. The conversations got louder and louder as silly stories were told of childhood memories. We sang the usual "Happy Birthday" song to Mother, and a customary Dutch tune to them both.

With a round of drinks held high for the toast, we sang, *"Lang zal ze leven, lang zal ze leven, lang zal ze leven in de Gloria, in de Gloria, in de Gloria, hieperdepiep, hoera!"*

Just before leaving the party to travel home, we made plans to see my relatives one more time after they enjoyed a few days of sightseeing in Oregon, and a quick trip to Reno, Nevada. It ***was*** a good plan!

*

Early Wednesday morning, June 23, Cousin Dom and my Dad flew from Salem, Oregon to Reno, Nevada for a 24 hour gambling excursion. It was one of those economical flights sponsored by certain hotels and casinos to attract a full load of passengers to patronize one or more of their establishments. In most cases, even with a purchased discounted ticket, you still had to show a certain amount of monetary bills in your pockets before you could even board the plane.

Dad and Mom had fun on similar trips and always looked forward to the next one. Neither of them were big gamblers, but they did enjoy a good game of black jack, and the freebies and discounts that went along with a trip like this.

Ineke's husband was supposed to have gone with Dad that morning, but graciously gave up his seat so our guest from Holland could go with his uncle. It was a unique opportunity for the two Dominicus Marinus' to go and do something fun together.

Having just checked into the hotel, Dad mentioned to his nephew that he felt "kind of tired" and wanted to rest for a few minutes before going into the casino. Just before laying down, he took one of his nitroglycerin pills and placed it under his tongue. His heart condition still caused some pain and fatigue every now and then, and he figured this was a prudent thing to do.

After a short rest, Dad said he felt better. They both went down to join the many other gamblers in the casino.

*

Late in the afternoon on that Wednesday, the phone rang at our home back in Pasco. I had only been home a couple of hours from my RN job working for a new oral surgeon in Kennewick, WA.

"Marja, Traci's on the phone," Mark said, handing it off before going back into the house.

My sister started out as she usually does with her greeting, then quickly lost her composure. She fell apart.

"Mar, Dad is in a hospital in Reno after having a bad heart attack." She broke down in tears.

"Oh my God, what happened? Is he going to be alright," I asked?

"He's unconscious and it doesn't look good."

As the details of what had happened earlier in the day became clear. Numb to whatever else was going on around me, my knees began to buckle. I slid myself down against the house to prevent a fall. Time seemed to stand still during those moments.

We gradually composed ourselves while we both tried to figure out what we should do. Details were minimal, and all of it second or third hand. With my medical background, I told my sister that I would make a phone call down to the hospital. I needed to talk to those in charge of our Dad's care to get some clarity regarding what happened and his current condition. I promised her that I would call Mom and the rest of the family, when I found out what the doctors and nurses had to say.

Holding my forehead in my free hand, tears began to fill my eyes. This was the dreaded phone call that none of us ever wants to receive, and the one nobody is ever ready for. I took a moment to pray after hanging up. "Dear Lord I need you again. Give me strength. I'm not ready for this. What do you want me to do?'

It didn't take long for Mark to figure out what was happening. He came outside to join me on the porch, helped me to my feet, and held me in his arms. I had never received a call like that before. Nothing could have prepared me for the shock of emotions of sadness, anxiousness, and fear that stabbed me in my gut with such force that it prevented me from standing upright by myself. Mark held me tight to prevent me from collapsing to the ground while primal grief flooded my face with tears.

*

The information that was given to us later that day was that Dad had barely placed his first bet on the black jack table when he collapsed onto the floor. It's not difficult for me to imagine what the scene must have looked like before and after the paramedics arrived. In my profession as a registered nurse, I have been involved in medical scenes like that before, just not in a casino. There was no doubt in my mind that among those patrons and casino employees who witnessed the event, or rendered assistance until medical help arrived, this would be the topic of conversation for days afterward.

After my phone call with Dad's nurse, I had a better understanding of the situation. Dad was defibrillated over 20 times at the casino before a life-sustaining cardiac rhythm was established. He was then rushed to the ER at St. Mary's Hospital in downtown Reno in critical condition.

The hospital chaplain had arrived to take care of my cousin, who spoke and understood very little English. They let him stay with Dad for quite some time until it was necessary to get him back to the hotel. It must have been extremely difficult for Dom to finally say goodbye and leave his uncle under these circumstances.

He was driven to the hotel to join the other passengers who had traveled with him on the plane. He would be flying back to Salem the next day, as planned, without his uncle by his side. Cousin Dom was left to figure things out on his own.

After talking with Dad's charge nurse, my next phone call was to Traci. I let her know that if Dad survived the night I would be flying down to be with him. She told me that Mom and our brother, Dominic (now 27), would be flying down too. After we hung up, I called Mom.

Her voice was soft, and I could tell she was just hanging on. I was expecting as much with all that had already transpired that day. She never wanted to burden any of us, but when I told her about my plans to be with her the next day in Reno, she did not try to talk me out of it. It was my decision to make, and her response was, "You should do what you think is best."

"Mom, I will call you tonight or tomorrow morning, and let you know about my flight arrangements. I am so sorry, Mom, for what has happened to Dad. Mark and I, and the kids, will be praying for you and Dad, and the rest of the family. I love you, Mom."

Just after our conversation, I sat down on the kitchen floor and began another wave of primal grief. I let Mark tell the children what was going on. I didn't have the strength for it.

Everything within me told me to go and be with Mom and my brother. My thoughts weighed heavily toward my cousin as well. I wanted to look after him as best I could.

Cousin Dom had just witnessed a traumatic, life-changing experience, having watched the uncle he was named after and loved dearly, collapse in front of him. He would be the only one in the family burdened for the rest of his life with the actual imprint in his mind of what really happened to Mienus van Lith. I just had to go to Reno!

I called the oral surgeon I worked for. "I won't be able to work tomorrow, and the next few days. My father had a major heart attack in Reno, Nevada. He is in critical condition in a CCU at one of the hospitals. I will be flying down with my mother and brother in the morning," I told him. Before ending the conversation, I asked for prayers.

The doctor was very sympathetic and understanding of the situation. "Take as much time as you need, and keep us posted. You and your family will be in our prayers," he offered.

Flight arrangements were made very quickly. I would be taking a very early morning flight to Portland. Mom, Dom, and I planned to meet at the airport and take a midmorning flight to Reno.

I called my brother to let him know that if Dad did not survive the night, I would cancel my flight and plan to drive down with Mark and the kids in a couple of days. We had barely unpacked from our weekend trip to the family reunion. Dom understood and wondered aloud if it would be necessary for them to make the trip to Reno if Dad died.

"Love you, Dom. We will get through this," I said through my grief.

"I love you too," he replied and hung up the phone.

That night, sleep was long in coming and short in duration. The anticipation of what was to come kept me wide awake during those first hours. All I could do was wonder if Dad was able to survive this heart attack or not. I knew what the odds were, and I just wanted to hurry up and get there to see things for myself, and try to be of some support to our mother. I hoped to help her ask the right questions of those in charge of Dad's care, and to fully understand the possible options and outcomes. I was trying to balance my words and actions as a daughter while processing it all as a nurse. It forced me to hold off my own grief.

I reflected on the times my folks and I talked about death. It was just one of many topics that usually revolved around faith and religious matters. It was never a morbid topic for us to discuss, and we never dwelt on it. It was just a matter of fact; we all knew we would experience death someday.

It sounded funny to me, the times Mom said that she was sure she would not die of a heart attack. She'd said, "I just know. That is your Dad's thing." Dad, on the other hand, said in no uncertain terms that, "When I go, I'm just going to turn the lights out!" I knew what he meant when he said it. He would just go…. period… exclamation point! As I laid in bed, I wondered, "Did Dad just dim his light today, giving us enough time to get to him before he flips the light switch off?!"

The long night was finally over. In the morning everything was pushed into high gear. No time to be tired. I called down to the hospital in Reno and talked to the nurse in charge of Dad's care. He had survived the night, and I was about to take an early morning flight to Portland, and then on to Reno with Mom, and brother Dom.

I had a few things packed from the night before, and quickly added what I thought I would need for a few more days. I had no idea what to expect, or how long all this would take. I just knew that I needed to come prepared and keep myself focused for my Mom and Dad's sake.

I could not give in to my own feelings. I put them aside. I had a task to do. Saying goodbye to my children was hard because I knew that they were afraid and in pain as well. None of us had dealt with such matters within our family before. This was all new. When a family member died in Holland, it never felt very personal. They were distant relatives to me. Though I did feel badly for Mom and Dad each time it happened. This time it was very close, very personal, and very different.

Mark drove me to the airport and gave me his usual blessing before I got onto the plane. It was always a cross on my forehead and a kiss goodbye. I told him I would talk to him often and give him as much information as I could as it developed.

"I love you, Mark."

"I love you too, honey." And then we parted.

Dom and our mother were waiting for me at the terminal in Portland. I could tell that she was in a state of manageable shock. Dom was doing his best to provide support to her as she held tight to his arm.

Somehow it seemed fitting that it was just the three of us flying down to be with Dad. Each of the siblings had to decide for themselves where they needed to be. It was not possible for all of us to go. Some were at the Oregon coast for a few days, while another was taking care of our cousin Bert and his wife Els.

Having all of us together would have been a lot for Mom to handle. She relied on Dom for what only he could provide her, and I guess I was there to provide whatever else was needed. I hoped my medical training would be beneficial as well. I wanted to be useful for my dad, my mom, my younger brother, and my cousin Dom.

We didn't have to wait long at the gate before boarding the plane. In less than two hours we landed in Reno. We got our bags and hailed a cab to the hospital.

Dad was taken to St. Mary's Regional Medical Center. Most fitting, I thought. He was in a Catholic hospital, established and run for many decades by Dominican sisters.

We were escorted to the proper wing and greeted by someone at the front desk. Dad's nurse told us that he was on life support, to prepare ourselves for what we would see. She escorted us to Dad's bedside and gave a brief report on what had happened and what was still happening.

Dad was being kept alive by the equipment and medications that he was hooked up to, of that I was very sure. The nurse told us that a neurologist would be coming by to examine him in a few hours, and would provide us with more information regarding his condition.

The three of us gathered around Dad and took turns talking to him through our tears.

Mom pulled herself together somehow, finding strength where there was none before. She could see the gravity of her husband's condition and said, "This is no way for Dad. No, Dad would not want any of this. We have to let him go!"

After 47 years of marriage, Mom knew Dad so well. It was as if she was reading his unconscious mind. Like finishing his sentences, she knew what her Mienus would want. She had a job to do for him, and she gave the impression that she was ready and willing to do what was necessary in order to help him.

Looking at my Papa in his unconscious state, I knew what was going to happen next. "I'm just turning my lights out," I imagined him telling us.

We began our vigil with our love, support, and prayers. We were blessed to spend what time we had with this patriot son, Dutch freedom fighter, survivor, adventurer, loving husband and father, and man of great faith, Dominicus Marinus van Lith.

Mom started giving Dad permission to die. Her words were so spontaneous and so affirming. "Ya, Mienus, you did a good job. You don't have to do anything else any more. You did a good job in your life, and for me and the children! You don't have to do this anymore!" she repeated many times, while she stroked his shiny forehead and brow.

I understood clearly the meaning behind her words. Dad had lived a full and extraordinary life, suffered enough, and now it was all done. It was time to go. Dom and I looked at each other through our tears, knowing we were experiencing the same event together, helpless to change the inevitable outcome. I will never forget those moments.

Since it would still be a few hours before the neurologist could see Dad, Dom and I saw an opportunity to slip away, and make our way back to the airport to meet up with cousin Dom. His flight was scheduled to depart for the return trip to Salem later that day. Before we left, we made sure that Mom was going to be all right alone with Dad.

We arrived about an hour before Cousin Dom's scheduled departure. We waited for him at the terminal gate. This was our first trip to Reno. We were amazed to see all the slot machines in the airport. While waiting for our cousin to arrive, I said to my brother, "Come on Dom. Let's put a quarter in those machines."

We wandered over to the closest slot machine, put in a coin, pulled the lever, and watched as the numbers and symbols spun. Within a few seconds, it stopped spinning and nothing happened, except that we lost our coin to the machine.

"Ok then, I got that out of my system. I don't need to do that again any time soon, I just don't see the point," I said aloud to myself, knowing my brother was listening. "Dad, what did you see in gambling anyway?" I added.

Within the hour, Cousin Dom finally arrived with the other passengers. I spotted him in the distance with his head down, following the others, just going through the motions toward the departing gate.

I ran toward him in the terminal, calling his name. He saw me running toward him. With a puzzled look on his face, he finally recognized me, still in shock from what he witnessed the day before. We embraced and burst into tears. My brother caught up and joined in the grieving.

I thanked him for being with Dad, and said that I was sorry for what he had just gone through. There was dread in his eyes and real unease. Was he feeling some responsibility for what had happened to his uncle? I did not know.

Before my cousin could say anything, I said to him, "This is not your fault, this is the way Papa would have wanted to go. It's ok!" I said it more than once so he would finally comprehend what I was saying to him. "It's ok to be sad and in shock, but it is not your fault. I am glad that you were with him. Dad was not alone. You were with him. It was meant to be this way," I continued.

Cousin Dom was genuinely relieved to see that we were there to give him support and comfort. Our time was very limited, maybe ten minutes was all we had before he boarded the plane to return to Salem. We said goodbye and gave each other one last big hug. I would not see him again. He and Bianca would be heading back to Holland in a couple of days.

Cousin Dom's first trip to see his relatives in America turned out to be quite different from what he no doubt envisioned. Though the first part of his trip was full of love, laughter, and storytelling, it ended with a very sad and traumatic journey, one he would remember for vastly different reasons. He had no way of knowing that it would include a goodbye to a man he loved, the one whose name he was given.

After leaving the airport, we quickly returned to St. Mary's Hospital to join our Mother at Dad's bedside. We'd been gone for less than two hours. It was all happening so fast.

Mom was pensive and composed while she waited for the neurologist. At about 5:00pm, the doctor arrived at Dad's bedside. Mom tried hard to understand the medical lingo the doctor spoke, and to make some sense out of the neurological tests he briefly performed on her husband. These tests were performed for our benefit, to demonstrate just how damaged Dad's brain had become.

Dad did not respond to any attempts by the doctor to cause pain, including a very stiff rub to the mid-sternum, which would normally cause anyone to grimace and pull away. The doctor demonstrated and explained details about Dad's condition. His body was still alive but his brain was dead. The doctor was making that very clear.

The lack of oxygen during Dad's resuscitation in the casino was the cause of his deep coma. I knew that all this information would make it easier for Mom to make that final decision to remove life support. It was only prolonging the inevitable. The three of us clearly understood what would happen next. It was time to help Dad turn his light out to us, so that an even brighter light could lead him toward the next journey he was about to take. Mom had the answers to what she already knew, Dad was gone.

Once the decision was made, we began the necessary phone calls to the rest of the siblings. I shared the neurologist's conclusions, conveyed Mom's decision to withdraw life support, and explained that Dom and I supported her. Though everyone was preparing in their own way for this outcome, it was still very difficult to let loved ones know what was about to happen.

Gert was the only one who had some reservations about the timing of it all. She was struggling with her desire to see Dad one last time before he died. After a brief discussion and a couple more phone exchanges, she made the sacrifice to stay in her home and let Mom do what she had to do for Dad. There was now reconciliation between all of us.

The nurses suggested we leave while they extubate Dad, and let him attempt to breathe on his own. Dom and I took Mom to the cafeteria for a quick bite. We all needed to keep up our strength. Soup, salad, and some tea was about all we could eat. We were gone about a half an hour.

Dad was breathing on his own, without any assistance, though it was labored. His body was working hard. We stayed with him, prayed with him, and said the loving and supportive words we needed and wanted to say. We gave him permission to go. Now we waited for all the medicine in his system keeping him alive to leave his body. He would run to the finish line on his own power.

After a few more hours, I could see that Mom needed to rest, her tank was on empty. This process of dying could take several more hours, or even days, and it was already taking its toll on her. She needed her strength now more than ever.

The hospital had a special building with small apartments for families such as ours, who needed a place to bunk for the night. We graciously accepted their offer since it was very close, only a couple of blocks away, and we did not have reservations to stay any place else. The nursing staff promised to call us if Dad's condition deteriorated further before our planned return in the morning. We wanted to be with him right away, and we could be there within fifteen minutes.

At 1:30am, after a couple of restless hours of almost sleep, the phone rang. I jumped out of bed and ran to pick up the phone before Mom got it. It was the nurse requesting our return to the hospital, as Dad was experiencing a sudden and rapid decline. "You need to come right away, it's going quickly now," his nurse said to me.

"We're coming as quickly as possible with our mother," I replied.

I was determined to commit everything to memory. For whatever reason, I felt it in my gut to do so. This was one of those moments that would be etched in my mind. Dad was about to die. Every detail, as much as possible, was to be observed and preserved for some reason.

*

I had a similar experience before the birth of my fourth child. After having given birth to three sons in less than four years, I had trouble remembering the details of each separate birth experience. What time were they born? What was going on around me? How long was my labor? How much did each weigh? It all got jumbled up over time. It was harder to separate the details.

To prevent that from happening with my fourth child, I was mindful to place the events of this birth into my long term memory: the water breaking at 2:00am, the car ride to the hospital at 3:30, the darkness and the cold outside. I remember the wheelchair ride, the elevator ride, the smells and the sounds down the hallway to my room. I remember almost everything of that labor and delivery, and finally the announcement, "It's a girl!" I wanted and needed to remember this. I did not know at the time that, unfortunately, it would be my last childbirth. Thank God for that memory.

*

We quickly changed and walked together the few blocks to the hospital. Dom and I sandwiched Mom between us, arm in arm, walking as fast as the three of us safely could.

We were anxious to say goodbye one last time to Mienus, husband, and father. We hoped that there might still be a chance for him to hear our words of farewell.

I began to point out things to my brother that could otherwise go unnoticed, in an attempt to help us both remember this moment, and never forget. I pointed out to him our surroundings as we walked, "We should never forget this walk Dom. The cool of the night, the streetlights shining our path, the concrete sidewalk that showed us the way as we walked with our heads down, listening to the sounds of our dewy exhales as we walked briskly back to St. Mary's. We just have to remember this Dom," I said. I knew Mom was listening.

Nobody said much more until we reached the front door of the hospital, only to find them locked. "We need to find the ER doors, these doors are locked for the night, let's hurry," I said.

Mom was anxious and dreadfully tired. The sliding doors of the ER finally opened for us and we quickly followed the directions to the ICU from this unfamiliar entrance.

We wanted to get to Dad in time. We managed to arrive within fifteen minutes of that phone call. Within that time, Dad's heart pumped its last beat, and we missed it within minutes. Dad did what he said he would do, "I'll just turn the light off!" He did it his way.

I was sad and a bit angry that the front entrance doors, the ones we were already familiar with, were locked. It was so much closer to where Dad was. If those doors had only been available, I think we could have made it in time, but we will never know for sure.

I then began to second-guess our decision to leave Dad until morning, but I knew Mom needed some rest. I just had to console myself with the thought that this was the way it was meant to be. Dad would have wanted us to take care of Mom.

"When did it happen? When did he die?" I asked the nurse. "Just a short time ago," she replied. Since we were not there at the exact moment, I asked the nurse to please show me Dad's EKG strip so I could see how and when it happen. I guess only a nurse would think to console herself like that, with an examination of an EKG strip.

She was good to accommodate my request and showed it to me. It did give me comfort. I saw how Dad's heartbeat became slower and slower over a few minutes, and finally stop.......! The IV medicine that had been administered to keep him alive long enough for us to join him, had finally cleared his body.

I knew he had not suffered any pain as he lived his last day and a half. Dad had already suffered enough in his lifetime, far more than anyone should ever have to. He was going to meet Our Lord in heaven soon, of that I was quite sure.

Looking up toward the ceiling, I was hoping that Papa was still in the room watching from above, knowing we rushed back to say goodbye. Talking to Dad in my mind, I said, "Have a glorious journey, and say hello to the family and the other saints in Heaven!"

My mind was flooded with thoughts I had pondered before. What is it like to actually die? Dad was, at this moment in worldly time, experiencing it all. Perhaps he was even at the ER door showing us the way. Though the tears were freely flowing between the three of us, I felt a sense of gratitude. God granted Mienus a peaceful death, and I was blessed to be there to witness it.

What happened next was amazing and miraculous to me.

The nursing staff suggested that we give them a little time to unhook Dad from all the tubing and clean him up a bit before we spent quality time grieving at his bedside. It was also suggested that we go to the cafeteria and get ourselves something warm to drink and collect our thoughts. Just before we left Dad, I made it my task to put his dentures back in his mouth. I wanted us to see him the way he always appeared to us in life, and not to have his face look retracted without his teeth when we got back.

We somberly entered the empty cafeteria and were warmly greeted by a middle-aged woman with a deep accent. We stood there for a moment, then ordered some tea. This woman heard my mother speak a few words to my brother and me and then asked, "Oh, I hear you have an accent, are you German too?"

I was a startled by her words, not knowing how Mom was reacting to her question, or even if the question registered any thoughts or feelings in Mom at that moment at all. Mom had been embarrassed to have an accent. She had worked very hard over the years to reduce it, not wanting to stand out as different from others around her.

I know that both my parents tried hard over the years not to harbor any ill will for the German people as individuals, but Germany was not their favorite country, to say the least. They both believed that they had to forgive their captors, but they would never forget the torture and hardship that they both endured under the Occupation and captivity.

I knew instinctively that this was not the right time or place to be drawing any comparisons to accents. I immediately took the initiative and said, "No, my mother is from Holland, and she just lost her husband, our father, a few minutes ago!" as I gestured to my mother and brother.

This seemed to have made an impression on the woman. With tenderness, she escorted us to a table. Shortly after, she brought us our tea as well as some treats to eat, something we did not order. She was so warm, so very kind, and provided us her very best service. Before we left, she looked at each of us, especially our mother, and gently said in her full German accent, "I am so sorry, so very sorry! *Sorry!* Let me know if there is anything else you might need."

Immediately, without warning, I was blessed with an overwhelming realization. "Oh my God, there it was. I heard it, and felt it. Another miracle. The last act of my father's life was to have his wife, and two of his children, lovingly waited on by a German woman who, with sincerity in her heart, said she was very sorry! Sorry! This was an incredible moment. I was wondering if anyone else in the room had any idea what just happened.

I looked at Dom and quietly asked, "Did you hear and feel what just happened? Do you know what just happened? Dom, the last thing left to happen on the day Dad died was for this German woman to wait on us and say she was very sorry?" I know that this woman was sorry for the loss we were feeling at the death of our loved one, but the meaning went far beyond this moment.

I did not mention it to our mother. It would have been too much for her to grasp at this time. I knew that much. It was for my brother and me to witness and to remember it for another time. It would be shared again at the right time for our Mom and for the rest of the family.

Dom looked at me and thought for a moment about what I said. I was hoping he understood the significance too. He was very pensive. This was a gift of grace, not just surrounding Dad's death, but for the suffering Dad and Mom experienced at the hands of the Nazis so many years ago. This was the final healing moment, the last chapter of Dominicus Marinus van Lith's life on earth. A moment of grace. Freedom!

*

Dad's funeral Mass was celebrated at St. Mary's Catholic Church in Shaw, Oregon. This country parish is located just a few miles from where Dad and Mom built their retirement home. Across the road from the church is a small cemetery where both planned to be buried next to each other when the time came. Dad was laid to rest on June 28, 1993.

Each of the son-in-laws were pallbearers. Included with them was Dad's nephew Bert, who helped to carry his uncle to the gravesite. The symbolic gesture, having a relative from Holland among the men, was most fitting.

Mother leaned heavily on her only son. None of us called him Dommy anymore. We stopped doing that sometime during his late teens. Now 27 years old, he was a strong and handsome man who stood by Mother and took care of her throughout the events of that day, and for the next several years thereafter.

After the reception in the parish meeting hall, the family gathered again at Mom's house to spend more time sharing our memories of Dad. The house was now engulfed with several flower arrangements that had been sent or brought back from the church. Several of the flower arrangements were filled with red, white, and blue flowers, the colors of the U.S. and Dutch flags. Many who sent flowers must have had the same intentions.

It's comforting to look at the pictures that were taken that day. Mother looked so composed, and so very beautiful in her blue blazer and white skirt, with her gray hair nicely arranged. Not surprising though, she always took time to look her best each day.

Many of the photos that where taken show family members smiling and laughing, and touching one another. Friends we hadn't seen in many years came to pay their respects, and to see what the van Lith children looked like all grown up, with families of their own.

I really wanted to share what happened in Reno with my sisters. With so many visitors in the house, and so many other stories being shared, I realized it was not the appropriate time. To fully appreciate the details and the blessings surrounding Dad's death, especially when the German woman cared for us, we would need to be alone. I had to wait for another opportunity.

You are free at last. Really and truly free, Dad.

Long shall you live!

Lang zal ze leven in de Gloria, in de Gloria, in de Gloria!

This is dedicated to Ineke, Gerrie, Suuske, Treesje, and Dominicus

and

The Third Generation Survivors

End of Part One

Mienus

Suze

Long Shall You Live
Part 2

Prologue

I was in my early 50's the first time I came across the term "Second Generation Survivor." To understand its meaning, I pulled up articles and research papers available on the internet and discovered that I am a part of a very large group of aging individuals who share a common background. We are the children raised by parents who were victims of unspeakable horror in concentration camps during the Holocaust of WWII. Our parents may have been able to heal much of the physical effects of the trauma they endured, but the psychological effects, tattooed in their minds would never fully heal.

Over the last seven decades, a great deal of research has been done by a number of specialists studying the physical and psychological effects suffered by Holocaust survivors. The knowledge gained has advanced the diagnosis and treatment of the effects of Post-Traumatic Stress Disorder (PTSD) and other illnesses.

During these same years, similar ongoing studies are examining and documenting the effects the Holocaust has had on second, and even third generation survivors. Two of these more recent studies have been important to me. One is presented in an article written by Tori Rodriguez, published on March 1, 2015, in the Scientific American magazine. It is titled, "Descendants of Holocaust Survivors Have Altered Stress Hormones" (Rodrigues). Another article was published on September 9, 2010 in Time's Health and Medicine by Jeffrey Kluger. It is titled, "Genetic Scars of the Holocaust: Children Suffer Too" (Kluger). I could identify with both of these studies, and wished this information had been available much sooner in my life. Maybe it could have prevented some of my personal struggles.

Part Two is a memoir containing some incredible events in my own life that were affected by the suffering my parents endured during the Dutch Occupation and the Holocaust. I share it for many reasons. The most important is to encourage other second generation survivors, and others affected by similar circumstantial trauma, to gain a better understanding of their upbringing, and achieve a measure of hope and peace.

All of us have options to help us cope. Option A: bury the trauma as deeply as possible and suffer in silence, Option B: hang on to victimization and let it take over lives, or Option C: turn to any number of resources for healing with the hope to find meaning, purpose, and peace for what was endured. I assume that many move in and out of each of these options throughout their lives, consciously or not.

Having introduced you to my parents, you know how Mienus navigated in and out of each option before finally remaining in Option C during his later years. Dad and Mom enjoyed many blessings in their adult years, and came to reconcile the pain and suffering they endured.

Like my parents, I see my life through the lens of my faith. I am a survivor many times over. Long Shall You Live became my story too. The deep trials in my life, and the adventures and miracles that I have enjoyed, have enabled me to move beyond the victimization of a war, and in the process, gain a large measure of inner healing. I've discovered my new passion, new direction, and dare I say, my own liberation. I would not be who I am without experiencing them all. I've chosen Option C.

My Passion and My New Direction

It was Good Friday, April 22, 2011, and I was sitting outside in a rocking chair soaking up some sun. I had made a commitment to myself to take the phone off the hook, turn the computer off, sit, and be quiet from noon to 3:00pm, devoting my time to prayer, reading, meditating, and listening to God. I try to doing something like this every Good Friday, but this year something happened that changed my life.

As you know by now, I was born into a Catholic family and baptized in that well-worn, little white dress. In my youth, I practiced the faith much like many others. I went to Mass on Sundays, observed all the traditions of the Church, and for a number of years, I felt I was just going through the motions. It took meaningful events over many years to finally convince me that God is real, and loves me very much.

On this day, I was recuperating from a second big health scare. My life was threatened, and my job was hanging in the balance of my recovery. I was weak, confused, and full of grief. I didn't recognize myself in the mirror or feel like the strong, outgoing, confident woman that I had always been.

Three hours can feel like a long time just sitting, especially when you are wallowing in self-pity. I had my cup of decaffeinated tea (no chocolate, it was lent), as well as a few religious books to leaf through, and my rosary. Ok, I was ready. "Here I come Lord, to spend time with you!" I said to myself.

The first hour went by fairly quickly. I did my daily scripture readings, prayed the rosary, and read a religious article. Now what? Hmm, at least it was warm outside, and I was enjoying the relaxing sounds of the babbling brook in our backyard. The birds were chirping and flocking around the feeder. The tulips were all in colorful bloom, and new growth was showing on all the trees and perennials. It was so beautiful, so peaceful, and just the perfect place to be inspired. But inspired was not what I was feeling. I was feeling lonely, weak, and uninspired.

I had a couple of religious magazines that I could read and more articles in my daily meditation booklet. I also had an old version of a book called, *The Lives of the Saints*, (copyright 1955, the year I was born). The reprints of this particular book have changed over time as new saints were added into the yearly cycle. Why I brought it outside with me that afternoon, I still couldn't tell you.

With lots of time left, I decided to pray for a new patron saint. Unless you have a Catholic background, it might be hard to figure out why I did that. As a Catholic, I believe the saints in heaven can pray with me much like our friends or family here on Earth. I was hoping I could find one to give me comfort during my health crisis. There are lots of patron saints for health issues.

"God, what do you want from me? I need some guidance," I prayed.

"You think He's gonna hear you?" my doubting mind asked.

Some people say that they've actually heard God speak to them. I was open to the possibility, but never experienced that before. I've received inspirational feelings and impulses that made me believe in the reality of God's presence within me, then wondered if it was real or just my own thoughts or imaginations. At the moment, in my current state of mind, I was very open to listening.

"Marja, pick up *The Lives of the Saints*! Turn to your birthday!" I did not hear an audible message, but definitely was moved by inspiration. I sat for a moment, and then heard the same message again. Without hesitating, I picked up the book and opened it to my birthday.

January 29, feast day of St. Francis De Sales, Bishop, Confessor, Doctor of the Church, and...Patron of Writers!? I laughed. "Really, you send me to a patron saint of writers?" I must tell you at this point that I had just written something very special that had greatly benefited me. To share more would spoil something I include later in the book.

I chuckled as I read the short bio about St. Francis De Sales. Still not 100% sure of what had just happened, I asked God what else He had in store for me now. Just like before, He said, "Now, pick up your monthly meditational, *The Word Among Us*, and open it near the back."

"OK then," I thought. With the same quick response, I picked up the magazine, closed my eyes, and flipped it open near the back.

The article that opened up to me was titled, "Take Your Time: The Gentle Guidance from St. Francis de Sales." So maybe I've never heard the voice of God audibly, but as my tears began to flow, there was no doubt in my mind that He had heard and answered my prayer. I was now introduced to, and friends with, St. Francis de Sales.

The next two hours flew by so quickly. Before I was aware of the time, my husband had come home from work and I couldn't wait to share with him what I experienced during those three hours.

What would I be writing? "Write what you know!" was the only direction I ever received during my prayers. I had the stories handed down by my parents, but as I wrote their stories, my life became clearer and more meaningful. "Write what you know!" never went away. And so begins Part Two.

Chapter 18

Mark

My husband was born in Nashville, Tennessee, on November 29, 1954, and given the name John Mark Henderson. He is commonly referred to by his middle name, Mark.

Just days after my sixteenth birthday, January 29, 1971, I saw my husband for the very first time. It was Tuesday, February 2, and I was returning to North Salem High School after passing my driver's license test. It was midmorning and I was just given my hall pass from the front office to get back to class.

I was visiting with one of my friends in the office when I spotted these two very attractive guys being escorted around the building by one of the school counselors. I thought they were student teachers by the way they were dressed. Nice slacks, button-down long sleeve shirts, and leather shoes were not the normal attire for students at my high school during the early 70's. The rest of us were wearing jeans and work shirts or other casual clothing. We were still trying to figure out when and where the next fashion trend was coming from, having just come out of the hippie 60's.

I was in no hurry to get to class that morning so I moved myself to a place where I could eavesdrop on these new guys and the counselor, and see if my hunch was correct.

Instead of being student teachers, they turned out to be new students from the Midwest. In addition to that, I found out they were juniors in high school, just like me.

I motioned to one of my classmate in the hallway and whispered, "Casslayne, I am going to the prom with one of those guys!" She laughed and said, "Don't get your hopes up, Marja." For the rest of that school day, I kept my eyes out for them.

The following day I walked into my third hour class, and there, sitting in front of my assigned seat, was one of the newbies from Missouri. I had one of the cute guys in study hall with me!

"Oh, I gotta meet this guy for sure!" I thought to myself. After a few moments of thinking how I was going to approach him, I leaned forward and said, "Excuse me, can I ask you for a piece of paper?" He looked at me, paused, and then said, "Yes, you can ask!" Then he turned away, went back to what he was doing, seeming to ignore my request.

After a few puzzled moments, I leaned over my desk and asked, "Where's that piece of paper you agreed to give me?"

"I didn't agree to give you a piece of paper, I answered your question. You asked me if you could ask, and I said yes," he countered.

Not knowing if I was getting off to a good start or a bad start, I had to finish working my plan. "Ok then, can I have a piece of paper?" I said.

"Sure, why didn't you just ask the first time?" He handed me one piece of paper and smiled at me as if he just won a cleverness contest. I couldn't tell if I had generated any future interest in me, or just lost any chance due to my dumb question.

When class was over, I thanked Mark for the paper and left the classroom wishing I could have a do-over of that first impression. "Hmm," I thought to myself. "I might just manage a second chance at a first impression." You see, the other guy in the hallway turned out to be his brother. Not just any brother, but his identical twin brother Mike. I had a second chance!

Over the course of the next couple of weeks, I figured out that the brothers left school right after the last bell and walked home the same direction that I did. So I started leaving right after school too, "happened" to run into one or the other of the twins, and walked together the few blocks toward my house.

I must have left an interesting enough first impression on Mark after all. He began to wait for me after school to walk me home. He showed interest in me during study hall too. I was starting to like this guy. Each time I saw him, the butterflies in my stomach acted up. We were two 16-year-old kids making a lasting impression on each other.

Unfortunately for me, I had very strict parents. They forbade me from going out on dates, even before I met Mark. I was "only 16!" That was their excuse for keeping me from boys. So Mark and I did the next best thing. We snuck around at every opportunity. We had lots of help from our friends. The only "real date" I was allowed on during our junior year was the junior/senior prom. "I told you I was going to go out with one of the new guys," I later reminded my friend.

I wouldn't turn 17 until January 1972, having completed 7th and 8th grade in one school year. Throughout my entire senior year, I was still not allowed to date, except for prom. Dad and Mom had some struggles with some of my older siblings, so to prevent, "those same mistakes," they were unyielding. So we continued to sneak around, month after month, and got pretty good at it.

Mark and I just wanted a normal dating experience. It should have been the time to discover who and what we were looking for in a relationship, slowly growing into the next phase of life as healthy adults. Instead, it was not a natural experience. The restrictions placed on us served to intensify our desire to be together, no matter what!

My parents and I had our ups and downs. I could be just as stubborn as them, maybe more. But not everyone had parents who had experienced the kind of hell that mine had. In their minds, they both were trying to protect me from harm. I know that now. But as a teenager, it caused hardship on them and me that otherwise could have been prevented.

At our graduation from high school, Mark and I walked next to each other during "Pomp and Circumstance." We sat next to each other during the ceremony for everyone to see, primarily my parents. This was our way of coming out of hiding, so to speak. We were proud to show everyone that we were a couple.

We were boyfriend and girlfriend, a fact my parents tried to prevent, yet were forced to acknowledge. They would no longer be able to deny what was obvious. We were 17 years old, and we were in love.

Even after I graduated, Mom and Dad still hung on to me, just a little looser. They didn't ask me where I was going quite so often, and they didn't check the odometer anymore when I came back with the car.

The ice jam was slowly melting between us. "We can talk about what your plans are for school and work and other things when you get back from Holland," Dad said to provide some peace between us.

Within a couple of weeks after graduation, I went on my first return trip to Holland. I figured, if they think I am mature enough to travel alone so far away from them, then I should be mature enough to make some of my own choices when I get back. So I thought.

Chapter 19

Dag Opa, Tot Ziens – Bye Opa, Till I See You Again

I was 17 years old when I bought my ticket to go to Holland. I was about to embark on my first solo trip to the Netherlands. My Tante Mia and my cousins, Leen and Els, would be my hosts.

This was only my second airplane trip. The plan was to spend the first two weeks in Vlaardingen, enjoy Germany the third week, and then relax the last few days at a beach house back in Holland. Oh how I was looking forward to this trip.

The day I was to depart, Mom answered a phone call from Martinair Airlines, the charter carrier of my flight. She was told that there was an unexplained delay and I would not be flying as scheduled. I would be notified when the plane was available. We were led to believe that this delay would only take a day or two before I could finally leave.

Mom sent a telegram to her sister, Mia, letting her know about the delay and assured her that I was still coming. She would send another telegram with the new day and time just as soon as we got the updated information.

As it turned out, Martinair called again within hours with the new itinerary. I would be leaving that same day, just a few hours later than originally scheduled. Mother immediately sent a second telegram to my aunt with the new arrival information. I would be on my way soon.

My new arrival time in Amsterdam was scheduled very early in the morning, around 5:00am. Tante Mia was planning to take the train from Vlaardingen to meet me, and arrive before my plane landed. Just before leaving the house, Mom grabbed a notepad and quickly wrote down the phone number of her brother, Anton Bruggeman, who lived in Amsterdam with his family.

"Now, if for one reason or another something unexpected happens after you arrive, give your Om (Uncle) Anton a call from the airport. I'm sure everything will be fine, but take this and put it in your purse," Mother said. I was just about out the door when she gave me this small piece of paper.

"I'm sure I won't need this, Mom! Someone will be there to meet me," I assured her.

"I'm sure you're right, but take it anyway. Take good care of yourself, and be good to your aunt and cousins, and say hello from Mom and Dad. I love you," Mother replied.

"I love you too. I'll see you guys in four weeks. *Dag, tot ziens*!" I said with a hug and a trial run of my Dutch. Bye, see you!

The trip to Holland was grueling. The plane could not have been packed any tighter. The chartered Martinair flight was able to offer big savings to flyers by adding additional seats to the already tight cabin, and no other frills during the hours in flight. I don't remember much besides it being a very long, very boring, and very tiring experience.

After several hours in the air, we landed in northeastern Canada for refueling. I was unaware that this was not a non-stop flight. It was very dark and very cold, and I was not prepared for this short layover.

This airport did not appear to be very large. There were no passenger ramps to keep us warm and dry when we got off the airplane. The cabin door opened, the ladder was lowered, and the cold air rushed in. We were escorted to a very small terminal to hang out while the plane was being serviced.

We were given an opportunity to exchange some US currency for Canadian ones, just in case we wanted to use the vending machines for food or drinks. I purchased what I thought I needed before re-boarding the plane for the rest of the flight. This layover took way longer than it needed to. Next stop, Amsterdam.

I was grateful to have a window seat, especially during the daylight hours. The first half of the flight I was able to see the landscape below. Now, back in flight, there was nothing but darkness outside. Crossing over an ocean for the first time was unnerving. We were 30,000 feet above the Atlantic Ocean, with nothing but water and ice below, which only served to add to my unease.

As we approached the isles of Great Britain, a dim, rose-tinted light grew on the horizon ahead of us. I was able to watch as the slow-rising sunlight got brighter and higher in the distance. I'd never seen a sunrise like this before. I was being welcomed by the new dawn in such a picturesque way.

We would be landing in Holland in about an hour. I was excited to get to know this small country, and experience the culture of her people first hand. As the plane descended toward Amsterdam, my eyes were transfixed as I peered through the window, full of anticipation. I saw a land filled with beautifully manicured fields and trees shading old-world farmhouses.

I continued searching below for the first thing that would really say to me, "This is Holland," not Oregon, or any other place that I had been to. That moment came at the sight of my first big windmill. I was so excited! "I'm in Holland! I was born in this country! I have family here waiting for me. Finally, it is my time to return!" I was thinking.

Descending even further with the land below coming into focus, I could see for myself what I had only been able to appreciate in books and pictures of the Netherlands. There were cobblestone pavers lacing through the streets of the towns. Small cars and many bikes shared roadways. There were houseboats and other boats mingled in the waterways that went on for miles. There were three and four-storied row homes covered in bricks of brown and red, with flowerboxes adorning the windows of each home. This is a country that builds new structures right next to buildings that have stood for hundreds of years. This was Holland!

There were very large ships traversing through a number of inland waterways. These same ships, when seen from land, appear to be moving through green fields instead of water. The illusion is so convincing.

Windmills dotted the landscape and every town had at least one tall steeple towering above the other buildings. I knew the bells in those steeples used to invite townspeople to come and worship.

The wheels of the plane lowered. Within minutes, we touched down at Schiphol International Airport in Amsterdam. I was more than ready to get out of the plane. It took more than twelve hours to get here, including the time we spent in Canada refueling and refilling the plane. The last time I slept was more than 24 hours ago. I now had the whole day ahead of me in this new time zone.

It was 5:00am in Amsterdam. Tante Mia, Leen, and Els would be waiting for me, ready to escort me to their home. My travel for the day would end in Vlaardingen, a short, 50-minute train ride away.

In 1972, airline passengers were still able to meet up with their family or friends at the gates of the terminals when they arrived. Security at airports was minimal compared to today's standards. I was expecting to see family waiting for me at the gate. Instead, we were all directed through customs and immigration checkpoints. I didn't know that arriving in a new country was not the same as a domestic flight.

Waiting in line to get my passport stamped, I noticed a large crowd waiting on the other side of a huge glass wall. People began to wave when they recognized someone. I kept looking for a familiar face. I knew I would recognize my aunt, having spent time with her back home, and I would recognize my cousins from their pictures.

I followed the other passengers through the line and watched as the crowd slowly dwindled. "It should be much easier to spot them now," I thought to myself.

Finally, my passport got stamped. I exited the customs area and continued looking for my relatives. "They must be sitting down close by, waiting for me," I thought. I stood still for several minutes just looking and looking, now hoping they were just late. "They will show up and say how sorry they were for being late, because of... I don't know, something!" The few minutes turned into several.

After a half hour, I wandered to the baggage claim area to retrieve my bag, hoping they were waiting for me there. On my way, I kept listening for the loudspeaker in the terminal to call out my name. Quite often someone's name would be called, so I figured, why not mine. They are obviously late or lost. Either way I was alone at 5:30am, in a foreign country, and this was not supposed to happen. I was feeling very seventeen.

They were not in baggage claim! Though I was concerned, I did not panic. I reached into my coat pocket where I had nonchalantly placed the handwritten note just before I left. As I walked to the nearest airport information desk, I unfolded the small piece of paper with the phone numbers that I wasn't supposed to need.

My first concern was whether I could communicate well enough to the ladies behind the desk to explain the predicament I was in. "Do you speak English?" I asked?

"Yes, we both speak English. What can we do for you?"

I explained the situation, including the delay in my original departure. "I just need to call my uncle and let him know I am here. I have an aunt coming to take me to Vlaardingen to stay with her. I'm not even sure my uncle knows that I was coming, but he would surely call my aunt to let her know that I am at the airport," I said with growing frustration and fatigue.

I showed them the note with my uncle's name and number. The women could see that I was quite apprehensive, and assured me that everything would be ok. They asked me to sit down in a chair not far from them, and quickly contacted someone else from the airport staff to join me. This person initiated the phone call to my uncle and handed the receiver to me.

The phone began to ring, and ring, and ring, and ring, when finally, a girl's sleepy voice said, "*Ja, weet u hoe laat het is*?" Do you know what time it is?

Now almost in tears, I said to her in my feeble Dutch, "Yes, I know what time it is! My name is Marja, and I just got off a big airplane from my home in Salem, Oregon. Tante Mia was supposed to pick me up and take me to Vlaardingen. My mother gave me a note with Om Anton's phone number, so I called. I am sorry to wake you, but can you please talk to your Dad and ask him to call Tante Mia and let her know I'm here?"

By now my cousin, Marijke was wide awake. I figured I better keep talking before she thought I was a prank caller and hang up on me. In the background, I could hear animated voices trying to make sense of what I just said. My Dutch wasn't as good as I had hoped, but the message became clear.

My Om Anton took the phone. I had never met him before, so it felt a bit awkward. After saying a few words of encouragement, he asked to talk to the person at the airport who was taking care of me. Listening to the woman beside me, I could tell that Om Anton was requesting assistance to keep me comfortable and safe, and that someone would be there soon to pick me up. After a few minutes, they hung up.

I was given something small to eat and drink, and was instructed to stay in the sitting area close to the information desk. Within a few minutes, the phone at the desk rang and I was called over. The call was for me. It was Tante Mia.

"Hello Marja. I am so sorry that you are there alone. I had no idea that you were here. I got your mother's telegram saying that you would not be coming today," my aunt said to me in Dutch. I could hear the anguish in her voice.

She went on to say, "Your Om Anton will be picking you up, and I will be taking the first train to Amsterdam and go to Anton's house. We'll take a later train back after you get a chance to visit your uncle's family."

I was holding back the tears at this point. The second telegram with the new flight departure had not reached to my aunt. It would finally show up two days later. A lot of good that did me. My concern and frustration finally gave way to relief and exhaustion. All the adrenaline rushing through me over the last hour had depleted any reserves I had left after the long flight.

Sitting alone with people constantly moving about me made it difficult to rest. I hung on tight to my bags and waited.

It may have seemed like a long wait, but within the hour, they finally arrived. Om Anton and Marijke picked me up and took me to their home.

We arrived at their four-story brick townhouse just before 7:00am. The entrance to their home was on the second floor, and occupied the top three floors of the building.

I was warmly welcomed. My Tante Margaretha provided a typical Dutch breakfast of sliced meats and cheeses, fresh bakery breads, *hagelslaag*, and tea or coffee. With no one in the house fluent in English, it was imperative for me to make it work. Speaking Dutch was getting a little easier, especially with a lot of hand gesturing. I remember asking several times, "Did I say that right?"

"You are doing fine," was their kind reply.

They were surprised at how well I was able to communicate. The last time they had seen me I was only 15 months old. Back then, most of what I was able to say was restricted to, "papa, mommy, car, moo, meow, woof, happy." You get the idea. Come to think of it, at that age I was already bi-lingual!

Tante Mia arrived later that morning with Els. As it turned out, one of Anton's children was having a birthday, and many of his family members were planning to come over late in the afternoon to celebrate. So instead of leaving for Vlaardingen in the afternoon, as was planned, we stayed the entire day in Amsterdam to celebrate, and then took an evening train to Vlaardingen.

My first day in Holland turned out quite different from the way it was planned. Had my aunt received the second telegram in time, I may not have had the opportunity to meet Mom's brother and his wife and several of their ten children.

I would be seeing some of them again during the last week of my trip. Tante Mia, Leen, Els, and I would be spending time at Anton's small beach cottage (emphasis on small). Something I was especially looking forward too now.

After recovering for a day or two from my long flight and the lack of sleep, the sightseeing began. I was shown all the sights that were important to the family: the bakery, the Visbank, the City Hall, the church, the house where I was born, the windmills, and so much more.

Several days were taken up visiting other aunts, uncles, and cousins. But the most important visit to me was with my Opa Bruggeman.

I had heard enough stories about my grandfather in my youth that I got a little nervous beforehand. I was warned by my Tante Mia and cousin Els not to have high expectations. "Opa can be real grumpy at times. He is set in his ways, and doesn't always like visitors taking up too much of his time. He can be very short with other children too. If a child or teenager calls him Opa out of respect, or because he is old, he frowns back and cuttingly tells them, 'I'm not your Opa!'" they cautioned me.

Opa lived in a quiet neighborhood in Vlaardingen in a nice retirement home. I knocked on the partially open door to Opa's living quarters. Tante Mia and Els were with me.

"*Ja, komen* (Yes, come in)," the voice said. I opened the door a bit wider, and with a little trepidation, stepped into his room.

I looked at him, smiled, and said, "*Dag Opa*? (Hi Opa?)" I assumed it would be ok to call my own Opa, "Opa!" At least I was hoping it was ok!

There, sitting in an easy chair, smoking a cigar, was a very well dressed and very handsome 83-year-old man smiling back at me, arms out to greet me. "Dag Opa!" This time, when I said it, it was no longer a question, but a young girl greeting her grandfather for the first time, with confidence.

I happily accepted his invitation for a hug. I sat beside him and held the hand he was not using for his cigar. Tante Mia and Els followed in during my hug. I looked at them with an expression that said, "That wasn't so bad!" Mia and Els formally greeting Opa and then sat down for our visit.

Midmorning coffee and tea was delivered to the room, along with some irresistible baked goodies. So typical! It helped to have an activity as simple as this to begin the conversation. Opa was in good health and very friendly with me.

The hour or so that we were together went very smoothly. I don't remember what all we talked about; it didn't really matter. We could have talked math problems for all I cared. I was just happy to meet my mother's father.

He was my Opa, whose blood runs through me. It meant so much to me, being in the same room with relatives. These were people I knew from pictures that were part of my history, and important to my life.

After the second cup of tea and another treat, the three of us stood up to say our goodbyes. We knew when it was time to go. "I want you to come back to see me again before you go back to your mother," Opa said to me.

I looked at Tante Mia for guidance. Then she told Opa, "We will come back again for another visit."

"I'll see you soon, Opa. It was so nice to meet you after so many years. I'll be back, Opa," I promised him. I was determined to keep that promise, no matter what.

An amazing thing happened after speaking Dutch for three or four days. I began to think in Dutch! English was always my first language, but after the full emersion, it was as if my mind flipped a switch. Even the inflections in my voice were changing as I listened to myself emulating the voices around me. What occurred in my head was surprising and exciting. Before long, even some of my dreams were in Dutch.

The first two weeks in Vlaardingen were a lot of fun. I got to experience Holland while shopping open markets, sightseeing, eating different foods, and riding around on scooters called "brommers."

Leen, Els, and I had a lot of independence while I lived with them. I had never experienced coming and going at will like that before. I never felt danger in any way with this new freedom. I was used to parents who held on tight and were not very flexible. I had a very strict upbringing.

One of my best memories of this whole trip was the day my cousins and I got on the scooters and hit the open road. The day was sunny and warm by Holland's standards. After packing some food and drink, we set out for what I thought would be a short ride. Instead, with Leen leading the small pack, we drove our scooters on the old roads throughout the countryside. These roads had lots of character, full of curves, turns, and ups and downs. The countryside was beautiful and green, with lots cultivated fields and wild flowers.

After riding more than an hour, I noticed we were approaching the waterway. The large cargo ship moving slowly in the distance was my first clue. When we finally got to the dyke, we stopped the scooters and found some benches where we could sit and eat our lunches. We were nearly fifteen miles from where we started.

We sat there for a very long time, watching ship after ship from around the world make its way into Rotterdam. I knew that this very large inland waterway was something very familiar to my parents. My father worked next to it before the war. This place, and so many of the smaller tributaries, was the center of so much life and industry to the people of Holland.

The three of us sat quietly with our own thoughts. It was an inspiring moment, almost a religious one for me. Perhaps Leen and Els were not having the same kind of experience as I was. Just having them there with me made it all the more special. I was completely satisfied that day.

On our way back to Vlaardingen we stopped at a little open market that served *potat frietjes* (french fries). We spent a few minutes debating what real "french fries" looked and tasted like. These fries were made of potatoes, but they weren't shaped like the fries back home. When I asked for some ketchup, my cousins playfully frowned at me, handed me a dip, and said, "You don't eat these with ketchup, use this." I was given a small container of mayonnaise. I shook my head in defeat, and enjoyed my "french fries" with mayonnaise.

Leen and Els belonged to a dance club in town whose members were all under 20 years of age. The club was created to teach different styles of dancing, and perhaps to keep adolescents out of trouble too.

Once a week, the club would get together and practice what they learned, and then dance the night away. I had a couple of occasions to attend this event. It was a safe environment to let loose, feel a little more grown up, and stay out of trouble.

I certainly drew some attention in the room, being the newbie girl from America. I had to learn rather quickly the foxtrot, waltz, swing, and other forms of dance, so as not to look inept to the club members. The guys knew how to lead, which made it easy for me.

I have to admit that a little alcohol helped too. Drinking alcohol was not illegal for kids our age, and smoking cigarettes was something just about everybody did. The place was lit up.

"Sure, I'll try one. Thanks." I accepted the offered a cigarette. Everyone else was smoking, why not?

The Dutch were, and still are, much more laid back about smoking and drinking at a younger age. "It's not a big deal here in Holland, because it is legal," I was told, to justify the behaviors. "When in Holland…!"

For the next few weeks, I smoked right along with the cousins and their friends. Stupid, I know, but it happened a long time ago. You know the old saying, "So, if everybody else is going to jump off the bridge, are going to, too?" In this particular case, I jumped.

After the first two weeks of my trip, Tante Mia, Leen, Els, and I took the train to Amsterdam. A tour bus was waiting at the station to take us to Wurzburg, Germany for seven days. What should have been a six-hour bus ride, turned into ten hours of misery and frustration.

Not long after crossing the border into Germany, our bus caught up to one of the longest lines of stalled vehicles I had ever see in my life. It must have stretched 30+ miles. Both East- and West-bound traffic were involved in the traffic jam.

It was so difficult trying to get comfortable on the bus, especially not knowing how long we would be stuck like this. The air-conditioning only worked when the engine was on, and the bus driver would alternate between comfort for the passengers, and shutting down the engine to save on fuel. The single restroom was heating up, and each time someone opened the door, the side effects would overpower the nostrils. This went on for hours.

When we finally made our way to the multi-car collision site, most of the evidence had already been removed. As soon as we were completely out of the traffic jam, the bus driver headed to the nearest rest stop to fuel up and allow the passengers to purchase things to eat and drink. Unfortunately, there were many other anxious drivers pulling into the rest stop, with the same intentions. After an hour in this new traffic jam, we finally hit the autobahn.

The landscape in Germany was beautiful. It looked very green and clean, much like Holland, but with more topographical features to enjoy. Germany has more mountains, hills, and forests. It also has many small towns full of Bavarian features so indicative to this part of Germany.

The countryside reminded me of the Willamette Valley in Oregon, especially the landscape surrounding the town of Mt. Angel. After looking out the window for several hours, it occurred to me that these Bavarian towns were even more picturesque because they were missing something. There was not one telephone pole, electrical grid, or wire to be seen. All these lines were buried underground, and it made such a difference. It was lovely.

We finally arrived at our destination, a small hostel in Ochsenfurt, Germany. This quaint town is located between Wurzburg and Nuremberg. Our hostel was located downtown, above a local restaurant in the main square. Els and I shared a small room, and Leen and Tante Mia stayed in another. There was a shared bathroom for several of the guests. Not exactly what I had expected, but we managed to make it work.

Tante Mia had planned a couple of bus tours to some of the local tourist sights. We enjoyed walking through castles, museums, and small villages, and ate lots of fresh cheeses, meats, and a variety of breads for lunches.

One day, we went on a wine tasting tour to some of the many wineries in the vicinity. At my age, this excursion was quite the treat. No one asked for my identification. It seems they weren't too worried about that in Germany either. They gave us a little bucket to spit out our wine after tasting it. I maybe used it once or twice when I didn't like the taste. The rest I swallowed. After returning from our excursions, we cooled off in the public pool located within a comfortable park setting.

Another one of our trips was to Nuremberg, the site of the Nuremberg trials that were held at the end of WWII. The Allied forces held a series of military tribunals after the end of the war. Prominent members of the military, political, and economic leadership of the notorious Nazi party were tried for committing war crimes against humanity. The most notable and highest ranking surviving Nazi official charged at the tribunal was Hermann Göring. Also on trial were several of his infamous cohorts.

The allies were not about to make the same mistake that was made after WWI, when the German government tried its own war criminals. These trials turned out to be a sham to the European people so horribly affected from 1914-1918. Too many of those convicted were given light sentences, and several would later become leaders in the Nazi party during WWII.

I was pensive the day we were in Nuremburg. It was unsettling to think about how Dad had been tortured and imprisoned, and how Mother had suffered physically and emotional from the hunger and cold living conditions, and the constant fear of losing everything during the Nazis occupation. My only consolation was knowing that many of those who had committed these atrocities had been punished years ago, and were not around to hurt anyone else. At least those were my thoughts at the time.

Some of these same feelings welled up again on the day we had an excursion to Wurzburg. We had a tour guide in the bus with us who spoke exclusively in German. Tante Mia could understand a fair amount of the language, just enough to interpret what was being said.

I was angry that this man did not speak Dutch or English to us. Every place I visited in Holland, and any other place where a tour guide was present, he or she spoke in the language of the visitors. I felt as though we weren't that important and didn't merit another language other than German.

My anger continued to grow. I was even more incensed each time he identified one building after another, from one town to the next, as having been bombed by the Allies. He went on and on about the tragic loss of life of the German people, and how much his country had suffered by the Allied forces.

Of course I felt badly for all the suffering of the innocent townspeople. At one point, I could not hold back my words and said, "Tante Mia, why is he talking to us as if this was our fault. Holland didn't start a war, they did. And it was the second time they started a world war!" I just sat there and sulked. Whatever food we ate, or museum or castle we visited that day gave me little pleasure.

The evening before our return trip to Holland, the owner of the restaurant and inn put on a dance for the tourists. I thought it sounded like a lot of fun. I was thinking about how much enjoyment I had at the dance club in Vlaardingen. With my new dance moves, it was a good time to exercise those skills again.

After dinner, the evening of our last day, the staff moved tables and chairs around to make room for a dance floor. Els and I went to our room to freshen up to look our best. We wanted to look nice for the young men of the town who would be coming to the party.

Tante Mia was waiting for us downstairs. Some of the locals had already arrived, including a few young men. "This looks like it might be fun!" I said to Els. She agreed that it looked promising.

The music started and a few couples got up to dance. Els and I got a drink, lit up a cigarette, and tried to look very cosmopolitan. We did attract someone interested in dancing, but unfortunately, the guy moving in our direction was not someone I wanted to dance with.

This very tall, much older man was maneuvering his way straight toward me. I looked wide-eyed toward my aunt for assistance and said, "What should I do if he asks me to dance!"

"You say yes, and dance with him. It would not be polite to decline. If you refuse, that means you are not interested in dancing with anyone tonight," Tante Mia warned me.

I objected. "But he is so old and very unpleasant to look at, and he's already full of sweat from dancing with some of the other ladies."

With a disapproving look on her face, Tante Mia leaned toward me and quietly encouraged, "Just be nice, and dance. Then watch for those younger men over there. They've been looking at the two of you, and I'm sure they will come and ask you to dance. They are just waiting for the right time."

As my prince charming approach our table, he gestured to me to dance with him. I looked at my aunt, still wondering what I was going to do, and stood up. His hand was very moist as he dragged me off to the dance floor.

To say I was uncomfortable just doesn't describe what I was feeling. It didn't matter to this man if I could dance or not. It really didn't matter because I don't think my feet touched the ground once during that whole song.

My first dance of the evening was with this large sweaty man who swept me off my feet, holding one of my arms straight out, forcing me to hang onto his neck and shoulder where most of his sweat was accumulating. When the dance ended, he swirled me around in a circle with his cheek on mine, and finally put me down. "Danke!" he said. "Danke?" I replied, just before I ran back to my table.

I could tell my aunt was proud of me. I did what I had to, hoping I might get asked to dance from someone younger, better looking, and with less sweat!

After running up to my room to freshen up, again, I returned and was approached by a nice young man who asked me to dance. My aunt was right. Sometimes you have to prove something to yourself, and others. Having agreed to dance with that "overly friendly" older gentleman, made it easier for other young men to approach me, without fear of being rejected. It was a good lesson.

*

Our trip back to Holland was uneventful. We would only be in Vlaardingen a couple more days before leaving for my Om Anton's cabin at the beach.

I still had two more events to look forward to before we left. I was going to keep my promise to my Opa, and then enjoy Els' birthday party, scheduled for the following evening.

Opa was waiting for me, cigar in hand.

"*Ja, komen,*" he said after I knocked. My aunt and I entered his room and I greeted him with a kiss on the cheek.

"Hello Opa! I promised I would see you before I go home again," I reminded him.

The midmorning tea, coffee, and goodies arrived within minutes. Just after that, a lovely elderly woman came into view. This must be Johanna, Opa's special friend.

The greeting was genuine and the conversation light. I was happy that there was such a sweet lady that loved my Opa. I could tell. Opa seemed happy. All was right in the world around him that morning.

After the first cup and cookie, Opa got up, walked to a cupboard and proceeded to pull out what remained of my Oma's special dishware, the ones given to her as a wedding present. He carried a few pieces, handed them to me, and said, "I want to give these dishes to you. They belonged to your Oma. We only used them for special occasions. Here, come help me get the rest of them."

I turned to my aunt and saw the surprised look on her face. "Oh, Opa, that is too much to give to me," I said quickly.

"They are yours now, and let me see what else I have to give you," he replied. I think he said that so that it would be easier for me to take his first gift and call it good. "Come look in here and tell me what else you can take with you," he added.

At this point, I knew that I would be taking home the last of my Oma's special dishes. I did not look at my aunt again for guidance. I could sense her disappointment watching as these dishes were given to me and not her.

My thoughts went immediately to my mother, and how I would make her happy passing these dishes on to her. She received nothing of her mother's belongings after my Oma died several years before. These thoughts I kept to myself.

The delicate dishes were made of ceramic, painted white and covered with a shiny glaze. The edge of each piece had a fine gold rim followed by a bold navy blue stripe that encircled the dish near the top. Evenly scattered between the blue stripes, were four groups of three hand painted pink roses and green leaves. The stamp on the back of the dishes read: BASSETT, with CZECOSLOVAKIA in a half circle beneath it. These pieces today are over 100 years old.

I thanked my Opa for his generous and very touching gift. After carefully packing them in newspaper and placing them in a box, we shared one more cup of tea and another cookie.

It was so hard saying goodbye to my Opa that morning. I knew in my heart that I would never see him again. I could tell he was thinking the same thing. Standing up, I reached with both hands and helped him up from his chair. No more bending over to hug him this time.

The stories describing Opa as an old grumpy man were not evident to me. He may have been so in the past, but the two times I saw him, he was kind and generous to the baby granddaughter that he never got to see growing up. For that, I am blessed.

Tante Mia and I didn't say much on the way back to her place. I quickly went to my bedroom and packed each dish carefully between my clothes, and closed my suitcase. The dishes belonged to me now, and I did not want to upset my aunt any further.

The following day we got everything ready for Els' birthday party. She had invited a few friends and our cousin Marijke, the one who answered the phone in Amsterdam the morning I arrived. She would be traveling to the beach with us the following day too.

The party was fun, but more adult-like than I was used to. We had a few drinks, had a few smokes, and enjoyed some music and dancing. There was no thought of getting pulled over by the police for drinking and driving. Everyone walked. My aunt made sure that we kept things under control.

By midnight the party was over. It was sad to say goodbye to friends I had made on this trip. I suspected that I would never see most of them again either. I was right.

With each goodbye, it became clear that the most important things we left behind when we emigrated, and the biggest sacrifice my parents had to make, far more than the country itself, were the people. I have relatives, lots of them, and I didn't even get to meet them all. I liked my Dutch family very much. I would miss them, and wondered if and when I would see them again.

My time in Holland was coming to an end. The last days at the beach, fun as they were, only reminded me that I would be flying home very soon.

Tante Mia, Leen, Els, Om Anton, and two other cousins from Amsterdam shared a last meal in the café at the airport before I boarded. They were there to see me off. As I made my way down the terminal toward the gate, I turn and shouted. "*Tot ziens*!" Till I see you again!

*

It had been a wonderful four weeks but my first trip to Holland was at an end. I was more than ready to get home and see Mark. We'd planned for him to fly into Seattle, Washington, to meet up with me. Mom and Dad never knew of our pre-planning. He was waiting at the gate when I arrived.

"I missed you so much!" Mark said to me during our first big hug. Four weeks was a long time to be apart.

"I missed you too," I replied.

We flew to Portland together and spent three hours waiting for a bus to take me back to Salem. I was originally supposed to be on that bus to Portland with the other passengers from Salem. When the bus finally arrived from Seattle, I would again travel with the Salem passengers, leaving Mark to drive home from Portland in his folk's car. Sneaking around was hard work, but the only way we could see each other.

While in Portland, I had lots of time to share my adventures with Mark. "It sounds like you had a great time, but I can only understand part of what you are saying. I don't think you realize that some of what you have been telling me was not in English. Not only that, but you have an accent you didn't have before," Mark mentioned with a confused look on his face.

I was surprised at what Mark had just said. I did catch myself throwing in an occasional Dutch word, but I thought I caught most of them. "I have an accent? Really?" I asked. It would take several more days before the controls in my brain dialed back the Dutch and dialed up the English. The accent dimmed and then disappeared.

Mark was surprised to see me light up a cigarette. That would take some getting used to. I told him that I didn't think I would be smoking very much or for very long. It seemed to make him feel a little better.

In my outward appearance, I was still the same girl I was before I left. However, my inner self developed some independence such as I had never enjoyed before. I liked the new strength I was feeling. Maybe it wasn't apparent to Mark at that time, but it would impact both of us soon. I was about to test this new sense of freedom when I returned home to my parents.

Chapter 20

Inner Healing, and Not Just on Sundays

I had ambivalent feelings coming home. Mom and Dad were happy to see me, and I was happy to see them, but we had lots to talk about.

As tired as I was, it was important to share my adventures with my parents. They were happy that I had been able to meet so many of my relatives on my trip. Tante Mia had done a good job arranging visits with both sides of the family, and I wanted to have my camera film developed quickly so I could give copies to Dad and Mom of their family members.

Prior to my leaving for Holland, Mother had asked me to pick up a few items she wanted. It was important to me to get everything she requested. They had gifted me with some graduation money and I wanted to give a gift back in return. After carefully emptying my suitcases, I presented Mom with her items. Mom and Dad were both pleased.

I talked about my visit with Opa Bruggeman, but avoided mentioning the gift he gave me. I went back up to my room and returned with one of the pieces of my Oma's special dishes. "Mom, Opa gave me something when I went to see him a second time. He gave me these dishes that belonged to your mother. I have several more pieces upstairs to add to this one. I hope you will enjoy them. I want you to have them. I will get them back someday, you know, later on!" I said while placing the small plate in her hands. Both of us understood what I meant by "later on."

Mother sat stunned for a moment. It was hard for me to figure out the reaction on her face. I asked her if she liked them.

"Opa didn't give them to me, Marja. He gave them to you, because he wanted you to have them, not me."

"But you deserve these more than I do, Mom! I'm sure he was thinking about both of us when he gave them to me," I presumed to say. This wasn't what I anticipated. I truly thought she would be happy to have her mother's dishes. My having been given what rightly should have gone to her opened up some old wounds of hers instead. Not only did this gift upset my Tante Mia, thinking she would inherit them, but it upset my mother too.

"Please, Mom. I want you to have them. Opa knew that I would be coming back to you with them. He didn't give them to Mia, he gave them to me because I was there. He must have figured that you would enjoy having something of your mother's. Please Mom. They belong to you because, through me, Opa was able to hand down something of your mother's. You take them now, and I will take them later on," I pleaded.

After another awkward moment of silence, she said, "I appreciate what you are trying to do, and I will keep them here for now and make sure you get them back when you want them. Perhaps Opa has mellowed some in his retirement, as you say, but I will always know that they belong to you. It's just how it is." It was decades later before we ever talked about those dishes again.

*

When Mom was in her late 50's, she prayed for inner peace to overcome the painful memories of having felt unloved by her father. At a prayer vigil she attended, she prayed along with the intercessory prayers of many others supporting her. Mother was blessed with a vision.

In that vision, she saw herself as a young child of two or three years old. She was in the middle room of the second floor of the bakery in Holland, where the family relaxed on Sundays. Her father was sitting in an easy chair and her mother was sitting in a chair across from him. She saw herself with a ball in her hand, and watched as she rolled the ball back and forth between her parents. They were playing with her, and all three of them were laughing. Her father and mother then reached out their arms to their little girl. She saw herself running into the arms of her mother, and then running into the arms of her father. Back and forth she went, over and over, enjoying abundant love.

"Your Opa did the best he could in his life," she said after telling me of her vision. "It was not easy living in Holland during his adult years. He was not perfect, but who of us is? He did not show his feelings, much like many men of his time. I was just a child who didn't see things as my parents did. That scripture passage in the Bible comes to my mind, the one that says, 'When I was a child, I spoke like a child, I understood like a child, thought like a child: But, when I became an adult, I put away the things of a child' (1 Corinthians 13:11)."

Mother was given a gift that gave her what she needed, to see her father through her adult eyes and a healed heart. There was peace knowing her father and mother both loved her.

Thirty-eight years after my first trip to Holland, when I was 55 years old, it was finally time to take the gift my Opa gave me. I found a note between a bowl and lid that read, "These dishes, with the blue edge with roses, are Marja's. They were given to her. She let me use them. Love, Mom."

*

After my Oma's dishes were safely placed in my mother's possession, I put away the last of the items in my suitcase, and left my bedroom with a pack of cigarettes in my hand and the small lighter I bought in Holland. "Ok, here goes, testing my new sense of freedom. What better way than to light up a cigarette?" I thought.

I lit up a cigarette on the back patio in front of Dad. Though he was down to less than one pack a day from his two-pack addiction of unfiltered Camel cigarettes, he still hadn't given up smoking all together.

Dad stopped what he was doing at the flick of my lighter, and stared at me when he saw me take my first puff. "Smoking, huh?" Dad asked.

"Ya. I kind of picked it up at Tante Mia's house. Everywhere I went, just about everyone was smoking. So I figured, what the heck, and tried one too. I probably won't keep this up, but for now, I am smoking a little," I answered. I could see the smirk on his face even while trying to look dismayed.

Mom heard what Dad and I were talking about through the open sliding doors. No question about what she was feeling. She looked really upset. I looked at her with my cigarette between my fingers and said, "I know you and Dad would rather I not smoke, but I'm not quite ready to give it up just yet. I got used to doing what everyone else was doing. I'm not smoking much, maybe a half a pack. That is all."

"If you insist on smoking at the house, the only thing I ask is that you do it outside. I don't want Dommy to be around it. He's already after your father to quit, and this is not helping," Mom said.

"Agreed!" I said in reply. Then I thought, "That went well! Let's see how far I can push this new sense of freedom."

Before I had a chance to spread my wings again, Mom and Dad wanted to talk about something else with me.

Dad said, "Since you have been gone for the last four weeks, your mother and I have had a lot of time to think about you. We know that you are registered at the community college to become a dental assistant, and we think that is a good choice for you. We also know that you have been seeing that boy on occasion, behind our backs, and we don't want you to have to do that anymore. We want peace between us. So your mother and I agreed to let you see that boy on Sunday afternoons for a few hours, here at the house." I could tell they were thinking it was a good compromise.

I sat thinking about what my Dad just said. I looked over at Mother, who was quietly waiting for a response to their peace offering. Dad was anxious for me to say something, and said, "Well, does that sound good to you too?"

I was afraid the look on my face must have looked like the smirk I caught on Dad's face after I lit up that cigarette in front of him. With a smile on my face, I looked at both my parents and said, "It sounds good to me. It's a good start. Now I only have to sneak around six days of the week! In addition, that boy's name is Mark, and you know that!"

At that moment, Mother stood up, held out her hands in supplication to Dad, and said, "Great, now what do we do? This isn't working," and went to the kitchen, leaving me alone with Dad.

"Marja, we think you should see other people, and not just Mark. You are too young to have a boyfriend. It could be years before you are able to get married, and this boy is just starting four years of college. You cannot date a guy for several years without getting too close with each other. You know what I mean. But if you met someone a little older, someone who was almost done with college or is already working, then that would be different. You could get married sooner," my father said, trying to convince me.

"Dad, I love Mark. He is such a good person. I know you would like him if you just gave him a chance. Please Dad, I love him," I replied.

For a moment Dad sat stunned, listening to my declaration of love for "that boy." I'm pretty sure Mom heard it too because I didn't hear anything going on in the kitchen the whole time Dad and I spoke.

"Listen Dad, I don't mean to be disrespectful to you and Mom, but I am going to Chemeketa Community College in a couple of weeks, and by next summer I will be moving out on my own after I get a job as a dental assistant. A friend I work with at Meier & Frank wants to get a place together to share in the expenses," I added.

At that point, Dad must have thought I went over the line by telling him of my plans to move out of the house the following summer.

"I don't think so. You are not allowed to move out until you are married," he stated. "That is the rule in this family. Not only that, but once you start working, you will be required to pay Mom and me a certain amount of your paycheck for room and board," my father announced.

"What? If you thought I was mature enough to fly half way around the world by myself, I hoped you would recognize that I am old enough to start making some of my own decisions. Please Dad? That's not fair. I am not a kid anymore. Why are you and Mom always so strict with me? I'm just doing what others do when they reach a certain age and need greater independence. None of my aunts and uncles I met in Holland are as strict with their children my age. Things are not the same there as they were when you lived there," I argued.

I didn't want to sneak around anymore. None of what I said seemed to make a difference to Dad. My need for lenience and my determination to be with my boyfriend in a healthier atmosphere didn't seem to matter to him.

"This isn't your Dad and Mom's first time raising a daughter just out of high school. You are my fifth!" he said, in case I forgot. Like most families, we had our fair share of trials. Though we had been living in this country for several years, we were raised with the "old country" mentality and rules. I didn't understand why, until I was older, and learned more about what it meant to be raised as a second generation survivor.

"It's my job to protect you from making mistakes. Your mother and I have made a few mistakes with the others in the past, but we are not going to make those mistakes with you. You do not have our permission to move away from home until you get married and that is the end of it," Dad announced with authority.

Then he ended the conversation by saying, "So Mark is welcome to visit you on Sundays, and I am sure that you will, more than likely, see him other times anyway. He will be leaving for Oregon State University in a short time, and you will be attending school here."

Not another word was spoken between us for much of the rest of that day. So much for making a lasting peace between us. I did the next best thing. To spread my wings a little wider, I went outside to have a cigarette like I promised. Before I made it to the door, I overheard Mom say to Dad, "Let's not worry too much about Marja and that boy, Mark. He will be at school, and probably will find someone else there, and she will meet someone else too."

*

I know now the motives behind much of my parent's thoughts and actions. Their overprotection of their children was, quite simply, what they thought they needed to do to keep us safe and alive. I may be generalizing to the millions of us raised by first generation survivors, but they simply did the best they could. Knowingly or not, to our fathers and mothers it was always about protection and survival. If you were affected too, I hope you can find peace and closure with your parents.

*

Mark and I spent as much time together as we could the last few weeks before he left for college. I spent more time at his parents' house than mine. It was better that way.

We both had jobs that kept us busy. Mark worked at a frozen food processing plant, and I worked in sales in the young adult clothing department of Meier & Frank department store in Salem. We started going to church together on Saturdays or Sundays too.

By the time Mark left for school, Dad and Mom had eased up with restrictions, and I venture to say, understood that I had a serious boyfriend. They never referred to Mark as "that boy" ever again. So I guess we all mellowed out some. I slowly took over the reins of my life while they slowly let go.

Mark came home almost every weekend to see me. He would get a ride home with a classmate of his, and then hitch a ride back to Corvallis if he needed one. For football games or other special events at OSU, I would drive the 36 miles to attend with him, and then drive back to Salem.

Even though we tried to spend as much time together as possible, those first few months apart were a confusing and difficult time for both of us. Our relationship was being tested.

I was confused and in pain, finding myself drawn in by the attention of an older man at the store where I worked. I was no longer sure where my heart was leading me. Mark was aware of my dilemma, and I knew it caused him pain.

On a Sunday afternoon in December 1972, before Mark returned to school, he came to see me during my break at Meier & Frank. In an effort to end both our pain, he intended to make things easier for me by breaking up our relationship so I might find happiness again.

Seeing Mark's love and self-sacrifice for my happiness made me physically sick, imagining my life without him. Through our tears and loving embrace, all of my confusion melted away. What had I been thinking? I could not bear to be apart from him, and it was through his self-giving that I realized I didn't feel the same about the other man. Now we both could heal, and find our happiness together again.

The Good Lord helped me find and keep that special man I was destined to spend my life with. He would be mine, and I would be his. It was a true moment of clarity, and I never looked back on my decision to choose my Mark.

*

In early 1973, we talked seriously about getting married, having just survived this rough period between us. We were 18 years old, ready and desiring to be husband and wife.

We started shopping for a ring during his spring break from school. Though Mark hadn't actually proposed yet, I guess we just understood. I was unaware that he purchased the ring we both liked soon after. Even though he was still making monthly payments, he did not want to wait any longer to give it to me, so he picked it up a few weeks later.

On an ordinary Saturday in May, I went over to his parent's house to visit like I normally did. When I arrived, Mark took me by the hand and up to the bedroom he shared with his twin brother, Mike, who also attended OSU. As we sat on his bed he reached for a little bag and handed it to me.

I started to smile and get exited even before I opened it. "Is this what I think it is?" I asked, eager to see what I hoped was inside.

"Just open it," he answered.

As I unwrapped the little box, Mark expressed his thoughts regarding the restrictions placed upon me by my parents, preventing me from moving out of their house until I got married. Having made up his own mind about such matters, he simply said, "So, let's get married! (Pause) I guess there's a better way I should ask you. Will you marry me?" Mark asked.

It was an exciting moment, not knowing what the protocols were for getting engaged. There was no detailed planning of our engagement, no special date, no fanfare, no big surprise party, no candlelight dinner, and no banner flying behind a small airplane for everyone to see that read, "Marja will you marry me?" Not only that, but there had been no asking permission of my parents either. We were simply two content, love-struck 18-year-old kids making the biggest decision of our lives. And I loved the sweet simplicity of that moment between us.

"Yes, of course I will marry you! I think of you as my husband already," I said as we embraced each other.

"I've been thinking of you as my wife too," Mark returned. Then he shared a special vision he had the day his family left Missouri to relocate to Salem. He was just 16 years old and not very religious at the time, but he was certain this revelation was from God. "I wasn't sad leaving Jefferson City when we did. I was excited!" he began. "I was alone in the back of the station wagon as we drove away from our house. An overwhelming confidence popped into my head. I wasn't sad because I just knew that I was leaving to go meet my wife. There was no question in my mind, and I was certain it would happen. I couldn't wait to meet her. Then I met you, and your interesting way of asking permission to ask for a piece of paper. Clever, I thought! It was you, Marja! Now look at us!"

My husband loved to share that story with others over the years. I never got tired of hearing it. Over time, he understood that it was the first moment in his life he felt such an assurance in his heart of the presence of God. And as I write this, more than 44 years after our sweet engagement, our marriage is a testament to our shared love and faith.

Later that day, after announcing our engagement to Mark's parents, we went to visit my folks, to share our happy news with them. We walked into the house and greeted Dad who was sitting in his easy chair watching TV.

"Hey, Dad. Is Mom here?" I asked him.

"Ya, she is in the kitchen," Dad answered.

Mother came into the living room when she heard me. "Hello Mark. What are you two up to today?" she asked us.

Mark and I were still standing when he announced, "Marja and I have something important to tell you. I've asked Marja to marry me, and she said yes! We went shopping for rings a few weeks ago, and I bought this one we both liked the next day, and I gave it to her this morning!"

Mom and Dad looked at each other, trying to get an idea what the other might be thinking before responding to us. I could tell that Dad was holding back a smile, well, maybe more of a grin. Mother on the other hand, looked frustrated. She looked at both of us for just a few seconds, then turned to Dad and said, "Well, maybe that will satisfy them both for a couple more years!" She went back to the kitchen, perhaps to think about what had just happened. I could tell she was still having a hard time dealing with my new independence.

"Sit down you two," Dad said to us. "So, you just decided to make this decision by yourselves, huh? Just the two of you?

"Well, yes sir, we did," Mark replied, assuming that was the way it was done. Neither of us had a clue that Mark was first supposed to ask my Dad for his permission to marry his daughter. But after Dad's comment, it became apparent that it was expected of any young man who wanted to marry his daughter. We know that now, but we sure didn't know it then.

"Mr. van Lith, I love Marja, and she loves me. We want to get married, and I hope you will give us your blessing," Mark honorably requested.

I could tell Dad was having to think fast for his next response. Everything seemed to be going quickly all of a sudden. "How and when do you intend to get married? You have only finished one year of college, and Marja doesn't have a full-time job yet," Dad remarked.

"I will be working at the cannery again this summer, and will make more than enough for college tuition. I still have some money left over from last summer. I will work as much overtime as they will let me, to save even more," Mark quickly responded.

I know mother was listening in the kitchen. She suddenly came back into the room to be included in the conversation. "You still have three more years of college before you can support yourself and Marja. How is that going to work?"

"Mom, I got a call from a dentist recently, who is in need of a chairside dental assistant. He called the college and talked to one of my professors requesting a recommendation for a student who will be graduating soon. They told him about me, and the dentist contacted me right away. He then made arrangements for me to finish my internship with him at his office. He will be hiring me after graduation. I still plan to keep working six hours on Sundays at Meier & Frank for some extra money. It's all falling into place. I will work for us until Mark gets his first nuclear engineering job when he graduates," I said, hoping it all sounded reasonable to Mom.

Mark quickly chimed in, "And, I will be commuting to Corvallis during the week. One of the engineering students in my class has agreed to let me commute with him. I would be the third or fourth classmate to join this carpool. We all have the same schedule, and I will be helping with the gas expenses."

"So, exactly when do you plan to get married?" Dad asked.

Mark answered, "We'd like to get married later this year. I will have nearly four weeks off for semester break from mid-December to mid-January. We are hoping for the first weekend after my finals. That will give us enough time during the summer to meet with Father Neuville for our marriage preparation classes."

"You both are so young still," Mother pointed out, thinking she needed to remind us of that fact.

"It didn't take me long to fall in love with Marja. It's been over two years already, and by the time we get married, it will be nearly three years. I know we are young, but we are mature and ready to get married," Mark declared to my parents, while holding my hand tight.

The short silence was confusing. Did we just win the battle, or just loose it?

Dad looked at Mom with a grin on his face. Mother just looked resigned. So I looked to my mother and said, "We will be living in Salem, Mom! At least until Mark graduates and gets his first big job. That's still two and a half years after we get married. Please, Mom?"

Though my response was aimed at my mother, Dad took the initiative and announced, "You have my permission. Now go and let me be alone with your mother."

I stood up and gave my Dad a big hug, and then went to my mother and gave her a big hug too. I was holding back my excitement out of respect for my mother. I knew it would take some time before she could accept the fact that Mark and I were getting married.

That summer, I coordinated most of the wedding plans while Mark worked long hours in the cannery. With some of his input, I managed to nail down the necessary arrangements before he began his second year at OSU. Though he was living in Salem with his parents, his studies and my new job made it difficult for us to see each other as much as we would have liked.

We kept our plans very simple. We arranged to be married on December 15, 1973, at 6:30pm. Father Joseph Neuville, the priest at St. Joseph's Catholic Church, would officiate. Along with our priest, Mark's father, an ordained minister of the Disciples of Christ denomination, would participate as well.

My sister Gert and a friend of hers offered to sing for the ceremony, and a high school classmate of ours would accompany them on the church organ. Mark's dad would begin the service with a short greeting. He would say a few words and then ask us to commit to each other before making our vows at the altar with the priest officiating. The wedding ceremony was arranged.

Mark had two groomsmen and four ushers. All three of his brothers were included. My Dad was not on board with having my four older sisters in my bridal party (for his personal reasons). I was very sad and disappointed, but I did not want to do anything that might displease my father at this point. Instead I asked two of my best friends to stand with me.

During one lunch break at the department store, I walked over to the bridal department to look for a wedding dress. I found my gown searching through the sales rack. I looked at the price tag, tried it on, and bought it. It was the first and only dress I tried on, and it only cost $65.

I showed Mom the dress when I got home. The next week at work, one of my co-workers offered to let me use her wedding veil. I thanked her and took her up on the offer. Mother made the bridesmaids' dresses just a couple weeks before the wedding, and reimbursed me the cost of my dress.

My colors for the event would be red, white, and green, to blend in with the Christmas decorations already in the church and at the reception venue.

The Holiday Inn banquet room was reserved for the reception. To keep it very simple, we would only have a wedding cake, nuts, mints, and light drinks. Just a few days before the wedding, Dad surprised us by adding a couple of cases of champagne for the guests to drink during the toast.

I didn't even think about having music at the reception. Thankfully, Christmas music was playing throughout the Holiday Inn the day we got married.

A photographer was booked for the event, but due to the church's policy, he was not allowed to take pictures in the sanctuary before or after the ceremony. He could only use his big zoom lenses from the back of the church to capture the images. The formal pictures would have to be taken at the reception.

I mailed out very simple invitations five or six weeks beforehand, with no RSVP's. I wanted to save money by not having to use extra stamps.

All the details for the wedding were accomplished very quickly. Dad and Mom never told me how much money they were able to spend on my wedding, so I kept the cost of the wedding to a bare minimum. However, that was not my number one motivation for being frugal.

I took care of the major planning and was prudent with my parents' money so they weren't constantly being reminded of the fact that I was about to get married. I lived in constant fear that at any moment they would wake up one morning and change their minds, and tell me that I could not marry Mark yet.

"If I get all of these things arranged quickly, it would be more difficult for them to call off the wedding," I thought. I was driven by a single purpose, "Hurry up, before it's too late."

Even though my relationship with my parents had improved, I was still living at home, and now paying room and board. I felt trapped, with my parents holding all the cards, so to speak.

With one foot moving forward into adulthood, my other foot was still dragging behind.

Adults don't normally live with their parents. Adolescents do.

Marrying my Mark was my heart's desire, and we were both determined to see it through. I don't know what I would have done if they suddenly forbade me to marry. Maybe I'd light up a cigarette and plan to elope. Probably not!

I did my best to obey them, and didn't want to cause them any more pain. Running away to get married was not an option.

Chapter 21

Our Wedding Day

I could hear Gert singing "Sunrise, Sunset," the song from the movie *Fiddler on the Roof*. During the song, both mothers were escorted to their seats, with the bridal procession soon to follow. When everyone was in place, the organ swelled along with my excitement. I looked at my Papa. He gave me his arm and proudly walked me down the aisle to give me away to Mark. I felt like I was dreaming, but in just a few minutes, Mark and I would be married!

St. Joseph's Catholic Church in downtown Salem could hold close to a thousand parishioners during Sunday Mass. The altar look so far away walking down that long aisle, and it seemed to take forever to get there. The majority of the pews were empty with only about a hundred guests in the church to witness our vows. Standing next to Mark was my seven-year-old brother, Dommy, holding the pillow with both rings attached. They both looked so handsome in their tuxedos.

Dommy and I spent more time living at home together then he had with our older sisters. I was the last of the girls to marry, leaving Dommy to be raised as an only child. My intention was to spend as much time with my brother as I could after I was married, to build more memories between us. Mark and I planned to visit our respective families at least once a week while living in Salem.

The reception was just as I planned, sweet and very simple. Unfortunately, while greeting our guests during the traditional receiving line, each hug and kiss made Mark and I look more and more disheveled, and we hadn't had our formal pictures taken yet. I wish we could have taken them in the church before the ceremony, but that was not possible. Just after the last greeting, the photographer whisked us into a hallway to capture the moments.

How shall I say this? The pictures were not kind to us! I was so disappointed with the way most of them turned out. I only bought a few of the photos, and never put them neatly into the wedding book I was given at my bridal shower.

We returned to the reception as quickly as we could. The photographer had taken so much of our time away from the guests, that some of them had left before we returned.

It was time to cut the cake and have the champagne toast. I cut the first piece and gave it to my new husband. Mark had a curious looked on his face just after I spread some frosting over his mouth with the first bite.

"Why did you shove the cake into my mouth?" Mark asked while grabbing for a napkin.

"I thought I was supposed to. I've seen other brides do that at other wedding receptions and on TV. I assumed that was expected! I'm sorry. I guess we should have talked about it first. I didn't even think about what we would do after we cut the cake. Sorry!" I answered.

Thankfully, Mark was quick to forgive me for messing up his face. Though he was tempted to pay me back, he was much kinder than I was to him.

It was time for the toast. Even though we were under age, no one dared to deny us champagne at our wedding reception. After the best man and maid of honor gave us their words of wisdom and congratulations, my dear Dad grabbed the microphone and delivered one more toast.

I can still hear the sound of my father's voice. I loved the thick Dutch accent when he spoke. These were the thoughts he shared, and the way he would have expressed them:

> *Marja and Mark, we wish you all the best. I know, Mark, that you will take good care of my youngest daughter, because I know how much you love each other. I can see it. It hasn't always*

been an easy road to get here, but we are here now, and happy for you both. Marja, remember, we will always be here for you and Mark, and your family. We pray that you have a happy and healthy life together. Stay close to God in your marriage, and don't ask us to babysit your kids when they come! [Laughter.] Now, everyone, lift up your glass, and give a toast to the bride and groom. Cheers!

Papa was so right about the journey getting to this day. We were raised during a unique period of time filled with lots of social and spiritual changes going on all around us. Many things still felt foreign to Mom and Dad, even after this many years in America. They relied on the parenting skills they learned in the "Old Country," even though they themselves were denied normal conditions during the war. They did their best, and indeed provided us with much more than what they had received from their own parents. This is what good parents strive to do.

The reception was winding down, but I still needed my first dance with my new husband, and then one with my father.

A soft Christmas carol was playing in the background when Mark and I moved onto the small dance floor. With so little dance experience together, swaying back and forth was about all we were comfortable with. We managed to include a few expected kisses, to the delight of our friends and family.

When the next song began to play, Dad came to dance with me, and Mark escorted his mother to the dance floor. I never thought about the father-daughter dance either, when making wedding plans. But somehow, when Jingle Bells started to play, Dad and I both chuckled together; it just seemed perfect. Mother seemed to get kick out of that moment too!

Everything went by so quickly. When it was time to leave, our wedding party packed up all the gifts and the top to the cake, and put them in several cars. They planned to join us for a short after-party in our little apartment.

Unfortunately, just days before the wedding, I had been driving my 1966 Ford Mustang on a dark and rainy evening, and rear-ended another car. I was the third person in the family to own this car. Ineke sold it to Sue, and she sold it to me, and now it was in the shop getting repaired. I still miss that car. She'd be quite the classic now!

One of Mark's groomsmen and his wife owned two 240Z sports cars and let us borrow one of them for our wedding, until our car was repaired. We were so grateful.

We said goodbye to the remaining guests and our families, then ran through the rice that was thrown above us. Driving off to our little apartment in this fancy Z car, still wearing our wedding attire, was kind of exciting. I was eager to wave to anyone who pulled up next to us, and shout out, "We're Married!"

There was a small problem. Nobody dared to decorate the borrowed sports car, so it wasn't obvious when we drove home that a newlywed couple was inside. In addition, it was another one of those very dark and rainy evenings. Still, how could anyone miss my voluminous borrowed veil, and not notice that we were just married? Honestly!

Not one car stopped near us at any stoplight. Not one car was ever in front of us, behind us, or next to us. There simply was nobody to wave to while in our wedding attire. I had an adolescent moment. "Bummer!" I thought.

We managed to pirate a couple of champagne bottles to share with the bridal party at our little apartment when they arrived with our gifts. Mark and I opened a few gifts before we popped open the bubbly. David Harrison, Mark's best man from Missouri, made sure that nobody had more than one glass to drink. He also made sure that nobody stayed too long. After less than an hour, he stood up and announced it was time to leave the newlyweds alone. What a good best man!

We were finally alone as husband and wife. "The reality will set in tomorrow morning, when I wake up and see him lying here next to me, for the first time. Am I still dreaming? Am I really Mark's wife?" I thought as we turned the light off.

We had the next two weeks off during the Christmas holiday. There would be no flying off to a fancy honeymoon in Hawaii. That happened nineteen years later and we would be 37 years old by then.

We managed to save enough money to enjoy a three-day weekend at the Oregon coast. However, that wouldn't happen until July, seven months after the wedding. We stayed at the Inn at Spanish Head in Lincoln City. We went to this same hotel ten years later for our wedding anniversary, only this time we had three little sons to enjoy it with us!

*

Like most married couples, we've had our ups and downs. A few were the size of a small hill, while the majority were no larger than a molehill. Gratefully the strains in our marriage were few and far between.

We adopted a rule to never to go to sleep at night without coming to some kind of resolution, even if it was only a temporary one, and may have taken half the night to get there. Mark would probably say that this rule was mostly mine, but he went along with it. When morning arrived, I was often amazed that the problem of the night before didn't seem that important anymore.

The very best advice ever given to us was to pray together each and every day. We pray in good times and bad, choosing love and forgiveness over anger and bitterness. Through prayer, we strive to overcome the temptations of this world designed to tear us apart. And there are plenty of those out there for all of us!

After all these years, this equation continues to bless us with even greater love. If anything major continues to fester, we both feel renewed and forgiven after making a good confession to a priest. Having received God's grace and mercy, it makes it possible to provide the same measure of forgiveness to each other that we receive for ourselves. We walk together in faith on this journey of life.

Mark has asked me to include some advice for married men who are reading this book. He says, "Be a man and tell your wife you're sorry, and heal her with love. Then watch what happens!"

Good advice, honey. Oh, and I'm sorry too!

"I knew that I was going to meet my wife." I love that part of Mark's story! What a blessing. Long shall you live, in the Gloria, Hip Hip Hooray!

An Honest Mistake

Mark and I kept our word to visit our parents at least once a week. In addition, we routinely sat with my folks in church on Sundays, to stay close. Seeing each other frequently was important. We all understood that we would likely be moving away after Mark graduated from OSU, making it impossible to see each other with such regularity.

While having to travel to and from Corvallis five days a week, Mark rarely got home before 5:30 in the evening. A small part of our weekend was reserved for family time, while much of the rest was devoted to Mark's studies.

I had more flexibility and would often go to see my parents during my lunch break from work. They seemed to enjoy my coming over to eat with them, and it did help me save a little on food expenses, too.

Six weeks after our wedding, on January 29, 1974, we went to my folk's house to celebrate my birthday. Dinner was always scheduled for 5 o'clock, so Mark came home early that day so we could be on time.

I was given a card with a financial gift my parents typically gave to each of their grown daughters on their birthday. Inside the birthday card was an endearing note of congratulations, along with the usual, "Love, Mom and Dad." What was also included with Dad's signature was a sentence that read, "Congratulations on your 20th birthday, you're not a teenager anymore!"

I was puzzled, not exactly sure what to say. I thought there might be some sort of joke that I was not getting, which would have been out of character, especially for Mom. Finally I said, "Happy 20th?"

"Well, that's your birthday, isn't it?" Dad replied.

"Dad, I'm only 19! Did you really think I was 20?"

Oh, the look on Dad's face was priceless. He looked at Mom, then I looked at Mom, and Dommy looked at me. "So you were 18 when you got married? You mean, I let you get married when you were 18?!" Dad burst out.

"Of course we did! What were you thinking?" Mother questioned him. "I knew she was only 18."

Dommy suddenly looked toward Mom and Dad with a confused and apprehensive look on his face, not knowing what might happen next.

With the palm of his hand now supporting his forehead, Dad admitted, "I think I lost track of how old you were. With all of my daughters, I just lost track. I can't believe you were 18 when you got married!" Just after he said that he began to laugh, and the rest of us joined in.

"Well Dad, if it is any consolation to you, when we got married, Mark was 19 years old for more than two weeks already," I chimed in, generating another round of laughter.

I'm not quite sure Dommy has any memory of that birthday. But I will never forget, how my father had miscalculated just how old, or rather, young I was when he gave me away in marriage to Mark.

It didn't take long for my parents to develop a lasting bond with my husband. I knew they would love him after they gave him a chance and got to know him. They loved him for the rest of their lives. Mark was their favorite son-in-law living in Pasco, Washington!

Chapter 22

Conditioned to Protect

We moved to Pasco after Mark received his Bachelor's Degree in Nuclear Engineering from Oregon State University in 1976. He landed several job offers from a large company in Richland, Washington to do nuclear fuel research and development at the Hanford site. Our original intention was to live in the "Tri-Cities" (Pasco, Richland, and Kennewick) for a couple of years before moving on from there. As it turned out, 40+ years later, having lived, worked, and planted deep roots in this soil, we still call the Tri-Cities our home.

Moving away from our family and friends was more difficult than I had anticipated. Just six weeks before leaving, I had given birth to our first baby, Benjamin Mark on June 9, 1976. We would be living nearly five hours away with no support system waiting there for us.

Mark and I knew how important it was for me to be a full-time mother and "domestic engineer" for our young and growing family. In less than two years, I delivered our second son, Matthew John on March 1, 1978. Timothy Michael made his appearance two years and eight days later, on March 8, 1980. After two miscarriages and a short break for me, our daughter, Jessica Suzanne was born four and a half year later, on November 21, 1984.

There was always talk of me going back to college for a degree *someday*. I had always assumed that I would provide a second income after all our children were in school full time. Hard work was not new to me, having spent the summer months in my youth picking strawberries, raspberries, and pole beans in the fields around Salem. After my 16th birthday, I began working part-time at Bob's 19 Cent Burgers before moving on to the department store, Meier & Frank, when I was 17. I was working as a dental assistant when Mark and I got married, and was pregnant with Ben during Mark's senior year at OSU. With three more children to follow, that *someday* kept getting pushed back.

*

Even before our last child was born, I was pursuing my passion for singing. Mark knew how important it was for me to sing. He was home alone with our children on many Friday or Saturday evenings when I sang professionally at all sorts of venues with a variety of musicians. That was in addition to the hundreds of weddings, funerals, and church services where I was asked to provide music. The last professional band I helped to create was together for eighteen years.

Singing was a big part of who I was, and I was often ascribed as, "the lady with the voice." It was a huge loss and a sad time for me when I needed to retire from music in my early 50's. More on this a bit later.

*

My music career was a big concern of my parents, especially for my mother. "You shouldn't be out there so much. Too many people know who you are. You should stay home and just be happy there," she said to me on a number of occasions.

If that wasn't enough for my mother to worry about, when our daughter Jessica started pre-school, I began taking prerequisite courses at Columbia Basin College in Pasco, planning to enter the nursing program when she was in first grade. I had completed all the preliminary classes and was accepted into the two year Applied Science in Nursing program in 1990.

With me in college, my oldest in high school, two in middle school, and one in grade school, life at home was quite busy. Mark was once again very supportive of my choice to become a Registered Nurse

(RN). We both knew that a second income would be very helpful when our children began college in just a few short years.

School was never really difficult for me when I was growing up. I received mostly A's, B's, along with a couple of C's during high school, not bad, not great. I would have gotten better grades if I had worked a little harder. At the time, I just wasn't that interested.

Going to school in my mid 30's was daunting. I was very motivated, and challenged myself to learn as much as I could. If I was going be a competent health care provider, I needed to master everything required of me. Those two years in nursing school were difficult, and to my surprise, a couple of the best years of my life.

During the last quarter of my studies, four of my instructors cornered me at the same time in the hallway, wanting to talk. At that moment I got a little nervous, thinking I might be in some sort of trouble. Respectfully, I follow them into an office. What else was I supposed to do?

Behind closed doors, with the four nursing instructors looking at me, I finally asked, "Ok, am I in any trouble?"

Each of them began to laugh, and one of them said, "No, No, it's nothing like that! We just wanted to ask you something. We have gotten to know you these last couple of years, and know how hard you have worked in school, and how well you have done. We've never had any of our nursing students represent the college at graduation, and that day will be here before you know it. We'd like you to consider representing the department as a commencement speaker. We would be honored to have you represent the college."

Silence! "Oh my, I wasn't expecting that. I'm honored that you asked me. That's really special. Dang, I wish that I hadn't given my public speaking book away when that class was over. I never thought I would need it again," I responded. We all laughed at my mistake. "So what does this entail?"

"Here's the information you will need," one of the instructors said as she handed me an envelope.

"I see you came prepared," I said as I took the paper.

"We were hoping you'd say yes," they replied.

I may not have agreed to their request had I known that, to speak at graduation, I would have to enter a speech competition, and then be chosen as a finalist from the group. Because it was an honor to be asked, I followed through and was one of three students chosen to speak at the college graduation that year.

Mom and Dad came up for my RN pinning ceremony and graduation in June of 1992. I was 37 years old. My last graduation was high school, 20 years before. I was hoping my parents would be proud of me.

This weekend would turn out to be one of the best of my life. I so enjoyed having my parents with me to celebrate this achievement. Within a couple of weeks I would be traveling to Tacoma, Washington, to take and pass my State Board exams, which allowed me to practice as an RN.

The evening of Saturday, June 13, the pinning ceremony was held. This event is a tradition for all nurses, when each new grad receives a special pin to wear on her uniform. I was excited when the ceremony began, knowing that family and friends were seated in the auditorium.

The music for this event was provided by my keyboard player and one of my best friends, Warren Tate. He and I had been in a band called Candleflame for eighteen years. In addition, we performed as duos for weddings and funerals, and provided evening entertainment in local restaurants, wineries, and other venues.

Warren played the traditional processional, "Pomp and Circumstance," as the nurses walked down the steps of the auditorium toward the seats reserved for them in front of the stage. It was a very dignified and formal procession. That is until I began walking down the stairs.

Suddenly, and without any warning, the music morphed into a slow and noble version of the song, "The old gray mare, she ain't what she used to be..." I nearly missed a step when I realized Warren had changed the music for my entrance.

As the crowd began to identify the new song, I looked over at my family who were shaking their heads and chuckling, and I hung my head in embarrassment. By the time I got to the bottom of the stairs, Warren had already flawlessly gone back to Pomp and Circumstance. The humor was not lost on anyone in the auditorium.

During the event, a couple of my classmates delivered humorous tales of the many adventures we shared throughout our years of study. Just before each nurse was pinned with the symbolic nurse insignia, there were a couple of honors presented. The first of the awards was given to the nursing student with the highest grade point.

The instructor presenting this award began by saying, "This award is presented to the student who has the highest academic achievements over the entire nursing curriculum. This person has given each of her patients the very best care. We have seen her laugh, cry, sing, and pray with her patients. I had the privilege of watching this nursing student care for one of her patients who was in severe pain. She asked her patient if she wanted prayers while they waited for her doctor to respond to the request for an increase in pain medication to deal with her intractable pain. I stood just outside the door of the room and watched as she held her patient's hand and began to pray. I witnessed her patient relax completely, and watched as her pain diminish."

As I listened to my instructor, I looked to my children and saw that they were getting excited. They pointed at me and mouthed the words, "It's you, Mom, it's you!"

The instructor continued, "This student has done all this and more, while raising a family of four children, performing music on many weekends, and volunteering her time to others. Accepting our request, she was chosen to be our first nursing graduate to represent the college as the commencement speaker tomorrow. You just heard her sing "Wind Beneath My Wings." The student awarded with the highest grade point average of 3.7 for the class of 1992, is Marja Henderson!"

I could not hold back the tears. Never did I think that I would receive this honor. I knew I had done well, but the 3.7 grade point blew me away. I thought to myself, "I'm not a dummy after all. Is it ok to feel this way? Will my folks be proud of me now?" My self-confidence improved a bit that weekend. It was time to celebrate!

Words of congratulations and lots of pictures followed. I was so happy my Dad and Mom were there for me, sitting with Mark and the kids. I knew I would look back and miss many things about the nursing program, but my time in a classroom as a student was over.

The following day crowned the end of my wonderful weekend. I don't remember much about graduation except for how much fun it was to give my speech. I had people laughing as I told what it was like to go back to school and graduate 20 years after high school. The very last thing I said in my speech was a tribute to my Mark. "Thanks for Maui-ing me!" I said intentionally. The following day my husband and I would be flying to Hawaii, finally, to enjoy that honeymoon we waited this long to take.

It was difficult to say goodbye to so many wonderful women and men who studied with me during my years at Columbia Basin College. The real education would begin at the end of the summer, when I would begin working in the labor and delivery unit at the local hospital in Pasco.

I was excited to hear what my parents had to say after taking part in the weekend festivities. They were there laughing with everyone else who recognized "The Old Gray Mare," as I walked down the stairs. They listened when I sang "Wind Beneath My Wings," to my husband and children. They saw my emotion when I received my award. They paid attention during my commencement address at graduation. They were there for me, and I was grateful. Yet, throughout the entire weekend, I was still looking for their approval like a child, and not a 37 year old woman.

"I am so thankful that you came this weekend, Mom and Dad. It means so much to me. So what do you think about the whole weekend?" I asked them both.

"Well, it was nice. You did a lot. We're happy you're done with school," Mom said.

"Dad, what about you? What did you think about everything?" I turned and asked him, looking for something a little more affirming.

"Well, you worked hard, and did a good job. Is it time to go back to your place yet? It's very warm outside in the sun," was his response.

We quickly wrapped things up and headed home. Mom and Dad gave me an envelope with a check inside, some spending money for our first big vacation alone together. "Love, Dad and Mom," was written at the bottom of the graduation card.

Finally I had to ask them both, "Are you proud of me?"

"Well, sure we are. It's just, (pause) we want to know if you are finally done. Are you done now?" Mom questioned.

I was puzzled by her statement and asked, "What do you mean, am I done now? Done with what?"

She went on to say, "You know, done with your education, and doing your own thing. Are you going to be home more with your family, or are you going to pursue something else now, that sort of thing?"

"I don't know. I haven't thought about it. I just finished a very difficult nursing program. I don't plan on going any further with my degree, if that's what you mean. But I'm not going to stop learning," I said, still a bit confused.

Dad went on to say, "What your mother is saying is, she thinks you have been thinking too much about yourself lately, and not about your family like you should. Your sisters don't go out there and do the kind of things that you do. They stayed home more."

"You are always doing something out in the public. We just hope you are done now, except for working part time. That's all," Mom added.

"I was hoping that you would be happy with my accomplishments, and proud of what I achieved," I said quietly.

"Of course we are proud of you. You are our daughter, and we are glad we came this weekend to see you and the family," they both responded in various ways.

I didn't like having to come right out and ask my parents how they were feeling about me and my accomplishments. Just once, I needed them to freely say they were proud of me. It took quite a while to get over my huge disappointment. It took several more years before I figured out the added meaning to the words they were really saying to me.

Their goal for each of their daughters was to have us finish high school, find a nice Catholic man to fall in love with, and settle down to raise a family. It was expected of us, and we were not encouraged to pursue much beyond that. By following these guidelines, we would not stand out as being different, unconventional, or exposed in any way.

I was not fitting smoothly into that mold. I was living out the American dream, as I knew it. I had a goal, worked hard, became an RN, got a new job, continued to take care of the family, and sang on occasion. This was not what Dad and Mom thought I should be doing.

By minimizing achievements and cautioning me from being "out there," they were attempting to keep me from becoming a target, thereby keeping me safe from harm. Mom and Dad were trying to protect me.

Over the many years as they unfolded their stories to me, I came to understand them with greater clarity. Because they were habituated into submission during the war years, by "keeping our noses down," "not drawing attention to ourselves," and being "like everyone around us," as they said, they didn't stand out. That is what kept them alive, and what changed them forever. By raising us to follow these rules, they showed their children love. <u>I am a second generation survivor.</u>

*

What was also evident was just how much Dad and I had in common. "You're just like your Father," Mom told me many times. She was right, though when she used that phrase, it never sounded like a complement. On the contrary.

Dad and I were both extraverts and got energy by involving ourselves with other people and new things. We loved to be the life of the party, wanting everyone to have a good time around us. We could both be stubborn and opinionated because of our strong values and convictions. We were easily drawn to others, gravitating to individuals who were different from us. Dad and I both loved to sing and harmonize. One of us maybe did a better job at it though! We both had a sense of adventure that was expressed in many different ways. We just plain loved life, and wanted to experience as much as we could, while we still could. Let me not forget how much love of God I had in common with both my parents. That common thread saved us many times.

*

Papa died twelve months later. It was the most pain I had ever experienced in my life. Oh, childbirth was painful, but the reward for my labor was a beautiful child each time. The laboring pain of losing my Dad left nothing but a huge hole in my heart. I plan to see him again someday, but not just yet!

Lang zal ze leven, lang zal ze leven, lang zal ze leven in de Gloria, in de Gloria, in de Gloria. Hieperdepiep, hoera!

Hip Hip Hooray!

Chapter 23

Life Without Dad

Dad had taken the time to plan for this probable scenario, where he would die before our mother. She would continue receiving a good portion of her husband's resistance pension. Financial concerns would not be an issue for the rest of her life. For that, we were all grateful.

Mother had many adjustments to make that were challenging for her. She was now responsible of taking care of the monthly bills, taxes, and major purchases, things Dad had done for them for so many years. Simple household repairs overwhelmed her. Fortunately, she had men in the family who lived just a few miles from her house and could come to assist in repairs when needed, and daughters to help her get familiar with her personal finances.

Though Mom tried to put on a good face, we were all aware that this was a very sad time for her, especially that first winter alone. The first holiday season only made things harder. "What's the point in Christmas decorations when you have no one to share them with? I just don't see it," Mom said.

Without her husband of nearly 48 years, Mom had little to look forward to. In the past, when she and Dad had a desire to get out and do something fun, they would make plans to take another cruise. That always worked to lift them out of the doldrums.

Knowing how much she enjoyed cruising, the siblings began to discuss ways to give her something special to look forward to. What better way than to plan a vacation?

Cruising

Many of the siblings were together at Mom's house for her first Christmas alone. Someone asked, "Mom, would you like to venture out in the spring and take a cruise with your children?" There was little need to convince her. She got her Holland America 1994 cruise brochure down from the shelf in the kitchen and started planning.

Mom made it through that first holiday season without her Mienus, and seemed to perk up after the New Year. Planning a vacation with her children may have had something to do with that. This would be a big step for her to navigate, one on a long list she would face that initial year alone.

All of the siblings, except for Dominic, were able to travel with Mom. Dom hadn't accrued enough vacation hours at his new job, and more importantly, he was a newlywed. A seven-day vacation in May was not going to work for him. So, it would be six women, three to a cabin, for our great adventure to Alaska.

The day of our departure finally arrived, May 21, 1994. I had a four-hour drive the day before from Pasco to Woodinville, Washington, where Sue lived. From her place, we still had another three-hour drive to Vancouver, Canada the morning of our embarkation.

We boarded the Holland America ship, the *MS Westerdam*, and set sail in the late-afternoon sunshine, enjoying the "Bon Voyage" party on the lido deck. The ship set course for the inside passage toward the lower SE territories of Alaska. This was the first cruise for the five sisters.

Something unexpected transpired on the first full day of our journey. Mother fell back into a parenting role, leading her daughters as if we were small children again. This began even before we got on board the ship.

We were five very capable adult women, ranging in age from late 30's, to mid-40's, falling in line under our mother's supervision once again. It was subtle at first, but after a couple of hours, Gert and I looked at each other with raised eyebrows, wondering if the others were feeling uneasy too.

"Is it just me, or have we all regressed about 30 years," Gert whispered to me.

"Ya, I've noticed it too. But I'm also sensing some tension within the group. It didn't make me feel very comfortable hearing, 'I'm not sharing a room with so-and-so,' just like when we were kids. I hope everyone gets along on this trip," I whispered back.

We did develop a few conflicts during the seven days at sea. Of course that's going to happen when you get six women of the same family in close proximity to each other for that length of time. But those conflicts didn't last long, and were outweighed by the whole adventure. In our family, the love we feel for one another makes the worst in us tolerable.

Our first day, we cruised through the many tightly knit islands of the calm inland waterways of British Columbia, Canada. We arrived at our first port of call in Ketchikan, Alaska. Ketchikan is known for its fishing, canneries, cool-looking totem poles, rustic tourist shops, and an early 1900's "red-light district!"

We saw so many bald eagles in Ketchikan. To my surprise and dismay, I discovered that our proud American symbol is a scavenger. I made my objection to Ineke, who was with me on a sightseeing boat excursion. "Bald eagles can't be scavengers, eating off dead fish carcasses! Vultures do that. They have to be majestic birds that fly or stand proudly for us to take pictures of, and put their image on our dollars and quarters!" I playfully demanded. Ineke just smiled at me.

The following day we spent in Juneau, the capitol of Alaska. Four of us walked to a popular attraction, the Red Dog Saloon, not far from the ship. It had a quaint rustic vibe to it, with walls covered with patron's business cards from around the world. After exiting through the red saloon doors, we hopped a tour bus to see our first glacier.

Mendenhall glacier is one of several glaciers created some 3,000+ years ago during what is commonly referred to as, "The Little Ice Age." As exciting as it was to see, this very slow moving river of blue ice was only the beginning of our glacial encounters.

In the early morning hours of the following day, the ship came to rest in the middle of Glacier Bay National Park.

"Fitting name," I thought, due to the many different glaciers that fed into it.

After breakfast, the six of us ventured out into the cold and drizzly weather to admire the natural beauty of the colossal icy cliffs of compressed snow and ice. The ice is so blue from the trapped oxygen tightly bound after thousands of years of freeze, thaw, and refreeze. The terminal cliffs reach hundreds of feet in height. At any moment, chunks of ice that had labored under the ever-changing structure could calve off, diluting the salt water below, and once again return to the lifecycle of water.

The last port of call before returning to Vancouver was the small town of Sitka. This town, like many other coastal towns, is home to several fishing boat skippers eager to assist cruise ship passengers on an early morning fishing trip. Hoping to snag a fresh King salmon or very large halibut, Gert, Sue, and I set out on one of these excursions.

Gert was the lucky one that morning, hooking and landing one of the largest salmon any of us had seen in the wild. She wore the biggest smile on her face for the rest of that day, and made sure everyone saw her walking up the gangway with her fish as her trophy. Sue and I came back with only stories to tell of the big ones that got away from us. It took me a long time to get over the three times I had a fish on the hook, only to lose each of them just before surfacing. I think maybe I'm still not over it.

Our last day at sea was filled with simple, introspective conversations between siblings, and meaningful time spent with our mother before disembarking the next day.

With a week of fun, adventure, rest, and lots of good food and family time, it was hard letting go of this experience. Though I missed Mark and the kids, I was bitten by the cruise bug, just like Dad and Mom had experienced several years before. This would not be my last cruise. I was sure of that! This was just the beginning of more adventures to come, only Mark didn't know it yet.

Saying goodbye to my sisters was hard. Saying goodbye to Mom was very hard. My consolation was to have seen Mom enjoy cruising again, and taking delight in her daughters for a whole week. We also got to see our mother receiving some gentlemanly interest on board, too. There was no shortage of dance partners for her every evening before dinner. I knew she was amused by the attention. The blushing on her face gave it away.

Mom would go on to take several more cruises. Each time she cruised alone, she made sure she was assigned a seat at a table of ten to twelve every evening in the dining room. It forced her to meet new people and be social. Other passengers who met her were happy to take her under their wings on excursions off the ship, as well as activities on board. She made up her mind to do the things she wanted to do, and grew more self-confident during those, so called, "golden years" of her life.

She managed a couple more trips to Holland. She also enjoyed hosting her sister Mia, and her brother, Anton, and his wife, when they came to visit her a couple more times. She even treated them to a cruise when they came. It was easy for her to share what she had been blessed with. "I'm just spending your inheritance," Mom said to tease us.

My folks had always been generous with their money, especially with their children. Throughout their lives, several charities benefited by their generous monthly donations. They understood how blessed they had been with the standard of living they enjoyed in the later years of their lives.

They were not financially wealthy, like multi-multimillionaires, or anything like that. They were just a middle-income couple who were wise in the way they chose to save and spend their money. They set a great example for the rest of us.

Following in Their Footsteps

Before I became an RN, Mark and I never had enough money to take fancy vacations. Most of what we did with Mark's time off was to travel down the Columbia River Gorge to visit our families and friends, and occasionally spend time at the Oregon coast.

During the summer of 1989 our new friends, Warren and Devi Tate, invited us to join them and their family for a few days at their favorite fishing and boating spot in Twin Lakes, Idaho. We fell in love with the camping and the boating. After this first trip a new tradition was established. We bought our own boat and continued the annual week-long trip to "The Lakes" with the Tates for the next ten years.

We did manage to take one big family trip in 1989, and it took us more than two years to save the money for this vacation. We took the children on their first plane trip to experience the wonders of Disneyland in California.

And there was one special trip Mark and I definitely wanted and needed to take. We traveled to Great Lakes Naval Base, located less than 40 miles from Chicago, Illinois. We planned to spend four days with our oldest son, Benjamin.

Ben signed up for the Navy during the spring of his senior year in high school. He left for boot camp in early December 1994. Late in January of '95, we flew to Illinois to attend what was known as "Pass and Review." This is a traditional ceremony at the completion of the Navy's basic training course. Ben would further his naval training and become a hospital corpsman. We were very proud of him for the five years he served this country. Fortunately for our family, the U.S was not involved in any major combat the entire time he served. He was honorably discharged in December of 1999.

A couple of years later, we managed a second trip to Great Lakes, this time including our other three children. We all enjoyed the sights and sounds of Chicago together.

*

In the spring of 1995, just one year after my first cruising experience, I secretly began planning a second exotic vacation. We hadn't had a vacation with just the two of us since our five days in Hawaii after graduating from nursing school. That was three years ago. With both of us working, we finally had some extra funds to treat ourselves to a week somewhere special.

Cruising, oh yes, that's where I was going, and Mark was coming with me. He never showed much interest in taking a cruise. All my efforts at explaining how much fun we would have and how he would love it fell on indifferent ears.

I knew that if I: planned it, got it all laid out, picked a good time to get away, and showed him how we could pay for it, then he would agree to give it a try. One thing I didn't have to worry about was who would watch the kids while we were gone.

By this time, Matthew (Matt) was 17 years old and a senior in high school. Timothy (Tim) was 15 and a sophomore, and Jessica was in 7th grade in middle school, just few days from her 11th birthday (having entered kindergarten when she was four years old).

I had pre-planned meals, friends who would feed the kids a couple of times, a car at their disposal, and extra cash for "just in case" things that might come up. Our best friends, Max and Michele Towne, agreed to check in and were given written permission to speak for us in case of a medical emergency.

"Look what I've been up to Mark. I know you've been reluctant to agree to a cruise, but hear me out, please," I said.

After showing him the details of this cruise to the western Caribbean, and seeing all the planning I put into this trip, Mark sat quietly for a moment and said, "It looks like you have it all figured out! How can I say no now?

I smiled at my Mark and thought to myself, "mission accomplished." After a big hug, I said to him, "You'll be hooked just like I was!"

After many years of sharing their rental cabin up at Twin Lakes, Mark and I reached out to our friends, Warren and Devi, to see if they would like to join us on our cruise to the Caribbean. They were much more excited than Mark was, and agreed to join us without hesitation. This would be their first cruising experience too.

We set sail on Sunday November 5, 1995, on the Holland America ship, *MS Nieuw Amsterdam*, leaving and returning from New Orleans, Louisiana.

We enjoyed two days at sea before arriving at the first of the scheduled ports of call, Montego Bay, Jamaica. Over the next three days, we enjoyed day trips in Georgetown, Grand Cayman Island, Cozumel, Mexico, and the Holland America Cruise Line's private island, Half Moon Cay. Our last day at sea returned us to where we started, back in New Orleans.

The beautiful islands, the fun activities, the wonderful food, and entertainment were everything I had hoped it would be. Mark and I had a wonderful time, and so did our dear friends. Mark would no longer need convincing to take another cruise. He was hooked. I was confident that it would not be too long before we would enjoy another week of fun and sun on a ship to somewhere!

Gold and Silver Cruising

On December 15, 1998, Mark and I would be celebrating our 25th wedding anniversary.

"We need to go on a special vacation together, you know, to celebrate our anniversary," I said to Mark.

"Let me guess. You want to go on another cruise, don't you?" Mark asked.

"That's a great idea! I wished I had thought about that," I answered with a wink. "You know what would be even more fun? Let's invite some family and friends to join us."

I began planning for our November cruise back to the Caribbean. We were already planning to renew our wedding vows at our church in December, with a reception to follow at our friend's winery in town. With both the cruise and anniversary, there was a lot to do to organize.

I engaged the help of the travel agent in Salem, Oregon who had facilitated all of Dad and Mom's cruises. After picking the cruise itinerary and date, and after getting the best possible rates and perks, it was time to make some phone calls and see who would like to join us.

We began by inviting our families. The only ones able to join us were my mother, Gert and Larry, and Gert's daughter, Katie. Other family members were leaving their options open. They still had a few more months before they would need to commit.

Three of my band members and their spouses signed up right away. When we mentioned the cruise to others, they began to look into the possibility. Over the course of the next couple of months, several couples heard of our planned vacation and wanted to be included. The numbers started to add up. As the time drew nearer, we had helped to fill eighteen cabins on the ship.

In this group of 36, roughly half of them had never been on a cruise ship before. Though everyone knew that Mark and I were celebrating our silver wedding anniversary, we were outdone by two couples in the group celebrating their 50th golden anniversary. We had two individuals ready to party on their 50th birthdays, and one couple outdid all of us by commemorating their 60th wedding anniversary on board the ship.

Never in my wildest dreams did I imagine bringing together such a diverse group of friends with so many important events in their lives to celebrate together. Not everyone in the group knew each other beforehand. But after sharing eight days traveling and vacationing with each other, new friendships were forged, and memories imprinted for a lifetime.

A Silver Surprise

Before I wrote about the events surrounding my parent's wedding, I never recognized details that were comparable to my own wedding experiences. Those connections popped out when I went back to proofread what I had already written.

Mom was choosing to love, and was still very naïve. I was young and in love, with few life experiences. She and Dad forfeited the normal dating customs, and worked instead to save enough to start their lives together. Mark and I were denied normal dating. We did what we could to be together, and fell in love in the process.

Both couples were forced to grow up quickly, but for very different reasons. We all entered into a commitment with someone we loved, but without the foreknowledge of what marriage would really be like, and where it would lead us.

Having siblings involved with the planning and participation in our weddings were denied both mother and me, because of circumstances we could not control. Mother's brothers and sisters were not all present at her wedding. My siblings were at my wedding, but scattered among the guests in different pews, not as bridesmaids in attendance for me.

Both of our weddings were very simple. There was little money to spend for either. Mom and I were both challenged with the lack of what we thought we needed, or perhaps to say it another way, preferred to have had for our special day. We both made it work, and moved forward toward marriage anyway.

What was most important was how God blessed us with his grace, led us to our husbands, and provided what we truly needed to live out our vows to the best of our abilities. What more could we possibly have wanted or needed?

Even with that understanding, I would have loved to have had a wedding like the ones I had been asked to sing for over 30-some years. It was such a privilege to participate in such a way, knowing that my voice contributed to one of the most important days of their lives.

For 20 years I longed for a do-over of my wedding. Our silver wedding anniversary would provide me with that opportunity. Submission and fear would not be a factor in any way with the decisions that had to be made. This time I could look forward to the planning, and the moment we renewed our vows to each other as mature adults. I knew it would mean so much more with a much deeper understanding of what we were promising again. I could hardly wait.

I could include my family in ways I was not free to on the day of our marriage. My daughter Jessica could be with me as we shopped for new and beautiful gowns to wear, and nothing would feel rushed or compromised.

Mark would have our sons, Ben, Matt, and Tim standing in birth order, towering next to him. Ben in his Navy dress blues, and Mark, Matt, and Tim wearing suits and ties. He and the boys had matured more handsome with time, looking more dashing than ever.

In addition to our own children actively participating in our celebration, some of my siblings planned to travel up from Oregon to participate in special ways. Mother came with Ineke and Lloyd and their daughter Lori, while Gert and Larry took the long way to Pasco, traveling with a guest from Seattle. They would all arrive the day before the ceremony

It was a very busy time for the band during the month of December. Candleflame had been booked long ago to perform the night before our celebration. Knowing that my relatives would already be in town, I made arrangements for them to crash a large company Christmas party in one of the hotels in Richland, Washington. They agreed to arrive around 9:00 pm, the time the music was to start.

Having just arrived hours before, Mother was too tired from the long winter drive, and chose to stay at the house. Candleflame was in the middle of our first set when Mark, Ineke, Lloyd, Lori, Gert, Larry, and someone else came walking into the ballroom. I nearly stopped in the middle of my performance when I recognized my cousin. I could not believe that the few invitations that I had sent to family in Holland would actually motivate someone to come all that way to be with us. But that is exactly what happened. I had just wanted to let them know I was thinking of them.

The last time I saw Dom Vredenbregt was at the airport in Reno, Nevada, five years earlier. The tears we shed then were due to the sadness and loss we both felt when Dad died so abruptly. This time our tears were for surprise, gratitude, and sheer joy.

What in the world would move Dom to fly over on such short notice to spend the weekend with us and fly back to Holland in less than 72 hours? I will never know for sure, but I'm convinced it was more than just celebrating our wedding anniversary!

I quickly called for a band break after two more songs. Leaving the stage, I made my way over to the table that was reserved. Hugs, kisses, and smiles were in abundance when I joined them. "What are you doing here? I can't believe you came," I asked my cousin in Dutch.

"Well, you invited me, remember? I'm here to celebrate with you and Mark!" he replied with a self-satisfying smile on his face.

It was hard to keep it all a secret. I knew someone was coming with Gert and Larry, but I did not know for sure who it was. Dom had just flown into Seattle from Holland earlier in the day. Gert and Larry drove up from Sweet Home, Oregon, the day before and stayed the night at our sister Sue's house in Woodinville, before picking him up.

We all talked for about fifteen minutes, the whole break. "You must be so tired. Please don't feel like you need to stick around. You need your sleep, Dom," I said to him.

"Don't worry about sleep. I'm ok. I can sleep when I get back to Holland. Right now, I want to be with all of you," Dom said gesturing his hand around the table.

After watching the band perform a few more songs, the family members stood up and made their way back to the exit doors of the ballroom. I waved goodbye while I was in the middle of singing another number, and watched them leave for the night.

We had lots to do the next morning to get ready for the party. I managed a short visit with cousin Dom and the others before heading over to the winery to help set up and decorate. Warren Tate was setting up his equipment to play some music during the festivities.

Mother was pensive that morning. I asked her what was on her mind. Initially, she said that nothing was wrong, not wanting to upset me. But with a little more prodding she admitted that she had some reservation about why my Dom came all the way from Holland to be here. Five years had already gone by since Dad's death, but seeing cousin Dom again stirred up a lot of uncomfortable and unhappy memories.

"What is he doing here?" Mom asked.

"He's here to see the family again. I sent three or four invites to the cousins in Holland who I thought might appreciate it. Now that we have gotten to know them better over the last several years, I thought it would be a nice gesture. Never did I think anyone would actually come, though. I must admit Mark and I are thrilled to have Dom with us," I answered.

Mother was not satisfied with my response. "Yes, but now I can't enjoy the day like I would have," she admitted.

Her reply said a lot. I thought for a moment before saying anything. I did not want to say something that might make her even more uncomfortable.

"I don't think this has anything to do with Dom, does it Mom? You know, the last time he was here, he was pretty traumatized too. I think this was a good reason for him to come back and see all of us again. He must have needed this for his own healing, Mom. I have an impression you still harbor ill feelings. Perhaps it's because you haven't worked everything out in our own mind." I said.

Through the tears she was trying to hide, she shared, "I was supposed to be with Mienus when he died. It was supposed to be me! I spent all those years with him, while his nephew was with him but a short time, and he was there and I wasn't."

"But you were with him before he died. You were just spared the trauma that cousin Dom witnessed. It all happened the way it was supposed to, Mom. Please try not to hold that against him. You know what it is like to need inner healing. Think of all those people you prayed with at Mt. Angel, for their healing. What would you be saying to them in the same situation you find yourself in right now? Dom probably needs you now, in some fashion, to help him to heal from his suffering and loss too. Don't you think that maybe he feels his own misplaced guilt at being the one with Papa when he collapsed?" I said, trying to hold back my own tears.

Silence fell between us. Something inside Mother released. She knew she was holding onto feelings that were somehow misdirected. She admitted, "No, I can't continue to hold onto the past the way I do. I guess I was all worked up again, thinking about what had happened with your father. Maybe I am still a bit angry at Mienus for something he didn't know would happen to him. Dom's presence brought back some of those old feelings again."

As she began to understand her thoughts and feelings, I gave Mom a big hug and said, "You can't be too mad with Papa either. Even he didn't know when his lights would turn off! I am so grateful that you are here for me and Mark. I hope that you can enjoy being with us, and maybe even find the strength to provide a measure of closure for Dom before he goes back to Holland. I love you, Mom!"

"I love you too, and I am glad I came," Mother acknowledged.

Re-do, Renew, Rejoice

We renewed our vows during the 5:00p.m. Mass on Saturday, December 19, 1998. Mark and I were the first couple in many years to avail ourselves of this special opportunity during a regularly scheduled Mass. From the beginning of the processional, it was clear to the congregation that this evening's Mass would be a little different from the norm. The brothers and sisters in Christ who routinely attend this particular Saturday evening service seemed genuinely please to be witness to our joy.

Mark and I processed into the church along with the altar servers, Jessica and my mother, who would be the readers of the Word, and the priest and deacon. Benjamin was the greeter before the service began and stood behind the side altar podium. Matthew and Timothy would serve as extraordinary ministers of Holy Communion. Gert joined Candleflame to sing at Mass. Ineke and Lloyd would be bringing up the bread and wine at the offertory.

Sitting in the front rows, along with my family members, were Mark's brother Dan, his wife Janet, and their sons, Scott and Austin. The severe cold winter weather did not stop them from driving down from Spokane to be with us.

Following Monsignor Pedro Ramirez's sermon, our pastor asked Mark and me to come forward to renew our wedding vows. Our children joined us in front of the altar.

Monsignor's remarks were very kind to both of us, and we appreciated what he had to say. Our four children stood very stiff until something funny was said, and they seemed to loosen-up a bit through the laughter.

Monsignor began with these familiar words:

"My dear friends, you have come together in this church so that the Lord may seal and strengthen your love in the presence of the Church's minister and this community. Christ abundantly blesses this love. He has already consecrated you in Baptism and now he enriches and strengthens you as you *renew* your sacrament of marriage. And so, in the presence of the Church, I ask you to state your intentions.

Have you come here freely, and without reservations, to give yourselves to each other in marriage? You better say the right thing here," our Pastor said amid the laughter.

"I do, um, we do, we did!" we stumbled.

Monsignor continued, "Will you love and honor each other as man and wife for the rest of your lives?"

"Yes, I will!" we both answered.

Typically this next question is only asked of newlyweds, but Monsignor slipped it in anyway.

"Will you accept children lovingly from God, and bring them up according to the law of Christ and his Church?" Laughter filled the church. "Oh, you already did that!" our pastor pretended, as if he didn't see we were flanked by our children.

"We do, and already did," we answered, smiling at our kids.

The priest continued, "Since it is your intention to renew your marriage vows, join your right hands and declare your consent before God and his church."

We were then invited to say our written vows to each other. "Ok, who wants to go first?" Monsignor Pedro asked us.

"I'll go," Mark said eagerly. He quickly pulled out a piece of paper from the inside pocket of his suit jacket. We turned toward each other just like the first time, and looked into each other's eyes, unlike the first time. He smiled at me as if no one else was watching and said:

Marja, thank you for joining me in marriage and being my wife for 25 years.

You are my best friend, my prayer partner, my daily companion, and my lover.

You are the mother of our children, and the center of our home life.

We have shared joy and sorrow, sickness and health, forgiveness and healing.

We have grown up together, and lived life to the fullest.

I renew my marriage vow to you today, and ask God to bless us with another 50 years of love and life together.

I was all choked up, and holding back from full-blown crying. Great! Now with tears in my eye, and having to follow the words my husband just said to me, I looked at the priest and asked, "You expect me to say something after that?" I then looked at Mark and said, "Next time, I go first!"

I admit, I was nervous at that point and a little embarrassed too. My children and everyone in the church heard Mark refer to me as his "lover," among other nice adjectives. Somehow, I knew that line would follow me to the reception later that evening.

Ok, here goes, my turn:

Mark. Before our God, our children, our future grandchildren, and for our family and friends, I say I love you, and gladly renew my vow to take you as my husband, and be your wife.

With God's love and faithfulness to us, I promise to be there for you every day of our lives no matter what life brings our way.

We've already been through good times and bad, shared riches and lived on a shoestring, been sick together, and been happy and healthy.

We've had our babies, and patiently wait to become Opa and Oma.

I want to share it all with you again, and ask God to continue to mold us as husband and wife, in His image, and for His plan for us.

I pray that God bless us with many more wonderful years together.

I promise to proudly walk by your side for as long as I live. And, when we are old and gray, I will love you even more. Grow old with me Mark. I hear the best is yet to be. Amen.

After we exchanged our vows, Mark and I kissed, and everyone in the church gave us a warm applause. I saw many people wiping a tear or two with a tissue. We both looked over at our children at that moment and could see the love, pride, and joy at what they had just witnessed. The "re-do" of our wedding was nearly complete.

Just after the final blessing of the Mass, our pastor invited those who would like to stay, to listen to the song I prepared to sing to my husband.

It was hard finding the perfect song to sing to Mark on this occasion. Oh, I had many songs I could have picked from among the variety of ones I had sung many times before, for brides and grooms at their weddings. But none of them spoke the words I wanted to deliver after 25 years. "Please Lord, I'm running out of time. Help me find the perfect song for my husband," I had prayed.

The very day of this little prayer petition, while driving in my car, I heard a beautiful song, one that I had never heard before. It was filled with just the right words to express the thoughts and emotions I wanted to convey to my husband. I pulled the car to the side of the road to wipe my tears and to find paper and a pen to write down the name and performer of this song. Another prayer was answered. I had found my song to sing.

By the time I got the sheet music, I only had a few days to rehearse with Warren. The song I sang to my husband was "After all these Years," by Jim Brickman, and sung by Anne Cochrun. I hope my readers will look up this song on the internet and listen. The words alone, though they are beautiful, don't deliver the same impact without the melody.

Mark moved quickly to the very front pew of the church and sat there by himself. After a moment of silence, I gestured to Warren to begin, and sang:

Here we are, after all these years.

Face to face, heart to heart, and I've loved you from the start.

But I never thought that we'd be standing here,

After all these years.

Here we are with another song to sing.

All these days pass us by as we watched our childhood fly.

And I'm still the one to share your hopes and fears

After all these years.

After all these years,

We still have each other, one to another.

After all these years, you're still the one, and I'm still here,

After all these years.

Here we are, with another bridge to cross.

Face to face, heart to heart, and I loved you from the start.

But I never thought that we'd be standing here,

After all these years.

After all these years,

We still have each other, one to another.

After all these years, you're still the one, and I'm still here,

After all these years.

And I've loved these days, all we've been through.

And I'd just like to say, I'm so glad it's been with you.

Here's one more song from the heart, for the laughter and the tears,

After all these years.

After all these years,

We still have each other, one to another.

After all these years, you're still the one, and I'm still here,

After all these years,

After all these years.

(Cochrun)

I was finally able to let loose my tears and enjoy the love, the gratitude, and the joy I was feeling. We were blessed with the best do-over ever! It far exceeded my dreams and expectations. Mark and I will always cherish the smiles of so many of the parishioners, and the many friends who thanked us for including them as witnesses to the renewal of our wedding vows. It felt like a little piece of Heaven. What a blessing for our family.

The joy lasted throughout the evening's festivities. We had a dessert extravaganza at the winery, and enjoyed the company of approximately 90 people, some of whom had driven many miles to be with us, not to mention cousin Dom who flew thousands of miles.

The icy cold wind blew outside through most of the evening, but did little to dampen the warmth of the hugs and kisses freely shared among friends. Many of our guests knew each other, and some hadn't seen each other in quite some time, adding to the enjoyment of the event and the Christmas season.

If our 25th wedding anniversary had been celebrated in Holland and not in Pasco, someone in the family, or one or more of our rowdy friends, would have stood up from their chair, lifted high the drink in their hand, and led the guests in singing *Lang Zal Ze Leven. Long Shall You Live.*

*

Two years later, having had such a wonderful time on our 25th anniversary cruise, Mark and I decided to invite others to join us for another cruise back to the Caribbean. We were joined with six returning couples, and added twelve new couples who wanted in on the fun.

Moving forward there would be other cruises to enjoy, as well as vacations in Hawaii and Mexico to warm us during the winter months. Like Dad, traveling became a need to feed my adventurous spirit.

We made an effort to continue with our trips to Twin Lakes, Idaho, but it was never the same after the kids went off to college. They had summer jobs and other interest with other people. We stopped going the year we spent most of the week by ourselves. We missed the joy of watching the kids having a good time boating, fishing, or being pulled behind the boat, not to mention the teenage summer romances. I was sure that at some point in the future we would return though.

Our large family reunions in Pasco had slowed down considerably. All the children were growing up quickly, and with their busy lives, it became more and more difficult to get everyone together. Naturally, my siblings and I had increasing demands within our individual families. They took precedence.

The extended family made it a priority to gather together for the wedding ceremonies of our many nieces and nephews, and there were several over many years. These events were the only times most of us were able to see each other.

As our own children went off to the military or college, Mark and I understood that we were at the beginning of the end of having our kids around us. The empty nest was not far off.

Benjamin was the first to leave us, six months after his high school graduation. Seven years later, he would move back to the Tri-Cities, having completed five years in the Navy, and two years working in Illinois.

Matthew and Timothy both spent a few years attending Columbia Basin College in Pasco before moving away to finish their degrees at Eastern Washington University.

By this time, Jessica was in her last year at Pasco High. She finished high school in 2002, and was only seventeen years old. She managed to save enough money to attend EWU as a freshman, and never came back home to live. Working each summer in Spokane, and living with her Uncle Dan and Aunt Janet, we would only see her on weekends, when she could manage that.

Our lives at home had changed so quickly. They call it the "empty nest," but it felt more like an empty void in the heart. It was a big change, but to help us with the adjustment, we bought a bigger boat to soothe our pain!

There was a time in our lives when we pictured ourselves spending more time with our friends. "Someday when your kids and our kids have all left home, just think of how much fun we will have doing the things we talked about doing. That time will be here before you know it!" We had made comments like this to some of our closest friends through the years.

Something strange happened instead. Once all the kids were grown and gone, all we wanted to do was spend time with them again. Our original plan wasn't working. Our children were getting married and having children. We just wanted to be a part of their lives in a whole new way. Maybe this is what is referred to as "the Circle of Life!" No one can predict just how to react, or how we are supposed to feel when we enter this new period of independence. Nope, I didn't see that one coming either.

Chapter 24

Time with our Mothers

Less than two years after Dad died of a massive heart attack, Mark's father, William Clinton Henderson, had a stroke. Even with the good nursing care provided him full time after the stroke, he died within the year.

With both of our fathers deceased, Mark and I knew how important it was to see our mothers as often as we could. It was not always easy. With each passing year, we watched as their health progressively declined.

*

Mom started coughing more than a year before Dad died. I remember him telling her to stop coughing one day, as if she had some control over it. She took over-the-counter meds, with minimal relief at best.

After Dad died, she began to see her doctor regularly about this cough. It would never completely go away, and seemed to be getting worse with time. He treated her symptoms and any obvious infections with prescription medications. After several months of treatment that did nothing to reduce her cough, her family doctor referred her to a pulmonologist.

Mom explained to her pulmonologist the strong family history of "some coughing disease" that her mother, and several others in the family had died from. Her doctor evaluated the symptoms and took her concerns very seriously. Different tests were ordered, yet even with the results, it was difficult to determine a correct diagnosis.

Eventually she was diagnosed with pulmonary interstitial fibrosis, compromised with chronic pseudomonas bacterial infection. High doses of antibiotics and steroids were often prescribed to treat these infections. It seemed to get better for a short time, and then reemerge in a cycle that continued for the rest of her life.

Mom did her best to live her life to the fullest, engaging in family activities, tending to her flowers, and taking the occasional trip. She never left without the medicine and breathing devices that made life more manageable. But the coughing continued to take its toll on her, and year after year, we could see her growing weaker and weaker.

We all did our best when Mom needed help during her very debilitating infections. There were many times when I'd go down to Salem on my days off to take care of her and help with her breathing treatments. Working two or three days a week gave me the chance to help out when I could. Sometimes I made arrangement to stay even longer.

My brother Dom was determined to keep the promise he made to our Dad as he laid in his coma in Reno. "Don't worry Dad! I promise to take good care of Mom," he'd said through his tears. He even went so far as to purchase and move into the house just behind our mother's homestead when it went up for sale. Moving his family closer made it much more convenient to look after her. Dom's family was happy in their home for many years, and they were a great comfort to our mother.

*

The last all-family reunion with Mom was in the summer of 2001 at our home in Pasco. With enough time to plan ahead, most of the family was able to attend. It had been four years since our last reunion, and the size of the family had grown several times with new babies.

Much of the reunion was spent watching the younger generations enjoying the pool and playing happily with each other. I enjoyed spending much of my time watching three of my older sisters, now grandparents themselves. I wanted to see how they managed their new role. It wouldn't be too many more years before my children would be entering into marriage and starting their own families, and I wanted to be ready.

The problem was, each of my sisters approached their role as grandparent in very different ways. One of them took the "I'm going to sit back and enjoy watching the new parents with their little ones" approach. She would help out when asked, but preferred to entertain herself watching the mayhem playing out around her.

Another of my sisters demonstrated the "I'm willing and ready to get my hands busy again with children" approach. I would watch her pick up a baby, sniff, and then proceed to change diapers with no need to consult the mother. When it was bath time, she was just as likely to grab one grandchild after the other, hose them off in front of her RV, while the rest of us watched the children scream and shiver in the cold water. Those same little ones quickly warmed up in the towel their grandma used to dry them. Immediately after, the little ones would go off to play some more, proud of themselves for having survived their Grandma once again.

The third sister revealed her style of grandparenting. She was more the "I'm here, I'm ready, just tell me what you need" style. She could be very hands-on, but mostly when the child's mother needed a break.

I was sure that when the time came, I would figure out what my style would be, and hope for the best. Just like many things in life, there's more than one way to get it done. Right, Mark?

Meal times were the only times we all gathered together in one place each day, holding each other's hands to say prayers before dishing up our food. The rest of the time, most of us navigated our days visiting within different groups that had formed around the property.

Mother was having a great time visiting and interacting with the family as they gathered around her. That is, until some of us decided to play a board game together.

The last evening of the reunion, a large group of us was sitting around the dining room table, ready to play a game. I don't remember which game we ended up playing, but I do remember it produced a lot of teasing and laughter. It was one of those times when jokes were told and funny family tales were disclosed, with little-to-no discrimination. Everyone was fair game.

Others heard the laughter and began climbing the stairs to see what was so funny. It got to the point where Mother was having trouble controlling the coughing that the laughter was producing. Suddenly, Mother gasped and made a loud groan.

"Mom, are you ok?" we asked.

"No, not really. Something popped in my back and I am in quite a bit of pain," she said, catching her breath and trying not to cough again.

Between the paramedic nephew, Erick, the battalion chief firefighter brother-in-law, Mike, and the RN, me, we helped Mom into a recliner, placed ice on her back, and gave her some anti-inflammatory medication to help ease her pain. After several minutes, she calmed down some, but it was evident something in her back was injured.

Mom refused to go to a doctor right away. She would go to her doctor in Salem if the pain did not subside in a day or two. We found out after her doctor's appointment a couple of day later that the x-rays revealed a broken vertebra in her mid-back.

It was a rather sobering reminder of Mom's frail body. The coughing over the years had worn her body to the point that playful laughter could cause her to break something in her back. She would need help for the next few weeks, until she had some healing and better pain control.

One by one, the trailers, the motorhomes, the campers, the fifth wheels, and the cars with their tents, peeled away from the driveway. The passengers in each departing vehicle would be entertained by the ever-dwindling crowd standing in front of the house.

Since our very first reunion in Pasco, there was a tradition to fulfill. When it was time to say goodbye and drive away, those of us still remaining at the house, would line up side-by-side in the grass nearest to Argent Road and begin the family wave. The first person standing to the right would bend from the middle and then stand up straight and throw their arms into the air. The lineup would follow one after another, creating the famous stadium wave so often seen at ball games. We continued the wave until each vehicle was no longer in sight.

By the time the last vehicle left, the only ones to produce the wave were our children, and Mark and me. Another wonderful reunion had come and gone, with promises of getting together very soon. None of us knew at the time that this would be the last big reunion with Mother at the center of us all.

Another baby would be arriving soon after this reunion. On September 2, 2001, Mom would be an Oma (grandmother) again to Dom's second child, Zachary Ryan van Lith. Her oldest grandchild, Rick Barnes, turned 30 that April, just five months before the last grandchild was born. Mother was 76 years old, and the name *van Lith* was passed on to another generation. Papa would have been overjoyed.

Our next Pasco family reunion would not happen again for another seven years. This is not to say that we didn't have large family gatherings during that time. As I mentioned earlier, between 2002 to 2005, we would gather to witness five nieces and nephews getting married.

With the five new "in-laws" married into the family, the clan grew even larger with the next influx of babies. There were two babies born in 2003, one in 2004, one in 2005, two in 2006, one in 2007, and four in 2008. Having consulted my calculator, that was sixteen new members added to the van Lith/Bruggeman family tree.

Fortunately for Mother, she still had the stamina to attend each of her grandchildren's weddings. It was also evident how much joy she experienced each time she was introduced to another one of her many great-grandchildren.

There was one very special time in 2005 when the entire family came together to celebrate. It was not for a wedding or for new babies. This day was to rejoice and give thanks to God for the life of our beautiful mother, Suzanna van Lith (Bruggeman). June 20, 2005 was her 80th birthday, and we wanted to shower her with love and affection.

We were all in attendance at Mass on Sunday. Gert and I sang during the service, as a gift to our mother. She always enjoyed listening to us sing together. Both of us shared a love of music that bonded us. We spent two separated weekends in Pasco recording a couple of tapes full of religious and Christmas music to give away as gifts.

Growing up, Gert and I weren't really that close. I was the youngest of the girls, and she was my older sister by six and a half years. Before leaving Pasco, after our first weekend of recording, she gave me a hug and said, "I'm so glad I came up to visit you and Mark. Spending this time singing together and visiting with you alone gave me the chance to get to know my little sister as you are now."

I was so grateful for what she said to me.

At the end of Mass, the priest invited our entire family to join him near the altar for a special blessing for our matriarch. Someone grabbed a chair from somewhere, and Mother sat reverently in the middle of her clan. Each of us laid a hand on her, and if someone could not reach her, they laid their hand on someone who was touching her.

What a beautiful moment we shared. We, who loved her the most, were strongly united through this blessing given to our mother. It was hard to hold back the tears. Most of us didn't even try.

Lunch and dessert were waiting for us at a local event room. We were four generations, sitting around laughing and telling stories. It was a memorable party. The small children and babies were passed around like another serving of dessert.

Prior to this celebration, each family member had been asked to create an original memory page that personalized our relationship with Oma, and described how she had impacted our life. We were all free to express ourselves however we wanted.

Gert integrated our pages into a book to be presented to Oma in honor of her special occasion.

Before digging into her birthday cake, Mother was presented with her book. None of the pages were alike. Some in the group wanted to show everyone what they had created and to read what they had written. Most of the pages were shared, causing laughter, tears, and usually both.

Through the handcrafted book, a common theme emerged. Though Mother was smaller now in stature than she was when she was young, in the hearts and minds of her descendants, she was a tower of faith, a woman of hope, and a model of Christ's love. She set the bar high for all of us to emulate. I am still endeavoring to catch up to the example she set.

Mom never expected to live to see her 80th birthday. Just a few years after Papa died, when the coughing became pronounced, I remember her saying, "Don't plan anything around me. I don't think I will be around to attend Erick and Sharla's wedding."

Well, she did make it to Erick and Sharla's wedding, and she made it to many other weddings and graduations after that. Yet, she still maintained that we should not count on her being around for whatever the next event happened to be.

April 11, 2015

This was the day I had hoped to finish writing this story. My heart was in it, my head was in it, but my time was not always my own. When my children call for help, all my immediate plans come to a halt. For the last four months, I have spent a great deal of my time being a mother and an Oma. It goes with the job description.

I thought for sure that April 11 was the day. Surely the significance of this day would not be lost on the reader. The whole purpose for telling this story was the importance of this day. So I thought.

"Never forget, don't let anyone ever forget!" were my marching orders. Yet, my true marching orders did not come from my father. They came from higher up. Sorry Dad!

My book's completion did not happen on the deadline I had set for myself. The completion came through another's time line. Only in hindsight will I know why it took me so long to finish a project I have so much passion for.

*

Over 70 years ago, on April 11, 1945, Domincus Marinus van Lith, was liberated from Buchenwald concentration camp, when four American GI's scouts walked through the front gates. The 6th Armored Division of General Patton's US Third Army would arrive in full force the very next day, with Patton himself arriving on April 13. To the younger generations reading this, they may think that was a very long time ago. To those of us Baby Boomers, we realize how quickly the time has passed.

We, the children of the "Greatest Generation," understand the tremendous debt we have to those who fought, and especially to those who paid the ultimate price. We are alive, and the freedoms that we have were preserved by their ashes.

I read a few articles and listened to a few commentaries commemorating this 70th anniversary. Sue sent me an article published in The Seattle Times on Sunday, April 12, 2015. It was her way of saying, "I know you are thinking about this too. Hope this helps you in some way." How my other siblings reminisced is known only by them. But I am sure they did remember.

*

Dad, today is a special day, and you are in my thoughts. I am so grateful that you fought for your life, never gave up, and held on. Many died, but you lived. There is no guilt in surviving. You held on not just for yourself, but for those of us that came after you. You lived so that we could be born. It was God's providential grace that you should live longer, so others could live. No one should question why. Someday we will all know. I pray that you are complete, and in union with the others that you have loved in this life. We have not forgotten you. I love you.

Your youngest daughter, Marja

May 8, 2015

Mom, I thought of you today. Vlaardingen was declared liberated on this day, 70 years ago. I discovered what you wrote about your early years in Holland in that black bag that had so much information about you and Papa. I am so glad you wrote what you did. This is the perfect place in the book to share it. I miss you!

Love, Marja

Mother's Own Words

Found 4/27/2014

Looking at the book, "A Mothers Legacy: Your life story in your own words," I realize how very different my life has been growing up in a different country, different culture, in an earlier time, when life was simpler, less complicated. It may look like I missed a lot, but I did not know better!

When I was born on June 20, 1925 in Wageningen, the Netherlands, I was given the name Suzanna Maria Elizabeth Bruggeman, after a sister of my father. I grew up being called "Suze." I was the youngest of six children, Herman, Antoon, Johan, Wim, Mia, and me.

When I was six weeks old, my family moved to Vlaardingen where my father had bought a business. It was a place with a bakery in the back and a bakery shop in front with a very small room in the middle with room for a table, six chairs and a desk. It seemed to have started out pretty well with my brothers helping in the bakery. But in the 1930's the depression came throughout the world, and the business went broke, and my father lost ownership. We were able to stay where we were after someone else bought the shop. The burden of doing business became heavy. I remember very well, the lack of money in the family.

The house [the bakery store building] we lived in was 100 years old and on a street lined with businesses. It was three stories high and had a basement where my mother had to cook! All of us kids slept in the attic. Our parents had the only bedroom.

The attic window looked out over other roofs, and the church with its watch towers. That church became very familiar to me. I remember as a little girl sitting all alone in the first pew for a long time, just looking at the tabernacle. No one at home noticed that I was gone. I did not realize it had gotten dark when the priest came, tapped me on the shoulder and said, "Shouldn't you go home?" I did go home after that, but no one missed me.

No one needed to tell me to go to church. I loved going, especially the devotions in the evening. I received my first Holy Communion and confirmation there. Then in 1946, Mienus and I were married there. My five daughters were baptized in the same church. My two oldest daughters received their first communion also. [Author note: Three oldest. Suuske did right before we emigrated.]

When I woke up in the morning there was always the smell of fresh bread. It was a very busy place, and my mother worked very hard too.

The house was not comfortable and business always came first. There was one room on the second floor where family could gather. There was only time for that on Sunday afternoon, for tea or a card game for my brothers.

Relatives lived too far away so we did not have much contact with them. I never knew my grandparents. They died before I was born.

I always walked to grade school. It was fourteen blocks away. In later years I had a bike to ride.

I grew up on simple food which, quite often, consisted of a one pot meal of potatoes, meat, and vegetables, except on Thursdays, we had no meat, and on Fridays we had fish.

My first job was in another bakery shop. I got two guilders [$0.50] per week. When the war came, I found out that the baker was on the wrong side, a collaborator. That was the end of that job. Later on, I worked in a shop selling shoes. During this whole time, I had gotten all my diplomas for sewing. I then worked in our bakery shop and started my own sewing "business," which kept me busy till I got married.

The war years, 1940-1945, had a deep effect on my life. I was accepted in an academy in The Hague to become a fashion designer. The start of the war brought an end to my apprenticeship before it even started.

I vividly remember how the war started for me. We woke up very early in the morning. There were many planes overhead. My brothers climbed on the roof to get a better view. Planes began to drop, what looked like big cigars, until they hit the ground! Parachutist began to drop too. My mother turned on the radio and heard that we were being invaded by the Germans. She got my brothers off the roof in a hurry.

Three days later, the bombardment of Rotterdam began! The next day I wanted to go and see what happened. So Mienus, (a friend of my brother, who would later become my husband), and I rode on our bikes the 45 minutes it took to get to Rotterdam to see it burning. It was a horrible sight. Unforgettable!

I was 15 years old when the war broke out and almost 20 years old when it ended. It squeezed normal life out of us. Peace was replaced with fear, oppression, and then hunger!

I remember living in Amsterdam for a few months with a family that had one child. They had a furniture store, but more important, they had food. I helped with chores and babysitting. When they did not have enough to eat, they sent me home. The last year of the war was the worst.

Before the hunger began, I continued spending time with my gymnastic club. When club members became too weak to continue, the club stopped meeting. Some of my girlfriends were so hungry, they ate tulip bulbs.

There was no social life to speak of. All civilians were supposed to be indoors by 7:00pm, or risk being shot to death. There was no dating or boyfriends. Most of the young men were shipped to Germany to work as slaves in labor camps, those that remained, lived "secretively" [hiding from the Germans].

Three years into the war, I met a young man in 'S-Hertogenbosch [a town in Holland]. I went there to visit my mother's sister and her family. She was my favorite aunt. He came to see me several times there, and we became engaged. Within a year, without explanation, my mother made me break off the engagement.

Later I corresponded a little with Mienus, who was in Buchenwald concentration camp from 1941 to April 1945. He was arrested for being in the resistance group, "de Geuzen." Resisting the Germans was punishable with death or concentration camp.

When he came back, we both worked hard for a year to get some money to get married, which we did on October 2, 1946. First we lived in an attic floor until I was pregnant with my third baby. Then we got a house to live in until my fourth pregnancy, when we got a nicer new house. We lived there until after the birth of my fifth girl. When she was 14-months-old [nearly 15-months], we left Holland for America.

We had a beautiful family and Mienus worked as a policeman, but he never felt like one in his heart.

After he was liberated by the Americans under General Patton, he always wanted to go to America. We finally left Holland in April of 1956. That was the hardest thing I ever had to do! I left everything familiar to go to a place I never heard of, with the responsibility to care for five little girls. I was the only one who spoke some English, which I had learned in school. [Author's note: Dad did speak minimal English, Mother was just better at it.]

This was the time that I prayed deeply, "Lord, if this is not good for our souls, stop it for any reason!" And I meant it!

We arrived in Salem in May 1956 and lived there ever since. I thank God for inspiring me with the preparations I made before we left Holland. It paid off.

The first years were rough. Thank God my mind stayed focused on success. I never gave in to sadness, I could not afford to. I wanted so much for my children to feel at home and I trusted in God for their happiness here.

When we were here ten years, God blessed us with one more child, this time a son. From the moment I was pregnant, I knew it was a blessing. Mienus picked me up from the hospital in our first brand new car!

Several years later, we bought a large property in 1975 and built a new house.

I find that God blessed us richly with success after our immigration to the USA.

Glory to God!

Written by Suzanna van Lith

She wrote this sometime in 2004 or 2005 when she was 79 or 80 years old.

When we give others the opportunity to share memories of their life, more often than not, they are happy to accommodate. Asking someone to talk about themselves, especially if they have been raised to not draw attentions to themselves, is a real compliment to them. When we ask to hear more, they recognize their own value and importance to others.

Everyone has a story to tell. I encourage my readers to spend time with their parents and grandparents while they are still alive, and gather from them a summary of their lives. You may be surprised to learn meaningful details that you never knew before. These memories would otherwise be lost, if no one takes the time to ask.

What lessons will you learn when you go back and hear the stories of the triumphs and the tragedies of earlier generations? It is so important to communicate the faults of the past for those in the future, so they don't compromise their world by forgetting, denying, rewriting, or simply stop caring, and end up suffering the same heartbreaks all over again. They shouldn't have to. Talk to them!

Rainbow Colors

It was time to bring the family together again. Seven years had gone by since our last all-family reunion in Pasco. In early 2008, I sent emails to the members, asking them to set aside the last weekend in July and join us at "Henderson's Acre."

With so many new family members added over the last seven years, three days seemed like a good amount of time to begin building memories for those who had no idea what they were in for when we're all in attendance.

I was a little excited and worried about having so many people at the house. How was this going to work now? Fortunately, some of the clan decided to take advantage of the motels that had sprung up near our home, providing us a bit more room for the others to park their RV's and tents.

There's something endearing when everyone is wearing a matching t-shirt that serves to identify and validate our unity. Thanks to our daughter Jessica, she managed the creation of this year's family t-shirts for everyone to wear, just like we had done in the early years. There was a sense of pride and belonging in those shirts.

Jessica and I decided on a rainbow theme for the shirts. On the front of the shirt, she fashioned a design that resembled a postage stamp. In the center was a windmill, and on the left side was written, "Nederland." Below that was written, "0.75 Euro." It was a fun design.

Each family would wear their own color. Jessica called dibs on orange (the Dutch color), for Mark and I, our kids, and their families. Each of my siblings had separate colors for their respective families. Together we had a red, orange, yellow, green, blue, and purple family. We nearly had the complete rainbow spectrum.

On one of the days when everyone was present, we donned our t-shirts, gathered in the big field next to the house, and had a large group picture taken Each individual family clustered together for the photo. The Henderson clan chose to separate into two smaller groups, so as to help balance the photo. We asked a neighbor to take pictures with the many cameras brought for that purpose.

The time we shared was bittersweet. On the one hand, we had never had so many in attendance, and we all had such a wonderful time. It was, for many of us, the best reunion ever. On the other hand, this was the first time we were without either of our parents. Mom was too weak to make the five-hour trip to Pasco. She was deeply missed, and we all were aware of the huge absence.

We knew she was thinking of us as much as we were thinking of her. We promised to show her the many pictures taken at the reunion. Many of those photos showed the activities of so many who had never experienced a reunion like this. They were either married in, grafted in, recently born, or too young to remember the last one. These kids were the third generation beyond Mienus and Suze, and we all had a hand in creating lasting memories.

Mother was given an 8x10, framed picture of our group shot. She took great delight in looking at it, and displayed it prominently in her living room. Even though we had a few family members unable to attend, we still had 54 individuals in the photo. Sweet!

None of us knew that this would be the last of the reunions held on Henderson Acre. Just six weeks later, after living on the property for 25 years, we sold the house.

Chapter 25

35 and 25

Most of us would agree, time marches forward very quickly. A month after our reunion in 2008, Mark and I traveled to Europe. It was a gift we had long planned for, to celebrate our 35th wedding anniversary. Ten years had already gone by since our Silver Wedding Anniversary "do-over." Poof, just like that, ten years!

*

During that time span, Mark and I witnessed Matthew and his bride, Ammie, join in marriage in November of 2003, at St. Aloysius Church in Spokane, Washington. Eleven months later we became grandparents (Opa and Oma) for the very first time, when Deacon Thomas was born.

In April of 2005, Timothy and his bride, Stacey, were wed at St John's Church in Elma, Washington. Our family was growing!

Mark and I had a bunch of grandchildren born between 2004 and 2008. Less than two years after Deacon was born to Matt and Ammie, William Dominic (Liam) followed in 2006. Isabella Kathleen (Bella), our first granddaughter, was born to our eldest son Benjamin, and Bella's mother, Joanie, in 2007.

After Bella's birth, four more little girls were born in 2008. Matt and Ammie's daughter, Eden Suzanne, was born in February. Tim and Stacey became parents to identical twins, Paige Marie and Chloe Lynn, just two weeks later in March. Jessica and her fiancé, Joel Morgan, delivered their first child, Amelia Suzanne, eight months later. Whew! Five granddaughters in a row within eighteen months of each other.

We were blessed with seven grandchildren in four years! I know it's not a world record, but it felt like one to us.

Mark and I wanted to be called Opa and Oma by our grandchildren. I had always intended to keep the Dutch version of "Grandma" for myself.

"Well, if you are going to be an Oma, then I will be an Opa," Mark stated. I was pleased!

Our children seem to appreciate using the Dutch version. They had an Opa and an Oma, and were happy that their children would have one too. The little ones can readily identify which set of grandparents are coming to visit by the way their parents refer to them.

Mark and I had lots to celebrate in 2008. In fact, our 50's were turning out to be the best decade of our lives so far. We were relatively healthy, with a growing family, and we were DINK's. For those who are unfamiliar, we were now Double Income No Kids! I retired from my music performances, and had more time to "slowdown and smell the roses." And change the diapers, spoil the little ones, etc.

*

It was September of 2008 when we flew to Rome, Italy to begin our three-week vacation. We were invited to stay for four nights at the Maryknoll Mission House, located in downtown Rome.

We have been benefactors for the Catholic Foreign Mission Society of America (known as Maryknoll) all of our married life. Mark and I decided to support this mission the way my parents had throughout their marriage. We became friends with a few of the priests and lay workers when they came to visit us a few times in the Tri-Cities. They had reached out and asked for help with their capital campaign to further the work of their missions around the world. We felt honored, and accepted.

During our time in Rome, we walked or took the subways to as many places as we possibly could in the three days that we spent there. We also visited the Vatican twice, once to take a private tour below St. Peter's Basilica, called the Scavi Tour, and again to attend an audience with Pope Benedict XIV.

The Scavi Tour begins three levels below the main High Altar of St. Peter's Basilica. There it follows a very narrow, stone-paved road that had been used by the early Christians and pagans two thousand years ago. This area was unearthed during WWII. Books have been written telling the story of the remarkable discovery of an early first century necropolis where pagans and Christians were laid to rest. As we progressed toward the High Altar above, the artwork painted within the burial chambers changed from pagan signs to recognizable Christian symbols of the crucifix, fishes, and grapevines.

Near the end of the tour, we were able to see and spend a little time reflecting at the site where, after his upside down crucifixion, St. Peter was laid to rest. His bones were discovered during the excavation in the 1930's, exactly where tradition had always said they would be found. Sometime after the unearthing, his bones were encased in what looked like a thick, clear, acrylic box, and place on a ledge of an ancient stone wall near where they were discovered. We could clearly gaze upon these remarkable relics. This tour was very meaningful, and one of the highlights of our vacation.

During our second visit to the Vatican, we were among an intimate group gathered to visit the Pope. It was just Mark and me, and about 10,000 other visitors. Like I said, an intimately large group of excited pilgrims from every continent in the world.

It was during this papal audience when I was touched by the universality of the Catholic Church. Oh, I knew that there were over a billion Catholics around the world, but to see so many of us gathered together, all followers of Jesus Christ, enhanced my belief and understanding of this powerful gift of the Church on Earth, handed down to St. Peter, and continuing uninterrupted for nearly two thousand years.

Every evening after returning to the mission, Mark and I would take off our shoes to soothe our blisters and go downstairs to the kitchen/dining area to meet up with some of the other guests staying there. We were with a very eclectic group, to be sure. We hung out with two priests from Cameroon, Africa, two seminarians from communist China, and briefly with a young man and woman from England and Norway. The majority of our conversations were with the two priests from Africa.

I'm not sure what I appreciated most during our time in Rome. Was it the marvelous sights we had seen, or the typical three-hour evenings of drinking wine and discussing significant Church and political issues impacting the world? These were some of the most intellectually stimulating conversations I've ever been a part of.

We learned so much of the growing Catholic communities all over Africa, and the state of the Roman Catholic Church in China. I was moved by the stories and the concerns these two seminarians shared with us. One of them gave me one of those rubbery bracelets. It read, "Pray for China," in both English and Mandarin. I wore it for much of our trip, and I still have that bracelet in a safe place at home.

We went to Mass in the mission house two mornings, and prayed each evening with our new friends before we went to bed. Looking at the two young men from China, I couldn't help but wonder if we were in the presence of future martyrs.

The authentic Catholic Church in China is lived out covertly, "underground" as they say. These seminarians were told that if they were ordained Roman Catholic priests, they would be arrested if they set foot in China. One of them in particular knew that he was called to the priesthood for the benefit of the faithful in China. There was little doubt in my mind that at least one, probably both, would return to China someday, risking their lives.

Saying goodbye to these incredible individuals was difficult. We kept in contact for a while, but over the years, it was hard to continue. Saying farewell to our host wasn't easy either. She was a great help to us during our stay.

As we left Rome for our next stop, Mark and I agreed that we would be back someday. Although we managed to see several famous sights, there was still so much more to see, and places where I would have liked to spend extra time.

"We'll see you again, Rome. We'll be back," I said softly as we pulled away from the train station. If Mark was paying attention, I was just loud enough for him to hear me.

The train took us to Civitavecchia, a metropolitan city close to Rome. It took me a lot of practice to accurately pronounce the name of that city. As soon as we arrived, we found our way to the second part of our trip.

As we got off of the train, we were within walking distance to the *MS Noordam*, a Holland America cruise ship. We were about to begin a ten-day voyage to ports of call on the eastern Mediterranean Sea.

Throughout the next ten days we enjoyed excursions that included: 1) Dubrovnik, Croatia, where we spent some time in the newer part of town, and more time enjoying the very old parts of this beautiful place; 2) The island of Corfu, Greece, a wonderful picturesque place where many Europeans go for their vacations; 3) Katakolon, Greece, where we traveled to Olympia, the site of the first Olympics; 4) Nothing prepares you for the beautiful island of Santorini. One day was not enough there; 5) Kusadasi, Turkey, where we traveled to the ruins of old Ephesus and the historic Virgin Mary house. It was there that St. John was thought to have taken Mary to protect her during the early Christian persecution; 6) Valletta, on the island of Malta, which exists thanks to the Knights of St John. They were the first to build the city as a defense and refuge for injured soldiers and pilgrims during the Crusades in the 16th Century. Many of these knights are honorably buried under the floor of the famous St. John's Cathedral that we visited; and 7) Messina, on the island of Sicily, a great place for us to rest.

With our time spent in Rome and the ten-day cruise, the first two weeks of our journey felt more like a pilgrimage than it did a sightseeing adventure, though we certainly had plenty of that too. We felt incredibly blessed having visited parts of the ancient world where important Christian saints had traveled, lived, and preached.

To say that this was the trip of a lifetime would be accurate, but I hesitate to describe it that way. At some point, Mark and I plan to spend time in Rome again, and then cruise the western Mediterranean. We'll make that another trip of a lifetime so we can check it off our bucket list.

The third and last part of our vacation was a five day trip to Holland. Over 25 years had gone by since Mark and I first visited the Netherlands. A lot had happened during those years. Raising a family, going back to nursing school, helping pay for our children's college education, and being present at every major event of their lives up to this point had consumed much of our time and resources.

*

Our first trip to Holland together was in 1983, and it was not something we had planned ahead for. At the time, Mark was working for a small research and development company. He was an engineering manager overseeing technology developed to determine the structural integrity of offshore oil rigs in the North Sea. Mark had already been on a couple of trips to London to meet with the oil company.

The owner of this R&D company was aware that I was an immigrant from Holland. He graciously offered to send both of us on Mark's next business trip to the oil rigs just off shore of England and Scotland.

Mark said the offer from the owner went something like this, "How would you like to take your wife on one of your next business trips to Europe? I'll give you a few additional vacation days if you need, so you can take her to Holland. I know you've never been there before, and I bet your wife would be happy to accompany you. I'm sure she will find enough things to do in London and Scotland while you work during the day."

Mark was surprised with this generous offer, and replied with gratitude and excitement. "That would be great. She's only been back to Holland once, but that was eleven years ago. I can't wait to let her know. Thank you very much."

What an incredible opportunity, an all-expense paid trip to Europe for both of us. Joining Mark for this eleven-day trip would be awesome, but difficult to manage. Unless I could find family members willing to take care of three little boys, I would not be able to accompany my husband for this generous offer.

We only had a few weeks to make all the arrangements for me to be able to go. In addition to childcare, my passport had expired and I needed a new one in a hurry.

Two of my sisters stepped up to help me. Traci agreed to take the boys for the first four nights in Salem. Ineke would pick the kids up in Salem, and care for them for four days at her home in Silverton. The last four days, Mark's twin brother Mike and his wife would take them to their place in Portland until we returned.

Just as soon as my passport arrived, there were no more impediments preventing me from traveling. I was finally able to get ready and get excited for this adventure. Mark and I were going to Holland, England, and Scotland together!

We left in August of 1983, just two weeks after moving into our new home on Argent Road, where we would spend the next 25 years raising our children. We were 28 years old, and going on (dare I say) a trip of a lifetime.

My cousin Els, was at the airport to greet us and take us to her home. We spent time with her mother and brother (Tante Mia and cousin Leen), and a few other relatives from Mom's side of the family. Unfortunately, we had minimal contact with anyone from my Dad's family. There just wasn't enough time to organize a larger reunion.

Mark finally got to see the important places in Vlaardingen that had meaning to me. It was a wonderful opportunity to share Holland with him. We would come back someday. I was confident of that.

*

Now, 25 years and a few hours after disembarking our cruise ship, we were flying to Holland for a second time. My hope was to visit cousins I knew, and meet many more that I hadn't gotten to know yet. These last five days were all about getting to know more of the family we left 52 years ago.

Our entire anniversary trip felt like three separate vacations. Both of us would have been very satisfied if all that we had planned for was Rome. If our trip had ended after our ten-day cruise, we would have been doubly satisfied. Adding this trip to Holland was almost overwhelming.

Our plans included three nights with cousin Els and two nights with cousin Bert and his wife Els. Now that we had developed a friendship with cousins from my Dad's side, I was excited to stay with Bert and his wife.

A couple of months prior to this trip, I had asked each of our host cousins to help me get in touch with our respective cousins. I wanted them to know when Mark and I would be in Holland, and if there was any way I could meet up with them. I was willing to do what I could to make it happen. I came with high hopes, but wasn't sure what to expect when I arrived.

Cousin Els picked us up at Schiphol, the airport in Amsterdam. We arrived mid-afternoon to the hugs and kisses of my cousin. Els and I remained close over the years. We are the same age, and spent a lot of time together when I was 17. She also stayed with us a couple of times when she flew over to visit my mother and siblings in Oregon and Washington.

Sadly, Els was going through a difficult period in her life at that time. I'm not sure which one of us needed this visit more, her or me. She and I needed each other, but for very different reasons. Fortunately, Mark was there for both of us.

Before we left the airport, another one of our cousins, Birgitta, joined us. I had spent time with her when I was 17, the morning I was alone at the airport waking her family up with a 5:00am phone call, and then weeks later at the beach.

After leaving the airport, we drove to a restaurant/bar just off of the freeway. It was a good mid-point between Vlaardingen, where Els lived, and Amsterdam, where Birgitta lived. We shared drinks, heavy appetizers, and good conversation. It was a great start to the five days.

That first evening, Els had arranged for a small gathering at her home. Two more of my cousins and their spouses, whom I had never met, came to see us. The evening was so enjoyable. We shared time with photos and a few stories of our lives. They were the only other cousins from Mom's side that were available during our stay. It was the middle of September, and many of our shared relatives were on "holiday," as they say. We call it a "vacation." It's the same thing.

We enjoyed some sightseeing with Els and her son Terry. Our favorite activity was relaxing on a tour boat that was navigating the Maas River in and around Rotterdam. Our last day with Els was spent revisiting important family places.

It was always special to visit the house that I was born in. The last time I had seen it, I had a chance to talk with the woman who was living there. She turned out to be the same person who had moved into the house right after we emigrated. During that visit, this sweet elderly lady invited me into her home and pointed out some of the things my father had built around the fireplace, and some ironwork that he had done on the outside. This time I just wanted to see how it looked, so many years later.

I knocked on the door to ask permission to take a photo outside of the house, and was greeted by the current owner. It was not the same woman anymore, but she was very nice and listened to my story, and allowed me to take a picture outside of the house.

Els suggested we call my mother that evening to say hello, and tell her about our visit. Mother talked with both of us. I was excited to tell her that we stopped by the house at #31, Vanderhemstrat to take pictures.

"Why did you do that?" Mom said.

"I wanted to see if the same lady was still living in the house. You know, the one who has been there since we left Holland. As it turned out, she doesn't live there anymore, but the current occupant gave me permission to take a few pictures. I just wanted another picture of the house that I was born in," I answered.

"But we never lived there! Our Address was #1 Vanderhemstrat," Mom clarified.

We started laughing at this point, just thinking about telling the woman in #31 why we were there, and asking to take a picture of her home. Now we had to go back tomorrow to get pictures of the correct house. I think I still have the pictures taken at #31 with the woman standing in the window smiling. I never did tell her I got it wrong.

The young man in #1 had moved in a few years prior, after the elderly woman finally passed away. It was a little more difficult to get permission to take a photo. He wasn't sure if his mother would approve.

We smiled and thanked him. After he closed the door, we quickly took a picture anyway, when he wasn't looking. I knew that the lady who had lived in that house for more than 50 years would have approved.

It's always an emotional time, saying goodbye. When there are more than five thousand miles between Washington State and Holland, the best any of us could say was, "Let's not wait so many years before we see each other again. I hope to see you soon. Thank you, and I love you."

On the afternoon of the third day, it was time to say goodbye to Els and her son. We hugged and kissed, and went to visit my father's family.

*

Our new hosts were waiting on the steps of their apartment for us to arrive. The tears of goodbye were replaced with hugs and kisses from Bert and his wife Els as they greeted us.

That evening Bert's sister, Ineke Vredenbregt, and her companion Peter Schenk came to visit us. It didn't take me long to figure out who Peter was. His father, whom he was named after, was also a survivor of Buchenwald, and a very good friend of my father.

Peter Schenk Sr. and Dad shared the same bunkhouse with several others from Holland. He was in the camp for a much shorter duration, just during the last few months of the war. He was so grateful to be with Mienus during this unbearable time. Dad took him under his protection, and the two of them did everything they could to keep each other alive.

After returning to Holland, Peter began working in the startup garment industry as a designer, something of a shared interest with my mother. Consequently, he and his wife became good friends with both of my parents.

Peter Schenk Jr. was very interested to talk with me about what we knew about our fathers' time in the camp. I saw how excited he became when sharing stories about his father's memories, and most especially of my dad.

He gave me a gift, a booklet called, "*De Geuzen*." This small book described in great detail the story of the Dutch resistance in Vlaardingen. The book also showed many pictures, one of which was a photo of the memorial in the town square across from the old courthouse. This monument was dedicated to the *Geuzen* resistance. I had no idea that the sculpture even existed.

Even though the book was in Dutch, it was invaluable to me. The seeds that long ago had been planted in me, encouraging me to write, were well watered that evening.

After Peter and my cousin Ineke left, we enjoyed a nice simple Dutch meal with our hosts, and had a few drinks in their living room before bed.

As relaxed as Mark and I were, Bert appeared to be fidgety. Finally Els said, "Oh, just tell her Bert. You aren't very good at keeping secrets. Tell her."

"I was trying to keep it a secret until tomorrow, but Els is right. I'm not good with surprises. We have made arrangement at the Novotel Hotel in Schiedam for several of our family members to come to see you and Mark tomorrow evening. Ineke and Peter came this evening because they were not available tomorrow," Bert divulged with a big smile on his face.

I put my fingers over my mouth in delight. "Oh Bert, thank you. How many are coming?"

"Well, quite a few I think. Many of them said they were coming. They were all happy to hear that you were in Holland, and wanted to see you and Mark. You know it has been a very long time since many of us cousins have seen each other all together in one place, too," Bert said. "Except for the occasional wedding or funeral, we hardly ever spend time together," he added.

"We are all looking forward to seeing whoever comes. I think many of the spouses are coming too," Els added.

I was so pleased to know about the planned reunion for tomorrow. Though it was disappointing not to have been able to see more of the relatives on my mother's side, it appeared that it would not be the same with the relatives on my father's side.

Knowing had its price. I had trouble getting and staying asleep, and not because the bed was uncomfortable. Our hosts had insisted on given up their bedroom for us, while they slept on cots in another room in their apartment. My sleep was disturbed because I was too excited to sleep, plain and simple. Ugh!

I don't remember much of what we did the next day. It just seemed to take forever for the day to progress and for the evening to come. Finally, after a light meal late in the afternoon, we left for Schiedam.

The Novotel Hotel had a perfect-sized room reserved for the reunion. We walked in with Bert and Els, into a growing group of middle and late middle-aged men and women. Several were greeting each other with the traditional kisses to the right and left cheeks and the smiles that went along with them. Many of the men gave each other the bear hugs so easily shared within this rowdy bunch of van Lith's. And then, it was my turn.

A small line began to form in front of me and Mark. After each had said their hellos to everyone in the room they had known all their lives, they turned their attention toward their distant cousin, me. One by one I was approached by individuals I had only known through stories and a few pictures.

Either before I got a hug, or just after, I'd ask this person, "Ok, who are you, and how are we related," or, "I am so happy to meet you, or see you again," which ever was applicable.

We would look at each other as if we were identifying facial features we may have in common. Or perhaps it was just to imagine what we may have looked like when we were both children and not middle-aged. Either way, the look was comfortable and welcomed. And this went on for quite a while as the relatives continued to gather for the evening.

The cousins that I was familiar with were so comfortable with me. They would place their hands on both my cheeks and welcome me back. I felt as though I was being pulled back into this unique and loving family. Of the nine brothers and sisters my father grew up with, seven of them were represented by my cousins.

I was hoping that the affection I was feeling was overflowing into each of the others in the room. Those who were related by marriage or friendship appeared to be sharing in the value of the moment too.

I came prepared with pictures to show of our family back home. I had asked each sibling to send me photos of their families that they may want me to share along with their greetings. Mark placed the assortment of images onto a thumb drive to take with us. It was an effective way for me to present the ever-growing American van Lith side of the family.

Three generations of van Lith's had developed over the last 50+ years in their absence. There were lots of smiles and laughter in the group, especially seeing the children of the children of their distant cousins.

I was eager to share the six beautiful grandchildren that Mark and I had already been blessed with over the last four years. I included a photo of my pregnant daughter Jessica, who was still incubating her first child. She would soon give birth to our fifth granddaughter. I'm sure I mentioned this earlier. Don't be surprised if it comes up again. I'm a proud Oma!

Timothy and Stacey's twins created lots of smiles, laughter, and oo's and ahh's. I told everyone that twins were bound to happen since my Mark has an identical twin, and Stacey's younger brothers are identical twins, too. Our grandchildren have even referred to Mark's brother, their great Uncle Mike, as their "other Opa."

Much like what had happened before, I was amazed at how quickly my brain shifted the language. It was a bit of a challenge, speaking Dutch, when most of my cousins spoke English to me in return. Mark was better able to keep up with the conversations, with one side in English, and me speaking Dutch-lish. He had heard many conversations spoken like that over the years, and even got pretty good at understanding bits and pieces of the Dutch language. Like before, my Dutch inflections even lasted until a few days after we got home.

After the eating, drinking, and lighthearted conversation, it was time to take several group pictures with the many cameras in the room. Looking at the images, the smiles on so many faces remind me of just how much fun we were all having. Perhaps some of the levity was enhanced by the free flow of libations, but I suspect that we would have had just as much fun drinking coffee or tea! I had no way of knowing that this drink theory of mine would be tested in the near future.

Soon after the cameras were put away, the party began to wind down. Before the relatives began peeling off, I reached for the microphone to say a few words before going our separate ways.

> *Saying thank you to each and every one of you for coming to visit me and Mark just doesn't begin to express how I am feeling. I know that many of you took time out of your busy day to celebrate with us, and others drove many miles to get here. We are both very grateful.*

> *We've so enjoyed getting to meet many of you for the first time, and for others, to see you again after so many years. It was a treat for me to be able to speak Dutch. I don't get that opportunity very often. You didn't make it easy for me though, many of you kept speaking English to me in return.*

> *You have all made me feel like I fit right into this family, like you've known me all your life. When I was little and growing up, I always knew that I had distant relatives. You and your parents were never forgotten, and now I know, neither were those of us in America. I am a bit overwhelmed with this whole evening.*

> *Mark and I will not wait another 25 years before returning to Holland. That is for sure. Having said that, I would like to extend an invitation, on behalf of the Mienus van Lith family. To any of you who would like to come to Oregon and Washington, and visit our growing families, and to enjoy some of the wonderful things to see and do in our country, you have a place to stay with your relatives in America.*

There were a couple of others who wanted to say a few words to everyone gathered, and specifically to me and Mark. Their words were full of gratitude and kindness toward us. I tried hard not to show the emotions associated with saying goodbye, but that was impossible. Tears were inevitable.

After the well wishes were expressed, I was handed the microphone again and added, "Good-bye is not what I want to say. Now that I know you, it is much easier for me to say *tot ziens*. Don't say goodbye, instead say, 'till I see you again.'"

Everyone was invited to write down their email addresses on a paper that was left on a table for that purpose. Each of them took the time to fill in their contact information before leaving. Now I have access to them, and they would be able to contact us as well. Bert and Els would see to that.

It was nearing 10:00pm, and morning would come too soon for those going back to work. The last of the hugs and kisses followed. I heard cousins making their own promises to get together with each other, which was music to my ears.

One of my cousins was more difficult than the others to say goodbye to. The moment Dom Vredenbregt arrived and walked into the room, I knew that he had driven nearly two hours just to get there. We both shared big smiles, and then he winked at me. That wink was special. There was something we both understood.

In Dom's wink to me, I hoped he was remembering the big hugs we gave each other at the airport in Reno in 1993. I also hoped that the words I spoke to him, on behalf of my whole family, had given him some measure of comfort just before his departure. He was at center stage to the tragic events surrounding Dad's sudden death.

I hoped that my responding wink was able to deliver my gratitude of just how special it was that he had traveled so far, ten years ago, to celebrate our 25th wedding anniversary.

Both events were momentous in my life, and I don't think either time was coincidental. Trying to comprehend the significance of those visits still makes me pause and wonder.

"*Tot ziens*, Dom. We will see you again. Soon I hope!" I said with assurance. There will always be a special place in my heart for my cousin, Dominicus Marinus Vredenbregt.

Just a handful of relatives remained to wrap things up. And I will be able to unwrap this memory any time I want, and leisurely relive this historic occasion.

Mark held me close in bed that night. He allowed me to talk about what I had experienced throughout the evening, and when my tears overflowed, he held me tighter. My own expectations did not prepare me for the emotions.

My heritage came to life as never before. The feelings of love and acceptance were intense, but I knew that I would come down to earth by morning. I would experience other strong emotions at the airport, saying goodbye to our hosts, Bert and Els.

But that was hours away. That night I would stay awake as long as I could to live in the moment. I would try to sleep on the plane, and I knew Mark would forgive me for his lack of sleep.

*

After we returned from our trip, we had two weeks to pack up 25 years of our accrued belongings. Midway through cruising the Mediterranean, our son Matthew let us know via email that our house had sold. "Holy Moses, Mark! That went fast. We only put the "For Sale by Owner" sign up a week before we left," I said.

I got to work right away preparing for our move. My first priority was to find a place to live. Next, I would obtain the necessary boxes needed for the move and storage. Our plan was to rent a home until we found property to build a new house on. Everything would be kept in storage except for the minimum of belongings we would need to live in the rental. Everything fell into place quickly.

Within two months of finding a smaller lot in a new development, we were under construction. Our new, one-story home would be in a quiet neighborhood, just a couple of blocks from the Columbia River. We made sure that the design of our home would be the perfect place to live in throughout our retirement.

Our new lot was just a third of an acre, and we would not be including a swimming pool this time. Our grown children can put their own pools in their backyards, and I hope they will invite us to join them when it gets hot outside.

Chapter 26

In Sickness and in Health

The thread within "Long Shall You Live," is weaving into a new, yet familiar path. As I had mentioned earlier, I was unaware when I began this memoir that my journey would be a part of it. The events in my life can never come close to what my parents endured, but I can shed another light on surviving trauma through faith, hope, and love. Like Mienus and Suze, I had these same options to deal with. Option A: bury the trauma as deeply as possible and suffer in silence, Option B: hang on to my victimization and let it take over my life, or Option C: chart a new course toward healing, with the hope of find meaning, purpose, and peace for what I endured. I eventually chose Option C, but not before I struggled within A and B.

*

Staying healthy in body and spirit had always been a priority for me, and was never too difficult to maintain. But in an instant, that changed. What began with an automobile accident, and the migraines that followed, my new priority was to find ways to cope with a cascade of events over many years.

Migraine headaches began in my late 30's. I was rear-ended by a driver going roughly 25 miles per hour. Initially, I thought that I had dodged a bullet. "Man, I'm glad he wasn't going much faster," I thought. Except for the stiff neck, I developed for a few days, I thought nothing more of it.

I settled with the insurance company of the at-fault driver about six weeks later, and bought my first computer with the settlement.

Three months after the accident, I woke up one morning with incredible pain and stiffness in my neck, and with a headache to add to my misery. I called in sick that morning, and went to the doctor with my symptoms. I was given a neck brace, pain meds, told to take anti-inflamatories, and if I didn't get better in a few days, to consider physical therapy. "You sustained a whiplash when you were rear ended. Did you settled your claim with the other driver's insurance already?" my doctor asked.

"Well, yes. I only had a stiff neck for a few days, and I thought that was the extent of it. When the insurance company called and offered me a settlement, I took it. That was six weeks ago," I replied.

"That's unfortunate. In that case, we will have to bill your medical insurance company. It's not unusual for these types of symptoms to flare up several weeks after a collision. A car doesn't need to be going very fast to cause this type of injury. A 25 mile-an-hour bump, as you called it, is plenty enough," my doctor stated.

I followed through with physical therapy, as well as chiropractic treatments, neither of which I'd ever needed before. After completing several months of treatments, I was able to tolerate the symptoms fairly well with some ibuprofen, stretching, moist heat, and icepacks. That is until I started getting migraines.

The majority of my headaches seemed to develop when my neck flared up, but the other times I was unable to identify the cause. The pain was always in my left upper forehead just above the hairline. In the beginning, I could sleep the headache away during the night, and it would be gone in the morning. But over time, that didn't work.

I managed the continuing pain with the standard treatment of rest, darkness, silence, cold packs to the forehead, and prescription pain meds. At the time, I only got really bad migraines once a month or so, and I was hoping they would go away in time.

In my mid-forties, about seven years after my first accident, I was hit by a high school student pulling out into the street from his school. This young man made a very poor decision thinking he could outrun the oncoming traffic. He chose to race across the two lanes to the other side without fully evaluating his clearance. He ended up causing a three-car accident, of which mine was the worst. The front end of my vehicle was rammed during his acceleration.

In the moment, I could see what was about to happen, so I veered into the oncoming lane (the next car in that lane was about ¼ mile away), pushed hard on my brakes, grabbed my steering wheel hard, and braced for impact. Fortunately for me, I was driving our truck that day. It was able to handle the impact, but it was not drivable afterward. The high school boy was not so lucky, and took the brunt of the collision. The front of his car was smashed like an accordion, almost to the front window of his car. I was told that he got this car just a couple of weeks before.

This painful incident set me back into the cycle of whiplash and migraines, and many trips to physical therapy and adjustments. Just prior to this new assault to my body, I had been relatively pain free for a year or more.

The headaches intensified during my forties and early fifties. They occurred more frequently, and could last up to four days. All I could do was stick it out and let it run its course.

The first day of a migraine I would be incapacitated to the point of not being able to think about food or drink. The second day I could sit up just long enough to eat and drink something, and get up by myself to the bathroom as needed. On the third day, I would force myself into the shower and put on some real clothes. Forget hair and makeup. I was still too tired to do much but sit and watch TV. My head would be very fuzzy and the fatigue was debilitating. Finally, the afternoon of the third or fourth day, my head would begin to clear, and I knew at that stage, I was nearing the end of my headache.

Mark could always tell when the migraine was abating. He could see it in my eyes. The best way I could described the experience to him was telling him, "It's feels like I'm coming out of anesthesia after surgery, but I can't clear my mind, and it hurts like H-ll. When my head begins to clear, it's as if someone opens up my head and sprays Windex on my brain, and slowly wipes away the fuzziness that covered it." I knew then that I was clearing out, and I could think again.

I tried a few migraine prescription medications in an attempt to prevent reoccurrences, with minimal success. Each prescription would either make me sick, or I would develop other nasty side effects. I was so unhappy, feeling like I had few options.

After a couple of years of putting up with a few different mediations that I could not count on to work, I asked for a referral to a neurologist. In the meantime, I continued with the different treatment modalities to relieve the pain in my neck and shoulders.

The neurologist was successful with a treatment that finally rid me of the cycle of migraines. God bless Botox!

Every three to four months, my forehead and area just above the hairline was injected with Botox. It was nothing I looked forward to, being poked multiple times in my head, but it was totally worth it. It worked to prevent the major migraines from developing.

On a rare occasion, I still got smaller versions, but they were much fewer in number, intensity, and duration.

The quality of life I was blessed with felt like a small miracle. I no longer worried about jeopardizing my nursing job like I had been. I knew there were a few fellow nurses who truly did not understand what I had been suffering with. There was not much I could do about that, but it made me uncomfortable each time I returned to work after those horrible days of headaches.

I hired a personal trainer to help me get into shape and help me strengthen my neck and back. I felt like I was in the best shape of my life. I had some muscle definition and felt good. For a while my injured neck and upper back didn't feel so bad. A far cry from where it had been. Come to think about it, maybe it felt that way because the rest of my body was sharing the aches and pains from working out.

Still, my poor neck would always need tending. I worked with a doctor at the surgery center who specialized in pain management. He treated my back and neck pain with injection to the damaged areas in the spinal column, hoping to stop the pain cycles that I was experiencing. For the next year or so, I required no treatments of any kind for my neck. It felt like small miracle.

Unfortunately, I once again began experiencing migraines after two years of relief. The return of my migraines was an unwelcome casualty as a result of the change of insurance providers where Mark worked. This new insurer did not cover the effective Botox treatment the neurologist had been providing me. Even though a great deal of studies had already been done to demonstrate the efficacy of Botox for this purpose, Botox had not fully been approved to treat and prevent migraine headaches. Because of that, the new insurance provider listed it as "experimental" and would not cover the treatment.

My neurologist worked hard to get the new company to approve the coverage for several of her patients that were now denied this service, to no avail. Not wanting to burden Mark and me with the financial hit of $6,000.00 a year, my only recourse was to return to prescription medication that at least gave me a chance of preventing and/or treating migraines.

There was one prescription that worked better than others, but I did not like the side effects. It made me feel jittery and made my heart race and flutter on occasion, making me feel very uncomfortable. There were times I'd have one of my co-workers take my blood pressure shortly after taking my prescription medication, and found it unusually high.

I felt I had little choice whether to use it or not. I had been enjoying stability over the last two years, and the return of migraines was going to jeopardize my job and affect the quality of my life once again.

The nasal spray form of this commonly prescribed medicine for migraine headaches gave me the best chance to knock out an oncoming migraine. The sooner I got the meds into my system at the first sign of an oncoming migraine, the better. The pills took too long. Usually it only took one dose, and the headache would abate. On a rare occasion, I would need to repeat the spray one more time, sometimes hours later.

I put on a good face to those around me, even as the age lines returned to my now moveable forehead. I had high hopes that Botox might finally be approved for treating migraines in a couple of years, and I was hanging on to that hope for the time being.

Mother reminded me that she began suffering with migraines in her forties. At some point, her headaches abruptly stopped, just as unexpectedly as they began. She said she thought they went away sometime in her 50's. Her words gave me another reason for hope.

Our marriage vows, "in sickness, and in health," were tested many times since that first accident in my late thirties. I hope I have been as helpful and kind to my Mark as he has been to me.

Life Happens

Life was good, except for those darn headaches. They still plagued me from time to time, and it seemed more triggers were involved than just the constant pain in the neck. Mark was not one of them!

Sadly, the same could not be said of our beautiful mother. Life was not so good. Her health continued to decline, and quite rapidly.

During her last twelve months, hospice nurses had been summoned to assist with Mother's struggling condition. Her lungs were so weak, and the frequent bacterial infections would result in more antibiotic treatments just to reduce the infection, but not cure it. At best, it gave her a measure of hope, which increased the quality of her life, if just for a short period of time.

She could no longer be left alone for more than a few hours each day. My sisters in charge of her finances hired a care provider to come each morning for a few hours. Breakfast and lunch would be prepared for her, as well as help with bathing, dressing, and light housework.

Dom continued living in the house behind her. He'd bring her dinner each evening and help her to bed when she needed him. This routine went on for many months. Dom continued fulfilling his promise to our father, but he was not alone.

We all did what we could, though none of us felt it was ever enough. Two of us had offered to have Mom move in, but there was no convincing her to leave her house for the care and comforts her daughters could provide in their homes. Gert and I tried many times to convince her. She could have been a part of the lives of many of her grandchildren, who otherwise were only able to visit her for a short time once or twice a year, if they were able.

Mother had expectations of each of her children during her last few years of ill health. "I don't understand why each of you can't just take turns living with me for one week, and rotating every six weeks, so I can stay in my own home. You are my children!" Mother would say to us. "You are my only family. There is nobody else!" she added. It was gut-wrenching to all of us, and impossible for six of us to share equally in what she was expecting of her children.

Each of us did what we could, as often as we could. Through our individual abilities, sacrifices, and yes, our guilt, we kept Mom in her home for as long as we physically were able to do. But time was running short, and I was needed by my own family.

*

Jessica gave birth to our seventh grandchild on November 22, 2008. Amelia Suzanne Morgan arrived just one day after Jessica's birthday. She was the fifth granddaughter, and was the apple of her daddy's eye. She was precious and feisty, and looked just like her dad, Joel.

Amelia had a tough time in the beginning, and Jessica wanted and needed my help every so often. I would oblige.

My fondest memory just after Amelia was born was the few nights that Jessica and I spent together in a double bed with this precious newborn baby sandwiched between us. I felt great joy and purpose in those precious hours when two women and a little girl bonded together. My daughter and I would look at each other and smile. "Let's enjoy this. It may never happen again." I said, and she agreed.

Joel was still recovering from a very serious car accident he suffered a few months before, and he needed his rest far more than we three girls needed our sleep.

I watched Jessica as she gave comfort to her colicky baby. We were living one day at a time, and if that didn't work, we took it one hour at a time. Writing about this makes me realize the many years that have gone by since this all happened. It feels like it was just a short time ago.

In the spring of 2009, we were surprised to find out that our granddaughter Isabella would be having a sibling in late December. On December 26, 2009, Logan Mark became our eighth grandchild. Sadly, Ben's relationships with Joanie fell apart not long after.

Now with eight grandchildren to love on, six still in diapers, I wanted to stay close to home and be available to my children when I could be of service. Life was busy between my job at the surgery center, my husband and home, and our growing family.

When it was evident that Mother needed someone with her during one of her very sick spells, and no one else was available, I'd break away to assist her in Salem for several days at a time. It became increasingly difficult to keep up with her progressing health needs. Mom required full time help, more than any of us could handle alone, especially during the winters. Though Dom was continuing his daily routine of help, it was impacting his life in an unsustainable way.

In August that year, my siblings and I called for a meeting with the Hospice nurse in charge of Mother's care. We needed to discuss the future care for our mother and the tough decision we had to make for her. We needed their help.

We planned to gather together in Salem for a meeting on Friday, August 14, 2009. Our goal was to share our thoughts and feelings surrounding our dear mother's declining health, and come to an agreement to secure full-time care. The half-day provider currently hired to assist mom was not enough to get her through the entire day and night safely anymore.

Mark and I planned to leave Pasco with enough time to visit Mom for a couple of hours before we attended the 4:00pm meeting at the hospice building. The poor night's sleep, the trip ahead of us, and the subject matter and purpose of the siblings meeting was more than enough to trigger the muscle spasms in my neck, and the beginnings of a migraine.

"Oh crap! I don't need this now. How will I function if I get one of my migraines?" I asked Mark. "I better pack my prescribed nasal spray and take a dose now. This is very poor timing. Very poor!" I said in distress.

Thank goodness the first dose seemed to abate the onset of a full-blown migraine. I made sure to pack a few doses to have on hand just in case. I hated to use the spray more than once in a 24-hour period. I did not like the way it made me feel. But I was not willing to risk being debilitated during this weekend trip. For now, I was ok.

The drive was beautiful as usual, and uneventful. We arrived at Mom's house and surprised her with our visit. We decided it would be better to stay with Mark's twin brother Mike and his wife Kelly, who lived just twelve minutes from Mom, in Stayton, Oregon. This would also allow my sister Sue and her husband Mike to have more room while staying with our Mother.

Mom seemed happy that she had company for the weekend. Other siblings came over in the afternoon to visit as well. Though her cognition was a bit compromised, I knew she figured we were up to something. She just let It go when we said that we were all getting together to spend time with her, as well as to plan for her continued care. She was too weak to go out to dinner with the twelve of us, but encouraged us to have a good time.

One of her biggest fears as she was aging and ailing was that her family would not stay close with one another when she was gone. In some ways, this gathering reassured her that we would stay in contact and see each other as often as possible. At least, I hope that was what she saw.

Well into the afternoon, I felt that migraine threatening to return. I decided to hit it one more time with another dose of my nasal spray, which was within the prescribed guidelines. No time for this headache. We had a meeting to go to, and soon.

We arrived a few minutes late for our 4:00pm meeting in Salem with the two hospice nurses. The last of the siblings finally arrived at 4:25pm. I could feel the tension in the room, at least that is what I thought I was feeling.

We took a moment to pray as a group. Everyone seemed to calm down a bit after our prayer, everyone but me. I wasn't sure what I was feeling, but something was wrong. Without warning, my heart began to pound in my chest, which made me feel extremely uncomfortable.

Typically, I have little trouble taking part in round table discussions. However, with the way my body was reacting, I thought if I just got my thoughts out quickly, I could relax a bit and listen to what everyone else had to say. So I began the discussion, and said my peace. Then I did my best to listen.

Each of us in the room was given a chance to communicate their concerns regarding our mother's deteriorating condition and the need for full time care. With the input from the hospice nurses, combined with our own observations and experiences, it was clear to all of us, that we needed to make a new care plan for our mother.

Mom would be moved to a wonderful, assisted-living community in Mt. Angel, Oregon. All of us agreed that it was the very best place for her. This would enable us to continue to be her children when we came to visit, as opposed to social service workers and nursing care providers. Though we knew it was the best decision we could all make, we also knew it would be very difficult for our mother. That made it much more challenging, and the decision gave us little comfort. We were all feeling sad for Mother's losses.

My Broken Heart

My concentration during the meeting was sporadic. The anxious feelings I developed grew with the increasing pounding in my chest. I tried simple nursing interventions to try to reduce my heart rate. I held my breath several times and leaned forward to bear down on my contracted tummy to no avail. Then I tried to focus on my breathing to relax and slow my heart rate that way. Still no help. I even tried rubbing each side of my neck along my carotid arteries to see if that would work. Nothing was working, and with an ominous feeling overwhelming me, I remained very still.

My teeth began to clench so tightly that I could hardly open them. My jaw was clamped shut. My body began to shiver as if the temperature in the room had suddenly dropped 30 degrees. My neck hurt, my chest hurt, and I felt like my heart was ready to jump out of my chest. Suddenly, I felt as if someone had just punched me in my chest with their fist.

This strange sensation caused my heart to slow down somewhat, but made my chest hurt a lot more. I still could not control the shivering. I knew something bad had just happened and I was in trouble.

"Mark, something just happened. Something is wrong with my heart. I need some help," I whispered. Mark just looked at me as if he didn't quite comprehend what I just said.

"Please excuse me for just a minute, but does anybody have an aspirin that I can chew quickly? I need one for my heart. I am having severe chest pains. Can one of you nurses please check my vitals? I'm not stable right now. Please hurry!" I requested.

Now everyone was looking at me. We were no longer discussing Mother, and I felt embarrassed and afraid that my siblings might think that I was just drawing attention to myself. Those old childhood feelings could still wreak havoc in my mind. I was not faking anything. I was just plain scared.

I quickly chewed Gert's aspirin, my blood pressure was elevated, and my heart rate was a bit high, but appeared to be slowing down. "Maybe, I just need to relax, and give it a little time," I thought.

"What do you want to do, Mar?" "Do you need to go to the hospital?" "Just relax for a little longer." "We are wrapping things up here soon." "I'm sure you will be alright after you have a couple of glasses of wine at dinner." "You look a little pale, but maybe you just need a bit to eat and some fresh air."

Nobody really knew what to make of my announcement, including me.

"I guess I am feeling a little better. Let's just get going soon, and see if my chest calms down. I think I would like that glass of wine," I responded.

Mark had asked me a couple more times if he should take me to the ER for a quick check. The hospice nurses were encouraging me to get looked at too, but the worst of my chest pain was abating after the initial punch, and I was still feeling more embarrassment than concern for my own wellbeing. Denial is an interesting phenomenon.

I wanted to move on to dinner, sure that it was what I needed to help me feel better. I promised the hospice nurses that I would go to the hospital if I still had chest pains much longer.

Mark helped me to the car and opened my door, just like he does for me nearly every time. He was concerned, I could tell. I tried hard to be normal again. At least my jaw wasn't clenching, and the shivering was gone. From start to finish, that foreboding lasted at least an hour.

I just wasn't hungry at the restaurant. I ordered a simple side salad, a glass of red wine, and some water. I picked at my salad.

I could hear conversations around me, but I was not participating in it. I was more pre-occupied with the chest pains that were not going away, and my poor posture at the moment. Both of my shoulders were drawn forward as if they were protecting me somehow. Leaning forward while sitting seemed to give me a bit of comfort.

I was totally lost. I had no idea what time it was. I saw that Mark had long finished his plate of food, and I decided it was time to travel the 20 miles back to Stayton and get to bed.

"Mar, you still don't look like your feeling much better yet. Promise us that you will go to the hospital if it doesn't get better soon. I would, however, advise you not to go to the Salem Hospital on a Friday night. That place gets crazy busy," Traci said to me.

"I promise!" I told her. I also assured the rest of the group that I would seek help in the event that my symptoms continued. "I hope I just need a good night's sleep and I'll feel better in the morning," I said to everyone, hoping that they would not worry about me.

A good five hours had gone by when I noticed my headache was returning. It had been four and a half hours since I used my second dose of nasal spray. It had been three and a half hours since I called out for an aspirin, and we were now on the road, going to Mike and Kelly's house.

"How are you doing, honey?" Mark asked me. He could tell I wasn't ok. "Should I take you to the ER in Stayton, just to be sure?"

"I think we better. My chest still hurts, and I just keep thinking about what I would do if one of my family members or friends came to me with the same symptoms that I have been experiencing. I'd be calling 911 and getting them some advanced help. If I was at work, I'd be calling for anesthesia to come and check on my patient," I said.

I began to cry at this point. What an evening. We really just wanted to go to bed and get some sleep, and now we were going to a small community hospital instead.

Mark made a quick call to his twin brother. "Mike, Marja and I are taking a quick detour to the ER here in Stayton. She's been having some chest pains that aren't going away."

"You're kidding. Well, that's not good. We'll be here waiting for you to call us back when you know something. Hope everything will be ok?" I could hear Mike say through the phone.

It was a bit chilly outside when we got to the hospital. I started to shiver again, which made me tremble. "Hurry with the wheelchair Mark. I don't want to shiver. I did enough of that at the meeting," I reminded him.

I was immediately taken to a room in the ER of this really nice little community hospital. I began to feel safe for the first time since the incident occurred.

The nurse began the chest pain protocol. She placed me on oxygen, gave me a sublingual nitroglycerine tablet, and held off giving me an aspirin because I already chewed the one Gert game me more than three hours ago. The ER doctor came in to talk to us while this was going on.

The doctor held off giving me any strong pain medication for the moment, and quickly ordered the routine blood work, EKG, chest x-ray, and a cocktail of Maalox and lidocaine for me to drink. There are a number of things that can cause chest pains besides the heart. Acid reflux is one of them, and this cocktail would help relieve the pain if that was the culprit.

After taking my vitals, which were normal, and reading my EKG and chest x-ray, which were normal, and noting that the cocktail didn't help, the doctor said, "I'm kind of scratching my head here a bit. I just don't think it's your heart. You don't look like a heart attack waiting to happen. You are young (53), don't smoke, height and weight are normal, you exercise, and you eat right. Huh, let's just see what your blood work looks like. I'll be back shortly. In the meantime, I'll have my nurse give you a little morphine to keep you comfortable."

Oh, that morphine worked just fine. My pain went from a 7 or 8, on the 0-10 pain scale, to a 2. I can handle a 2. I was living with a 2 to 4 most days from my previous whiplashes.

Another 20 minutes went by, the ER doctor suddenly opened the curtains like a stand-up comedian eager to make his audience laugh.

"Well, my dear, it's a good thing you came in to see us. The blood work came back, and you are having a heart attack!" he announced.

"No, what? No! Are you sure? You said I didn't look like the type to be having a heart attack," I countered with denial.

"Your troponin levels are elevated, indicating the cause of your pain. I'm sorry, but you are indeed having a heart attack. I've called for an ambulance to take you to the Salem Hospital, where they are preparing for your arrival. They've already got a room for you. I really am sorry, but they will be able to figure this out, and take good care of you there. They are better equipped than our little hospital here. I'll be back in just a few minutes. I have some paperwork to get ready," the doctor said before leaving the room.

Everything in the room stopped for a few seconds. In those moments, something profound happened to me. I looked to my right, where my Mark was standing. He was stunned into silence. I thought to myself, "People die of heart attacks. I could die tonight and be separated from my husband, children, and those eight grandchildren." Then in the next second I looked away to my left and thought, "But tonight I might be with my Lord Jesus in Heaven."

"Where do you want to go?" I distinctly heard in my head. In the next moment, I looked at my Mark and silently prayed, "Not tonight Lord, not this night!"

Mark and I looked at each other in silence when I returned his gaze. "We'll get through this, honey," he said to me.

"I know we will, but I am scared Mark. People die of heart attacks. I don't feel like I am going to die. In fact, in some ways, I am relieved to know that what I was feeling was real, and really happening. This wasn't supposed to happen. I've tried hard to take care of myself, and still I get a heart attack? Honey, I know it is 9:00 already, but I think we should let our children know what's going on, and ask them for prayers."

"I'll give them a call, but first I would like us to pray together before I call the kids," Mark pointed out.

Mark's prayer over me was simple and full of praise and thanksgiving. He praised God for His protection, and offered thanksgiving that we were led to the ER. We both prayed for the doctors and nurses to take good care of me, and asked for a full recovery. We prayed to God for courage and strength, and to help us to live our lives according to His will. I thanked my guardian angel for protecting me once again, and asked for my angel to stay close. Mark placed the sign of the cross on my forehead, much like he has done so many times before.

I think the nurse was just on the other side of the curtain, and heard us praying together. Just after we ended, she came into our station. She was shaking her head, back and forth, and said, "I did not see this coming. No way did I think you were having a heart attack. I just never know what I am going to encounter working in the ER. I will remember you!"

"I'm feeling a little better. If I have to leave in an ambulance, I better at least have good-looking EMT's," I said to Mark and the nurse. They both laughed.

While we waited for the ambulance to arrive, Mark was busy making phone calls to each of our children. No one wants a phone call like this. I knew that each one would worry and react in different ways.

I knew that Jessica would want to drop everything and drive seven hours from Spokane to Salem to be by my side. I knew that Matt and Benjamin would be more pensive, and lean on their families and close friends for support. I knew that Tim would reach out to his wife and his siblings for comfort, and say a few prayers for me and Dad.

The receiver on the phone was loud enough that I was able to hear each of our children's reactions when Mark called them. Mark's conversation with Tim was kind of sweet, and went something like this:

Mark: "Mom's had a heart attack, and we are heading to the Salem Hospital in a few minutes?"

Tim: "Is Oma going to be ok?"

Mark: "Mom had the heart attack!"

Tim: "I know, Oma, right?"

Mark: "No son. Oma did not have a heart attack, your mother did."

Tim: "Mom did? Ohhhhhhh! Stacey, it's my Mom!"

Tim's response was priceless. Mark went on to explain what had happened, and told him I was doing ok, and that he would continue to provide updates in the morning.

Mark reached out to his brother and one of my sisters, to let them know what was going on. Both were upset to hear that it was my heart and not acid reflux.

I remember thinking, "Well, now everybody will know that what happened in the meeting was not an act to draw attention to myself, but was a real emergency!" What a thing to be fretting about at a time like this. What a childish reaction, afraid that my sisters were thinking I was being melodramatic. They gave me no cause.

Moments later, two EMT's arrived in the ambulance. I was hoping for a similar experience to our elderly friend, MaryAnn. She and her husband were celebrating their 60th wedding anniversary when we were celebrating our 25th on the cruise ship. She suffered a heart attack onboard the ship and was whisked away in a helicopter to "somewhere in Cuba." She had these handsome young military men in uniform taking care of her. She said she'd thought she had died and gone to heaven!

I wasn't quite so lucky. One of my guys was a very short and skinny young fellow, who looked like he just got out of high school. His mate was about six and a half feet tall, and looked like a sumo wrestler in training. But, hey, they were in uniform, and were so sweet to me and very professional. They kept me comfortable and made me laugh during a very stressful, 25-minute drive back to Salem. "More morphine, please!"

"We're going to drive at normal speed without the emergency lights on. So don't race to the hospital, Mr. Henderson. In fact, why don't you go on ahead and wait for us in the ER. We will be passing through there on our way to the cardiac unit. You might even be able to meet us up on the floor. She already has her own room waiting for her," the EMT's suggested, and then walked out of the room to bring in the stretcher.

Mark leaned into me and said in a quiet voice, "I don't think so! If I get passed by an ambulance with lights and alarms blaring on the way to the hospital, I will be keeping up with that ambulance. I promise to drive carefully though."

"One more cross on my forehead, please," I requested.

Mark obliged, and included a kiss along with it. "I'll see you soon, honey. I love you," he whispered.

"I'll see you soon. I love you too," I whispered back.

Nothing can really prepare you for a life-threatening incident. I don't remember everything of what happened that first night in the hospital after my admission. What I do recall is giving the doctor and nurse my medical history and my medication list, and explaining the details of what I had experienced before, during, and after the meeting.

The doctor did a quick examination, looked at my medication list and asked me a variety of questions.

"So what time was your last dose of the prescribed nasal spray?" the cardiologist asked.

I thought for a bit and said, "Let's see, that was about 1545. It was right before we left for the meeting I was telling you about."

After his examination and reviewing my medical history, the doctor said, "I think I know what happened to you. I'm going to order an echocardiogram right away, and see if my preliminary diagnosis is correct. I believe you had what is called a 'Broken Heart' heart attack, also known as a stress-induced heart attack. It's not very common, but you present with some of the classic symptoms. It is not related to coronary artery disease (CAD). It is a completely different sort of event that caused the attack on your heart. I'll explain more to both of you after the echo is completed. While we are waiting for that, I will write some orders for the nurses. How's your pain level at the moment?"

"Right now, it's about a 3-4, but when the pain medication wears off, it jumps to a 7-8," I answered.

The doctor looked at my nurse and said, "I want her very comfortable tonight. Give her a dose of morphine and start a morphine drip, and..." I stopped listening after that next dose.

The sonographer came sometime later. He completed the procedure in about 20 minutes, and then left. The clock in the room read 2030 (10:30pm).

The cardiologist returned a second time and began to explain, "My hunch was correct. You had what is known as a Takotsubo Cardiomyopathy, which is the medical term used for the 'Broken Heart' heart attack. This type of cardiac event results from an increase in what we call catecholamines, when they are quickly released within your body. If the conditions of extreme stress from physical or emotional distress are present, these catecholamines (adrenaline), can cause damage to the heart, just like what you experienced."

Mark was invited over to view the video of the damage to my heart, captured by the echocardiogram machine. The doctor explained, "What happened to your wife during this attack is shown here at the bottom of her left ventricle. This is what a healthy heart looks like pumping normally. This is your wife's heart after the attack. The apex, or lowest point of her left ventricle, is ballooned out quite a bit, making it difficult for her heart to push the blood up to her right atrium. This is why she is short of breath and has pain. In a woman with your wife's medical history, I'm quite sure it is not related to CAD. But to rule that out all together as a possibility, we are scheduling a cardiac catheterization for tomorrow to look at the arteries that supply her heart."

"Is my wife going to be ok? How do we treat this condition?" Mark asked.

"She's pretty sick right now. Her blood flow (ejection fraction) is down to 30%. That's way too low, and we are treating her with some medication to assist her heart. We are monitoring her constantly, and supporting her oxygen and her pain.

"The good news is the treatment for this is a few weeks of solid rest and pain control. The heart will heal itself, and she should be fine after that. In addition, I will send her home with a prescription of a Beta Blocker to take each day. Whatever external stressors she had should be reduced, and don't ever let her use that medication in any form for her migraines, or Sudafed, or anything over-the-counter (OTC) that may increase adrenaline ever again. That is very important now," he said to instruct and warn.

"We will continue to answer all of your questions during her stay. For now, I suggest you let her try to get some sleep, and you take care of yourself. It's been a long day for both for you. The staff here knows to call me if anything changes. I'll see you in the morning," he added. The two men shook hands before the doctor left the room.

With a kiss and "I love you," Mark left me, and drove back to Stayton to be with his twin brother. It was nearing midnight when he finally left.

I got bits and pieces of what was done and what was said in the room, but I did not get a clear understanding of what had happened until morning.

It is very difficult to sleep in a cardiac care unit, with all the machines making all those beeping sounds, and the alarms going off each time my IV bag was empty, or when my tubing crimped. Let's not forget the squeeze to my arm every so often, and another thermometer placed in my mouth just as I was dozing again. Even with all that, I gave thanks to God for directing me to the ER after my three and a half hour delay. I mean *denial*. I learned my lesson. You got symptoms like I had, you call for an ambulance, period!

"I want to be with you in heaven someday, Lord, but not today, not tonight," I thought, all alone in my room. A sense of peace and assurance filled my spirit as I drifted off for much-needed sleep. I would not die tonight.

Mark and I had agreed that I should receive the sacrament of the sick before undergoing my angiogram. During one of my night nurse's rounds, I reminded her to check on my request. She told me it had already gone out, and I should expect a priest sometime in the morning.

It's humbling to be a patient when you are a registered nurse. This experience helped to remind me to be kind and empathetic with every person I encounter, and to provide my very best care to each of my patients, much like I was receiving here.

Not long after Mark arrived the next morning, a priest showed up with a little carrying case. After a short visit, I asked if I could receive the sacrament of the sick and receive communion. My angiogram was scheduled for later in the day, and I was given the ok from the nurse to swallow something, but to do it soon.

This priest was more than accommodating. He moved an over-bed table toward him, lowered it, opened his case and started unloading its contents. It didn't take long to figure out that he was setting up the table to say Mass. We were having Mass in my room. "Holy Moses!" I said.

I was feeling well enough to fully participate in the service. It lasted a mere fifteen minutes with just the three of us in the room, and it certainly helped that he kept the sermon very short.

Next, the priest anointed me with the sacrament of the sick. What a wonderful gift that was. Just listening to the words being read during the rite made me feel so peaceful and my soul clean. I didn't like being in the hospital with a sick heart, but since I was here, I wanted to avail myself with as much grace, encouragement, and healing that I possibly could. It made me think of how Dad was feeling just before his open-heart surgery. I remember what Dad said to the priest who anointed him. "Whatever happens now, it doesn't matter, because I am clean as a whistle on the inside, thanks to you!"

Later that afternoon, my cardiologist arrived to perform the scheduled procedure. I listened to him explain what was about to happen, and then signed the consent form giving him permission. I was just praying that he would find nothing else going on with my arteries and heart.

I did not want to be awake for this. I was already pretty groggy from the medication they had me on, but I didn't want to remember the experience. I had been through enough already. "Can I get some Versed after I get into the room, say, maybe 3-4 mg please?" I asked. Oh, it's good to be a nurse and know what to ask for at a time like this. They obliged. "Thank you!"

I woke up in my room and opened my eyes enough to see my two sisters, Sue and Gert, sitting near the window. I did not engage in much talking initially. I just wanted rest.

I could hear the doctor discussing his findings with Mark and my sisters. Just as he had already predicted earlier, there was no evidence of CAD. My vessels were clean, so to speak. With his diagnosis now confirmed, the only thing left to do was one more echocardiogram scheduled for the following day. If he saw enough improvement in the blood flow of my left ventricle, he would discharge me the next day, on Sunday.

"Your heart is already showing signs of improvement. Your ejection fraction is in the low 40's already. That's a good sign. You will need to rest, rest, and get more rest for the next two weeks. After that you may begin light activity and slowly increase your activity as much as you are able during the following two weeks. Then you should be fine to go back to work. Follow the instructions the nurse will give you, and be sure to follow-up with a cardiologist in the Tri-Cities within this next week. Let us know where to send copies of your medical records from this hospital. Other than that, you are free to go," the doctor instructed.

Then he added a stern reminder, "And remember, don't ever take that medication again, and the other med's we talked about."

We couldn't think of anything else to ask the good doctor. We thanked him for his care. After all the discharge instructions were reviewed, and with all the paperwork in hand, we left the hospital in the late afternoon.

"Mark, I want to see my mother before we go to Mike and Kelly's house," I said.

Mark smiled at me and said, "No problem. Let's go see your mom. Sue and Mike are still there, and I think Gert might still be there too."

Mom was sitting in her favorite chair when Mark walked me into the room. I was so exhausted. I gave Mom a quick hug and sat down for a short visit. I had no knowledge of what happened after our meeting on Friday. I wasn't there to take part in any of the conversations with Mother regarding her impending move into assisted living in Mt. Angel, Oregon. I didn't ask, and none of us talked about it.

She was very concerned about me, but also seemed very confused about the entire weekend's events. It was a lot for her to take in. I assured her that I was already getting better, and not to worry about me.

"Please Mom, try not to worry. I'll be ok. I know what I need to do to continue to get well. I promise to call you when we get home, and continue to keep you posted on my recovery. I would appreciate your prayers though. You always seem to have a direct prayer line to God, while mine often feels like a long distance phone call," I said with a smile.

She got my meaning and blushed through her smile. This seemed like a good moment to leave, with a little levity between us.

Hard as I tried, I could not hold back my tears. Not only was my heart broken from some major adrenaline release that would eventually heal, but broken just looking at how frail our mother had become. That would take much longer to heal.

Compromised with age, Mom's severe coughing spells and progressive lung disease over such a long period of time had made her so very fragile. It was difficult to see the changes in her, and I was sad knowing that her world would soon get even smaller.

The hospice nurses where surprised that she had lived this long. I'm not sure if that was a good thought or a sad thought. We all let her know that her life still mattered to all of us, even as she questioned why God had let her live this long.

I truly believe we were doing what was right for Mom and I have no guilt, just sorrow. She would leave us in the very near future, of that I was sure, and it would happen in God's and Mom's time!

Mother would be moving into her home-away-from-home in a few weeks. I would be moving as well, at about the same time.

*

Rest, rest, and more rest. That's what the doctor said. That's not so easy when, just three weeks after my Takotsubo Cardiomyopathy, we were moving into our new house.

Thank the good Lord for family and friends. Two of my dearest friends, LeeAnn Roach and Maureen Vincent, spent the last day in our rental house helping me with the deep cleaning. I wanted to leave the house cleaner than when I moved in. My friends were lifesavers to me.

As the three of us were cleaning, others were moving all the boxes out of the garage. I was excited to see what was in each box I had so quickly packed away eleven months earlier. It almost felt like Christmas.

I did my best not to overdo it, but I probably did anyway. My heart would always remind me when I was not being kind to it. The chest pain would return, and it scared the "you know what" out of me.

I was able to return to work after about five weeks, and continued the treatment that my new cardiologist in Richland prescribed for me. I still had a fair amount of pain, and continued to experience strange quivering feelings in my chest every now and then.

I liked my new cardiologist, but it was obvious that I was the first patient he had ever treated with Takotsubo Cardiomyopathy. I felt like a rare specimen during my doctor visits. Every time I had an appointment with him, he would open his computer to look up my condition and see if he could find more information to make sure he was treating me properly. I was someone he was learning from, and that's not what I needed. He didn't exactly make me feel very confident in his care, but at the time, I didn't know where else to turn.

There really was not much research or information about Takotsubo, and the information there was had only been around for the last ten to fifteen years. Not long ago, medical schools were not even providing information on this disorder. Consequently, there were not that many doctors who were well trained in the care and treatment of my condition.

Over the next several weeks I spent a great deal of my own time researching and reading as much as I could find on the internet. And what I did read convinced me that something had happened to me other than just stress on the day of my attack. Lord knows I've experienced much worse stress before.

I had my suspicions. "Why was I given strict orders not to use my migraine prescription anymore, in addition to some OTC that could increase adrenaline in me?" I pondered. I needed to find some answers.

*

We were growing very comfortable in our new surroundings, but it was our first Christmas that officially bonded us to our home. My previous decorations seemed new again. I used many of them in different ways and in different places within the home. It felt good to purge many items that just didn't work for me anymore. I chose a simpler approach to decorating by using only our favorite pieces. The outside was another story.

Mark meticulously installed clear white lights all around the front and sides of the house. We decorated the new trees we had planted in the fall with clear lights. We had just enough time to landscape the front yard before the cold weather prevented us from doing anything in the back.

The feeling of Christmas lasted much longer with the arrival of our eighth grandchild. Our sweet grandson, Logan Mark, was our favorite Christmas present.

There was much to be thankful for in 2009: we built and moved into a new home, welcomed our third grandson who helped to close the gap of the disproportion number of granddaughters, took positive steps to aid both of our ailing mothers, and survived a serious health scare. The events of the year generated a big change in me. There was a lot on my mind as we prepared to ring in the New Year, 2010.

Chapter 27

Just When We Needed Her!

"I'll get it!" I yelled when the phone rang. "Hello?"

A woman's voice replied, "Hello, my name is Sister Francis Marie, and I am calling for some help. I met your husband, Mark, at your church last summer, when I came to your parish to talk about my Adopt-a-Priest program. He was very kind and told me that if I ever needed anything when I was in Pasco, to give him a call. I'm driving up to Pasco from Berkeley, California for a couple of weeks during my Christmas break from my studies at the Dominican School of Philosophy and Theology. I have lodging for the second week I'm there, but not for the first week. Would you be able to let me stay with both of you for that first week?"

I was unprepared when she called, and the only thing I could think to say was, "Who is this again?"

Sister Francis Marie took it from the top, and started all over again. After I listened more intently, I excused myself for just a moment, and went to talk to Mark.

"Honey, there's a nun on the phone who says she knows you, and that you told her she could stay with us if she ever needed to. She wants to stay with us for a week during her Christmas break from school," I said to him with a puzzled look on my face.

"You remember her, don't you honey? At the end of the Mass a few months ago, she gave a talk to our parishioners about her Adopt-a-Priest program. Remember? There were so many parishioners who wanted to participate that by the time she left, Sister had most of the priests of our diocese adopted from our parish alone. That was when we adopted Fr. Fox, and committed to pray for him every day for a full year. I remember talking to her after Mass and I told her that if there was anything we could do to help her when she is in Pasco, to let us know. She quickly wrote my name and phone number down in her little book."

"So, what do I tell her? She wants to stay with us the first week, and then go to someone else's house for the second week. We've never done anything like this before, you know, for someone we don't really know," I said, as if that made a difference before we decided what to do.

"Tell her yes!" Mark replied without hesitating.

"OK, then! We have a nun as a houseguest for a week sometime after Christmas, and into the New Year," I replied.

I took my hand away from the mouthpiece of the phone, hoping that she didn't hear everything I was trying to whisper to Mark, and said, "Of course you can stay with us. You are more than welcome!" I did my best to make it sound sincere.

I gave her our address and our cell phone numbers, and wrote down the itinerary of her planned visit. Our conversation ended, having just made a sweet-sounding nun very happy.

It is amazing how deeply our lives changed after a simple request by a stranger, and an act of hospitality by my Mark. Moving out of our comfort zone to embrace a new experience by accommodating a guest in need turned out to be one of the biggest blessings in our lives.

Within the first couple of days after Sister Francis Marie arrived, Mark and I both felt a great friendship developing. We spent the first two evenings mesmerized by how God had been working in Sister's life. She seemed quite interested in us as we shared our journey of faith, and the family that we have been blessed with.

"Mark, I was just thinking!" I said, just after he turned off the light on our nightstand.

He leaned back over to turn the light back on and said, "OK, what are you thinking about now?"

"I don't want Sister to leave at the end of the week. I want her to stay here with us the whole two weeks. I like being with her, and I think she likes it here too. We have these two extra bedrooms and there's really no reason for her to pack her things and go somewhere else. Can I ask her to stay?" I questioned.

"It's fine with me. Give her the option and leave it up to her. I like her here too. It feels right. Now, can I turn the light out, and go to sleep?" Mark said, reaching for the light a second time.

"Great! I just hope she wants to stay with us. She's our first houseguest in our new home, outside of our children, and she's a nun! It's kind of special, don't you think?"

"Yep, kind of special. Good night honey!"

"Good night Mark!"

The next day at dinner, we asked Sister Francis Marie to stay with us throughout her entire two weeks. Apparently, she had been praying for us each day, and hoping we would ask her to stay. We began to understand that this was just the beginning of a long-term relationship. "I wonder what she had been praying for on our behalf," I thought to myself.

I knew that Sister had plans for most of her two weeks in Pasco. Much of her time was spent down at the church. She would leave in the morning and go to St. Patrick's to say her morning prayers, and be there for the daily 8:00 mass. On the mornings when I went to Mass, we would visit for a short time before she devoted the rest of her day helping to do anything and everything she could around the parish.

Much of her time was spent restoring and painting the large statue of Jesus and His Sacred Heart. The restored statue stands regal on the shelf just to the right of the altar in our church. The image is so beautiful again, thanks to the handiwork done by Sister Francis Marie.

She made many new friends during her stay, each wanting to spend time with her. The two weeks went by very quickly and I knew it would be hard for her to leave when the time came.

Before Sister Francis Marie left us to go back to California, we made sure to let her know that she was truly welcome to stay with us again when she came back to Pasco.

She smiled and said, "I was praying for you again, as I do each day now, and asked God to let me stay here with you again someday. To hear you offer your beautiful new home to me is a real blessing, and I would love to come back. It is so peaceful here, and I can feel the love of God through you both. You are a gift to me."

Her words to us were very humbling. We fell in love with Sister, and she loved us in returned.

Sister was not ready to leave us at the end of her two weeks stay, just as I predicted. But it was time for her to travel back to Berkeley and resume her Master's Degree studies in Philosophy and Theology.

I was packing some food for her two-day drive when she came into to the kitchen.

She was sad and had tears in her eyes when she said, "I am hoping to come back to Pasco after school lets out for the summer. I was wondering..."

"Of course you will stay with us," I quickly interrupted her, my eyes welling up. "We both want you here with us, all summer if you like!" Just then, Mark walked into the kitchen finding two women in tears.

We prayed one more time together before she left. The sendoff was much easier now, knowing that in a few more months, Sister Francis Marie would live with us for the summer, and share some more of life's journey together again.

We walked her to her car and gave her hugs and a blessing on her forehead. Sister was more than a friend to us now. She was family!

It's hard to explain the change in me. We'd hosted other overnight guests in the past, and enjoyed the time we spent with them. However, I did not experience the same emotions of peace and joy that I felt whenever Sister was around. I guess this is how it feels when the Good Lord blesses you with the gift of hospitality. Hebrew 13:2, "Do not neglect hospitality, for through it some have unknowingly entertained angels." Food for thought!

Sister is now a part of this story. It would take writing another book to describe the incredible journey she has shared with us and the many fruits of Grace bestowed on our family. She was sent to us to take under our wings. We accepted her and our lives have changed forever. She came at the right time for the peace and healing my body and spirit needed.

Not long ago, our son Matthew mentioned, "Next time you get a call to take care of another nun like Sister Francis Marie, please give her our phone number so we can have her with us!" We all laughed, knowing that he and his siblings had witnessed the effect that Sister has had on our lives too.

"Long shall you live, in the Gloria, in the Gloria. Hip Hip Hooray."

2010 Uneventful?

The new year had gotten off to a wonderful start. There was no way of knowing whether the rest of the year would continue to surprise and inspire us. Would the year be smooth sailing and uneventful? Or would it shake us up and present "opportunities for growth," a phrase Mark is known to use when referring to new and difficult challenges at his work.

The phone rang the morning of my birthday, January 29. You might say that there's nothing unusual about hearing from someone on your birthday! To which I would reply, "No, not usually, but this year had already produced unusual."

"Hello, Marja? This is Father Pitstik," the priest said.

"Well, good morning to you. What a surprise! It's nice to hear your voice. What moved you to call me today?" I asked him.

I could visualize the smile on his face through the tone in his voice when he said, "You popped into my head this morning during my morning prayers. Something inside me thinks that today is your birthday, so I thought I would call and wish you a happy birthday. And if it's not your birthday, I'm calling to say hello, and find out how you and Mark are doing."

I was stunned for a moment, then began to laugh, "Father Pitstik, it is my birthday! How did you know? I haven't talked to you since I made that weeklong silent retreat in Spokane a few years ago. I remember seeing you briefly in the cafeteria. You were visiting your mother and sister, as I recall," I said.

He asked about what had been going on in our lives, and how St. Patrick's was doing. Then I asked him to fill me in on what was going on in his life.

"Well, I went home during the holidays and got a chance to see some family and friends before I returned to Oregon. I'm in the middle of another wonderful year of teaching the seminarians at Mt. Angel Abby. I've been teaching for a couple of years already," the priest mentioned.

As soon as he said Mt Angel Abby, my jaw dropped. This priest that I had known for many years, ever since he was an associate pastor in Pasco, lived just across the road from where my mother was now living. Now I was doubly astonished on my birthday.

"Oh my Lord! Father, you live right across from my ailing mother. We just relocated Mom from her home in Salem to The Towers just a few months ago. I wish I had known that you were in Mt Angel when I visited her late last year. I would have called you to come and visit!" I said with amazement in my voice. "Father Pitstik, this is one of the best birthday presents ever. God put me in your mind today, not just because it is my birthday, but to provide me with a spiritual lifeline for my mother."

These words came out of my mouth so fast, and probably too loud for my friend's ears. I was beyond amazed with this timely phone call.

Even though there was a retired priest living at the The Towers, I asked Father Pitstik if he could visit my mother and provide her some spiritual comfort. She was receiving communion almost every day, but the resident priest didn't spend much time with her.

"I'd be happy to meet her and tell her of our friendship. I have many seminarians that rotate visiting the residents at the Towers. I will ask your mother if she would like a seminarian to visit her weekly, or more if she wants," Father Pitstik graciously offered.

We talked a while longer, both of us feeling blessed. We both knew without a doubt that God was working today in a very obvious way. The Good Lord answered a prayer of mine, and perhaps that of my siblings too. None of this was a coincidence. None of it! It was nothing less than a small miracle.

*

During a break in the inclement winter weather, Jessica, Joel, and little Amelia, came down from Spokane for a weekend in February. Jessica was excited to tell us that she and Joel had set a date for their church wedding. They had begun marriage preparation classes with a priest at Gonzaga University, who was a good friend.

To accommodate both sides of the family, August 14, 2010 was the chosen date, and St. Aloysius Catholic Church in Spokane, Washington was the chosen place for their nuptials. Mark and I were indeed excited for our daughter and future son-in-law. He already fit right into our family.

Jessica and I got to work right away with the wedding plans. I really didn't have much to do though. She has a degree in Marketing and loves to do this kind of stuff. The only constraints on her part were to stay within the budget we provided for the wedding and reception.

The lifetime of picturing what it would be like watching our daughter walk down the aisle with her father was now just months away.

By the time Jessica and Joel get married, it will have been more than five years since Tim and Stacey got married, and nearly seven years since Matt and Ammie wed. As much fun and excitement there was when our sons got married, there's still an additional emotional component involved when your only daughter marries. You "let go" of sons, but you "give away" your daughters. It sounds old fashion, but it was still relevant to us.

*

The first springtime in our new home was upon us, and that meant some hard work landscaping the rest of the front and back of our new property. I did as much as I could without stressing my heart too much.

I thought about my heart almost every day. Even though months had gone by, and I was taking medicine for my heart, I still experienced strange feelings in my chest more often than I should, and was hesitant to do anything to increase my heart rate, out of fear.

My first reaction whenever I got cold enough to shiver and before my teeth began to clench was to jump in a hot shower to make it all go away. I was just living day-by-day, trying to avoid any kind of stress. Do you know how stressful trying to live without stress is?

During a mid-morning break at work, I was sitting alone in the break room with my finger on a carotid artery counting my heartbeats. My chest hurt and I felt anxious. One of the surgeons happened to come into the room for some coffee and asked how I was doing.

"I don't feel all that great, Doctor. My chest hurts a little, but I'm sure it will get better soon," I answered, thinking that reply was sufficient.

The doctor looked me in the eye and said, "You need to go to the ER now. I know you had some trouble last fall, and we don't want to take any chances with you."

"I don't really want to go, Doctor. It does this every once in a while, and then goes away. I just never know what sets it off," I replied through the few tears that I had been holding back.

"Stay right there!" The doctor ordered, and walked back to the recovery room of the surgery center.

My supervisor walked across the street with me into the ER of the hospital. I refused to go in an ambulance. I didn't want to make a scene.

Mark arrived within a half hour, relieved my supervisor, and sat next to me in the room I was occupying. All the tests came back negative for another heart attack, but I was admitted to the hospital for overnight observations and periodic blood work to see if my troponin levels increased over time.

The nitroglycerine tablet I was given for chest pains was now producing a major migraine headache, so pain medications were ordered. It wasn't long before it was apparent that the cause of any chest pain was not my heart. The remainder of my stay was pain medications for the severe migraine that had been induced.

I missed the rest of my scheduled work that week. I was sick in bed with a migraine that lasted four days.

There were other times when my heart began to beat fast and flutter for no apparent reason. It would produce a similar adrenaline rush that was so familiar to me now. When the rush came, I did everything I could to relax and let it pass.

My search for answers led me to an endocrinologist to see if we were missing a component to why my body was reacting the way it was. Every test that was necessary to rule out a possible cause was negative. My condition was not caused by an imbalance of my endocrine system. I struck out again.

I relived my Takotsubo event many times in my head. Did I have to live in fear like this for the rest of my life? I needed help to figure this out.

After failing to find information on the internet that might help me better understand what happened to me, I concluded that I needed to go back to when it all started and look for the cause on my own.

The cause was stress. I understood that. Usually sudden and severe stress. I understood that too. Now what was I doing that day? I was worried about getting another migraine right before the long drive and hospice meeting. But I had experienced many migraines before and never had cardiac problems, at least none that I could identify. There was a fair amount of stress dealing with the needs of our aging mother, but we were meeting to make plans to help with the care of our mom. This was a stress reducer. I've had much greater stress than what I was having on that day.

I thought about the warnings the cardiologist in Salem gave me, and then reread the bold written words in my discharge instructions. DO NOT TAKE [BRAND NAME OMMITTED] FOR MIGRAINES, OR ANY OTC WITH PSEUDOEPHEDRINE, LIKE SUDAFED.

Most of us just glance over the pharmacist's medication information sheet that comes with our meds, instructing us on what they are prescribed for, how to take them, and possible adverse side effects to look for. These instructions can be readily understood by most people.

However, the pharmaceutical company inserts that come with our medications have so much clinical information included that even some physicians can find it difficult to read and fully comprehend. It surely was not written to be read by the consumer.

It became important to my investigation to read the small print so neatly tucked in every box of the migraine medication that had been prescribed for me. I was shocked to read all the side effects. I recognized so many of the cardiac symptoms described as side effects that I got sick to my stomach thinking about what I had taken for prevention and relief.

These were the same symptoms I had experienced when I was first prescribed this medication. It was the reason I stopped taking it then and began to look for an alternative treatment. After the Botox injections that were effective but denied to me, I suffered with the side effects of the medication again, with the hope that it would prevent the four days of illness. I was afraid not to.

The stress that I was experiencing the day of my heart attack was not from the normal stressors that I had been living with already. The stress was from the side effects that were caused by the medication. It must have generated the sudden release of adrenaline that caused damage to my heart. I was sure of it. I just needed validation.

I stuck to my convictions about what happened on August 14, 2009. I told my cardiologist what I suspected, and he agreed that it was more than likely the medication.

Now, what was I going to do with this information? I wondered how many other people have been damaged by this drug in similar fashion, and may not have known. As in my case, the side effects turned out to be much worse than the migraines.

Not long after I figured out what happened to me, I heard about a similar case that happened to a woman whose husband worked with Mark. In a conversation the two men had after my attack, Mark's coworker mentioned that his wife had a heart attack in the emergency room ten years earlier.

This couple had gone to the hospital to get some help to treat a severe migraine headache she was suffering with. Within minutes after receiving an injection of the same medication I had been on, she suffered severe chest pains and was sent to cardiac unit to be stabilized and monitored for 24 hours. The doctor determined that her heart attack was a direct result of the injection.

I called his wife on the phone and told her my story. She said that she still experienced occasional heart flutters, discomfort, and an occasional fast heart rate, but nothing like she experienced after the injection. The doctor didn't call it Takotsubo Cardiomyopathy. Ten years ago, they didn't know what it was, or very little about it at best.

I tried to put all this information behind me and go on with my life. I felt confident that I could learn to control these random episodes of adrenaline rushes and chest pain, and as long as I stayed away from certain medications, I should be just fine.

*

At the beginning of summer, Timothy and Stacey announced that they were expecting another child near the end of the year. "Is it just one or two?" I said with a smile.

"We already had an ultrasound and we only saw one beating heart," Stacey divulged.

Number nine grandchild was on his/her way! This just never gets old! Uneventful? Ha!

Sister Francis Marie came to stay with us for the whole summer. She got to know the rest of our family throughout this longer stay, and began to feel like she was part of all of us too. Most of her time was spent working at the parish though. She had a wonderful effect on everyone she encountered. It would have been unfair to keep her to ourselves.

All the wedding arrangements for Jessica were done, for the most part. I was delighted to have been involved in helping her find the perfect wedding dress. The very first dress she tried on at the very first place we shopped at turned out to be the one dress that all other gowns were compared with. We went to three or four stores in Spokane and ended up right back where we started, and bought that first dress. I was excited for my daughter. She would be a beautiful bride.

The Road to Goodbye

The first time I went to visit Mom in her new surroundings, I stayed in a guest room. It was a nice room, but I was not comfortable. Much of the night I was thinking about Mom tucked away two floors down, knowing she wasn't happy. I was aware that her dementia and her lungs were getting worse, and I knew that she just wanted to go home. It was her heavenly home she really wanted to go to, and she would often question why it was taking so long for her to get there. I was sad for her, for myself, and for the rest of the family.

It was exhausting each time I drove down to visit. I had been making the same four and a half hour trip all of my adult life. Usually it was once or twice a year. Now, it was every three to four weeks.

After Mother was moved to Mt. Angel, I stayed with Ineke and Lloyd a few times. They lived in Silverton, Oregon, roughly twelve miles from where Mom was. I couldn't remember a time when I had both of them to myself. Staying with Ineke was a treat. It enabled me to salvage some enjoyment from an otherwise sad and stressful visit with our ailing Mom, and Mark's mother, who was also sick and in a nursing home.

Mark's twin brother Mike and his wife opened their home to me a few times when I traveled alone. Staying with them added another 20 miles each way, but it was worth the extra drive. They always made me feel so welcome, and Mike would fix the best breakfasts each morning. It also helped to know that they understood what we had been going through, visiting both of our mothers. Mike would spend time with his mother once or twice a week, and he was running on empty as well.

When no one was able to take me in, I'd travel the extra 25 miles to stay at Mom's empty home in Salem. Her house was still full of her belongings. There were only a few things she could take with her to furnish her small room in Mt. Angel. Even so, without Mom and Dad living in the house, it felt very empty. The void could only partially be filled with memories of a time gone by, adding to my loneliness and sadness.

Our children were aware of how often one or both of us were traveling down the Columbia River Gorge. They all knew we were worried about our mothers' declining health. We never kept anything from them. Most of our children hadn't seen their grandmothers in a long time, and were expressing their need to spend time with them too.

Mark's mother, Doreen Henderson, had been living in different retirement homes for several years already. Fortunately for both of us, her current residence was in Woodburn, Oregon, just eight miles from Mt. Angel.

I could write a whole chapter about my mother-in-law, Doreen. I will summarize by saying she was a unique and unconventional woman, with artful talents, and a flare for writing. She was a free spirit with a strong devotion to God, and I loved her.

Doreen suffered a heart attack in early July of 2010. She remained in the hospital for over a week. The social services from the hospital worked to find a place for her rehabilitation. Sadly, her attending hospital physician, having consulted with her regular doctor, wrote orders for her discharge back to her assisted living facility in Woodburn.

She resided in a facility where the elderly would only need medium assistance, and we were aware that they were not equipped for any kind of medical rehabilitation. When talking on the phone with the residence manager, she was quick to add that they were trained and available to assist in end of life care. The hospital physician was aware of this information when he wrote the discharge orders.

Our most recent visit with Doreen was less than a week before her heart attack. Having talked with her, and with her resident manager, we knew it was time to go to Woodburn and assess things for ourselves, yet again. Did we need to do battle and insist on cardiac rehab, or was it time to call for hospice care?

Mark finished work early on Friday and we drove to Woodburn that same afternoon. When I saw Doreen, it was apparent that she would not be able to recover without cardiac rehab, and also apparent that she was too sick to begin any restorative treatment in her current condition. Doreen was dying. We just didn't know how long she would labor.

"I don't understand why they brought me back hear, Mark. First, they were looking for another place for me to rest and recover, and next thing I know, I am getting in an ambulance and I'm back here again!" Doreen said between labored breaths and coughs.

Looking for the appropriate words to say, I turned to Mark and then to his mother and suggested, "Mom, your body is really weak since your heart attack. You're unable to participate in any rehab because you are too sick right now, and in a lot of pain. I know this might be difficult to hear, but I think we should consider the help of the hospice nurses. You know my mom has had their help for over a year and a half already, and they have provided her with very good care. With the kind of pain you have, and the labored breathing, even with the increase in your oxygen they have been providing you, you are just too weak for rehab. They can take care of all you need to remain comfortable."

Hoping to help his mother understand her true condition, Mark added, "Marja and I talked about this kind of help for you, Mom, before we even saw you. I know you want to get better, but first you need to take things one day at a time, and with the help of the hospice team, they will be totally in charge of your medication and anything else you would need to be comfortable. Perhaps, in time, if you get well enough, they can re-evaluate what your needs are, and figure out if you still need to be under their care or not."

Doreen was quiet, pondering what we both said. I'd never seen her so solemn and pensive. Much of her life revolved around her asthma, her aches and pain, and a growing list of other maladies. She could bounce between extremes of feeling really bad and sorry for herself, to "woo-hoo, look at me, I can dance!" This was a big part of who she was. But at this moment, she was like a young child who needed her parents to love her, and do what was right for her.

"So they would give me whatever pain medication I needed to stay comfortable?" she asked us. "And, there is a chance that I might still get better, and if I don't, they will still keep me comfortable?"

"Mom, there is always a chance, but you are pretty sick right now, and your heart is not doing very well anymore. And, yes, they will keep you comfortable. You won't be alone. You have so many people here who love you, and will do what they can while you try and get better. Mike and Kelly will come to check up on you too, and we'll come back in a couple of weeks, after Jessica's wedding, to see you," Mark and I said, taking turns finishing each other's sentences.

"When will hospice care begin?" Doreen asked. "Can they come right away?

"We'll call them right away, and help to get you signed up for their special care. We'll also call Mike, Dave, and Dan, and give them an update on your condition. Please Mom, try to rest now, we'll be back shortly," we said to assure her.

*

Ben and Matt were already in the process of planning a road trip to go see their Oma and Grandma. Once they were told just how sick both of the matriarchs of the families were, they knew they could no longer postpone their trip.

Tim had just finished with the annual summer hay cutting at the farm of his in-laws, when he got word of Ben and Matt's decision to travel. He quickly phoned his brothers to say he wanted to join them. They planned to leave in a couple days, in the middle of the week. They planned for a one day, down and back trip. The only way they could do that was to leave very early in the morning, spend as much time as they could with both Oma and Grandma, before driving home after dinner.

*

I was very apprehensive thinking about my three sons traveling together in one car. I was still feeling a bit traumatized from a recent car accident I happened to arrive upon just seconds after the impact.

Unless you are a trained firefighter, EMT, police, or paramedic, it is extremely rare that you would ever need to render assistance during a medical crisis. Most medical providers, such as doctors and nurses, are very rarely called on to assist at emergencies outside of medical facilities. You'd have to be at the right place at the right time to witness an event that calls for some sort of intervention.

Not long after I became a registered nurse, I began finding myself at the right place at the right time for more than my fair share of emergencies. I've been one of the first, if not *the* first person to stop at automobile accidents on city streets and interstate freeways. I've been asked to help with health situations in airplanes, during seizures, and even someone fainting outside of work. Once my arms caught an elderly woman collapsing in church, and upon finding her nonresponsive, shouted, "call 911!" I have lost count of these chance encounters, and less than a week before my sons were planning their road trip, I found myself, once again, in the midst of chaos.

I've been trained for life and death situations, not only as a nurse, but as a volunteer chaplain in a Catholic hospital. It is a very humbling experience praying with, and then praying over an individual when you witness them taking their last breath. Fifteen years with a pager has humbled me many times.

On my way home from work this particular day, I was ending a phone call with Mark, who happened to be home before me. "I just turned onto road 68 from the freeway. I'll see you in a couple of minutes. Love you!" I said. That was my plan, a couple of minutes. That's all I had left to get home.

Just as I was ending the call, I noticed two trucks, and a couple of stopped cars throughout an intersection. Some men were, standing, walking, or running toward one of the trucks. A couple of people were on phones and others were pointing at something. It was a cold and extremely rainy evening, and these men were quickly getting soaked.

I slowed my car to a crawl when I realized the middle truck had been in a collision. After rolling down the front passenger window I shouted out, "Is everyone ok? Anybody hurt? I happen to be a nurse."

"No, we need your help! There are two women in that car and we can't get the doors open. Please help us!" a couple of the men yelled to me.

"Oh Lord, here I go again," I thought to myself, as I pulled my car forward and out of the traffic.

I quickly tied a plastic head covering under my chin, one that I always keep in my purse for days like this. I questioned for a split second if I needed my CPR mask, also in my purse.

Two of the men came running to my car and pointed toward a small embankment at the edge of a field. There was a car that had been pushed down into the field by the truck in the middle of the road. Each of them took me by the arm and quickly escorted me down to this vehicle.

While they were rushing me to the site, they began to tell me, "This car just ran the stop sign and was hit by that truck while he was going the speed limit, 45mph. He didn't have any time to even slow down. Some guys are trying to get the doors open on the small car, but they can't get any of them open because of the damage.

"Has 911 been called, and how long ago?" I asked them.

"We've already called them but we haven't heard any sirens yet, and it's been a couple minutes since we saw the accident," one of the men replied.

I was hoisted over a barbed wire fence that was downed by the car, and waded through the muddy, torn-up ground to where the two injured women were. Still trying to open the car doors, I asked again, "Time? How long it has been? Tell me again!"

"Maybe three or four minutes already. Here comes a guy from his house with a 2x4 piece of wood. Oh, and there's another guy with a crowbar," someone else said.

I looked at the two women inside the car to see if there were any signs of life. Both had been unconscious since the impact, and the woman next to me in the front passenger seat was looking pale. "What is taking so long? The fire department is just a couple blocks away!" I said in frustration.

The men were frantically working on the doors with the crowbar on one side, and the 2x4 on the passenger side that I was standing next too. "Guys, guys, be careful. Think about what you are doing. We don't need anyone else to get hurt by the broken glass, or a broken 2x4," I shouted.

I could see the panic on the men's faces. These women were dying right in front of us, and we couldn't get to them. Just then, a fire truck rolled in without sirens, just lights. "We need the Jaws of Life, quickly. We can't get the doors open," I yelled to the EMT/firefighters. They yelled back, "We don't have any in the truck, but we have what we need to get the doors open."

They immediately opened the driver's door to extricate the driver. I asked if she was alive, and one of the EMT's said he thought he felt a pulse. I then said, "What about this one?"

"She's dead," he said.

The passenger door was finally opened by one of the bystanders. I quickly looked for a pulse or any other sign of life, and I found none. I knew too much time had be lost before we were able to get to either woman, but I needed to go through the protocol for my own benefit. All the attention was going toward the driver, and no one was coming back quickly for the woman I was left with.

Even the men who had been at my side helping me down the muddy embankment, were now walking up the small hill, leaving me alone with my patient.

"I will not leave you," I said, to the woman. Taking her hand, I began to pray for her and her companion now in the ambulance. I prayed for all the men who had tried desperately to help, and for the medical professional doing what they do best. They try to save a life when and where they can. Then I prayed for her family and friends who would deeply mourn when told who they lost today.

Still holding her hand in mine, I stroked this woman's forehead with the other hand, and said, "I am not leaving you to be alone. I will stay with you until someone comes to relieve me. You are not alone. I'm so sorry for what has happened. I'm still here, and staying with you."

Finally, after another few minutes standing in the soaking rain, two EMT's returned to where I was. "Are you here to take care of her now," I asked. They nodded, "yes," and one of them helped me through the mud, and up to the road to where my car was.

"Oh good, you're home. I was just getting ready to get in the car and look for you. I thought there may have been an accident or something," Mark said just after he heard the door to the garage open.

Completely wet and completely spent, I said, "There was an accident and I watched two women die. One was for sure, but I don't think the other one is going to make it from the way she looked."

"Oh my God, what happened?" my husband asked as he helped me take my wet coat and shoes off.

I broke down in tears and let most of the tension that had built up throughout the last half hour dissipate. I relived the entire incident and then rested in Mark's arms. I don't remember much of the rest of the evening.

We found out later that both women died soon after the driver of the truck impacted the driver's side of the small car. The woman driving did not stop at the stop sign, nor did she even slow down, and both women were killed. The last time I saw the truck driver, I witnessed a traumatized man, without outward injury, but in a state of shock, knowing that he was involved in a fatal accident.

*

Though I knew in my heart that my sons would be careful on the trip down the Gorge to see their grandmothers, my head was thinking about all kinds of reasons why this was not a good idea. Then the phone rang.

"Hi Mom, its Jessica. Guess what? Joel is insisting that I go down to Pasco tomorrow before the guys leave for Mt. Angel, so I can go with them. I wasn't planning to go, but Joel said he'd take a couple of days off and stay home with Amelia. He'd rather I drive with my brothers than drive down by myself. I need to do this too. It's right before the wedding and I might not ever see Grandma again, from the sounds of it. I really need to see Oma and Grandma."

"Oh, great! Now all of my children will be in one car for a ten-hour round trip adventure. Wonderful!" I said sarcastically.

"Mom, we'll be fine. Nothing's going to happen. I'll make sure whoever drives, drives safely. We're not kids anymore, Mom," she said to patronize me.

I knew that she was just trying to assure me, but I had to let her and the others know that I would be worried until they were all back in their homes again!

"We'll call you every couple of hours," Jessica promised. "Good, then I only have to call you every opposite hour!" I added. We both laughed to help relieve my anxiety, exacerbated by the accident the week before.

Jessica drove to our house in Pasco on Tuesday, July 20, 2010. Bright and early the following morning, Matt picked her up with Ben and Tim already in the car. Waving and watching your four grown children drive away is unnerving. It was hard not to think about the upcoming wedding. "Oh, Dear Lord, please keep them all safe!" I prayed. I waited a full hour before I made the first call. From then on, we alternated check-ins.

The kids first drove to Woodburn to visit their Grandma Doreen. Jessica knocked at the door, walked in and found her grandma looking very pale. She could hear the fluid in Doreen's lungs that she was working hard to clear with each cough. Ben walked into the room just behind his sister.

Doreen recognized Jessica right away and then noticed Ben. "Jessica darling, I'm so happy to see you and Joel. I wish I wasn't so sick at the moment. It's hard to talk," she said in between fits of coughing.

"Grandma, this isn't Joel. It's Ben! We drove down this morning to see you. Matt and Tim are here too," Jessica announced.

"Hi Grandma!" Each of them took turns saying as they bent over to kiss her on a cheek.

"You all came to see me? This is wonderful. I've been thinking about you and the rest of the family. I'm not feeling very well, but talk to me and tell me how you are all doing," Doreen said laboring through each word.

Each of them took turns getting close to Doreen, and gave updates of what had been going on in their lives and their families. Doreen laid quietly listening to what they had to share.

There were moments when little was said, while the staff tried to keep up with Doreen's needs. She appeared to be quite distressed and anxious. At times, after a severe coughing spell, she would lay breathless for, what seemed to the siblings, a very long time. A few times they thought that their grandmother had just died. And then she would breathe again.

They each handled the moment in their own unique ways. Some had difficulty holding back the tears, while others were deep in their own thoughts. Each of them mentioned later, that they were pretty sure that their grandmother was dying, and they would be saying goodbye for their last time.

One hour was enough for Grandma Doreen and her grandchildren. She was struggling, and needed to rest. The last of the kisses, and "I love you's" were given and received. The four of them quietly left the room, giving way to the staff assisting Doreen through her immediate health crisis. "Goodbye Grandma!" each said as they left the room.

It was noon and that meant lunch. The tears were gone for the moment, and it was time for more lighthearted conversation. I wish I could have been a fly in the car, listening to the banter between them. I can only imagine. What I later found out was that they were having fun at my expense.

Each time I phoned them for an update, and before they answered, one or more of them would say, "Let me guess. It's Mom again!" and the eyes would roll, and the amusing comments would begin again.

Oma was resting quietly in a chair when the four of them knocked on her open door and slowly approached her. Mom looked up to see her four Henderson grandchildren standing tall in front of her.

"What are you doing here? This is such a surprise," Oma said to them.

"We're here to see you! We just had a visit with Doreen, and now we are here to see you. How are you?" they said.

Mom tried hard to put a good spin on how she was really feeling, but it was getting more and more difficult for her to do. She told them that she gets tired a lot, and doesn't always remember things like she used to. But, like Grandma, she wanted to know how each of these grandchildren and their families were doing.

The conversation was light, and when it became too tiring for her to talk, they decided it might be a good idea to take Oma for a nice walk outside. It was a beautiful July day and the blackberries on the bushes that lined the back of the property were ready to be picked.

They took turns pushing their Oma's wheelchair. Breathing the fresh air and having her grandchildren pampering her lifted her spirits. I know that the couple of hours she spent with these grandchildren, who lived the farthest away, helped her feel special and loved.

Before they each said their goodbyes, they took turns sharing loving remarks with Oma, and included the hope of seeing her again soon.

Oma smiled and said, "I love you too. I'm so glad you came to see me. It was such a wonderful surprise. Jessica, I am sorry that I won't be able to be there for your wedding, but I will be praying for you, and I'll be with you in spirit. Be sure to drive carefully. I know your mom must be worried. Goodbye."

"Bye Oma! Love you!" each of them said in return.

Today was a good day with Oma. They felt a little better after seeing her. Though she looked frail, her spirit was good. They knew she was declining. It was very apparent when they picked her up to place her in and out of the wheelchair, and felt just how light she had become. But when they told her that they hoped to see her soon, they really meant it.

The four of them set off to the pizza parlor in Silverton, where they would meet up with several family members who had planned to join them. Gert and Larry, Traci and Jim, Dom and his kids Alexis and Zack, and cousin Lori and her little son Jack, were making it a priority to join them for a late afternoon dinner.

One last round of goodbyes followed the pizza and short visit at the restaurant. This time, they were happy to hear, "See you at the wedding!" from each of their relatives.

The drive back to Pasco would take over four hours, depending on who was driving. They wanted to return by 8:00, to allow enough time for Jessica to drive over two more hours to her home in Spokane Valley before it got too late.

During the time our kids were traveling home, Mark was at a business dinner at a winery in Prosser, 30 miles outside of Pasco. I was attending a video series down at the church, and would be checking in with the kids during the break at 7:15pm.

"Hey guys, where are you at?" I asked Matt when he picked up the phone.

"We're just a few miles from the bridge outside of Umatilla. We should be home in 30 minutes, give or take," he replied.

"So, how was the visit at the pizza parlor? Did you say hello to everyone, like I asked?"

"Oh, the visit was great, under the circumstances. We are just physically and emotionally drained, and are ready to get home," Matt replied. "How's Dad doing?"

"Fine, I think. He's in Prosser at a dinner meeting, and I am at the church watching another video of the Theology of the Body series," I said. "I haven't seen him after work yet. Why?" I asked.

"Mom, you haven't heard yet, have you? Grandma died this evening just hours after we left her! Dad called to see when we would be home, and then told us that he just got a call from the manager where Grandma lived. She told Dad that Grandma died late this afternoon. We're all kind of in shock right now, thinking about what just happened, and the fact that the four of us went down to see Grandma and Oma today," Matt replied.

I was shaken by the news and said, "Oh my God, I can't believe this. Honey, be careful driving the last few miles home. I am so sorry kids, but so grateful for your last visit with her. I need to go son, and call your dad. I love you guys."

"We love you too, Mom," Matt said just before ending the call.

I returned to the meeting room in the parish center and told our pastor, Fr. Barnett, what had happened. Someone else would have to be leader in my discussion group tonight. I needed to go home right away.

Before leaving, the group of about a hundred parishioners stood up and prayed for Mark and me, and our family. "Thank you," I said through my tears, and left to call my Mark.

Mark was already home waiting for me. He didn't want to call me at the church, and planned to tell me about his mother when I got home. We hugged each other for comfort. I cried but he did not. We shared the same peace between us, knowing that Doreen was no longer in pain. Her suffering was over.

Not long after I got home, our children walked through the front door. We listened to them share the events of the day, and how they were handling the whole experience.

"I can't believe that we saw Grandma right before she died. We were meant to go down today. I'm forever grateful that Joel encouraged me to go down with my brothers," Jessica said.

The six of us didn't spend too much time together. They had families to get back to. They would find comfort in their own way with them.

Before Jessica left, she gave her Dad and me a big hug, and with tears in her eyes said, "Grandma was never going to make it to my wedding anyway. We knew that. Somehow, she lasted long enough for our visit. I know this was her way. Now I'll feel her at my wedding even more." We both smiled and agreed.

"Please, Jessica! Call us when you get home. We won't be able to sleep before then anyway. We still have to pack for our trip to Portland. Grandma's body is there, and we both want to see her before she is cremated. We will meet up with Mike and Kelly, and clean out Mom's room, and we'll be staying at their house if you need us," Mark said.

I can never recall a time when my adult children had ever been together like this. They will never forget sharing the gamut of emotions, and a lifetime of memories during this hastily planned quest. They said their goodbyes to Grandma, and did the same with Oma, just in case.

Mark and I were left alone to comfort each other. There were still no tears in his eyes, just sadness and wonder. He tends to hold tight to his emotions. Perhaps seeing Doreen's body tomorrow and going through all of her belongings in the same day, might help him open up his grief.

I know Mark worried about my heart, which only compounded his own stress, which in turn caused me added stress. It's a vicious cycle, and an enigma. Right now, life was almost more than we could manage.

We stayed in Stayton after we went through Doreen's belongings. Because she had specific instructions in her last will and testament, which included no funeral or newspaper announcements, we simply called the brothers and their families, along with a few other relatives and friends, and planned for a gathering at Mike and Kelly's backyard on Saturday, July 24, 2010. This would be a celebration to remember Doreen Lillian Henderson, and to complete the last chapter of her life with love.

"I'm just grateful that she is not suffering anymore, and praying that she is at peace," Mark said to reassure me when I mentioned his lack of tears.

In some ways, I understood his feelings and reactions. Like my mother, Doreen suffered for a long time, and Mark grieved long before she passed. I recognized it, because I'd been grieving a long time for my own mom. I knew I would be grateful when she no longer suffered.

So far, the second half of 2010 wasn't slowing down from the pace established in the first half. On the contrary. The strain was greater and Mark and I were holding on the best that we could. We had faith that God wouldn't give us more than we could handle. But He was getting pretty close!

Chapter 28

"I Can't Wait!"

From start to finish, it took four days to sort through Doreen's belongings, coordinate the memorial service, and part ways with family and friends again. During those busy days, I managed a few trips to Mt. Angel to see my mom. I needed to spend this time with her, hoping each visit was as meaningful for her as it was for me.

"Mark, I'm going to take off for a few hours to go see Mom again. I finished putting Doreen's pictures together on the memory board for tomorrow's afternoon's gathering. It looks like most of the arrangements are pretty much done."

I entered Mom's room and found her sleeping in the recliner with her legs propped up. Having seen her less than a week ago, I was not expecting to see her look so much weaker. I quietly said, "Hi Mom. I told you I would be back soon. I just didn't think it would be quite this soon."

When we hugged, she said, "It's good to see you again, Marja. I'm always glad to see you." Her voice was very soft and a little hoarse.

I assumed that one of my sisters may have told Mom about Doreen's death, but I still thought I should tell her myself. I sat on the floor in front of her and gently placed my hands on her knees and said, "Mom, Doreen passed away just hours after the kids saw her on Wednesday. She didn't suffer very long, and was surrounded by the hospice nurse and her care providers where she lived. Our kids were the last family members to see her. They were pretty shocked when they heard what happened, and so grateful to have been blessed to see her and tell her they loved her before she died. The whole timing of that day was really quite remarkable."

Mother just looked at me for a moment, smiled, and then whispered, "I'm so glad for her. I can't wait."

Her remarks startled me. I wasn't ready to admit it, but Mother was in the process of dying. Seeing all the signs in her words and actions, I was no longer in denial. She was allowing it, getting ready for it, and just could not wait.

Just last week, I watched her in the dining room before I entered the room. Mother just sat in her wheelchair pushing her food around on her plate; none of it was going in her mouth. Oh, she may have taken a bite of chocolate pudding to give her an ounce of pleasure, but she wanted nothing else.

When she spotted me entering the room, she looked at me, pushed the wheelchair away from the dining table and said, "I want to go back to my room now." I was not about to burden her with my will by attempting to persuade her to eat something she had no desire for anymore.

Today, the day nurse told me that Mom was eating less and less, and sleeping more and more. She needed total care now, and could no longer walk at all.

The two of us didn't say much during our visit. I placed my head in her lap, she placed her hand on my head, and let me cry. After a couple minutes of silence, she asked me to help lay her on the bed. She was light as a feather.

She picked up the big black rosary Dad had used for many years. She paused for a moment, looked at it, and handed it to me saying, "I want you to have this. I don't need it anymore."

"Oh, Mom! Not yet, you still need it. But I promise to take it when you don't need it anymore. I promise. I would love to have Papa's rosary. If you would like, I brought my own rosary to pray with. Would you like to pray together again?" I asked her.

"I'm too tired to pray with you, but I can listen with my eyes closed while you pray," she replied.

"I'd be happy to. You hang on to Dad's rosary, and I'll use mine. In the name of the Father, and of the Son, and of the Holy Spirit..." I began to say the Glorious Mystery of the holy rosary. It was Friday, and we normally would have prayed the Sorrowful Mystery, but I just couldn't pray that one with her at the moment.

Mother dozed throughout the entire 20 minutes I prayed. Once in a while I could see her lips moving in response, but not much.

"Mom, I'm going to leave now. You need your rest. I promise to come and see you on Sunday before we go back to Pasco. Mark will be with me then too. I love you Momma."

"I love you too, Marja."

For the past six months, each time I left her, I'd walk out of the room and weep. It felt like it was always the last goodbye. I had been grieving for quite some time already. "How long Lord? How long?" I would pray.

Not in Suze's wildest dreams did she ever expect to live to be 85 years old. She outlived all of her family members and was sad to be the last one left. *"I can't wait!"*

After the Sunday morning Mass at St. Mary's Church in Stayton, Oregon, Mark and I headed to Mt. Angel to see Mom again. I told him about what I had observed and what the staff had shared with me about her recent decline. We both accepted the inevitable outcome. We just didn't know how much time was left, and wanted to make this a very meaningful visit and goodbye, just in case.

August 1, 2010 was a beautiful day in the Willamette Valley. The half hour drive from Stayton was postcard beautiful.

I was remembering the many drives to Dad and Mom's place on Christy Court. "That's Christ with a Y," they'd point out whenever they gave out their address. Mom and Dad would always stand behind the big picture window next to the front door, looking out for us to arrive. I was also thinking about the last time Mom was able to stand alone at that window waving goodbye. That was not long before she moved to the Towers.

When we reached her room, we found her asleep in her chair, just like I found her two days before.

"Hi, Mom," Mark and I quietly said.

"We both came to see you, like I said we would," I added.

Mom seemed pleased, but had a distant look in her eyes. "Hi Mark. It's good to see you. I'm so sorry about your mother," she said as he gave her a gentle hug and kiss on the forehead.

"Thanks, Mom. I'm just so glad our kids got a chance to see her before she died. That was such a blessing," Mark replied.

Mother agreed that the weather was perfect for a wheelchair ride around the facility. We stopped now and again, so as not to tire her out too quickly. Our last stop was at a water feature that included a babbling brook and pond. With the large trees shading us and the sound of the water dropping from the stones, it was a perfect place to rest and get lost in our thoughts.

After our walkabout, we decided to take Mother to the deck on the top floor of the building. The panoramic landscape of hills, trees, and farmland were at their peak beauty. The large baskets of multicolored flowers scattered around the chairs and tables on the deck provided an up-close opportunity for Mom to reach out and touch the colorful eye candy that she loved so much. Every summer Mom used to hang or place several baskets, much like these, on her own patio. She had a green thumb when it came to caring for her plants.

We didn't stay very long on the deck. It was clear that we needed to take her back to her room. She would always let you know, maybe not always in words, but by her demeanor and appearance. We could tell.

"I want to lay down now. I'm tired," Mom said. So Mark lifted her out of the wheelchair and together we gently placed her onto her bed.

I put Dad's rosary near her hand in case she wanted to hold it while she napped. We asked her if we could pray with her, and for her, and she was most agreeable. Our prayers were simple and direct. We prayed for God's blessing on our mother, and a safe trip back to Pasco for us. We gave thanks for her life and how important she'd always been to us and our kids. We ended with the Lord's Prayer, a Hail Mary, and a Glory be.

To help me understand the last years of her life, and to give meaning to her suffering, I had one more question to ask her. I looked at her and said, "Mom, with all that you have gone through in your life, and all that you know now, did God answer your prayer 54 years ago before we immigrated? You know the one where you asked Him to make it clear to you, that by following Papa to America, it would be best for your children's faith. Are you glad we came?"

It did not take long for her to reply. "Oh yes! God did answer my prayer, and I am very glad we came to America. Look at what He has done for all of us. Yes, it was a good thing."

"I'm happy that we did too, Mom. Thank you. Thank you for everything! You've been a wonderful mother, and I love you so very much. Please forgive me for any pain I brought you," I was quick to add just as my tears began to flow.

"There is nothing to forgive. I love you too," she assured me in a sweet whisper.

The last thing I still needed was her blessing. First, Mark and I both took our right thumb and traced a cross on her forehead to bless her, and asked for her blessing in return.

"Jesus bless you," she said as she lifted her hand to do the same.

I could not hug her like I used to. She was too frail. So I bent over her bed and placed my arm gently on her pillow, and kissed her mouth and cheeks. Mark followed with his own kiss.

"Goodbye, Mom. I'll send you pictures of Jessica and Joel's wedding. She will be a beautiful bride. I'll talk to you soon. Bye, Mom, I love you," I said and slipped out of her room.

"I love you, Mom. Goodbye," Mark said. It was time to leave her.

"How long, honey? How long?" I cried.

"I don't think it will be too much longer, honey," Mark answered. I fell into his arms so he could support me through another wave of primal grief.

The drive home was somber. We talked off and on, and listened to music in between. One of our CD's has a variety of Celtic, classic, and easy to listen to favorite melodies. One of my favorite songs began to play. Every time I listened to it, the melody would make me cry, especially coming home from a visit with Mom. As soon as the first note played I'd grab the nob and crank up the volume.

"Time to say goodbye!" I'd sing, then continue to join my voice with Andrea Bocelli and Sara Brightman as we stretched for those high notes together. Back then I could still reach them when I was inspired. I was caught-up in the moment with my eyes closed, waving my arms as if Bocelli and

Brightman needed me to conduct. Mark said little, and simply allowed me to soothe my grief in my own way.

My normal routine was to call Mother and tell her we got home safely. Not wanting the phone to disturb her, I called the nurses station and asked them to quietly let her know that Mark and I were home.

*

I knew that some of my sisters were spending more time with our mother. I would call them and get an update each day. She was still getting up to sit in her chair for several more days, but that would end soon.

As a nurse and volunteer chaplain, I knew that there was no way to predict the exact day or time when someone in Mother's condition would die. It could take a couple of weeks, or it could be just hours. Some people rally in strength, and enjoy a few extra quality days, while others just close their eyes and don't wake up.

The Way to the Wedding.

With Jessica's wedding just days away, it was important for me to remember the days leading up to Matthew's marriage to his beautiful bride Ammie, and to Timothy's marriage to his lovely lady Stacey. The time leading up to these two events were filled with such joy and excitement. Nothing else was consuming my energy, and nothing could prevent me from feeling the normal emotions I imagine most mothers experience letting their son's go to build a family of their own.

I felt compromised as we approach Jessica's wedding. Her special day was affected by emotions that I needed to turn off and on when necessary. The moving forward in life, and the taking away by death, became a battle mitigating my joy, and suspending my grief.

Like the birth of my fourth child and the events surrounding the death of my father, I felt a strong need to remember the events surrounding our daughter's wedding. I knew that in order to look back and experience the abundance of blessings bestowed that day, I needed to imprint as much of it as possible so as to relive the memories again in peace and happiness. So, I did just that.

I also needed to commit to memory, as much as possible, everything surrounding the end of my Mother's life. I knew that she was very close to the finish line, and that I would want to remember it all for a later time, a time when I could grieve in peace. So, I did that too.

With Mother heavy on my mind, I encouraged Jessica to try to spend her time and energy getting ready for her joyful event. I would try to do the same, because this is exactly what Mother would expect us to do. *"Honor your Father and Mother!"*

*

Nearly everything on Jessica's wedding list had been completed. There were just a few things she was making for table decorations, and a few gifts to buy for her bridal party. When her bridesmaids arrived from out of town, she planned to spend as much time as she could with them, which would of course, include her bachelorette party in downtown Spokane.

With everything ready to go, Jessica could focus on getting things prepared for the arrival of Joel's family. They were flying in from Iowa and several would be staying at their house. She had to postpone her own grief, knowing her Oma was dying.

I was having a difficult time with my prayers. Do I selfishly ask God to keep Mom alive long enough for Jessie and Joel's wedding, and for the six days I was committed to caring for their 20-month-old Amelia while they were on their honeymoon? Or do I selfishly pray that Mom's suffering would end today, so there would be enough time for her funeral before the family came up for the wedding? Either way, I felt selfish. It all seemed depressing because the child in me didn't want her to die at all.

"Lord, I don't know how to pray right now. You know my needs, and the needs of everyone involved with the wedding next week, and those family members caring for Mom right now. Please help me to trust in your care for all of us, and that your will be done. I pray for mercy and comfort for Mother in her last days. Please send us your peace. Amen."

Then I quickly added, "Oh, and Dad, pray with us. Mom's coming to join you soon."

After my prayer, I had another good cry. There is something so cleansing about tears. Expending the energy it takes to cry seems to purge the body and spirit of the garbage that builds up inside through bitterness and grief. It causes us to inhale deeply the air around us, which, when open to it, allows a renewed Spirit within. I inhaled a lot, just to get more.

The rest of the week had its own distractions. I worked on Monday and Tuesday at the Surgery Center, and tried to live as peacefully as I could. On Wednesday and Thursday, I drove down to Lourdes Medical Center Chapel in time for the 11:30 Mass. Many of the same people who attend each day knew what was going on in my life. They were there with open arms and added prayers on my behalf, invoking, "Lord, hear our prayer!"

I knew from reports that Mom had stopped eating entirely, and was only drinking sips of water to quench her dry mouth. She was in and out of consciousness, and spent most of her time asleep. Her breathing was more labored, and she could no longer get out of bed.

Ineke and Gert phoned with an update just six days before the wedding. "Hey Mar, it's Ineke. Gert and I thought it best to call you and let you know that Mom is laboring quite a bit, and Gert and I are planning to spend the night with her. We brought our sleeping bags and they have mattresses for us to use on the floor."

"Oh Ineke, should I come down? I can be there in just a few hours," I asked.

"No, Mar, don't drive back down. You told me about your last visit, and it sounded like you had already said your goodbyes. Stay in Pasco and save your energy for Jessica's wedding. Gert and I want you to know that, no matter what happens here, all of us are still planning to be there for the wedding. So please don't worry about that. It will be a special time for Jess, just like the other family weddings, OK?"

"OK! Let me say a few words to Mom just one more time, please," I requested.

I could hear Ineke telling Mom that I was on the phone and wanted to say a few words to her. She held the phone across Mom's cheek. I could hear her struggle to breath. Then I heard her whisper, "I lo-- " and then she took a short breath.

"Oh, Momma, I love you too. I can hear you. You don't need to say anything," I offered.

I could hear Ineke and Gert speaking loud enough for me to hear. "She's smiling Mar. She mouthed 'I love you,' and it was meant for you." They were tearing up on the other end of the phone line.

"Be not afraid, Momma! I know you want to go, and I want you to go to. You don't have to do this anymore. It's OK, Momma. Remember us down here when you get to Heaven, and say hi to Papa. Tell him that I keep finding his pennies. He'll know what that means. Goodbye Momma. I love you," I said to her for the last time.

Ineke got back on the phone and said, "This is the most lucid I've seen her all day. She didn't even open her eyes when we got here, and she smiled when she heard your voice, Mar. I know she would not want you to drive down again. Just stay there and be with your family. You were with Dad when he died. We will be with her now."

Mark held me through my tears until I ran out of them. I don't know how long I sat by myself after that. Time had no bearing, no significance. I waited to move on until I had my fill of breathing in that special grace that always gave me peace.

*

I've had my share of bedside vigils during my time as a volunteer chaplain. I've watched how family and friends react to the unstoppable progress toward imminent death.

Some just sit and spend their time deep in thought, while others run out of the room. Still others spend their precious time talking about all kinds of stuff to whoever appears to be listening, in an effort to avoid the obvious. Some are brave, and some are afraid. Some weep, some cannot.

From one culture to another, grieving can come in many different forms. There can be open wailing at a bedside vigil, while other rooms will be so quiet that you only hear the breathing of the dying. People's cultures may vary, but when losing someone you love, the pain is always there.

What little wisdom I can share with you that might help guide you through one of the most important events in your life, losing someone you love, is this: your loved one is alive until the very last moment. Love them with kind words and loving touch, if you are able. When it is time, give them permission to go; they most likely can still hear you. Limit touching them after your consent or saying your last goodbyes. Your actions should match what you say, otherwise it can send mixed messages.

Lastly, live in the moment and take care of yourself. Look for the sweet little details that may give you comfort later on. What time of year was it? Were there decorations of some kind? Was it cold in the room, or warm? Who was with you? What did the room look like? Who were the people that cared for your loved one? Ask for their names so you can personally thank them later. Whatever you do, look for something good, and don't forget what it was. These are your future memories, and will become a part of the story of your life.

*

For the next two nights, Ineke and Gert stayed together and slept on a mattress on the floor next to Mom. Both were quite exhausted by now. Many times they thought Mother had passed away, only to be startled by the sound of another breath.

They took shifts during the day, giving each other the time to shower, eat, and check in with their families. The siblings were contacted daily with the progress Mom was making. One of us would get a phone call from Gert or Ineke, and then volunteer to call the others, so they didn't have to report all over again.

Dom and Traci came by for short visits to relieve both Ineke and Gert. Each time they left, they made their peace with Mother, and gave her permission to go. Sue stayed close to her family in Duvall, Washington, getting support from them.

On the third day of the vigil, Gert needed to go home and be with Larry. She was too exhausted to stay. Ineke, somehow, still had some reserves. She had been able to take a much-needed nap during the day. On Tuesday night, Ineke stayed alone with our mother.

The next night, with all of her reserves spent, Ineke was unable to stay with Mother. Her health just didn't allow it. She planned to return early the following morning.

Around 2:00am, Thursday, August 12, 2010, the phone rang in my bedroom. Before I answered it, I said to Mark, "Momma just died!"

"Hi Mar, this is Tra. Mom died within the last half hour," she announced tearfully.

I instantly recalled the time Traci called me with the sad new about our father seventeen years before. The vigil was over. Mom died with none of her children sleeping on the floor in her room. Perhaps this was her way of sparing her children from the actual event, much like her husband had done. She was cared for by the loving staff who had surrounded her for the last eleven months. Mom was never alone.

Later that morning, so as to not wake them in the middle of the night, I called our children with the news of their Oma's death. Though we all knew it was coming, it is still difficult to announce the death of a loved one.

Jessica said to me on the phone. "I'm sorry, Mom! I'm going to miss her so much. Just like with Grandma, this was the only way that Oma was going to make it to my wedding. Now they will both be there in spirit."

She was right. Neither would miss this important day. It was Suze and Doreen's way to the wedding.

The relatives in the Netherlands were notified that same day. They did not have to wait for a white envelope with a black border to arrive weeks later. Those times had long gone.

Great Joy to Overwhelming Sorrow

Family members arrived just as they said they would for Jessica and Joel's wedding. The majority of them came on Friday, the day after Mom passed away. Mark's side of the family arrived on Saturday, the day of the wedding.

There were genuine feelings of joy among the siblings. We intentionally set aside our grief to celebrate the sacramental union of our daughter and her husband. Of course there were moments of tears, but overall, it was a relief to be focused on a celebration of life, as opposed to what we had all gone through over the last several months.

The moment Jessica stepped out of the limousine, she literally took my breath away. I had never seen my daughter more beautiful. Her dress fit the curves of her frame just perfectly, and her hair was styled up in curls and waves that flawlessly framed her face. Her eyes were enhanced with the longest lashes I've ever seen. She called them "extensions." Who knew?

Little Amelia was in my care while her parents were preparing for their big moment to arrive. I took her to see her mother in the bridal room so the two could spend some precious time together before the ceremony.

When Amelia saw her momma all dressed up, she placed her little hands on her momma's cheeks and just stared into her eyes. Our little granddaughter knew how beautiful her mother was. They both stood before a long mirror and enjoyed the images that reflected back. Jessica took delight watching her daughter prance around in her pretty new dress.

Father Hightower from Gonzaga University had spent many hours with Joel throughout the previous year. For a couple of months before their wedding, Jessica gathered with them for their weekly marriage preparation. He had become very good friends to both of them, and was happy to unite them in marriage. He had already baptized Amelia when she was just six weeks old. She looked like an angel wearing the nearly 100-year-old handmade gown from Holland that her mother, her Oma, and her great Oma had worn.

St. Aloysius Church in Spokane, Washington, accommodates up to 1100 people, with a center aisle that is very long. Benjamin and Matthew escorted me and Amelia up the aisle toward the altar. It took a while before we finally reached the first of our two hundred guests already seated near the front. Amelia hung on to me tightly, concerned and confused with so many eyes looking in her direction.

I almost forgot to watch Mark walk our daughter down the aisle. I was trying to distract Amelia long enough so she would not take off running toward her dad, who was waiting to escort Jessica to the altar. With just seconds left, Matt's wife, Ammie, took Amelia into her arms just in time for me to see my daughter and her dad smiling as they walked past me. I watched as my husband gave our daughter to Joel.

There were extra candles lit and placed on the edge of the main altar. They represented the grandparents that had passed away, most notably, Oma Suze and Grandma Doreen. They were there in spirit, and many of us felt their presence.

All of Jessica's planning produced a joyful occasion. Timothy and his Aunt Gert sang beautifully together as Warren Tate accompanied them on the organ and keyboards. Mark and I were overjoyed watching our daughter marry the man she loved, and watched as Joel loving gazed at his bride.

The steeple bells in the towers began to ring, a traditional practice at this church. This was to signal that the new Mr. and Mrs. Joel and Jessica Morgan were about to leave the church for the first time as husband and wife.

They stepped through the doors to the delight of the cheering guests already waiting for them outside. Walking arm in arm, Jessica raised her bouquet into the air as if to announce, "Be happy with us! We're married!" After mingling with their guests, and a few more photo ops, it was time for Joel and Jess to enter the waiting limousine to spend a few moments together before heading to the reception.

Of all the possible venues for the wedding reception, they chose the McCarthey Athletic Center at Gonzaga University, where Joel worked.

As the assistant athletic director at GU, Joel knew every inch of that building. Everyone who worked with Joel understood that the basketball court was considered holy ground. Nobody dared to consider using it for a wedding reception, until now!

It helped that he and the basketball coach were fishing buddies and loyal friends. Even with that, and the coaxing of his co-workers, it took a while for Joel to agree to the offer, and the extra perks that were included. Jessica and Joel's wedding reception would be an exception to the rule.

It would have been difficult for Mark and me to provide the additional benefits at any other venue. Each table was graced with a large centerpiece filled with tall hydrangeas, roses, lilies, bluebells, and more, and easily stood three feet tall. The professional chef and all the waiters provided excellent food services for the occasion, and added such elegance to what was already a beautiful event.

This was a wonderful day, full of happiness, joy, pride, love, and laughter. The bride and groom got to celebrate with a number of family members, and several friends, many of whom had traveled long distances to be there. We will always be grateful.

The lows of the last three weeks were set aside for the highs of this wonderful day. All the drama and sad tears were gone for now, replaced with tears of joy. I was living in the moments and did not think too much about tomorrow.

Mark's emotions finally conquered him while he danced with our daughter. When the song ended, someone else took his place for the next dance. He walked right over to me and said, "Look!"

I looked around for what he wanted me to see when I realized it was him that he wanted me to see. "Oh Mark, you're crying. You did it! You cried at Jessica's wedding!" I said hugging him through the last of his tears. I can hardly remember the rare moments when my husband cried. This moment will never be forgotten. My heart was overflowing with love for him that day.

Typically, a bride and groom are among the first to leave their wedding reception. These newlyweds enjoyed every moment of their day, and were in no hurry to have it end. The adults with small children were some of the first to leave after the wedding cake was cut and shared, and the first few music selections were danced.

Not long after, we said goodbye to those who had long drives ahead of them, and needed to get home at a semi-reasonable hour.

Mark and I hung in there long enough to thank most of the guest before they left. As our siblings were leaving the reception, we said that we would meet up with them shortly, and spend some time with them at the hotel.

Before we left, Jessica and Joel came to us and expressed their gratitude for making it possible to have such a wonderful wedding day. After the hugs and kisses, we finally left the reception to decompress before going to bed. That was the plan, to decompress!

Meeting up with four of my sibling was more difficult than I anticipated. One of my sisters, Traci, was unable to attend. The rest had come to celebrate Jessica's wedding and provide support for me and my family.

I suppose it was necessary that they also came with plans to discuss the upcoming funeral for our mother. I just wasn't ready to give up on this incredible joy, and wanted it to last until morning.

But grief cannot stay compartmentalized and conveniently tucked away. The conversation about the many wonderful blessings of the day inevitably turned to a discussion surrounding our mother's funeral. We had a few important decisions that still had to be made. There would be no more wedding joy. It was replaced with overwhelming sorrow.

At some point, I remember saying, "I have experienced such a rollercoaster of intense emotions in the last days and weeks. I guess if I my heart can handle all this turmoil, I should never have to worry about another stress-induced heart attack. I can't imagine dealing with anything more stressful."

There were additional stressors going on in conjunction to the obvious ones already mentioned. It only supported my theory that I had nothing more to worry about with my health. I beat this heart thing, this Takotsubo Cardiomyopathy. Once was enough.

*

Fortunately, Mother had planned ahead for her funeral Mass, including which scriptures were to be read and what music she wanted to be sung. Everything was prearranged at the funeral home as well. Her foresight was a gift to her children.

Mark and I had already committed ourselves to taking care of little Amelia while her parents were on their honeymoon in Hawaii. Amelia had never been without her mother for any length of time. Mark and I knew that we would be the best ones to care for her; she was always so comfortable around us.

She was a sweet, loving, precocious little girl, with a heavy dose of toddler mischief, and was bound to keep us very busy. To make it easiest on Amelia, the plan was for her to come to Pasco on Sunday evening with her parents, after Joel's family flew back to Iowa. The newlyweds would fly to Hawaii out of the Pasco airport the next morning, and return to Pasco on Friday. They would either drive back to Spokane the next day, or travel to Oregon for her Oma's funeral, should the developing plans accommodate it.

My siblings and I were split down the middle as to when to have the funeral. After several painful attempts to postpone the funeral just two extra days, to Saturday, August 21, the decision was made to have the funeral on Thursday, August 19, 2010, just five days after the wedding.

I was not mentally or physically prepared to take Amelia down to Salem for my mother's funeral. I had never experienced this level of conflict and sadness before. I didn't even know how to pray to resolve the crisis within me. This was something new and confusing. I finally made the decision not go. It was too much for me.

Through the love and prayers of my husband, children, and many others, they were able to convince me to take a leap of faith. They would provide the extra help I needed to care for Amelia. Our dearest of friends, Max and Michele Towne, let me know that they were planning to follow us down to Salem to attend Mother's funeral, and would help us out in any way they could.

Tim was going to sit next to Amelia in the back seat of our car. Mark's brother Mike offered his house for the four of us to stay. Matt and his family were also coming, and offered to help. Jessica and Benjamin were not able to attend on Thursday. They were the only grandchildren of Mom's who could not be there on the day that was selected for the funeral.

Just a couple of days before we were to leave for Salem, something moved me to stop and gaze at the white infant baptismal gown hanging in my bedroom. I remembered the list of names Mother had written of all the family members who were baptized in this dress. I removed the list of names that I had taped to the back of the shadow box, and slowly read each one.

I then understood that this white gown had a story to tell, and I was determined to tell it. I sat down to write the story, and planned to share it at Mom's funeral.

At a Catholic funeral Mass, the casket is draped with a white sheet referred to as a pall. It is a reminder of the white baptismal gown a new Christian wears as he or she becomes a member of the mystical body of Christ. This pall, in some sense, brings the believer full circle, from new life celebrated at baptism, to the new life experienced through physical death. Not everyone has their original white gown of their baptism, but Mom did, and I was going to let her have it back one more time.

Amelia, who was not the best long-distance traveler at her age, could not have been a more perfect passenger. She was entertained by her Uncle Tim, and slept a good deal of the trip. She fussed very little and when she did, there was always somebody to help her. To me, this was a small miracle, and a true answer to so many others who were praying!

The evening we arrived at Mike and Kelly's, I quickly set up Amelia's sleep area, and Tim and I hurried off to Mt. Angel. We were just a minute late for the beginning of the recitation of the rosary at the Towers where Mother had passed away. Most of her friends who lived there were unable to attend the funeral the following day. They were there to say the rosary instead.

The next morning, the descendants of Mienus and Suze van Lith, gathered at the entrance of the sanctuary at Queen of Peace Catholic Church in South Salem, Oregon. Everyone in attendance was given a handout to follow during the funeral Mass. It also included the names of the grandchildren participating in some fashion. In addition, my brother Dom was prepared to say a few words of reflection before the funeral Mass began.

I positioned the baptismal gown next to the crucifix already placed on top of the white pall on the casket.

I did not prearrange with anyone to say a few words of my own before the service began. Just after displaying the little white dress, I told my siblings that in addition to the dress, I would follow Dom's reflections with a story to share. Dom and I were together when our father died, and now we would stand next to each other behind the podium for our mother. It seemed fitting, and it was my personal contribution for Mom's funeral.

After Dom's well thought out tribute, I stood before the podium and read:

Suzanna Maria Elizabeth (Bruggeman) van Lith

Funeral Mass

August 19, 2010

The Little White Dress

First generation: Hermanus Bruggeman (1916), Antonius Bruggeman (1918), Johannes Bruggeman (1919), Wilhelmus Bruggeman (1921), Maria Bruggeman (1923), Suzanna Bruggeman (1925).

Second generation: Ineke van Lith Barnes (1947), Gert van Lith Helvey (1948), Sue van Lith Remington (1949), Traci van Lith Tuor (1951), Marja van Lith Henderson (1955), Dominic van Lith (1966).

Third generation: Lori Barnes along with her brother Rich and sister Cheri, all baptized (1976), Erick Bishop (1971), Krista Bishop (1975), Katie Bishop (1976), Jennifer Loacher (1974), Mackenzie Cummings (1979), Chris Cummings, was too big for the dress in (1983), Benjamin Henderson (1976), Matthew Henderson (1978), Timothy Henderson (1980), Jessica Henderson (1984), Alexis van Lith (1997), Zachary van Lith (2001).

Fourth generation: Deacon Henderson (2004), Liam Henderson (2006), Eden Henderson (2008), Paige and Chloe Henderson (twins, 2008), Amelia Morgan (2008).

The most important things in Mom's life were her faith in God and His Church, and her husband and children. Mom was not present to see her own children born again at our baptisms. Dad took us to the church the day after our birth while Mom was still recovering. Both of them wanted our baptisms so much that she sacrificed her attendance so that we could enter the Church as soon as possible.

At my last visit with mom, Mark and I prayed the rosary with her, something she did almost every day of her life. We talked about our immigration from Holland, and the sacrifices she made for her children to move to America for Dad. I reminded her about her prayer to God, the one that she told each of her children when it seemed the right time. She had prayed that if leaving all her family and all that she knew behind would bring about the salvation of her children, then she would freely sacrifice and pass through the door to a new life in America. If it would not be beneficial to our spiritual wellbeing, then her prayer was to slam the door shut.

Before we left I asked her, "Mom, did your prayer get answered, and are you happy we left Holland?"

"Oh yes. God answered my prayer," she replied without hesitation.

Her last seventeen years, after Papa died, were filled with great physical suffering, and yet full of grace and joy. She offered everything up to God for our salvation, pointing the way to Christ.

She prayed that we would all be one in faith and love. She joined her suffering with Christ's for the sake of her children, and for her descendants, of which there are many.

Mom and Dad passed on to us their faith in Jesus Christ and His church. She taught by example, that we should follow God's will for our lives and be willing to sacrifice for our children.

She prays for us even now, that all may be one in Christ. Mom, thank you for the gift of your faith, rest now in peace. We can take it from here!

Someday the little white dress will be too old and frail to wear. Someone will place it in a new shadow box and display it in their home for future generations to admire, and ask questions about it. But not yet!

Isabella and Logan Henderson were later baptized together in 2012, too big for the dress. Still to arrive, and later baptized in the little white dress were: Tyson Michael Henderson (2011), Sadie Elaine Henderson (2013), Dominicus Howard (Nic) Morgan (2011), and Charles William (Wim) Morgan (2013).

*

This is the story of the little white dress. It is more than just fabric and traditions. It's also the meaning it conveys. It represents the faith of the believer in Christ, the hope for eternal life, and the parental love that this garment embodies that moves forward in time and does not separate us after death. Placing the gown over the pall on Mom's casket was the first time the actual baptismal gown was used in this way. It did not just remind us of her baptism, it touched her when she was an infant. Maybe a new tradition will spring forth from my gesture.

There was no way for Mother to prepare for the grueling physical marathon she ran the last several years of her life. We were privileged to witness her last sprint over the finish line. Her goal was the hope promised to all of us, to be raised again to eternal life with her savior, Jesus. I have no doubt that many of those she loved who finished the race before her were cheering her on.

Lang zal ze leven in de Gloria!

Long shall you live in the Glory!

It is not intended for us to just finish the race, but to win the race, and help carry others over the line with us. From generation to generation, that gift of faith is what we endeavor to pass on to our children and our grandchildren.

*

After the funeral, Suze was laid to rest next to her Mienus. Both bodies lay side by side in the picturesque country cemetery across the street from St Mary's Catholic Church in Shaw, Oregon, where they were members for over 30 years.

The rest of this day was spent catching up with several of the nieces and nephews and a few family friends who had gathered at Mom's house. Amelia continued taking the whole experience in stride, and managed to find a few other children to play with.

My siblings and I took time out to gather in Mom's bedroom away from everyone else. We had business to attend to, which included reading over Mother's last will. I did not interact much, other than to ask a few questions.

Ineke handed each of us a small box of jewelry along with a handwritten note from Mom that had been placed inside each of our boxes. She had taken the time to identify specific jewelry that she wanted each of us to have. In a few short words, she was able to tell us why she wanted us to have each of the items.

I think we all felt like Mom was with us in spirit, making it easier to deal with the matters at hand. Her last gift to us was having planned ahead in order to streamline the upcoming distribution of her belongings. It was so important that her family remain close to each other after she was gone. She didn't want there to be any major disputes when it came to dividing her estate.

Before going our separate ways, we agreed on a date when we would come back together and begin going through the house. Mark and I would drive back down in mid-September. I hoped that I would be in a better frame of mind for the job that lay ahead.

We were back in Pasco the next day, in time to deliver Amelia to her parents. The trip was uneventful, which meant Amelia was a super passenger. She was amused with Uncle Tim's attention. Thank you, son!

It's an interesting undertaking going through a lifetime of our parent's belongings. Most of us were unaware of what Mother had kept in drawers and closets. To see what things Dad and Mom felt were worth saving was eye opening. Many items they valued were not treasured in the same way by all of their children.

There were surprises. Mother had taken the time to place one of our names on some of the items we had forgotten about, or had never seen before. Knowing each of us as well as she did, I can imagine her looking at something and saying, "I want this to go to (a particular one of her children)." Finding our name on items felt as if she had just handed the gift to us, and we were supposed to figure out why. Some things were obvious, others, not so much.

There was a large black garbage bag in the closet in a spare bedroom. The bag was well over half filled. It contained every card, every small photo, and every handmade drawing from her children and grandchildren. There were letters from family and friends from Holland that she didn't want to part with. Each of us had the opportunity to retrieve what we had once given Dad and Mom.

There was one item that was a complete surprise to me. Neatly tucked away with other memorabilia of her mother's was a hand-written note to me from my Oma. I stared at the light blue folded piece of paper and could hardly read my Oma's message. I have no memory of ever seeing this small letter.

I am able to read some Dutch, but the penmanship in Holland during the early 1900's was not at all like what I was taught. It was hard to read, and the ink on the page had faded. Ineke and Gert read some of the note, the rest I had to figure out on my own. Using a magnifying glass and a computer translator, I painstakingly worked through her message.

There is no date on the letter, but from her written words, I can postulate that she had to have written it in the fall of 1961.

> *Dearest Marja,*
>
> *I was very happy with your letter. It was well written, and your handwriting so good. You are already six years old since January, and going to the big school. Your mother is happy with you. Your mama has it good with all of her children in school now. Learn a lot Marja, and write me back.*
>
> *A big kiss from Oma. Good bye, Marja*

Suze's mother, my Oma, died several weeks later on December 30, 1961.

My Oma's letter is now displayed behind glass in a small frame, and sits on a shelf next to a picture of my mother and father in the living room of my new home. Now that it is translated, I no longer worry about the inevitable fading. Soon it will reach a point where it would be impossible to decipher any longer.

It was a small miracle that all of the siblings managed to be satisfied with what we each had been given, and what we had taken for ourselves. On occasion, if two of us wanted the same item, we would barter together. It was a peaceful process, full of, "Look what I found!" "Who wants this?" "Oh, good lord, I had forgotten all about that!" And, "You should have this."

I was surprised at how differently we placed our own value on any particular item. Some of us appreciated newer items, while some looked for the old. We each received a number of artworks that Mother had created. It's exciting to see them hung up or displayed in other ways in each other's homes.

Returning home with some of the oldest items, some I'd never seen before, and many I remembered from my youth, was so gratifying. The big old blue Dutch bible filled with the famous Gustave Dore biblical drawings, so recognizable to those who have seen his distinct work, was mine. Nobody else wanted it!

Now as I walk past my curio in the dining room, I can see the bible, the book of saints, and my Opa van Lith's well-worn missal he took to every mass. There are a handful of Dutch to English, English to Dutch translation books that Dad and Mom relied on before and after leaving Holland. Looking at these keepsakes makes me smile every time.

The old rosary that Mother had wanted to give me before she died is now displayed inside my shadow box that holds the white baptism gown. I took ownership of it the morning of the funeral. Just before we closed her the casket, Ineke and I gently removed the rosary that was intertwined in Mothers' hands, and I took it for my own just as I had promised her.

Looking at the crucifix attached to the rosary, I understood just how much Mom and Dad had used it in prayer. The center of each of the stained, dark brown wooden beads was now worn down to the pre-stained, light brown wood they were made from. In addition, the only thing left from the corpus on the cross was the nailed left hand of Christ. It was as if they had prayed Jesus Christ right off of the cross!

I can't imagine a better distribution of an estate than what my siblings and I had undergone. We were mostly done after our second trip at the end of October. Then, some of my snowbird sisters headed south for the winter.

We placed Mom's house on the market in early 2011, and would finish the job of removing what was left to keep, give away, or purge in the spring.

Having grieved the loss of my mother for so long already, I did my best to move quickly through the process of grief by refocusing on Mark and our growing family. Mother told us how happy she was for Doreen, and how she couldn't wait for it to be her time. Though I will always miss her, I really was happy that she was finally at peace. The sting of grieving was no longer deeply painful. Each day was better than the next.

Before too long, Mark and I would no longer travel down the Columbia Gorge like we had for so many years. That time would come after the sale of Mother's house. We were ok with a trip once, maybe twice a year, but we needed a well-deserved break. What better way than to plan a trip before the end of this *very eventful* year, 2010.

*

I could think of no better way to relax and enjoy a week of warm weather, than a cruise to the Caribbean. We'd been to the Caribbean on three other cruises, but with so many different islands and ports-of-calls, and so many different ships to try, every vacation was different. This time, I was planning for us to sail through the Eastern Caribbean islands.

Now, with something fun and relaxing to look forward to, we went about our daily lives of work and home. We spent a good deal of time with our children and grandchildren. Tim's wife, Stacey, was advancing nicely with her second pregnancy (their third child, due in January 2011). Jessica and Joel announced that they were pregnant with a sibling for Amelia in May of 2011. To our great delight, grandbabies #9 and # 10 were on their way!

We were closing in on the holidays and our planned vacation. Mark and I were just nesting in our home, giving us a little more time to rest up. 2010 was a year like no other, and I was ready to top it off with a fun and *uneventful* cruise. Right?

Chapter 29

What Are the Odds?

I'd been so caught up trying to do the right things for my extended family that I had neglected my own wellbeing in the process, and that's not a good thing. The accumulated stressors were taking a toll on my health.

My energy level was very low. I had trouble sleeping, and I was still experiencing these unusual sensations inside my chest and abdomen. They were random occurrences that often led to a pounding heart rate, and would remind me of the way I was feeling just before my heart attack.

I stayed far away from the medications I had been warned against, and was faithfully taking the prescribed meds my cardiologist thought might help me. Even so, there were times things got out of control. The occasional adrenalin surges scared me enough to call a friend over to my house and be with me until the symptoms abated.

I began to seek other doctors who might be better able to diagnose what was happening. I was referred to other specialists for further evaluation. None of them were able to identify the cause for these episodes. In the meantime, I relied on my nitroglycerin spray when the pain in my chest warranted its use.

Moving forward, I tried not to let these symptoms get the better of me. "I'm stronger than that. I will simply control them with my will."

So I thought.

*

My will told me to spend some more time on a cruise ship in the warm Caribbean. On December 3, 2010, Mark and I flew to Ft. Lauderdale, Florida. The next morning, we were shuttled to the cruise ship terminal and boarded the *MS Eurodam*. As they say in the Caribbean, "No worries man." We were just looking for some relaxation, sun, fun, and some good food and drinks in Puerto Rico, St. Thomas, and Grand Turks and Caicos.

Vacations are meant to refresh one's body and soul, and cruising is one of my favorite ways to do that. In addition, they have become an adventure of the unexpected, something that I have come to appreciate just as much. When an impulse stirs inside me, it usually involves reaching out to another person. It is during those moments when some of my best adventures begin.

*

Mid-week of our cruise, the ship docked at the port in San Juan, Puerto Rico. We got off the ship in the morning, and enjoyed a walking tour of the section of town referred to as Old San Juan.

The classic old-world Spanish architecture was present throughout this part of town, and was enhanced by the array of rich colors on the buildings and the cobblestone streets. Walking along on this sunny day, the multicolored facades of the buildings, and the blue tiled bricks making up the streets and walkways made for a beautiful contrast. These blue bricks were taken from some Spanish galleons. They were originally used as weight stabilizers on those old ships.

Positioned just beyond the city was a vast, open field of grass that drew visitors toward a massive seaside fortress know as Castillo San Felipe del Morro, "El Morro" for short. This enormous, four-hundred-year-old structure, constructed over many years, stood 150 feet tall, and was built on a cliff just above the sea. It included an even taller lighthouse that illuminated the waterway into the harbor for friendly ships, as well as potential foes lurking below.

Within the massive stone walls were multiple layers of carved out rooms that housed many of the military soldiers and their leaders. It included many supporting rooms for food, munitions, medical bays, and even a chapel. Turrets were built on the strategic corners of the structure, and numerous cannon and gun ports were scattered across different levels of the fort.

For hundreds of years, El Morro protected the island population from invading forces. It now stands as a landmark that speaks of a bygone era. This engineering achievement will no doubt survive several more hundreds of years.

After a late lunch and a walkabout through the shopping district in town, Mark and I were making our way back to the *Eurodam*. Before we walked all the way back to the ship, Mark left me for a few minutes to use the restroom.

While waiting, I walked a little closer to the moored ships at the docks, and stopped near an open sitting area where others were also enjoying the scenery around them. At one table sat two older gentlemen talking to each other while family members stood around them. I got the impression that they were traveling on one of the other cruise ships docked in the yards.

I did not intend to eavesdrop, but it was not difficult for me to clearly hear what these men were saying. I heard them reminiscing about their years in the U.S military. My ears perked up and I began to listen more intently. Part of the conversation went something like this.

"Yes, it's hard not to think about those years sometimes. So many in my company were killed on those beaches," one of the men said.

"We lost a lot of men fighting in the countryside as we pushed through France and into Germany. I still think about them. How can anyone forget what we had to do? Even after so many years, you can't forget," the other man said.

I stood up and moved a little closer to this ongoing exchange. I have an inherent interest to know whatever I can about the war years and the men that fought the "war to end all wars!" My curiosity peaked when hearing words like: Normandy, D-day, freedom, and liberation. That was enough to embolden me to walk right over to these elderly GI's. I had an important question to ask them that was itching to come out, and I could wait no longer.

"Excuse me gentlemen, but I could not help but overhear your conversation about your time in the military. You, sir, talk as if you were in Normandy on D-day. Were you there?"

"Why, yes I was," the man replied, looking curiously at me.

"And you sir, you were fighting to liberate the towns during the march toward Germany?" I asked the other man.

The man looked at me with his puzzled look, and answered, "I was."

I completely forgot that others were standing around the table; I was so focused on these two elderly men. "I just need to know if either of you happened to have been in Buchenwald in April of 1945 with General Patton?" I asked, hoping I wasn't out of line in doing so.

The old GI to my right looked directly at me and said, "I was there in April of '45 with General Patton."

Both men, and apparently their families, looked at me as if it was my turn, and then I said, "Oh, thank you both for your service and sacrifices during WWII, and thank you for saving my father's life, and so many others. You helped to liberate my father from Buchenwald after surviving there for more than four years. Thank you!"

The surprise and amazement of what I had just announced was profoundly expressed by both of these men and their families, and it was not long before tears began to flow. During this emotional encounter, I remember hearing someone say, "Dad, did you hear what she just said? Oh Dad, she just thanked you for saving her father! This is so incredible and special, Dad!"

Though it felt like a long time had just transpired, in reality the entire exchanged lasted but a few minutes. I thanked them again for their military service and the sacrifices they made.

Mark reappeared, and after I looked at each of the elderly GI's one last time, we walked back to the ship. Mark could tell that I was crying and asked, "What are you crying about? Who were those people you were talking too?"

"The most amazing thing just happened, Mark," I answered, grabbing his arm.

As we walked back to the ship, I told him about the exchange I had with the two GI's. Mark understood what caused the tears and the excitement that he had walked in on. The way I see it, being at the right place at the right time to experience such an amazing, small world encounter, is nothing short of a miracle.

Before we arrived at the gangway, I saw and picked up an American penny on the ground. "Dad, you're thinking about me again, aren't you? Did you just watch what happened? I found someone who was there!" I said to Dad in my thoughts.

"Another penny, huh?" Mark asked when I showed him what I picked up. "Why does that not surprise me!?" he added with a smile.

When something wonderful happens in my life, I just need to talk about it with Mark. Then, after I have exhausted him, I'm ready to talk about it to whoever else will listen. I guess it's my way of wanting to share the blessings that I am feeling at the time. Fortunately for me, Mark has been a pretty good listener for the last 40-some years, and I have some really patient friends who will listen too.

Sometimes we need to be reminded of just how proud and respectful we should be toward the men and women who served in the military, especially during times of war and great sacrifice. Those in my generation were raised by the men and women who fought during WWII. We called them Dad and Mom. But over time and a couple more generations, many refer to them as "the Greatest Generation." Rightly so!

It was a war that needed to be fought, and needed to be won. The noble cause our country fought and died for was to destroy a "Culture of Death" perpetrated by the likes of Hitler, Stalin, Mussolini, and their minions.

These men and women did what they did so others could live in peace and freedom, and not suffer under socialism, communism, or totalitarian rule.

I realize that others may disagree with my assessments, but when you were raised to understand what it was like to lose those fundamental human rights we so casually take for granted, it becomes too easy for someone to come along and rewrite history, or worse, follow the same ideologies that would repeat the horrible mistakes of the past.

What's that old saying? Oh yes. The definition of insanity: doing the same thing over and over again, expecting different results.

*

The remainder of our adventure at sea, was filled with warm weather, some shopping and sightseeing in St. Thomas, and a relaxing play day on an island in the Bahamas.

After spending our last day on the beach, it was time to gather up our belongings and start packing our bags for the next day's departure. After that, we could relax and enjoy our last dinner and evening show. Why does a week's vacation have to go so fast?

*

We were on the flexible dining schedule, and typically reserved a table for two at 6:00pm. About half of the guests chose this way of dining, as opposed to a set schedule for either an earlier or much later dinner in the evening. Mark and I were content to stay with the same table for most of our week, but larger groups were often seated at a different table every evening.

Other than small talk with those seated in close proximity to us, we pretty much focused on each other. Our last evening though, we were celebrating our 37th wedding anniversary and shared a bit of champagne with a few passengers next to our table.

Unlike the beginning of our cruise, we no longer felt the need to stuff ourselves by ordering something from the appetizer section, the soup or salad column, the main course, dessert, and the after-dinner drink with a piece of fine chocolate. By now we had figured out how much we should eat, and avoided overeating.

We've been on enough Holland America cruises to know that the Indonesian waiters bring a special dessert to surprise guests celebrating birthdays or wedding anniversaries. They light a candle on the small cake and then sing a song in their native language.

Nearby was a large table, big enough to accommodate up to twelve passengers. Every evening throughout this cruise, a different group of passengers ate there. The last evening was no different.

This night there appeared to be a birthday celebration for the matriarch of the family gathered around her at this large table. The waiters brought a cake, placed it in front of the elderly woman, and with several servers gathered around her, began to sing her their song. I recognized the tune immediately and began to sing along. I sang the song in Dutch, the way I have always heard it sung so many times before.

Lang zal ze leven, lang zal ze leven, lang zal ze leven in de Gloria, in de Gloria, in de Gloria. Hieperdepiep, hoera!

During the singing, my eyes connected with a woman about my age just to the left of the elderly woman. This woman was singing her heart out in Dutch just like I was. We smiled at each other, and pointed a finger at the other, guessing we both must be Dutch.

Immediately after the waiters finished the song and well wishes, the same waiters walked the few steps to where Mark and I were sitting. A similar small cake was placed before us and the waiters sang once again, this time to congratulate us on our anniversary. Here we go again.

Not one to miss a song, I joined in and watched as the same woman from the larger table stood to sing along too. When it was all done, we pointed at each other and Mark and I soon had a visitor at our table.

"Hello there. I saw you singing that song in Dutch too! We were celebrating my mother-in-law's 90th birthday," the woman said during her greeting.

"Hello, my name is Marja, and this is my husband Mark. We are celebrating our 37th wedding anniversary," I said while reaching for a handshake.

"I'm Johanna, but everyone calls me Joke [pronounced **Yō**ka]. From the looks of it, it appears you are from Holland too!" Joke acknowledged.

"Yes, I was born there and then immigrated to the United States. Dad wanted to become an American after the war," I said.

"We immigrated a couple of times, once to Australia for a couple of years, back to Holland for a short time, and then finally to Canada. I don't remember much from the first passage, but I have a few memories of the second voyage," Joke went on to say. "So, did your family come over on a Holland America ship like ours did?"

I thought for a second and said, "I don't remember hearing that our ship was a Holland America ship. We came over on an old freighter that was converted to transport immigrants back in the 50's. It was called the *Groote Beer*."

There was a surprised look on her face when she said, "We came over on the *Groote Beer*! What year did you guys immigrate?"

"Oh my goodness, what a coincidence. We came over in 1956. When did you guys come over?" I asked.

Her eyes got even bigger, then quickly said, "We came over in 1956!"

Now this was getting very interesting. The *Groote Beer* made many voyages throughout the year, so I said, "We came over in early April of 1956."

Suddenly Joke's jaw dropped, and the look on her face told me the rest of the story, but it was still exciting to hear her say, "We came over in early April of 1956!"

I stood up quickly; we looked at each other, and gave each other a big hug. We must have made quite a scene hugging each other as if we were old friends, and making all kinds gestures in our excitement. Mark stood up too, and Joke's husband quickly came over to see what all the commotion was about.

In the short time we were together, we gathered so much information about each other. Joke's husband John, quickly grabbed his camera from where they had been sitting, to photograph this moment between Joke and me. Anyone looking at the photo can see the complete surprise at having just met another person who, as small children almost 55 years before, emigrated from Holland to the Americas on the same ship. I treasure the expressions on our faces. I was tearing up and had my right hand over my heart in sheer amazement (or protection).

Joke and I exchanged email addresses and physical addresses. Though we were 99% sure we had come over on the same ship, we wanted to do some research when we got home to be certain. There could only have been one trip made in early April.

What are the odd of ever meeting like this? It boggles my mind even still. If any slight deviation of events had occurred that evening, we would never have met. If they hadn't been assigned that table, we would never have seen each other. If there were no birthday or anniversary to celebrate, we would have gone unnoticed. If one of us had our backs to the other, I would have been singing in Dutch by myself. If we were both shy individuals, we would have never pointed at each other. I could go on and on with the events of that evening, let alone the entire seven-day cruise. What are the odds? Beats me. But it was clear to both of us, we were meant to meet.

I wish we had spent more time together. Just like meeting the GI's in Puerto Rico, the minutes together seemed longer than they actually were. To this day, I have yet to see Joke and John again, but we shared an incredible moment in time, and years of emails back and forth. John and Joke Burrows, who live in a small suburb of Ottawa, Canada, are now our friends.

Flying home after our vacation gave me lots of time to think about the events of this extraordinary cruise. I had no idea I would be connecting to my past with not one, but two small world encounters.

Mark and I were just hoping to enjoy a well-deserved break from the tremendous highs and lows that enveloped us in 2010. As it turned out, my life would never be the same again.

Winning and Losing

Soon after we returned from our cruise, the emails back and forth from Canada and Pasco began. We were excited to get to know each other, and to provide details of the progress we were making with our research. We both wanted to know for sure, what we already knew, that we were on the same transatlantic voyage in April 1956.

I made phone calls to my sisters, Ineke and Gert, to see what they remembered about the voyage. Ineke was able to verify that the *Groote Beer* first landed at a pier in Halifax, Nova Scotia, Canada, two days before we arrived in New York City. Joke and John were able to identify the lighthouse that can be seen in a picture that Mother took of Dad and the five daughters sitting on the deck of the *Groote Beer* docked in Halifax.

Each time Joke and I sent or received another email, it would contain more information that confirmed our having immigrated together. The final verification came when we were both able to find the ship's registry of the passengers list for April 3, 1956. All of the van Lith family was listed, and so was Joke's family. Within that first week, we had the evidence of what we already knew.

Our emails became more personal with each exchange. In one of our earlier letters, we shared the death of our mothers just months apart, mine in August and hers in October. I then began to think that our mothers had something to do with our encounter.

Joke and I amused each other as we envisioned our mothers looking down on us from above, trying to figure out a way for us to meet on board the ship. Day after day we passed by each other unaware of our connection, only to frustrate our moms each time.

Finally, our mothers had only one last chance to get it right. "Ok, you make sure your daughter sits facing this table, and I will make sure mine is facing your daughter. Those waiters better bring my daughter's mother-in-law her birthday cake before somebody leaves, and Joke better sing *Lang Zal Ze Leven* in Dutch!" Joke's mother says to my mother in Heaven. It was a fun fantasy (or was it?).

"I'll do my part, and you do yours, and the rest is in God's hands! Oh listen, they're singing. Wait for it...Hip Hip Hooray!" I imagine the mothers saying.

It gets easier, as I get older, to recognize the hand of God, and the many miracles that occur, not just for me, but for so many people I encounter. When you know how to ask for them, and you have eyes to see them, miracles happen all around us.

Some miracles can knock you over the head so there is no way to deny them. Other miracles can only be seen in hindsight, and with the eyes of faith to see how the Good Lord has been working all along. As far as I am concerned, it's a miracle you are reading my story right now. I'm just a very ordinary person, with an extra-ordinary story to tell, with the hope that others will be encouraged.

With no doubt left in our minds that Joke and I had cruised together so many years ago, we both had the same thoughts about writing our story and telling Holland America what transpired on our most recent cruise onboard the *Eurodam*.

December 17, 2010

...I agree that we should tell our story and show our photo to Holland America cruise line. I would love to show them some of our old photos from our immigration...tell me more about your family and why your parents made the journey. I love a good story.

More later, Marja

December 17, 2010

...I find this whole encounter incredible, and feel we should let HAL [Holland America Lines] know about this chance connection of 50 odd years later...

Cheers, Joke

December 21, 2010

...I loved reading about your story. What pioneers our parents were. Not sure I would have the same courage...I'm going to wait till after Christmas to work on my end, writing our joint story to HAL...

Cheers to you also, Marja

December 21, 2010

...I found your story about your parents' background very moving. My dad went into hiding during the war since the Germans would pick up any available strong lad to work in the factories as you know...My Dad loved the Canadians after they were liberated and would exchange eggs and bread for cigarettes. My parents got married in '46, and had absolutely nothing except a house they had to share with another family...

Cheers, Joke

December 31, 2010

...I had a great image this morning, in my head, thinking about our meeting and imagining our mothers watching from Heaven, and how all the parts began to fit together for each of us to meet. I imagined them cheering us on and excited when it happened. The whole thing still could have fallen apart if you or I had our backs to each other at the dinner table. So many events had to fall into place just right for it to happen the way it did. I am still amazed. Christmas was a little sad though, missing my Mom this year. But I am very sure she is enjoying Christmas like never before. It's always Christmas there!

Talk to you soon, Blessings, Marja

January 10, 2011

...John found some more interesting information on the Groote Beer, which I will forward to you...lots of great pictures and the history of the ship. He is trying to come up with a winning way to tell our story.

Cheers, Joke

January 10, 2011

...We are Oma and Opa to #9 on 1/6/2011. We have another boy. That makes 4 boys and 5 girls. His name is Tyson Michael and looks a lot like his father, our son. This grandparent stuff just never gets old. Our daughter Jessica is expecting a boy in May. That evens up the score again...I enjoy looking forward to our next exchange.

Tot Ziens, Marja

The correspondence continued between us. Sometime twice a day. I guess we both thought that we had a great PR story for Holland America, and that when they read about us, they might think it cool enough to at least give us a discount on our next cruise, if not a free one.

*

With Mom's house ready to close on the sale soon, the conversation between some of my siblings and me involved the possibility of doing something fun to honor our parents. We promised our mother before she died that we would always remain close in each other's lives and support one another. What better way to honor Dad and Mom than by spending time on a cruise together, something they loved too.

Mark beat me home from work on Thursday, January 13, 2011. I found him in our office at home. He turned to me with a big grin on his face and said, "You are not going to believe the email that was sent to us today. You have to read this."

It was an email from Holland America Cruise Line. The subject read: "Enter to win a 9-day Classic Transatlantic Crossing for Two." I continued to read, to see what it was all about. When I finished, I looked at Mark and said, "Can you believe this? I've got to enter this contest. There's no way I can lose. The timing of this is incredible. I'm gonna forward this to Joke, my sisters, and Dom, and tell them to get excited. We're going cruising in July!"

To win the cruise, each contestant was asked to, "tell us about your most memorable Holland America Line transatlantic crossing, and win a 9-day cruise for two from New York to Rotterdam." In 2011, HAL was celebrating 40 years of providing transatlantic voyages, and this contest was part of it. In the email it advertised:

2011 Classic Crossings:

Share in joyful transatlantic traditions of the past, from big band dances to a bon voyage sail away party. Be enlightened by special guests and entertainment, meet distinctive guest chefs, and receive a celebratory gift and much more on these unique and extraordinary journeys!

The winning entry would be announced sometime around April 11, 2011. The winner would cruise from July 12 through July 21. During the nine day crossing, there would be one stop on the seventh day in Cobh (Cork), Ireland. The *MS Rotterdam* would embark from New York, New York, and disembark in Rotterdam, the Netherlands.

Knowing it was an essay contest was a bit intimidating for me. A couple of years prior, I had written an editorial that was published for our local newspaper, sharing my thoughts on the hot topic of immigration. I spent hours writing that. There were also a few of my letters to the editor printed in the same newspaper. Oh, and there was my college graduation speech I wrote, but I never considered myself a writer of any means beyond that. I just knew I needed to do a good job if I had any chance of winning this contest.

There was a flurry of emails sent between Joke and me, and my siblings and me. It felt like we were all on board with the idea of going back to Holland together. I encouraged Joke and John to enter the contest too. With both of us writing about our shared encounter, it might help. Who knew?

I was recovering from a surgery during the latter part of January and into February, and had some extra time to focus on writing. The emails between Joke and me slowed down from one or two a day, to around three per week. It was hard to keep up the pace we had set for ourselves early on.

January 31, 2011

Hey Joke. My birthday was fun (29th). Thanks for singing Lang Zal Ze Leven in Dutch! ... I got to hold the newest baby and love on his twin sisters...Thanks in advance for your "little Token." Can't wait to see what it is...I think your story makes for a great read. I especially like the part where you write that it was like seeing a long lost friend. That is how it felt and how it looks on our photo. I wish we could have spent just a little longer together and taken more pictures including our husbands. It all happened so fast that night...Please, someday, we would love to enjoy a winter festival like the one you are describing. Man, that sounds like fun. Someday maybe, huh?...

Have a great rest of the day, Marja

Joke and I both got our entries in before the deadline. We got notification that our entries were received, so now we just had to wait. Our emails had slowed down to one every week or two. We'd learned a lot about each other, but in many ways, we are still strangers. We live so far apart, but we kept on going as email buddies.

March 14, 2011

Hi Joke. Yes I am still here, busy as ever... When I am done with our taxes, I will be working on a presentation I will be giving to a couple of 8th grade classed at a school in Richland on Monday, the 21st. I was asked to participate and talk about WWII and the concentration camps. I am the "show-and-tell" portion of one of the students who picked this subject matter to give a report about...I came home from Salem a few weeks ago to clean out the rest of Mom and Dad's house, and brought back some real treasures they kept about Holland and the times during the war...I found original photos of Dad in Buchenwald and a lot of great material I can share. I reread one of the many newspaper articles, from years ago about my father. The last line of the article Dad said that, "we should never forget what happened, and won't as long as he lived, and his children and grandchildren live." I felt Dad nudging me when I read that article again, and feel called to share the story to any classroom that would want me, just like my folks did. It is a privilege...Sorry for the delay in responding to your last e-mail. Every time I get one of yours, I look at our photo and it makes me smile.

We'll talk soon again, Blessings, Marja

April 12, 2011

Hi Marja. Well I guess if we are going to make the return journey to Holland, we are on our own...no news from our end of things, so there is still hope you may have won? They were supposed to let the winner know by today, and the day is almost half over. Hope you had a wonderful time in Mexico... (I still think our story warrants being published somewhere in the HAL brochures!!!!)

Cheers, Joke

April 12, 2011

Greeting to you. Our trip was very relaxing...I guess I am disappointed we didn't hear from HAL. At least we had fun exchanging information and thoughts. I may still give them a call and find out who won the contest. I think we will stay closer to home and enjoy our boat and the river this summer. I did like the idea of traveling to your neck of the woods sometime in the near future. What do you think? Washington State is a wonderful place to visit too. This is wine country! We also have Mount St. Helens, Grand Coulee dam, beautiful scenic rivers and mountains, with family in the Seattle area to help us explore. Sound interesting to you?...Say hello to John.

Tot Ziens, Marja

Like Joke, I figured we would have heard by now if either of us had won the cruise. I'm of the mindset that, if it's meant to be, it will happen. If not, then it wasn't supposed to happen. That's not to say that I wasn't disappointed. I just get through life a little easier when I think philosophically like that.

*

What was finally clear to me, after returning from our last cruise in mid-December 2010, was the need to make a big change in my life. After working nine years at the surgery center, I decided to quit my regular part time job and place myself on the per diem list, to work when they needed me, and I was available. Not only was my head prompting me to make this adjustment, but my body was too. I was worn out.

I still worked at least one day most weeks, but I could tell that things didn't feel the same anymore. I wasn't enjoying my job like I had in the past, but I could not imagine quitting my profession altogether.

I had agreed to work on April 13, 2011. When I got home that afternoon, I went about my normal routine, changing out of my scrubs, checking the mail, and checking the phone for messages. The light was blinking on the phone, indicating I had at least one message while I was away.

"Hello Maria. My name is Mary S. from Holland America Cruise Line. Would you please give me a call? I look forward to hearing from you. Goodbye."

"What time is it?" I said to myself. "Oh, it's only 3:30. Mary better still be there!"

I sat for a minute before picking up the phone to call HAL. I knew why she was calling me. I just knew!

"Hello Mary? This is Marja, I mean Maria. I don't normally go by my formal name. I was surprised when I listened to your message."

"Hello Maria. I'm so glad you called me back. I wanted to talk to you right away. I want to let you know that you are the Grand Prize winner of the free cruise contest. We all loved your story, and were secretly hoping that you would win," Mary said with a great deal of enthusiasm.

Deep down I knew I was going to win, but it was a wonderful surprise to finally hear it. So much so that I was glad I was sitting down. "I am so excited to be the winner. Mary, I knew I had a good story. The events that occurred on our last cruise were truly remarkable," I told her.

Mary went on to say, "The committee that chose your entry included our president and CEO, Mr. Stein Kruse and the Cruise Critic Editor-in-Chief, Carolyn Spencer Brown, along with other judges on the panel. Your friend Joke's entry was also picked as one of the top 30 to be published in a souvenir book for the transatlantic voyages."

"Oh, I am happy about that, and I know Joke will be excited too. I won, I am so excited!" I said again.

The tone and enthusiasm in Mary's voice took me to another level of excitement. She went on to talk about the press releases that would be coming out in another day or two, and all the different internet sites that would be carrying my story.

I continued to listen as Mary talked about another Grand Prize winner from the Netherlands. Holland America Line had two contests simultaneously, and we both received free cruises. The press in the Netherlands would also be publishing the results of the contest. The winner representing Holland would leave from Rotterdam to New York, and as the America winner, I would be on the returning voyage back to where it all started at the pier in Rotterdam. I was given the chance of a lifetime, to retrace my immigration journey.

I had no idea that being the Grand Prize winner would take on a life of its own. My story was going to be published and shared over the internet. My insides got a little too excited at that point. Mary kept up the pace by saying that, "Sometimes government officials, or even some in the Royal family love to make appearances for such occasions!"

I don't remember what all was said after that. My heart began to race in my chest, my teeth began to clench, and my body began to shiver. I needed to end this conversation as quickly and gently as I could. I hung in there a bit longer to wrap things up. I was thinking, "I don't like what I am feeling. I need to hang up before this adrenaline rush gets out of control!" But I suddenly ran out of time. It was too late.

The punch to my heart was abrupt and too familiar. My shoulders instinctively pulled forward to protect my heart from further damage. I managed to wrap up the conversation, thanked her for everything, and was told that someone would be in touch with more details soon. And then I hung up and began to cry.

"No God, No! Not again. It was never supposed to happen again. I knew I was going to win, I knew it. But my heart, Lord, my heart hurts again. Please protect me," I prayed.

I made my way onto the couch in the living room. It was late enough in the afternoon that I knew Mark should be on his way home soon. I was going to tough it out until he got home. I held onto the phone just in case I needed to call 911 for help.

Mark came home not long after the attack, and found me reclining. "I'm home, honey! Are you OK?" he asked.

"I've got some good news and some bad news. I got a call from Holland America Line. I won the cruise, just like we thought I would. When the lady from HAL sounded more and more excited, and began filling my head with all kinds of stuff, I became overly excited too. Then I got anxious, when I began experiencing the adrenaline rush and chest pounding. I tried to stop it, but I couldn't and now I'm having another heart attack just like before. I'm scared Mark, it hurts. I can't believe it happened with good news. It wasn't supposed to happen again," I told him through my tears.

"I knew you were going to win, now let's get some help. We should call for an ambulance. When did this all happen?" Mark calmly said.

"I'm not sure. Maybe 15-20 minutes or so. I haven't taken anything yet. Can you get me an aspirin to chew while you are calling 911?" I asked.

Mark left to get the aspirin and said, "Just try and relax. I could tell just looking at you that something had happened. I'm going to get one of your nitroglycerin tablets too."

Things happened quickly. The local EMT's arrived within minutes of the call. The fire station is just a mile away. It's unnerving to hear the sirens of the ambulance and fire trucks coming when you know they're coming for you.

I told them what happened, and after they quickly assessed my condition, the conversation turned to my having just won a free cruise. These guys knew how to distract me enough to lighten the mood during a very stressful intervention. I was able to relax enough, knowing I was in good hands for the ride to the emergency room in Richland. I must also add, these EMT's fit the profile I had in my mind. "Now this is what EMT's are supposed to look like when they come to the rescue," I was thinking. I'll just leave that for your own imagination, ladies!

All the vital signs and the tests run in the ambulance and hospital confirmed what I already knew. I was experiencing another Takotsubo Cardiomyopathy. The ER doctor had never seen this happen to someone experiencing really good news before.

The following day I underwent my second Coronary Angiogram. Even though everyone was pretty sure of the diagnosis, the cardiologist insisted it be done to make sure we were not missing anything, *again*. I was released after I recovered from the procedure and when nothing else was found, I was told to rest, rest, and rest some more. My heart should heal like after the first time.

2011 was beginning to feel much like 2010, but for different reasons. I had my gallbladder surgically removed in January when a doctor thought he found the cause of my weird symptoms. Unfortunately, the discomfort in my chest and upper abdomen never went away, and my gallbladder seemed pretty normal. Now I was recovering from my second heart attack, and having a difficult time with the whole thing. My adrenaline and heart continued to act up and scare me. I was thinking about my heart several times each day. My cruise to Holland was in less than three months, and on top of that, Jessica was about to have her second child in just a few short weeks. I wanted to be well enough to help out when the baby was born.

Saturday, April 16, 2011

Hi Joke and John,

Are you sitting down? I won the contest!!!!!!!!!!!! They called me on April 13th with the exciting news. They did mention your entry as being one of the top 30. There were well over 500 entries. It occurred to me that this award came on the exact day that the Groote Beer arrived in NY 55 years ago. Everything was so overwhelming. I would have emailed you earlier, but something happened to me as I was talking to the HAL representative. Are you still sitting down? I had a heart attack during the phone call. The lady was telling me how excited everyone was, and then went on and on about my story and plans for its publication and promotion, and then I became a bit overwhelmed and started getting chest pains. I suffered a rare, stress-induced heart attack 1½ years ago that I believe was the result of some medication I was taking for migraine headaches. I thought it would never happen again, but it did...OK, now breathe again! I will recover again after 2-3 weeks' rest. This attack doesn't seem to be as severe as the first one, and my heart should fully recover.

I know that the good Lord has a plan for my life and that He is allowing these events to happen for a reason. My faith is strong and I am so grateful for what He is doing for me right now, even though I do not understand it all. What a journey. I would appreciate your prayers...

My siblings are seriously interested in going together with me and Mark, and I am extending the invite to you and John as well...

Joke and John, thank you for being a big part in this journey. I look forward to getting to know you better with time, and seeing you both at some future date.

God bless you both, Marja

April 20, 2011

Hi Marja,

Well, what can I say??? John called me while I was visiting my daughter and he was so excited to tell me you had won the contest. He had read it online and couldn't wait to phone me. I am so sorry about all your medical related problems...What a scare for you...Here you were all excited about a happy event only to be struck down by an over excited heart. You must have felt like being in another world...As for us, we have made other plans when it seemed we were not the winners, and as I mentioned before, John had already booked his big canoe trip for the same time...I will try and phone you later when I get back from choir. It is just too exciting to spend time typing when there is so much to talk about...You are right though, someone up there is looking over you!!! I will certainly keep you in my thoughts and prayers. Talk to you soon I hope!

Cheers for now, Joke

April 20, 2011

Yeh! I am so glad to finally hear from you guys. It is so strange to see our picture out there for the whole world to see. And then to read the comments of people kind enough to read it and be happy for us, even to the point of tears. And then today, I found out that the woman we contracted to build our house in 2009 has family members (grandfather and Uncle) who were in Buchenwald very near liberation day, and helped the prisoners. They were so traumatized by what they saw that they could not share the experience with their family. This story keeps getting add-ons to it.

Tot ziens, Marja

April 20, 2011

Hi again,

The newspaper wants to run an article about the story. I need to give them permission to use the photos, and I am asking you for permission to use the photo that John took. I know you already gave permission to HAL, but this is a related story that needs your consent as well. OK?...I am having fun with the comments that the story is generating. Our story makes some of the people cry, they are so moved. Just the reaction we were hoping for...What a day this has been. Hope to hear from you soon.

Tot ziens, Marja

The local newspaper ran a front page article with pictures the following morning, April 21. I sent a copy to Joke and John so they could enjoy reading the account, and sharing it with their family and friends.

Mark was so protective of me after I won the contest. He could see how very tired I was at the end of each day, and tried to remind me that it had only been ten days since I was rushed off to the hospital.

It's difficult to explain the extreme highs and lows of emotions I experienced during this period. I just hoped to be able to enjoy the upcoming cruise back to Holland as I had wanted to. Now my goal was just to live long enough to make the trip. I did my best to control my emotions to avoid another one of those uncontrollable adrenaline rushes. I was not always successful at doing so.

I began doing more research on my medical condition with the hope of finding a way to control it, whatever "it" was. Even as I did everything I could to get well, there were a couple of times that awful adrenaline rush reared up for no apparent reason. It would force me to lay down with the phone next to me, and try to hold on. After 20-30 minutes, my heart pounding would wind down as the rush of chemicals retreated.

The best way that I was able to describe these occurrences to my cardiologist and others, was that it felt like an instant, exaggerated, fight-or-flight occurrence. It's like something really scary happens, and you either want to turn around and punch somebody, or run away as fast as you can. The symptoms always ran the same pattern, and had the same affects. When they got to the point that I would begin to shake and grit my teeth, as if I was cold, I would jump in the shower and stand in very warm water to calm myself down.

I sought diagnosis and possible treatment from an endocrinologist, only to run into a dead end. All the tests were negative for any adrenal causes. My cardiologist was running out of suggestions, and simply monitored me during this recovery.

With a new grandson soon to be born, I reached out to a psychologist to help me control the panic and anxiety that I knew was developing because of my condition. I did not feel stable enough without something to rely on to help me for the week or so I would be helping my daughter after her baby was born. And that was right around the corner.

I got some relief from my 6-8 visits with the therapist. He gave me some mental exercises to make use of whenever I felt the panic developing. Most of the times when I used the relaxation techniques, I got some relief.

May 9, 2011

Good morning Joke,

I wish I could say that my grandson was here, but Jessica and Joel have made two trips to the hospital only to be sent home. I have been living out of my suitcase in my own home for several days already...She is sooooo ready to have this baby...So far three of my sisters are joining us on the cruise. They plan to call our brother and other sister and encourage them to come too...

Tot Ziens, Marja

May 23, 2011

Greetings Joke,

I was in Spokane for eight days with my daughter Jessica, and her new baby Dominicus Howard, born on 5/13/2011, one day before my Dad's birthday. He is named after my father, and will be called Nic. Cool huh? Mom and baby are doing great...They don't have me on the schedule at work at the surgery center until mid to late June. I'm deciding if I really want to go back or not. Still praying about that one...

Talk to you soon, Marja

June 7, 2011

I am starting to get excited about the upcoming trip. I think New York will be a lot of fun. Hope to see you there. This is a wonderful opportunity to get to know each other while we all (siblings included) have fun together...I am working tomorrow for the first time since my "you know what" attack! I have mixed feelings about going back...I still think I might be moving in another direction in my life. I am buying another rental house and I think I will quit my nursing job and just manage the rentals...

Cheers back, Marja

I quit my job as an RN. June 8 was my last day. Nobody at work, and nobody at home knew. It was apparent to me from the moment I arrived for work that I was done.

I could not worry about my unstable condition while I was taking care of my patients. Emergencies at work could happen at any time, and I needed to be prepared.

I said goodbye that day, just like I always did to the doctors and nurses I worked with, and to some of my favorites in the front office. This goodbye did not include "See you later."

Thankfully, I was alone in the dressing room when I emptied my locker. That made it easier on me too. As I walked out the side door, just past the break room, I turned around and quietly said, "Goodbye Surgery Center. Thanks for the nine years. Goodbye everybody." Nobody was there when I walked out the door.

I was not sad. I was relieved. I knew it was the right thing to do, and I had peace. I was blessed to have such an obvious answer to my prayer.

June 24, 2011

Good morning Joke,

We leave for our trip in 2 weeks. I can't believe it's so soon...I quit my job a couple of weeks ago. Mark told me afterwards that he was hoping I would make that decision. That was a relief as well. I didn't know he felt that way. He wanted me to come to that conclusion by myself. I am at peace, and I still have plenty to do.

June 29, 2011

Hi Marja,

You must be getting really excited about your trip. On top of that, you have made a decision regarding your future and should feel good about retiring. There comes a time in your life when there are so many other things that become important, and work is not necessarily one of them. I hope you enjoy your new-found freedom and am sure that the time will quickly be filled with all your other pursuits...As for the New York trip, I am afraid I am not going to be able to make it...So, enjoy the time with your siblings. Have a great trip and I would be happy if you could pick me up a copy of the book they are printing for the occasion. I also expect pictures so I can share the trip vicariously...

Cheers, Joke

*

My Most Memorable
Holland America Line Transatlantic
Crossing Story

Maria Dominica Henderson

Pasco, Washington

(Published in the Holland America souvenir book for the cruise.)

Part I

My name is Maria Henderson, and I can't wait to tell you a story that spans nearly 55 years and two amazing Holland America cruises. My story begins with a tale of my first and only transatlantic voyage from Rotterdam, Holland, to New York City.

The year was 1956, and I was not quite 15 months old. I was the youngest of five sisters. My memory of that voyage is from the stories my parents and sisters told, and from the pictures that are now archived in our family photo albums. On April 4, 1956, we set sail on the *SS Groote Beer* (*Big Bear*), a Holland America Line ship used at the time to transport immigrants to the United States and Canada. The ship was nothing like today's luxury cruise ships that are designed to treat passengers with the very best of every accommodation. That voyage was not like today's cruises that cater to our vacation spirit, but an undertaking to establish a better life for my parents and their children.

We were assigned two separate quarters with my mother and her five daughters in the women's section, and my father in the men's section. With some pleading from my father, and kindness shown to our family, we were given a stateroom with a small porthole and three sets of bunks. I slept in a buggy that we brought from Holland. All of our belongings were tucked away in a 6'x6'x6' wooden crate buried in the storage hold of the ship. Meals were cafeteria style, and activities were minimal. Throughout the nine-day voyage, all my family but my father and one sister got very sick. We landed in New York City with the Statue of Liberty in the background. A very long train trip across the country would eventually deliver us to our new home in Salem, Oregon. This trip was not like any of the six other cruises that I have enjoyed with Holland America.

Why would we leave everything behind and start over in America? There were many reasons, but Dad's desire was to become a U.S. citizen. My father was so filled with gratitude to the American GI's in General Patton's army because they liberated him from Buchenwald concentration camp in April of 1945. He was an active part of the first wave of the resistance movement in Vlaardingen, Holland. He was getting ready to blow up the shipyards in Rotterdam to prevent the Nazis from using it, when he was captured and nearly killed. He was soon sent as a prisoner to Buchenwald in Germany, and forced to work hard labor for his captors. He was 20 years old when captured, and was liberated the month before his 25th birthday.

Eleven years and five daughters later, our immigration number came up. Our future was in America, and Holland America took us there. We would become the distant relatives to all our extended family that still live in Holland.

Dad was a war hero and a true patriot to the people in Holland. On September 16, 1981, my father received the National Medal of Freedom Award and was awarded the Resistance Cross by the Queen of Holland. There is a monument created across from the courthouse in Vlaardingen dedicated to the resistance fighters of which my father was a surviving member.

After my father retired, my parents, Dominicus and Suzanna van Lith, spent most of their vacations cruising with Holland America all over the world. Even after my father's death in 1993, Mother continued to enjoy cruising with Holland America. Because of my parents' many adventures cruising, several of us siblings followed their example, and are enjoying cruising. My husband, John Mark, and I have no desire to cruise with any other line. Why would we? I go way back with Holland America after all.

Part II

What makes this story so special are the events that unfolded on our most recent Holland America cruise in December 2010 that reconnected me to my heritage and my first voyage.

On December 4, 2010, my husband and I boarded the *Eurodam* and enjoyed a week in the Eastern Caribbean. We were celebrating our 37th wedding anniversary. After our tour of old San Juan, Puerto Rico, we were walking back to our ship when I overheard two elderly gentlemen sitting together by the pier talking about their involvement as GI's during WWII. They had family with them, but I just could not resist approaching them.

I said, "Excuse me gentlemen, I could not help but overhear you talking about the war. Did I hear you say that you were at Normandy for D-day?"

"Yes I was," said the first gentleman.

I then asked both of them, "Were either one of you in the Buchenwald in April of '45 with General Patton's army?"

The other gentleman then said that he was there in April of '45.

I looked at him and said, "Thank you sir, you helped to liberate my father from Buchenwald, and saved his life!"

The families of these men were astonished. I again thanked both of them for their service and, with tears in all our eyes, wished them well.

This connection to my past was profound, but even more was in store for me on this special cruise.

On our last evening at sea, we were escorted to our table in the flex-dining area. Near the end of our meal the waiters and stewards brought a cake to the table of ten just to the left of our table. This was a new group of people we had not seen before. The cake was for the elderly matriarch's birthday. The *Eurodam* dining room staff sang a familiar Dutch tune to her in their native language, and I joined in by singing the same song, Lang Zal Ze Leven, in Dutch. Just after that, the staff came to our table with a cake and sang the same song to celebrate our wedding anniversary. This time the younger woman saw me singing the song in Dutch. We made eye contact and smiled across our tables. She then came over to our table to say hello. What happened next was extraordinary!

We introduced ourselves and confirmed that, yes indeed, we were both immigrants from Holland. Johanna Burrows and her husband, John, live in Canada. Johanna (nicknamed Joke) asked me when we emigrated. I told her 1956. She smiled and said that was the same year her family emigrated. She then asked if my family came over on a Holland America Line ship.

I said, "No, we came over on an immigrant ship called the *Groote Beer* (at the time, I did not know that the *Groote Beer* was a Holland America Line vessel).

Joke's eyes got big and said that she came over on the *Groote Beer*. Then I got a little more excited.

I said cautiously, "But we came over in April of '56."

From the expression on her face, I knew. I started to shake, tears welled up and started to flow as I waited for her response.

"We came over on the *Groote Beer* in April of 1956," Joke exclaimed!

We both began to shake and hugged each other at that moment. We realized the tremendous odds against us ever meeting, and even greater odds meeting on a Holland America Line ship during, what turned out to be, our second cruise together. John took our picture at that moment. You can see the emotion and excitement on our faces. Everything had to have happened just the way it did that last night for us to meet.

Joke and I have become e-mail buddies and discovered many things we have in common. We have also confirmed that we truly were on the same ship almost 55 years ago. Our letters just kept getting better and better with more information of that first voyage. We found the passenger list with all of our names on the registry. Joke's family disembarked in Halifax, Canada two days before we arrived in New York City. One of our family photos shows us on the deck with the Halifax lighthouse in the background.

We both lost our mothers last year. I truly believe that our mothers had a hand in Joke and I meeting each other. The odds are just too amazing to think about. We shared and fantasized about reliving our transatlantic voyage, only this time in reverse. In addition, my siblings and I have been trying to figure out some special trip we could take to celebrate our parents' lives, in gratitude for the huge sacrifice they made for us, and to honor them both. Then, my husband found the Holland America Line e-mail invitation for this contest that might just provide such an amazing opportunity.

Do I deserve to win this contest? No more than anyone else. It would be a wonderful gift and a blessing. By the same token, winning would not be as complete without sharing my journey with my siblings and my new friend Joke. We all made the original transatlantic voyage together almost 55 years ago. What an honor it would be! What might the odds be after all? I guess you will let us know. I do believe in miracles.

The End

Silly me. I managed to live long enough to pack my bags and get on a plane to New York City, where I would enjoy three days and three nights before boarding the *MS Rotterdam* bound for Rotterdam, Holland. So far, so good!

Though I had hoped for all my siblings and their spouses to enjoy this once in a lifetime trip retracing our immigration of 55 years ago, only Ineke and Traci followed through and accompanied Mark and me. There were four of us, and a whole bunch of relatives waiting to see again. In less than two weeks, we would be back in Holland.

"Hip Hip Hooray!"

Chapter 30

55 Years in the Making

A couple of weeks before our cruise, I sent a mass emailing to my cousins. It was an invitation to come and join us for a family reunion the day we arrived in Holland. I referred to the event as the "55 year reunion of our immigration." My hope was to see many of our relatives at the Novotel Hotel in Schiedam for a mid-morning gathering of tea, coffee, and treats. This was the same place we gathered the van Lith cousins together when Mark and I vacationed in Europe three years prior.

The email responses came in slowly, but picked up the pace the closer we got to our departure. By the time we left for New York City, I knew that there would be quite a crowd coming to celebrate with us. Some of them were on vacation but planned to return early just to attend this gathering. I finally lost track of the total count.

*

The day of our journey finally arrived. Saturday July 9, 2011, Mark and I were packed and ready to go on another trip of a lifetime. Three years ago, we referred to our European trip as the trip of a lifetime. I can get used to these adventures. I might need to coin a new phrase though, say maybe, "another bucket list venture...of a lifetime."

Aside from worrying about random adrenaline surges and my heart, I had nothing else to worry about. Granted, what I was worried about was no small matter. The concern still controlled much of my thoughts and actions, and I knew I still needed to get to the bottom of these health issues.

Mark and I shared a light breakfast in the airport in Seattle, then went to a coffee bar for coffee and tea, and headed to the terminal to wait at the gate for our departure. After about an hour of reading and waiting, I decided to walk around the shops in the terminal. As I walked away, I felt as if I stood up too quickly. I became dizzy and very jittery. I tried to brush off the feelings, and kept walking.

"What is wrong with me? Why am I feeling like I'm about to pass out?" I thought to myself. Within minutes of walking about in the first store, I began to experience another exaggerated fight-or-flight syndrome. My heart began pounding in my chest, my arteries felt like they wanted to explode, and my head was in a spin. I was in trouble and needed help now. "This is not good right before boarding a plane. Not good at all!" I was thinking.

I was having some difficulty walking back to where Mark was. I finally got to him and immediately sat down. Mark turned to look at me and knew something had happened. "What's the matter?" he asked.

"Mark, I'm afraid. I can't control what I am feeling. Even the relaxation exercises are not working." I said. I lay down on the floor to see if the symptoms would abate, with no results. With an hour before our flight was scheduled to take off, I told Mark that I needed my vital signs and an EKG taken just to be sure.

We walked to an airline information desk and asked the attendant to call for the airport paramedics. They arrived within a few minutes and proceeded with the chest pain protocol. I felt like I was experiencing an out-of-body moment. This was not supposed to be happening. Not now!

My heart was beating fast and my blood pressure was pretty high, and they advised me to go to the hospital. They asked me what I had been doing when my symptoms first began. "Mark and I were just sitting at the gate sipping our coffee and tea, and reading our books. I got up to go shopping, and as soon as I stood up the symptoms began," I said. Suddenly, a light bulb went off in my head.

I still had my cup with me. I took the lid off, and saw two bags of caffeinated tea in a 16oz. container. There was just enough left at the bottom to see how dark the tea had gotten. I looked at Mark and realized what had happened. Ever since my last heart attack, I'd been plagued with a lower threshold for developing that adrenaline rush. All it took was a double shot of extra strength caffeinated tea to plunge me into this health crisis.

The EMT's had me sign a waiver when I refused to go to the hospital. I still had some time to wait for my symptoms to subside. It was a risky decision, but I was pretty sure I had figured out what the culprit was, and even felt relieved having something tangible to blame for it. I was determined not to miss our flight.

We boarded the plane 30 minutes later. Though my symptoms were not entirely gone, they were much better. "This I can handle!" I said to Mark.

He was relieved, but still a little concerned. "I guess you'll be giving up anything with caffeine in it. Lucky for you, they have decaf teas."

"That's fine with me, "I announced, "but just shoot me now if I ever have to give up an occasional piece of chocolate!"

*

The flight was uneventful, thank God! Nobody needed a doctor or nurse inflight, including myself. I got to enjoy a couple of movies, and then poof, we were on the east coast just across from New York City, in Newark, New Jersey.

"I'll have that drink and dessert now," I said to my sisters who were waiting for us in the hotel restaurant bar where we were staying. They greeted Mark and me with big hugs and gifts. "Nobody said anything about gifts! What's with that, you guys?"

Ineke had made one of her beaded bracelets for me and one for Traci. Traci's husband, Jim, surprised my sister with gifts for the four of us. We were each given a light blue t-shirt with an embossed circle on the front that read, "1956 IMMIGRATION 2011 CELEBRATION." What a thoughtful and special surprise. We'd wear them on this trip for sure!

We had two full days to see as much as we possibly could of New York City. We went to Mass at St. Patrick's Cathedral, had lunch in Rockefeller Center, took a cab to Times Square, walked a lot, and took another cab to the Empire State Building. I told Mark that when we reach the observatory, I wanted to play out a scene where two lovers see each other and run into each other's arms, never to part again. The most I got from him was one raised eyebrow.

It felt like there were a *million* people on the observation deck. With everyone crowding each other, there was no way I was going to live out my fantasy. So I just stayed close to Mark and kissed him instead.

We had dinner in the restaurant at the bottom of the Empire State Building before hailing a cab back to Times Square. What do people want to do in the evening in Times Square? They go to a show on Broadway. Mark was a good sport, joining us to see "Sister Act." I think he enjoyed watching our reactions to the production more than the production itself. Both were rather entertaining.

The morning of our second day at the Marriott Hotel in Newark, New Jersey, we boarded a bus for a full day of sightseeing. Before being dropped off at the New Jersey ferry terminal to get on a ferryboat to Liberty Island and Ellis Island, we drove past several sights in Hoboken, including the famous Carlo's Bakery.

Sharing Ellis Island with Mark, Ineke, and Traci was rather emotional. The exhibitions in the museum, and the historic accounts of so many future US citizens was humbling to see and to read about. Included was a display showing what a cabin stateroom looked like on board an immigrant ship, like the *Groote Beer*. It was very sobering to see, especially for Ineke.

"It looks just like I remembered it. Those bunk beds look just like the ones we had to sleep in. Look how small the space is, and there were seven of us. You had the best sleeping space, Marja. You got the buggy in the middle of the room." We stood quietly in our own thoughts before moving on.

As we were leaving the museum, we came upon a bronze statue created by Jeanne Rhynhart. It beautifully portrays the image of Annie Moore from Ireland. She was the first immigrant to arrive and be processed at Ellis Island. This seventeen-year-old girl stands smartly dressed in a jacket and skirt, holding on to the brimmed hat atop her head, while securely hanging on to her small bag of belongings.

Annie is looking off into the distance, absorbing the sights and sounds of this new land that she would soon call home. Wondering where her mother and father were in the crowd, she stayed very close to her two younger brothers who traveled with her. No longer a child, she was a responsible young woman whose story would be told, and her image memorialized for many years to come.

After lunch, we boarded another ferry to Liberty Island, home to the famous iconic statue. The closer we got to the island, the sheer size of Miss Liberty became apparent. The Statue of Liberty is one very large woman, standing on an equally impressive granite pedestal. She kept Mark busy taking lots of pictures.

Comparing my parent's photos taken from the ship in 1956 to the images Mark took 55 years later, the statue has not changed. The early photos were in black and white, and were taken from a distance. The statue was surrounded by gray clouds and misty fog that morning. Now, in the middle of a sunny July afternoon with the blue sky and fluffy white clouds framing her from above, we see her in color, radiant in the greenish-blue patina from the oxidized copper that envelopes her. What an unforgettable image, so majestic, and so reverent. This journey in reverse order, has given me an appreciation of the millions of people who admired the Statue of Liberty for the first time as their ships entered America.

Fortunately, we live in a time where resources are available to research our heritage. When we learn about our ancestors and where they came from, we learn more about ourselves. Even now, stories like mine are being written by those who are eager to keep the legacy alive.

The bus driver was waiting for us at the ferry terminal when we returned. We set off to New York City, to spend a few more hours sightseeing the many landmarks. Our tour included: Central Park, Strawberry Fields memorial, The Dakota resident building, Trump Towers, the many different burrows throughout the city, and Grand Central Terminal. Our last stop was to Ground Zero, to pay our respects and see the progress on the construction of the 911 Memorial sites, and the Freedom Tower that was pushing ever higher toward the sky.

Sitting by a window on an upper floor of the building just across from Ground Zero, we were able to see an incredible view of the entire area under construction. The images were quite different from those played over and over again on the television, of the horrible events on 9/11/2001. No one with memories of that day can ever forget the incredible violence and horror that killed so many innocent people and dishonored our country in that cowardly terrorist attack. We all knew that our lives would never be the same again. "Never again, never forget!" I can almost hear Papa saying.

I am grateful that my father was not alive to see what happened that day. I'm glad he did not have to see us go to war again. I'm glad he didn't have to witness the many events of the last several years that have changed the fabric of our society and the world around us.

I'm glad Mother and Dad are not here to see some of history repeating itself. Is it possible that we haven't learned from the mistakes of the past? I pray that we have. It's up to us now to do everything we can to prevent another Holocaust, and put an end to the hate and terrorism perpetrated on so many innocent victims who just want to live in peace.

The four of us were glad to leave Ground Zero. We actually stayed too long. It had already been a very long and emotional day. Time to get to bed for some well-deserved rest before beginning our cruise back to Holland. We had many more memories to create ahead of us.

*

Midmorning the day of our departure, the bus came to the hotel to pick up several passengers heading for the cruise ship. My sisters had their fancy phones with them, snapping selfies of us and putting them on their Facebook pages. There apparently were several friends and family members interested in following our adventures. That little "like" button was adding up with each beautiful or crazy picture that they posted.

Mark and I got separated from my sisters with the many passengers checking into the *MS Rotterdam* at the same time. We were in one line, and Traci and Ineke pulled ahead of us in a faster one. We eventually found each other on the lido deck at lunchtime.

After the lifeboat drill, we joined other passengers at the bon voyage party that was already underway. Free champagne was being served, and many cameras were busy capturing the event and the ship.

"Would you like us to take a picture of you together, and then perhaps you could help us with a picture of the four of us?" Mark or I asked other passengers standing close by. It's so easy to be friendly with others enjoying the same experience.

Cruise ship departures are typically fun events. Leaving New York City on the *Rotterdam* was especially exciting. In the midst of the late afternoon party, the familiar three blasts of the ship's loud foghorn sounded. It was time for me to do what I always do. I like to lean over the rails to watch the dock crew release the big docking ropes and throw them into the water. No longer fixed, the crews crank back the tethers into the ship. Now the Captain and officers slowly moved the behemoth away from the dock and into the Hudson Bay, toward the Atlantic Ocean.

There was a lot to watch as we moved east. So much history to gaze on, so much to think about at a time like this. I had no idea when I woke up on January 1, 2011, that I would be on a cruise ship retracing my tiny footprints back to an earlier time and place. Mark took the initiative to record the events so that the three of us girls could enjoy living in the moment. I could tell that Ineke and Traci must have been preoccupied with similar thoughts as me when I look at these pictures. Sometimes we would look at each other and just smile, knowing we were sharing this together.

We prepared ourselves as best we could for the nine-day voyage with only the one stop in Ireland on the seventh day. The reality of seven days with no land in sight was rather daunting.

We heard reports about the bad weather the ship encountered when she departed Rotterdam nine days earlier. Some crew members and passengers on their return trip back to Holland told us about the very rough conditions they experienced upon entering the North Sea. They met with very stormy seas for the first couple of days, and were inundated with fog for much of the journey. The beautiful weather we were enjoying at the beginning of our leg of this historic transatlantic cruise was a far cry from what they had experienced.

Ineke and Traci shared a verandah stateroom, similar to the one Mark and I had. After unpacking and exploring the ship, my two sisters enrolled in a few activities that were scheduled for each of the days at sea. From early morning hours to well past midnight, there is always something to do onboard a cruise ship to keep you as busy as you like.

Mark and I preferred to spend our time leisurely together. After a day or two, we developed a routine that included a few activities we both enjoyed, and a lot of down time for reading. We enjoyed quiet times and simple things, like curling up in an easy chair by a window up in the Crow's Nest Lounge or library on the ninth deck, forward of the ship. We did a good deal of reading there. Mark easily finished nine or ten books, the usual amount for him.

Every evening we gathered together at the La Fontaine dining room on the lower promenade deck. After dinner, we'd stroll to the front of the ship to the upper promenade deck, to find good seats in the showroom balcony.

The evening entertainment was always first rate, and I know at least three of us enjoyed every production. The other one of us was a good sport, though, it just wasn't his cup of tea.

Mark was rewarded after each show with a return trip to the Crow's Nest Lounge. We would recline in the comfy leather lounge chairs again, but this time he would order a shot of some special brand of smooth Scotch on the rocks or neat, and I would indulge in my personal favorite after dinner drink, a warmed cognac liqueur, Grand Marnier.

The only other times we share these special nightcaps are on Christmas Eve, Christmas day, and New Year's Eve. Ok, maybe for our birthdays and wedding anniversary, too. Ok, maybe a couple other times per year, but not many! That way it remains a special treat to us.

Installed on a wall on one of the promenade decks was a navigation board showing the ship's location and route on the world map. In order to avoid the stormy weather the ship encountered leaving Rotterdam, the Captain ordered the ship to take a more southerly route.

To my surprise, the ship's new direction for the first five days was heading straight toward the west coast of northern Africa. That seemed to be a very long way from Ireland, but I figured the Captain must know what he was doing, and if he needed my input, he would let me know.

Thanks to Captain Rik Krombeen, we only experienced one evening of rocky seas during the entire voyage. The four of us laughed ourselves silly watching each other attempt to navigate the dining room like drunken sailors, just to get to our table.

Sometime late on the fifth day, the ship changed course to a more direct route to Ireland. Looking at the navigation board, it was easy to see when we made the big turn. "Bye bye Africa. It's not your turn yet. I'll experience you some other time," I thought to myself.

"No question about it," as Dad used to say. We were very happy that the majority of days crossing the Atlantic were smooth sailing, thanks to the actions taken by the officers on the bridge.

On Monday, July 18, 2011, our sixth full day at sea, we prepared ourselves for the following day's activities at our one and only port of call. Mark and I wanted to get up early to enjoy breakfast in our room. This would give us more time to sit out on our verandah and take pictures of the Irish coastline before the ship came to rest at the dock.

In the cool and slightly foggy early morning hours of Tuesday, July 19, 2011, the *Rotterdam* slowly approached historic Ireland. The ship had turned into a large bay and was in quiet waters now, hardly making a wave.

As the fog began to lift, the morning sunshine and puffy white clouds were a welcome sight to Mark. The dispersed lighting on the picturesque towns and landscape we passed provided opportunities for perfect pictures. We came to rest at the pier in the town of Cobh, in Cork County.

Cork is the largest and most southern county of Ireland. As the ship came to rest at the dock, the gangway prepared for the passengers to disembark. The four of us had already signed up to take a bus tour around Cork County, and to spend time at the Blarney Castle and Gardens.

We gathered at 0800 in the ship's large showroom to wait for our excursion number to be called. We were excited to feel land after our full week at sea. Stepping off the ship, we found our bus quickly and seated ourselves near the front. Once again, my sisters took out their phones and began to take some more selfies of us to post on their Facebook pages.

Though it was the middle of the summer, the landscape was filled with lush green foliage and scattered colorful wildflowers. There's no shortage of precipitation here.

We enjoyed our tour guide, a well-prepared, older lady with a playful sense of humor. She had "many a story" to share with us in her colorful Irish accent. In between the landmarks and artifacts that she would point out, she incorporated one of her many Irish songs, and invite us to join in. Surprisingly, many of us in the bus knew quite a few of the songs, and complied with her request. We sang along with her, to everyone's delight.

After traveling over an hour, we stopped to visit a very old Catholic Cathedral. Old, in Ireland, is ancient by United States standards. Many of the grand churches, cathedrals, and castles are more than 800 to 1,000 years old. This served to increase my interest in our next stop, Blarney Castle.

The Tale of the Blarney Sisters!

There was a time, not long ago, when three beautiful sisters, and one very handsome man, endured a long and arduous journey to the land of Ireland. They traveled by foot nearly 300 miles (make that 1/3 of a mile from the parked bus) to the "Gardens of Blarney." Much to their surprise, while walking among the lovely gardens, they came across a very old structure known as the Blarney Castle. "How interesting to have named this large structure after these lush green gardens," one of the maidens said.

Upon entering this castle, they saw many inhabitants of other strange lands, who were following each other, one by one, up a winding stone staircase. They did so because they could not climb them two by two. You see, the stones were too narrow, and someone might have fallen.

The three sisters and their handsome companion began to climb the 1,000 steps (100 steps), one after another, after another, after another…until the four reached the very top level. Much to their surprise, there in the midst was a kindly chap who seemed to be some sort of greeter. Everyone called him "Whitehair." They did so, I believe, because he had white hair.

As the four travelers followed the inhabitants of other strange lands ever closer to the greeter, they witnessed a very peculiar ritual. One by one, the inhabitants of other strange lands lay down upon the stone walkway, and gave themselves over to the care of Whitehair.

The crowd stood in awe as each person was helped to lean way back, until they looked like they had lost their head into some opening in the stone wall behind them. Whitehair was strong. He made sure that no one fell through the opening in the wall that was really, really high up. Sometimes Whitehair seemed to enjoy helping others, while sometimes he was afraid *he* might get hurt.

"Why are these people doing this?" the sisters asked each other.

"They do this to receive the gift of eloquent speech and flattery. If you stay among these people of Ireland long enough, you will hear for yourself this form of speaking. They are a gifted people," the handsome companion said, as if he knew what he was talking about.

"What must we do to receive this eloquent speech?" the sisters asked.

"You must follow the lead of these others, and do what they do," Handsome replied.

As they approached the opening in the stone wall, they noticed how smooth the wall was right behind the hole. "Sir, what must we do to receive this gift we hear about?" one of the sisters asked.

"Just lie on your back and trust me. I will help you to bend your back way over as you grab the iron bars. To prevent falls, the bars were installed a long time ago, so don't worry. Trust me! Then you must kiss the stone in front of your face," Whitehair said.

"What stone, sir?" one sister asked.

"That stone!" Whitehair answered.

"Why?" second sister added.

"Because that's why you paid, I mean, that's why you traveled such a long distance, to kiss the stone," White hair answered.

"People have been coming here for a very long time, so long that it has made the stone smooth. Come on now, let's have you do this while this guy over here takes your picture," Whitehair went on to say.

Each of the sisters and their handsome companion took turns risking their very lives while wrenching their back and neck to get in just the right position to reach this stone and kiss it. Just moments later, the three sisters began to speak with Irish accents, and with such flattery.

"Lassie, ye did that the best!"

"Nay, sweet lady, ye did it better!"

One of the lasses asked Whitehair before the descent to the bottom of the castle, "So what do we tell those in our land, how we received this wonderful gift of eloquent speech and flattery?"

"Tell them, missy, ye kissed the Blarney Stone!" Whitehair called back to answer them.

"Sisters, we must forever memorialize this moment by calling ourselves the 'Blarney Sisters!' What do ye thinks, me sisters?" the youngest lassie asked.

"Why, tis a wonderful idea, ye are so clever, so ingenious," the two older lassies agreed.

"Ye flatter me! I am humbled." I said, uh, I mean, she said!

"I wonder why they call it the 'Blarney Stone.' Is it not enough that the Gardens, and the Castle already have that name? Come sisters, I think it's time to go shopping," I, *oops*, she proposed.

Ok, maybe I did flatter myself telling this story, but it only proves that the gift is real.

*

Perhaps my tale is just a *wee bit* embellished. I am simply allowing myself creative liberty to tell of our adventure in Ireland in such fashion. Me thinks the Irish would approve!

It is true that we called ourselves the Blarney sisters that day, and the legend of the Blarney Stone is fairly accurate. Before the iron safeguards were installed a long time ago, you had to trust those who were holding your legs so you did not fall through the hole. And there really were quite a few inhabitants of other strange lands!

We had so much fun laughing as each of us attempted to kiss that big stone. It was quite scary, actually. When you lean way back, you realize just how high up you are. You can see far into the distance the beautiful lush green woods and fields, but it's an upside down experience. Needless to stay, you don't want to stay in that position for very long.

We did manage some souvenir shopping. There were wonderful stores located across from the gardens. I was tempted by the beautiful Waterford crystals and the wonderful wool plaid fabrics displayed in so many different ways. But, my pockets were conveniently empty of cash, and I held on tight to my credit card.

I have a collection of Christmas ornaments from the many different places Mark and I have traveled to over the years. Every cruise ship, every port of call, and every country visited is represented on our tree. I can't help but smile when I place my Irish ornament on the tree. It brings back fond memories of that day in Ireland.

After the tour, the bus driver dropped us off at the docks in Cobh, and we wandered around in the small stores located near the pier. As we wandered our way back to the ship, we noticed the life-size sculpture displayed on the main entrance to the docks. There they were again, Annie Moore and her two brothers, memorialized at this port. It was at this dock, Annie and her brothers embarked on their journey to immigrate to the United States.

The same artist created both statues, which were unveiled in 1993 at both locations, here in Cobh, Ireland, and the other on Ellis Island. This time, Annie is looking over her right shoulder, as if to imprint the last few images of her beloved Ireland before setting sail to her new homeland on December 20, 1891. Annie's hands are resting on her two brothers standing in front of her. The oldest is stretching his left arm and pointing toward the west. The youngest boy is looking straight ahead and clutching his small bag. They would arrive in New York on the evening of December 31, and be the first to be processed through Ellis Island on January 1, 1892.

Another famous departure took place at the port in Cobh. On April 10, 1912, after leaving Southampton, UK, the *Titanic* sailed to Cherbourg, France, to pick up more passengers, and then headed for Queensland, Ireland, now known as Cobh. The last passengers and supplies were loaded, and the *Titanic* headed west toward the fateful encounter with the iceberg just five days later.

When the MS *Rotterdam* left Ireland, we knew we had only one full day left before completing our transatlantic cruise. Tomorrow was day eight, and early the next morning, we would arrive at our destination, nine days after we set sail from New York. The time went by very quickly. It always does when you are having fun.

We said goodbye to the fertile green land of the leprechauns, and to the Blarney sisters. It was time to be ourselves, the Dutch sisters, and handsome companion.

Bonifide

The next day I was no longer thinking much about the cruise. Now I was looking ahead to our time in Holland. When I start packing for the disembarkation, I begin to detach from the cruise I had been enjoying. I'm never ready for a journey like this to end, but knowing that relatives were coming to see us the following day made the inevitable departure process a lot easier.

Just before our last dinner onboard, I received a phone call from a staff member of the cruise line in charge of passenger relations. Apparently, I had a call from someone in Holland who was representing a hotel located next to the pier in Rotterdam. This individual asked to talk to me personally.

Hotel New York now occupies, what was for many years, the headquarters of the Holland America Line's main office complex. HAL had been there at the pier for many years before moving the main offices to Seattle, Washington.

A new venture began for this building in the early 1990s with the renovations and restorations for the now famous hotel. The Holland-Amerika Lijn marque still dominates the top front of this historic landmark in Rotterdam. It now boasts a sought-after hotel and restaurant.

"Hello, this is Maria Henderson. I actually go by Marja though," I said when I answered this unusual call. Having no idea why I would be receiving a phone call on the ship, I was very curious to hear what the person on the line had to say.

"Hello Marja, my name is Carl Deckers. My wife and I have been commissioned by Hotel New York to put together a commemorative book about the heritage of the Holland Amerika Lijn, here in Rotterdam. We read your winning contest entry, and loved it very much. Your story would be a wonderful addition to our book. These books will be given to guests who stay at the Hotel New York as a souvenir when they leave. We would like your permission to include it."

"Am I to understand that this publication is different from the one that Holland America put together of the top 25 entries to the contest?" I asked Carl. I wasn't completely sure they were not one and the same.

At the beginning of the cruise, each of the passengers received a special gift for sailing with HAL to commemorate 40 years of luxury Transatlantic Crossings. They were presented with a wonderful souvenir book of the top 25 contest entries.

It was a wonderful feeling to see my entry published in such a fashion. My story was the first entry and appeared under the heading "Grand Prize Winner." Just knowing that many people would get a chance to read something that I had written about my memorable experience still makes me smile. Johanna (Joke) Burrows' entry began on page 20. She received a copy of the book in the mail.

"This is a completely different book from the one you are describing. This one is exclusive to Hotel New York. The hotel continues a relationship with HAL by maintaining the landmark building and its legacy. We were aware of your remarkable story and knew right away we wanted to contact you to get permission to publish it in ours. The book will include other historical pictures and memories of how Holland Amerika Lijns has changed so many people's lives over decades," Carl said, to answering my question.

I looked at Mark, who was doing his best to hear the conversation. I quickly filled him in on who it was and what was requested of me. "It's up to you, honey. You'd be published on two continents," he said with a grin on his face. I just rolled my eyes for a second, then lifted my brow thinking, he was right. This whole experience kept giving me more surprises.

"Well, it would be an honor to be included in this memory book for Hotel New York. I will give you permission, with two stipulations. We need to exchange email addresses so we can communicate, and I need a promise from you that I will be given a copy of the book you are putting together just as soon as it is published. Deal?"

"Of course! Thank you so much for giving your permission. This is strictly being used as a gift for the hotel guests and will not be sold for profit," Carl said to make sure I knew that I would not be compensated in any other way. I was happy to give permission. I knew money was not part of the equation.

After exchanging emails and reiterating our intentions, I ended the conversation and put the phone down. I looked at Mark again and smiled. "You're *bonafide*, honey!" Mark declared.

"I sure am bonafide!" I agreed. We were both smiling with pride.

It's just a silly line we've picked up from the film, "O Brother, Where Art Thou," an adventure comedy released in 2000. Those who have seen this famous movie will comprehend our use of the word "bonafide." It's a part of our vernacular now.

During our last dinner onboard the ship, I was excited to tell Ineke and Traci about my phone call with the request to have my story included in the legacy book of the old HAL building at the pier.

"She's bonafide," Mark said, and then went on to explain the meaning, just in case they had never seen the movie. We then spent some time during our meal one-upping each other with funny lines from other movies.

Our family has an innate ability to recall lines from comedy movies and repeat them verbatim. Quite often we can deliver these lines with the same accents and mannerisms originally acted out in the film. We've been doing it for years. It never gets old, and we generate much laughter each time. I will admit we can be a little annoying to those married into the family who were not blessed with the same ability. You know who you are!

After our bags were packed for the following morning departure, it was time for bed. I had trouble sleeping that night, just too excited I guess. My mind kept wandering in many different directions. Dad and Mom were prominent in my thoughts. I could tell Mark was restless too. Probably my fault!

Finally, after dozing on and off throughout the night, Mark got up and opened the heavy glass door out to the verandah. I turned to look at the clock because it was still so very dark outside. It was just before 0500.

"Honey, get up! We're out of the North Sea. The ship is just about to turn into the Dutch waterway, passing the Hoek van Holland!" Mark said with excitement.

I quickly dressed and joined him on the verandah. The weather was very brisk that early in the morning. It was still quite dark, with just a touch of the pink dawn beginning to peek through. The fog was light, the kind that burns off as the sun warms the air.

"Come on, Mark! Let's go to the lido and get a better view."

"Fine with me. That way, I can get some coffee," Mark returned.

Besides us, there were less than a handful of people getting coffee and tea at the beverage station in the lido restaurant. There was another handful of passengers roaming around on the outside deck.

While Mark was busy taking pictures, I paced back and forth, from port to starboard, not wanting to miss anything. When that wasn't good enough, I climbed the steps to the next deck to find a panoramic view. My excitement was controlling my every action.

After exiting the English Channel, the MS *Rotterdam* moved smoothly through the Nieuwe Maas River. In order to be safely docked at the pier in Rotterdam by 0800, the ship traveled a slow eight to ten miles per hour for the 20-some nautical miles. At this speed, she barely made a wake in the water.

This early in the morning, most of the passengers were still sleeping, but not for long. They would be receiving their wakeup call soon enough, they just didn't know it.

By about 0545, the captain of the ship decided it was time for the surrounding towns, to know that the flagship of HAL was returning to her homeport in Rotterdam. The long and very loud fog horn blasted through the quiet morning air. The echo it created moved across the still water between the tall buildings, lasting for several more seconds after the release of the horn. It was fascinating to hear.

With more light, and another blast or two of the horn, the ship came to life again with more of her passengers peering out their verandahs and filling up the observation decks. Mark and I decided to go back to our room and ready ourselves for the room service we had ordered the night before.

While standing out on our balcony, we spotted Ineke and Traci peering out, taking in the Dutch landscape like we were. We waved to each other, then I headed to the phone to call them. We agreed on a time and place to meet to complete the last part of our return trip together. I was imagining Dad and Mom would be standing with us.

We dressed in blue jeans and proudly wore the light blue embossed t-shirts custom-made for this occasion. These shirts added something special. As excited as the moments were, sadness managed to sneak in too. I was missing our other three siblings. I had so hoped to commemorate this reunion with them. It didn't happen that way. I guess it wasn't meant to be.

I excused myself and headed for the big screen monitoring the ships' exact location. No longer was there a small dot identifying her position on the world map, but a map showing us traveling through the harbor with the names of the towns and major ports along the way. I was curious to see how much further we had to travel. To my surprise, we were less than a mile and only one more bend in the waterway from Vlaardingen. After that, the ship would travel just a few more miles to reach Rotterdam.

I hurried back to tell the others how close we were to Vlaardingen. We all moved to the port side of the ship just in time to see the town's big windmill we recognized from our previous visits.

"Mark, look over there. That's where my Opa and Oma were standing when the *Groote Beer* travelled past Vlaardingen as we were leaving Holland," I said as the ship moved closer to the dock where Dad's parents waved goodbye 55 years ago.

Looking more closely, we noticed a car parked on the dock with headlights blinking on and off. "I wonder if someone from your family is greeting us with their car lights," Mark speculated.

"I bet you're right, honey. How cool is that! Someone is obviously signaling the ship. I'm going to assume that those people in that car are welcoming us back. There are a bunch of relatives who know that we are on board this ship. They knew what time we would be arriving. I just have that feeling those lights are for us. I hope I'm right. I wonder who will be there to greet us at the dock." It wouldn't take much longer to find out.

Just past Vlaardingen, the ship took a turn to the left, and in the distance, we were able to see the old Holland Amerika Lijn sign in bold letters on the Hotel New York. "That's where we left, that pier just to the left of the old HAL building," Ineke said.

I was looking ahead to see where the ship was going to dock. I just assumed that after all these years the old dock used for so many emigrants of a bygone era, would be out of commission.

The *Rotterdam* was heading straight for the dock next to the hotel. With just a few modern additions, this pier is the same one pictured in so many of our old photos.

"This is awesome you guys. We've come full circle. We're going to disembark on the same pier we left from. And look, there are people waving on the dock!" I said all excited.

"That looks like Els and her husband," Traci announced. "It looks like there's another couple too," she added.

"I bet that's Els' brother Leen," Mark guessed.

"Oh, for sure, that's Els and Erwin, and Leen and Grada. They must have gotten up really early. It's only 7:30am, and they had to drive 45 minutes to get here," I said.

We began to wave, whistle, and shout to draw attention to ourselves. We must have made a quite a scene, but I didn't care at this point. It didn't take long for our cousins to find us on the big ship. There was no way they could have missed us.

Our voices traveled undisturbed over the calm water and cool air. Even before we reached the dock, we were able to hear each other's greetings. This was so much fun!

It took several more minutes for the ship to come to a complete stop. When it finally did, I didn't need to look at my clock to know that it was 0800. These mariners know what they are doing. It's always masterfully planned, and executed with such precision.

Long before any of the passengers began the disembarkation process, the pier crew and the ship's docking crew had already been hard at work getting everything ready for the travelers to leave. Behind the scenes, the hotel staff and shipmates were doing their part cleaning and restocking, getting the ship ready for the new passengers to come on board. It would all be finished in just a few hours. The tired crew would then put on their smiles and begin greeting their new patrons, and the process would commence all over again.

Our relatives at the dock knew it would take some time before we could join them. The passengers having connections to other commercial transportation, bus, train, or airport, were permitted off the ship first. We were disembarking and staying in Holland for a few more days. It would be a couple more hours before it was our turn to leave.

Having been with my sisters for the last twelve days, it wasn't until we were gathering our luggage that it hit me. After our reunion and lunch with our host families, we would be going our separate ways today. I didn't really know when I would see Ineke and Traci again.

Mark and I would be spending three more nights in Holland in Ouddorp, a small town on an island in South Holland with roughly 6100 residents. Els and her husband were living in a nicely refurbished, older brick home in walking distance to the ocean. They owned and managed a clothing store in the middle of the downtown that enjoys an influx of vacationers year round.

Ineke and Traci would be staying two more nights with our cousin Dom. He and his wife live in a town of about 23,000 people called Nuenen. The painter, Vincent van Gogh spent two years in Nuenen, creating several of his most famous pieces there.

It's also very close to a much larger municipality, Eindhoven, about a two-hour car ride southeast of Rotterdam. Eindhoven is the town Mienus went to when he first returned to Holland after he was liberated from Buchenwald, waiting there for Vlaardingen to be liberated.

Leen, Els, and their spouses were waiting just outside the luggage terminal. The excitement was infectious. The smiles and open arms progressed to the much anticipated hugs and kisses. Bert and Dom were on their way, but had not arrived yet. Traci gave them a quick call to let them know we were off the ship, and where they could find us. Within a few minutes, we saw our two cousins hustling quickly in our direction, eager to envelope us with our next round of affection.

The reunion was scheduled from 1030-1230. It was only 0930, so we decided to make our way to Vlaardingen, and use this short window of time to visit those meaningful places significant to us. We wanted pictures of us together at each stop to commemorate our journey.

Our first stop was the town square in Vlaardingen. There in the basement of the longstanding courthouse was the old police station where Dad was taken after his arrest in 1941, and where he later worked as an officer after the war. We walked up the steps of the courthouse to stand were our parents did when they were first married.

After taking some pictures, we made our way across the street to the WWII memorial commemorating the members of the *Geuzen* resistance of Vlaardingen, and the eighteen who were shot and killed in front of Dad shortly after he was imprisoned at the *Oranjehotel* in Scheveningen. The ten of us spent our time quietly reflecting as we walked about the statues and read the plaques. I was thinking about the many stories Dad and Mom shared about the tragic events that occurred in this town square and around Vlaardingen.

Our next stop was a must-see for Ineke. She wanted to go to the Visbank by the canal and eat a raw herring with Dom and anyone else who might want to eat a raw fish in the middle of the morning. Though it was tempting (*not*), I was more interested in chocolates and cookies at this hour. I also didn't want the smell of fish emanating from my mouth knowing that, in just a short time, there were many hugs and kisses waiting for us at the Novotel Hotel.

Ineke and Dom had a great time posing for the cameras. Both of them standing with their right hands holding the herring above their open mouths, anticipating that special moment when that fish slithered down their throats and were fully consumed. They held themselves in that traditional pose just long enough for the cameras to memorialize the magic moment. I still gag just writing about it. But in my heart, I knew that Ineke was making Dad proud. Ok, now that Ineke was content, we could move on to the site of Opa Bruggeman's Bakery.

This was my fourth time visiting the building that was a business and a home to my mother's family. Looking at it again, it seemed so small to have accommodated both. It hasn't been a bakery for many years, but it still appears to have occupants in the living quarters above the storefront. Time for a couple more photo ops.

#1 van der Heimstraat, was our last destination before the reunion. I would not make the same mistake I did three years ago, when I went to #31 on this street, thinking it was the house I was born in. *"Why did you go there? We lived in #1 van der Heimstraat!"* I can still hear Mother saying.

The rain began to fall just as we arrived at our old home. Like the times before, we knocked at the front door to ask the occupants for permission to take pictures. Ineke, Traci, and I stood under a couple of large umbrellas, still keeping the #1 visible.

Though we packed a lot in the one hour racing from one sight to another, I can spend as much time as I want looking at the pictures that were taken that day, and enjoy the moments all over again.

"There it is, Mark. I recognize that building," I said as we approached the Novotel Hotel in Schiedam. Looking out the window of Els' car, I was able to identify several family members entering the building.

When Mark and I were in Holland the last time, we were celebrating our 35th wedding anniversary. That was just three years ago. When the van Lith relatives came out to see us back then, many of them were strangers to me and I was to them. This time was different. Now I saw them as family with my eyes and my heart.

We walked into the section of the restaurant reserved for us. There were already a couple of handfuls of middle-aged individuals with big smiles ready to greet us. Some brought old pictures to show of our shared lineage. They were great opportunities for each of us to talk about our aunts and uncles, and omas and opas. Some of my cousins were not as proficient in English as others, and were more comfortable speaking Dutch. It was a good time for Ineke, Traci, and me to speak Dutch again. With Dutch and English spoken around the room, it got a little crazy keeping up, but the three of us managed.

Coffee and tea was provided, and trays of sweets were placed on surrounding tables for all to enjoy. It added to the festive atmosphere we were all feeling.

One of the Bruggeman cousins took us aside to look at some larger photos of Mom and Dad, and Mom's siblings and spouses. Mom had passed away less than a year ago, and had been the last surviving sibling of her generation. There in birth order were two sets of images of each of the Bruggeman aunts and uncles. One set was when they were first married, and the second set was of them in their later years. It was a very touching display, and we were all grateful to see them together again like this.

More and more of the van Lith and Bruggeman families arrived. Some brought gifts for Ineke, Traci, and me. Many of the same cousins from the van Lith gathering three years ago were back again, and others were added. There was a wonderful turnout from the Bruggeman side of the family this time. We could not have been any happier with the response we received at this reunion. As always, the more the cousins arrived, the louder we got.

The rain had stopped, even before we arrived at the hotel. To diffuse the volume of all the conversations, the door to the courtyard was opened, inviting many of us outside. People began to gather in groups to get caught up with each other. Most of them had not seen each other like this since Mark and I were here last time.

Just as before, when it was apparent that everyone who intended to come to the reunion was accounted for, we were given access to the same conference room as before. With everyone together, I began by thanking them for responding to my invitation, and how much it meant to the four of us that they were here to see us again.

Most of the family had read my HAL entry on the internet and were excited that I had won. Were it not for that, this reunion would not have happened.

Ineke, Traci, and I planned ahead to share some of our family photos, and the families of Gert, Sue, and Dom too. It was a proud moment for us to show them how many more distant relatives they all have in America.

Our pictures produced lots of laughs and "oohs and awes" as we shared each of our growing families. Mark and I had only six grandkids when we did this last time. Now we had ten. My cousins don't see that many grandchildren in one family much anymore. Mark and I just keep counting our blessings, and blessings, and blessings...!

Earlier I wrote about a theory I had regarding my Dutch relatives. I postulated that we would be able to have as much fun at a gathering with simple beverages and without spirited drinks. This morning's celebration proved my hypothesis was correct. We all had a great time. The fact I was able to prove this still blows my mind.

Having said that, there was a suggestion that it was time for a spirited toast before everyone parted. Most were content to cheer with their coffee or tea, while a few decided it was time to enjoy something else to drink, something usually reserved for evening hours.

We toasted our return. We toasted each other. We toasted the fact that anyone in the group is welcome to visit us in Washington and Oregon, and that they had a bed to sleep in. We toasted our elders, and toasted a safe return. "*Tot Ziens, allemaal*! Till we see you again, everybody!

Lang zal ze leven, lang zal ze leven, lang zal ze leven in de Gloria, in de Gloria, in de Gloria. Hieperdepiep, hoera!

Long shall you live in the Gloria, Hoorah!"

After spending two wonderful hours with our cousins, it was time to say goodbye. Not sure when Mark and I will return to the Netherlands. Then again, I didn't foresee this return trip coming so soon after the last one.

We had to say goodbye to Ineke and Traci too. I love the memories we created with each other, retracing our immigration voyage. I was sure we would see them and the rest of our siblings before too many months went by. That's what we do.

Mark and I spent two more days at the home of Els before flying back to Washington State. The weather cooperated as we meandered around a couple of small towns, strolled along on the beach of the North Sea, and drove around a part of Holland we had never been to before.

Our final goodbye was in the warm embrace of our host, Els, just after she dropped us off at the airport in Amsterdam. "*Tot Ziens,* Els and Holland! Till I see you again!"

Mark and I would have other grand adventures, but not before finding out what was physically wrong with me.

Chapter 31

Houston, I Have a Problem

"It was never supposed to happen again! Now I'm just hoping to live long enough to go on our transatlantic crossing," I said to Mark.

That should remind you how well I was coping.

Something happened to me that changed my life. I was determined to understand what it was, and how to prevent this "something" from happening to me again. If what I suspected had actually occurred, and could be corroborated, I might be able to avoid this "something" from happening to others who could potentially be at risk.

Not long after returning from Holland, I began obtaining copies of my medical records of the last few years. Now that I was no longer working as a nurse, I had more time to devote to researching my health issues.

The more I surfed the internet for information about stress-induced heart attacks, the more I realized what little information there was on Takotsubo Cardiomyopathy. I tried all kinds of different word combinations to pull up other medical sites that might help me find more.

This discovery phase was not healthy for me. The quest I put myself through pulled me inside a vortex I could not escape from. The more I researched, the more upset I got. Many times it would trigger the overactive fight-or-flight syndrome, resulting in a rapid increase in my heart rate and anxiety. The symptoms caused me to worry about my heart throughout the day, stressing me out even more. The physical, emotional, and spiritual battle was taking its toll, and all I could do was take a nitroglycerin tablet, lie down to calm myself, and hang on.

It was not long before my body got to the point where this "out of control" cycle would manifest itself more frequently, and without warning. I could be sitting quietly in church and this unholy cycle would make my heart begin to race and my chest hurt like h-ll, for no apparent reason, and I would grab my little nitro.

I could be watching a chick-flick and the unwelcome cycle would invite itself to join me, and I would take my little nitro.

I could be in the middle of normal household cleaning and the dirty little cycle would mess things up for me again. Out came my little friend, nitro.

The decades of singing before hundreds, sometimes thousands of people, should have been enough experience to control my fears and anxieties. Each time I'd walk on stage, grab my microphone, and begin to sing, my pre-performance jitters would vanish. It was an energizing experience, empowering me to do my best, and have a lot of fun in the process. Unfortunately, none of it prepared me for what I was living with now.

Most people experience appropriate feelings at the proper time. Healthy people laugh when something is funny. They cry when they are hurt physically or emotionally. They run away or fight when they feel threatened. We feel loved in a warm embrace of someone who really cares about us. And for me, I feel all warm and fuzzy eating a wonderful piece of dark chocolate along with a sip of some good merlot. These responses are appropriate, and considered normal.

When something troubled me, I could always count on Mark to listen. If he was away on a business trip, I knew I could count on a best friend to fill in. I've never been one to hang on too tightly to negative thoughts. That's too stressful. Talking was my way to work through problems and release tension. Some would say that I talk too much, and they might be right. What can I say?

I did not like how I sounded when I ruminated about my health and my research. My normal coping skills were not working. Every time I spoke about my health predicament, it only caused me more problems. It was hard to control my emotions, and I no longer recognized myself.

Having already consulted with different specialists, and finding no definitive cause for these exaggerated fight-or-flight symptoms, I was getting frustrated. I just needed to buck up, and get ahold of myself. Why does the old movie *Airplane* suddenly come to mind? With the infamous line, *"You need to control yourself! Snap out of it!"*

Trying to manage these random events only made things worse. I did everything I could think of. "Don't laugh too hard or work too hard. Don't get scared and don't worry too much. Just stay calm, say your prayers, find your peace, and whatever you do, STOP THINKING ABOUT YOUR HEART!" I demanded of myself.

Instinctively, I must have known that what I was experiencing as a result of my anxiety, was panic. I did not want to admit it to myself. I thought I had the inner strength to control these attacks. But then, I never thought I would experience two Takotsubo Cardiomyopathy's either.

I am not ashamed to acknowledge that I've sought the help of a psychologist in the past. I would imagine that many second-generation survivors, like me, have needed this kind of support. I've had some very good experiences with therapy, and some not so good ones, too.

As a Christian, I found it difficult to work with a therapist who did not speak my Christian language, or believe in the authentic Healer. I needed someone who shared my values and common belief in God. That was the only way this was going to work for me this time around.

I was referred to a gentleman with a PhD in psychology. Our goal was to reduce the number and decrease the severity of my panic attacks without the use of medication. This therapist was exactly who I needed. We both felt free to share parts of our spiritual journey, which helped us to create a healing environment.

With a better understanding of the physiological effects during a panic attack, and reinforcing some relaxation techniques to help control them, my confidence returned, somewhat, and my anxiety did improve, *somewhat.* After our six visits, I was sure I could do this. Right?

Since I knew as much about my heart condition as my current cardiologist, I lost confidence under his care, and began to look elsewhere.

One early morning I awakened with a message that popped into my brain. "Get up and turn on your computer, and do an internet search using the two words "Takotsubo" and the name of my medication. This is not the usual way I wake up. I'm rather slow, and just want to stay in bed a few minutes longer. But I was instantly wide-awake and compelled to follow the impulse that woke me.

The very first site to pop up on the search was from a woman writing to a doctor at the Texas Heart Institute in Houston, Texas. She was asking a question of a cardiologist by the name of James T. Willerson MD. She asked, "I have been diagnosed with Takotsubo Cardiomyopathy. Is there any evidence that this can be caused by the prescription that I took for headaches? Thank you."

I was stunned. My jaw dropped. "I'm not alone," I said to myself. This had happened to others. I've already mentioned the man who Mark knew from work, who, after hearing about my first heart attack, told him about his wife's similar experience ten years earlier after an injection of the same medication in an ER for her a migraine headache. The doctors didn't have a name for it, but knew that her attack was a side effect of that med.

"Now we're getting somewhere!" I said to myself. I was eager for more information about what I long ago suspected. I knew what happened to me back in August of 2009! "I need to contact Dr. Willerson."

*

I introduced myself to Dr. Willerson's receptionist at the Texas Heart Institute, and told her why I was calling. I was placed on hold, and within a couple of minutes I was talking to the doctor's office RN. I explained to her how I found Dr. Willerson, what had happened to me twice, and what I thought was the initial cause. She told me that she was going to get the doctor on the phone for me.

"Oh my, I wasn't expecting to talk to the doctor right away. I just wanted to see if he could take my call when it was a more convenient time for him," I said quickly.

"Don't worry about that. He will want to take your call," his nurse replied, as if she had been instructed to do so.

He was so very king and generous with his time as I told him my story. He said that he knew what happened to me, what I probably had been experiencing now, and that my doctor had prescribed the wrong medication to treat it.

This kind and soft-spoken doctor said he was quite familiar with Takotsubo, and the medication I had been taking for my migraines. He offered to consult with my cardiologist in Richland, WA. Then he said he would be happy to take me on as his patient if I wanted to come to the Texas Heart Institute for diagnosis and treatment.

"Thank you so much for taking my call and giving me some hope. I need to know what happened. My husband and I will want to see you as soon as your schedule will allow," I told him. "Until then, I'll have my cardiologist consult with you. He can't answer many of my concerns, and obviously isn't sure how to treat me," I added.

"Hold on for a minute while I get my nurse. She will provide the information you will need, and will give you her direct number to schedule an appointment that works best for both of us. In the meantime, stop taking your beta-blocker, and have your doctor prescribe this calcium channel blocker instead. Have your doctor call me, and be sure to tell him what I said. Don't worry, we can help you. Good bye," Dr. Willerson said.

Oh my Lord! This man didn't even know me, and just spent fifteen minutes of his valuable time on the phone with me. I was so relieved. Someone had just thrown me a lifeline while I was drowning. I needed to see him. I needed his help to get my life back.

Mark was more than agreeable to fly with me to Houston to help me get some answers. He was weary of living with the uncertainty, and how it was affecting both of us. He never complained, but I knew he wanted his wife back! My appointment was scheduled for early October 2011.

I went to the internet to find out about this person I was willing to fly to Texas to meet. I was blown away by the caliber of this man's resume. He had become one of the most accomplished cardiologists in the world. In addition to his practice, he served in many capacities, as author, teacher, and head of departments, sought-after speaker, and on and on. He has achieved countless honors and awards, and has fourteen patents that are attributed to him from the discoveries he's made over 50 years of research,

No! It was not a random thought I generated that morning when I woke up. It was a gift. Dr. Willerson took my call, and now I was his patient.

On October 3, 2011, I was scheduled for an early morning appointment with Dr. Willerson MD at the Texas Heart Institute in Houston, Texas. We arrived the day before to get settled in at the Residence Inn for the next few days. We walked more than a mile to locate the Heart Institute among the maze of other well-known hospitals. In total, these buildings create a huge medical complex that goes on for blocks and blocks in all directions. Neither of us wanted to get lost before my appointment, which could have been very easy to do.

Our plan was to stay in Houston for two or three days before driving down to Galveston, Texas, to spend a couple of days just for some fun. We would return to Houston and fly home the following Saturday, October 8.

The morning of my appointment was filled with some paperwork and some tests and x-rays that had been pre-ordered. By mid-morning, the test results were available and I was called into a room.

To my surprise, a foreign intern studying under Dr. Willerson was the first person to see me. Apparently, she was my intake doctor.

Her mannerism was very abrupt. She stood right in front of me, less than arm's length from my face. She talked at me, not with me. She said she "knew what happened to me." All this was without asking me much of anything.

She *told* me I had this Takotsubo from stress. "Right, you were under a lot of stress at the time, right?" she said.

As I attempted to describe what happened and what I suspected, I was abruptly interrupted. "No, no, the medication had nothing to do with it. You were under a lot of stress, right?" she brazenly said again, this time with intimidation.

I looked over at Mark for some clue as to how I was to respond to this person. We didn't come all this way for this kind of unprofessional treatment. From the look on his face, he must have seen something in me before I recognized it myself.

I began to shiver uncontrollably, clench my teeth, feel ominous, and develop chest pains. Oh my God, this woman had just induced a big panic attack. This was not what I was expecting to happen. I just wanted to see the friendly gentleman who talked with me on the phone a few weeks before, Dr. Willerson. I did not appreciate my voice being ignored, and to be given a lecture as if I knew nothing about Takotsubo Cardiomyopathy. Are you kidding? I've spent months researching this syndrome.

With my eyes, I pleaded with Mark to protect me. Just then, the intern stepped closer and said in a loud and stern voice, "Calm down, you must calm down!"

It's really not smart to tell a patient, already trying to calm herself down to prevent a panic attack, to CALM DOWN! I tried very hard to use the relaxation techniques that my therapist taught me, with no avail. Mark told the woman to leave, and stood by my side during the 30 minutes it took for this panic attack to subside.

In the middle of this episode, Dr. Willerson came into the room. He found me in this state of panic and asked me if my chest hurt. I said, "It does now!"

The good doctor spoke softly, calming me enough to listen to him. "I am going to admit you into the hospital. It would be prudent to monitor your heart at this time. I will make sure you are well taken care of, and we will evaluate your condition and treat you accordingly. Is that agreeable to you both?"

I was embarrassed that he was meeting me for the first time in the middle of this attack. Mark mentioned the behavior of the intern on my behalf, which made me feel a bit better about myself. I did not want the doctor to conclude that I was some crazy woman seeking attention, especially when it came to my health.

"Doctor Willerson, we came a long way to see you, and if you think my wife should be admitted, then that's what we will do," Mark replied.

"I just want to get well again. My world feels like it's getting smaller and smaller with this fear I live with now. I'll do whatever you think is best while we are here," I added to what Mark just agreed to.

What a turn of events. This was not what I had anticipated. Here I go, back into a cardiac care unit for monitoring. In hindsight, I must admit, that this whole episode was probably a blessing in disguise. But, I still didn't appreciate the way the intern treated me. She did not feel like a blessing in any way.

Over the next four days, I was under the care of five different doctors, and was monitored very carefully. I had the best cardiologist and a great gastroenterologist, both of them wanting to make sure we were not missing any overlapping diagnosis to my symptoms.

On the second day of my stay, I underwent my third cardiac angiogram in two years. This test, *once again*, showed that I do not have any coronary artery disease (CAD). The cause of my chest pain and my previous heart attacks were not a result of CAD. But I already knew that.

On the third day, Dr. Willerson came to talk to us with his conclusions. His diagnosis was coronary artery vasospasm.

"What caused this condition? One day I was fine, and the next day I was in the hospital with a heart attack," I asked.

"Your first Takotsubo Cardiomyopathy was a result of the medication you took that day to prevent a migraine headache. I have seen this a number of times with the use of this medication. It can cause coronary artery vasospasms. Our research was able to convince the pharmaceutical company to add stronger warnings in their literature. In your case, like in others, sometimes otherwise healthy individuals can develop these vasospasms. That is what happened to you in August of 2011. The excitement you experienced on the day you won the cruise was enough to produce the vasospasms again." Doctor Willerson explained to us. "I must admit, this second episode was very unusual," he added.

To help prevent or control vasospasms, I was prescribed medications to strengthen my heart. "I will be out of town the rest of the week, and will be leaving you in the care of Dr. Shephard (not really his name, but I like it!). Your GI doctor has ordered a couple of procedures for tomorrow. Depending on the results, I think that you can be discharged on Friday. I want to see you back here in one year, unless you need to come back before that for any reason, and you or your doctor can call anytime," Dr. Willerson said just before leaving.

I got rather emotional and said, "Thank you so much for accepting me as your patient and helping me. My questions have all been answered. You validated my suspicions. I knew it was the medication, and it upsets me to think that what happened to me has happened to others, too. If I had known about these side effects, I would never have used it again. I didn't know what else to do after the only treatment that was working, the Botox, was denied me after two years of success," I added while wiping my tears.

Mark reached out to shake the doctor's hand and said, "Thank you, Doctor Willerson, for all your help. We'll see you in twelve months."

The following day, I underwent a couple of very uncomfortable GI tests to check for esophageal motility disorders and/or GERDS. Because both tests were negative, my gastroenterologist was sure that my pain was not GI related. I was relieved.

What he did prescribe was a mild antianxiety medication to aid in the prevention of these panic attacks. Even though we all understood what happened physiologically, the effects of mental distress were just as important to treat. The steps I had taken with therapy were not enough to stabilize the panic. Though I was stubborn about it, I agreed and was grateful.

What a week this had been! On the fifth day, I was discharged from the hospital with the results I was searching for, and we flew home the next day. I guessed Galveston would have to wait for another time.

The first cardiologist I had been seeing was no longer my doctor. We parted ways amicably soon after returning from Texas. He knew that I needed someone who had better knowledge about my condition. I was fortunate to find another doctor in the Tri-Cities with much more knowledge and experience dealing with what I was suffering with.

After my twelve-month follow-up with Dr. Willerson, I felt confident enough with the care of my local cardiologist to part ways with the man who helped me regain my life. With Dr. Willerson's help, and that of my new doctor in Richland, I am doing quite well. My anxiety and panic attacks have almost completely abated.

We spent a weekend with our daughter and her family just a few weeks after I had been prescribed a better antianxiety medication. As we were getting ready to leave, Jessica smiled at me and said, "You're not so afraid about your health anymore. You haven't mentioned your heart or any other symptoms this whole weekend. On top of that, your sense of humor has returned. Mom, you're back!" I knew my life had returned to a new normal.

"You're right, Jessie. I am back, and I feel normal again. Finally, I feel hopeful, and I am so grateful. The Good Lord answered my prayers," I said, stating the obvious.

Mark added with a subtle smile, "He answered my prayers too!!"

I looked at him and said, "I do recall something about, for better or for worse, in sickness and in health, till death..."

Mark quickly interrupted and said, "I remember. I wasn't going anywhere with what I just said. Just remember when it's my turn, and I need your patience and help." After all the hugs and kissed, we waved goodbye. The weekend was fun and not consumed with my health. Halleluiah!

Intermission

I thought it best to stop writing and begin the first of many rounds of editing. Having spent nearly three years working on this story, roughly four hundred pages under my belt, I thought it prudent to remember what I had already written.

It is a humbling experience to proofread your own work. There was a good amount of editing in the early chapters. With so many different ways to describe things and events, and more than one way to make a point, I reworked until I was satisfied. I have since learned to break things down, and not be too complicated with how I tell a story. Unfortunately, I've not learned how to do that in normal conversations. My family and friend will tell you as much.

To my delight, I did not want to stop reading. It was as if I was doing so for the first time. I cried when I was supposed to, and laughed when the author wrote something amusing. I wanted to know what happened next, and how would it all end. I still do! It felt like an out of body experience knowing that I had done the research, and I was the storyteller. Silly! I did not see that coming.

Obviously, I've been thinking a lot about my parents since I started this project. Researching and writing this story has given me a better understanding of the many dramatic events in their lives, and how their extraordinary experiences impacted my siblings and me.

Watching my children and their growing families, and feeling the aches and pains of daily life, I am reminded that more than two-thirds of my life expectancy is behind me already. Looking through the rearview mirror at my past, it's uplifting to see the many people who were there during the milestones, and the unexpected things that have contributed to my growth as a person, mentally and spiritually. It's good to reflect and examine these things.

I still feel a little embarrassed, integrating my extraordinary life events into this story. But my fingers just kept on writing. I continue to trust in the intercessions of my patron saint, St. Francis de Sales. The Good Lord introduced me to him, and I hope and pray that my words will have meaning and purpose for others as well.

Guardian Angels

I do not believe in random coincidence, luck, accidents, flukes, quirks, or any other way of saying the same thing. Rather, I believe in opportunities, guidance, faith, encounters, interventions, and a Divine plan. Good or bad, nothing happens without a purpose. Nothing! That is what I believe.

There was a plan and purpose for the protections that spared Mienus and Suze's lives a number of times. Foremost was having been saved during a most difficult period in time when those around them perished, and later from their health issues that almost went undetected.

As for me, so far I've had more than my fair share of automobile accidents, several very close calls, two heart attacks, and other extreme moments that have caused me to pause and say, "That was close!" After a while, I really started to wonder if I had a sign on my back that said, "Hit me!" Seriously, how many time can I dodge "the big one?"

*

I will always need some kind of treatments to take care of my back and neck from the multiple whiplashes I sustained. Thanks to neck injections I underwent a few years after my second accident, I was fortunate to enjoy relief for several months. Sadly, a third rear-ending at a gas station began the process of treatments all over again.

As a result of the injuries to my neck and back, my singing voice weakened in my late 40's and early 50's. Physical and Speech therapy was not effective enough in preventing the pain and stress in my throat. No amount of warm ups and singing was going to stretch out my voice box and vocal cords to their pre-injury state.

I discreetly began to pull back from singing engagements during those years, too afraid that the changes, so apparent to me, would become all too obvious to others. I didn't want people to feel sorry for me. I stopped performing before it became too obvious that, "the lady with the voice," was now just their friend who used to sing a lot.

Sometimes I wake up with the ability to sing like before, and it is a gift when that happens. It doesn't last very long, and I can't count on it. I imagine most people just figured that after 35 years of professional singing, I deserved to slow down, and they would be right, too.

*

After each accident, there came a time when the insurance company representing the "at fault" driver wanted to settle the claim. I learned the hard way the first time not to represent myself when it came to dealing directly with car insurance companies.

I received a timely phone call from an attorney one day, for some other matter. After a couple of phone exchanges, I decided to meet with this man to discuss settling my third accident.

My appointment was on May 30, 2012 at 11:00am. While driving to the attorney's office, the unthinkable happened, just blocks from his office building.

On a busy commercial street, surrounded by businesses and restaurants on both sides, my peripheral vision detected a car that was quickly accelerating from a side street. The driver was attempting to cross four lanes of traffic at once. A moment later, the car vanished from my view, causing me to question whether I actually saw what I thought I saw.

Suddenly, as if someone else was in the car, I heard a voice clearly yelling, "Move toward the center, MOVE!" At the same moment both my legs were moved toward the console and my body leaned to the right. In that action, my face turned slightly in the same direction just as the speeding car slammed into the driver's car door.

The impact propelled me to the right and up toward the roof of my car, slamming my head against the roof. The accelerating force propelled my car from the center lane clear over to the far right lane, narrowly missing another car. Everything felt as though it was occurring in slow motion. I can still visualize the extreme bowing of the window next to me just before it burst into thousands of pieces.

The pain to my head was excruciating. I began spitting out tiny fragments of glass that had entered my mouth as I was screaming during the impact. My body began to shake and I knew I needed help badly. No one on the road stopped to help me. People just drove past very slowly, but when they saw that I was still alive, they moved on.

I began to worry about my heart. I unbuckled my seat belt to reach for the phone in my purse, now covered in glass on the floor of the passenger side. I dialed 911 thinking that no one else cared enough to do that for me.

As I hung up the phone, I heard a voice. Peeking through my broken window was a kind young man in uniform who walked over to me from the Military Recruiting Center across the street.

"Are you ok? I heard the car crash from inside my building!" the serviceman asked me.

"No! I'm hurting and I am worried about my heart. Thank you for coming to me. Nobody else stopped to help me. Please stay with me, don't go!" I pleaded.

We heard the sirens in the distance heading toward us. "Are the others in the car that hit me ok," I asked the young man.

"They appear to be. Someone is talking to them right now," he replied.

I had enough time to find my nitroglycerin tablets in my purse, and place one under my tongue, just as the ambulance, police, and firefighters arrived. They did a quick assessment on me while I explained what had happened, and where I was injured. A firefighter began using a "Jaws of Life" tool to open the damaged door to extricate me.

"Stop, there's more glass spitting at me. I think I can climb over the console and you can help me out there," I shouted. After someone assessed my neck, they agreed.

I made my way to the passenger door on the other side, and grabbed my purse off of the glass-filled floor. I always keep an up-to-date medical history and certain medications in my purse for just such an occurrence. As a nurse, I recognized how difficult it can be for patients to provide complete and accurate information under normal routine circumstances. Add an emerging health crisis, and it is nearly impossible, especially if you are alone, to remember such details.

The ambulance took me to Kadlec Medical Center in Richland, WA. This time, my body's natural fight-or-flight reaction seemed to be protecting me instead of damaging my body as it had in the past. It provided a measure of pain relief as well. I thought my head was the only thing injured during the accident. Only when I calmed down enough in the emergency room, did I begin to feel the other effects of the crash.

As I was helped into a hospital gown during my intake, the nurse pointed out several areas of contusions and abrasions over the upper parts of my body. I had glass particles falling out of my shirt and hair, and other glass stuck inside my bra and waistband. I could feel my back begin to seize up from when I was slammed back into the car seat after I hit my head.

While removing my slacks, I could hear glass dropping onto the floor. That was not the only place the broken glass particles had entered.

"How in the world did I get broken glass in my underwear?" I asked rhetorically. The nurse didn't respond to my question, but did ask me if my left thigh hurt much.

"Actually, yes. I'm starting to feel more pain there now too.... Holy cow! Look at the size of that bruise on my thigh," I said, now surveying my lower extremities. "Why did I not feel that before?" I added, knowing full well the answer.

My left thigh had a huge contusion, the size of a grapefruit on the outside. I hardly remember being hit by the crushed door, my head hurt so badly.

I had given Mark's name and phone number to the nurses so he could be notified. I also gave them my son Matthew's cell number. I had someone call both of them from the ambulance, and then again after I was admitted to the ER. Messages were left both times.

More than a couple hours went by before I got a return call from Mark. Apparently, he had been in meetings all afternoon and was unaware that I had called. Matthew finally listened to his messages and quickly called his Dad to see how I was doing in the hospital. He figured his Dad must be with me by now.

Mark had just gotten into his car to come home, and was just about to listen to his messages when his phone rang. "How's Mom doing after the accident?" Matt said.

"What are you talking about, son? What accident?" Mark shot back quickly.

Matt went on to describe what he knew, based on the message that was left him on his phone. Mark finally called me to say he was on his way.

There's something special about having temporary amnesia that helps to get you through trauma. It is another way our bodies help us cope until we can deal with what has happened. It was only after Mark joined me in the ER that I began to remember more and more of the sequence of events that landed me where I was, with a range of injuries that could have been much worse.

After spending several hours at the hospital, I was discharged with instructions that included a follow up with my doctor for any further care, and a prescription for pain medications if I needed them.

I continued to find small fragments of glass in my hair and mouth even after we had returned home. One such fragment was imbedded in a tooth, and I could only get it out of my mouth by chewing it into sand, and rinse it out. I would later need a new filling for the hole it created.

I gave Mark the information the police had left me at the hospital regarding the whereabouts of our car. It was important for both of us that he located the car and take pictures of it, for obvious reasons. We both needed to see the damage.

Bummer. We had planned to keep the Acura for many years, but the car was totaled. We later found out that the impact was so hard that the entire front console was shoved a good three to four inches to the right, and the cost to repair the damages was not feasible.

Relaxing in my own bed with the help of those pain pills, I began to cry and relive the accident over and over again. Of the (now) four accidents, this one was by far the worst. I kept ruminating, "Why? Why did this have to happen again?

After a couple of days, Mark and I went to pick up a rental car to use until we bought another car. He insisted on the only large vehicle available, a suburban. He wanted to help me feel comfortable and protected.

After filling out the necessary papers, we walked around the car to check the current body condition before we drove off. I was first to notice something comical about this vehicle.

"Mark, get over here and look at the license plate!" I said. "It seems appropriate, don't you think?" I added.

It took a couple seconds before he figured it out. "Yep! It pretty much sums it up," he replied. The license plate began with the letters "Y-ME," followed by a couple of numbers.

We both found something to laugh at. How ironic to drive away in a car that shared my sentiments. "Why me, Lord? Why me?"

The months of recovery that followed were very similar to what I'd required in the past. My physical therapist, my chiropractor, and my massage therapist have gotten to know me quite well over the years. I feel like I have singlehandedly kept each of them in business with the number of times I've needed their services.

No one is exempt from experiencing difficult times. Each crisis, discomfort, pain, sorrow, disappointment, or grief I've had has taught me that nothing happens without a reason. How I reacted and what I learn from them has helped me to grow in virtue.

Each one of my difficulties has forced me to examine what's important in my life. It encourages change that I would never have undertaken on my own. One very important lesson I was allowed to learn is that I am not in control and I am not alone.

When I am weak, I know when and where to seek my strength. When I feel alone, I reach out and allow others to be with me physically. When that is not possible, I let them in spiritually, especially loved ones who I know continue to pray for me even after death.

My guardian angel is BIG! I can close my eyes and remember the incredible moments my angel was there to keep me safe. This appointed heavenly representative guards me daily, and nudges me to stay on the right path in life.

I smile now when I think about the near misses. My angel can push me out of harm's way, or shout "Move" and "Watch out!" any time. Thank you, Guardian Angel. I know you are with me all the way to the finish line!

There are many angels that have surrounded my loved ones throughout life, even if they are not aware. Thank you Lord, for all these guardians!

Lang zal ze leven in de Gloria, in de Gloria, in de Gloria!

Chapter 32

Leaving, But Not Forever

Every year Mark and I plan a seven-day vacation in March or April for some needed rest and relaxation. This year was no different. Fortunately for me, I planned well to have my T-bone car accident the month after we traveled. (*Sarcasm, right?*)

"Welcome home, Mom and Dad. How was your trip to Mexico?" Timothy asked while he placed our bags into the trunk of his car.

"We had a great time, like always. Nuevo Vallarta is perfect this time of year," I replied.

"Great! Stacey and I might be moving to China at the end of the summer," Tim announced without a prepared warning.

Mark and I glanced at each other trying to see if the other heard the same thing or not. "What are you talking about? You're kidding, right?" I immediately asked.

"Stacey and I were looking at the Washington State teacher's job site to see what other music and biology positions might already be posted for the next school year. We've both been feeling like we are ready for a change. There were a couple of postings, including a music educator's position in Shanghai, China, at a private British International School called Nord Anglia. We talked about the possibilities for a couple of days, and then Stacey said to "go for it." Timothy said with excitement in his voice.

"Seriously? You're not kidding are you! You can't pick us up at the airport after we've being gone for a week, and then blurt something like that out without any warning! Couldn't you at least have waited till we got home first?" I said playfully and with mixed emotions.

Tim said that it was not a "for sure" proposition. They were just exploring the opportunity, but he was planning to submit his application, "just to see what happens."

"Good. That should give me enough time to figure out how we are going to talk you out of this moving-to-China business!" I said.

Just days before my car accident, Tim announced that he had been plucked from a group of about 65 other applicants from around the world, and was offered the music educators position in Shanghai, China. His family would be moving sometime in early August, less than three months away.

It was time to call Stacey's mom, Teresa, and figure out how we were going to convince our kids that this was a bad idea. Of course we both knew in our minds that this was a wonderful opportunity for Tim's career, and possibly for Stacey as well. However, it was a really bad idea for our hearts.

"Ok, you two can go, but the grandkids have to stay!" both Teresa and I said in jest to the parents of our shared grandkiddo's.

This would be a plea that would go unheard. We knew we would not be able to convince them to change their minds. Our only consolation was in knowing they would be home during the summer months, and it was only a two-year teaching contract.

Before the Tim Henderson family left for overseas, we opted to have a family portrait taken of our whole family.

*

We had tried doing this for the last couple of years, but each time we arranged to have pictures taken, we got another pregnancy announcement from one or two of our children. A family portrait would be incomplete within a few months with the arrival of a new grandchild. I hate when that happens! Just kidding. My arms are big enough to hold as many grandchildren as Mark and I are blessed with. The portraits would just have to wait!

*

The youngest of the ten grandchildren, Dominicus (Nic) was already fourteen months old, and nobody had any announcements to make. Our beautiful family portrait now hangs regally on the wall designed for it in our great room.

Letting go of Timothy and his family was extremely difficult for me. At the Pasco airport, we said our goodbyes. I got lots of hugs and kisses from Paige, Chloe, and Tyson. I took one long look at the twins and their little brother, who was only nineteen months old. I knew that when we would see them the next summer, they would have changed quite a bit. No, I did not see this one coming.

Thoughts of my two grandparents waving goodbye to their five little granddaughters, gave me an even greater appreciation of the sacrifices they were asked to make when we left Holland, now more than 56 years ago. I knew that my son's little family, going off on a two-year adventure, would be coming home again. I knew they were not leaving to become Chinese citizens. I knew we would be apart for only several months at a time. I knew we could talk and see each other on the computer a couple of times each week. All this in such stark contrast to what my two Oma's and Opa's had to deal with. Goodbye was forever for three of them, and for my Opa Bruggeman, he would have to wait a very long time to see us again.

Mark and I continue to pray every evening for the safety and wellbeing of each of our children and their families. During our separation from Tim and his family, praying for the Good Lord's guidance and protection took on an even greater urgency.

Did I mention that our family portrait was complete at the time we had it taken? Well, technically it was. It's just the rest of didn't know that baby number eleven wanted to be in the picture too. Didn't see that coming either!

It Just Never Gets Old

Just a couple months after Tim and Stacey left for Shanghai, China, we got a joyful announcement and big surprise, that they were expecting another baby due in March of 2013. I'm sure I've said this before, but I'm saying it again. This just never gets old!

Mark and I have found that one of the best remedies for maintaining our physical and mental health from all the aches and pains and trails of life is by keeping up with little children full of energy, mischief, carpet pile-on's, and lots of hugs and kisses. I highly recommend this form of treatment for those who want another chance to feel saturated with innocent love again. It does wonders for the mind and body.

*

Christmas felt melancholy in 2012. I think each of our children felt the void of not having our whole family together at some point during the Christmas season. In the past, if we were not all able to be together for Christmas Eve at our home, we found a day that was close enough when we could all get together. We made it work, but not in 2012.

When there is an emptiness that needs to be filled, leave it to the Good Lord to fill it. During our Christmas celebration, Joel and Jessica announced that they were expected their third child near the end of the summer.

Throughout their pregnancies, Stacey and Jessica were always accommodating when I asked to see their growing baby bump when we talked face-to-face on the computer. I wanted to enjoy the experience of these two gestating grandchildren, like I had with the first 10.

Sadie Elaine, our darling little China doll, was born on March 26, 2013. The granddaughters now outnumbered the grandsons, six to five. Even though it was not a race of any kind, I think Mark secretly hoped that Jessica's baby would be a boy to even the score again.

When Tim and his family came home for summer break, Sadie was just ten or eleven weeks old. They went to stay with Stacey's parents for the first part of their two-month hiatus. Fortunately for Mark and me, we had just purchased a motorhome and coincidentally felt compelled to take our maiden voyage about the same time they arrived back in the States.

For about five hours, Mark had very little control of our new vehicle. It pretty much drove itself west until we got to a farm in Montesano, WA. To our great surprise, three beautiful children came running down the gravel driveway to meet us with wide open arms for the needed hugs and kisses that we were all eager to fill.

Paige and Chloe had gotten much taller and more mature. Both of them had British accents that made us chuckle. Tyson was a big boy now, full of stories to tell us about the things they had been doing in China and how he liked his pre-school.

Tim and Stacey came walking down the driveway behind the children with a bundle in her arms. Not wanting to ignore my son and his wife, I quickly said in one big breath, "Hi son. Hi Stacey. It's so good to have you home. Ok, where is she? I want to hold little Sadie."

One look at our newest granddaughter was all it took. It was love at first sight! She was made from the same mold as her three older siblings, and was such a gift to all of us. They may have left for China a family of five, but came back to visit us a family of six.

Someday, Sadie will have to frame a copy of her birth certificate and hang it on a wall in her home. It's all in Mandarin with small English subtitles below each line. She's all American though. Her parents had that taken care of immediately after receiving Sadie's original paperwork.

When it was our turn to have Tim's family with us in Pasco, our house was filled with our children and grandchildren, off and on, for over three weeks. We managed to provide enough space to bunk at the house by putting together our own campground. Between our motorhome, Matt's camping trailer, a tent, three bedrooms, and a large sofa sectional in the family room, we had just enough space. We could have sleepovers whenever we wanted.

Moving about was getting more difficult for Jessica as she neared the end of her pregnancy. Joel, Jessica, Amelia, and Dominicus managed a trip to Pasco for a three-day campout. Joel was very protective of his wife, and only agreed to come down if she promised to lay low.

A week later, on August 1, 2013, Charles William was born. Like his big brother, he was given a family name, this time from his father's side of the family. And, like his older brother who goes by a shorter name Nic, this new grandson would be called Wim. Wim was the name of my mother's favorite brother who died of tuberculosis as a child.

Wim was two days old when he came to meet his aunts, uncles, and cousins all gathered in Pasco. Tim's family would be leaving in a few days to travel back to Stacy's family before flying back to Shanghai. There was no way Jessica was going to let them go without having them meet baby Wim.

The week before flying back to China, several of us traveled down to Ineke and Lloyd's property in Silverton, Oregon, for an all-family reunion. This was the first reunion since our last big one in Pasco, just before we sold the house.

The new venue provided plenty of space for the 60-some family members coming to enjoy each other once again.

"Remember how Mom worried that we would not get together as a family after she was gone? We promised her that would never change. I hope she can see us now. I hope both Mom and Dad can see us now!" I mentioned to Ineke and Gert, as we sipped our morning coffee and tea in front of one of the many RV's encircling the field.

Gert said, "I remember, Mar. Look how special and important it is for us to get together like this. It's our turn to pass on the love of this family, and let the younger ones know just how special they are to everyone here. I especially enjoy watching how each of us embrace each other's grandchildren, like their own. And what a blessing to see the men and women our children have become. Some may have had problems along the way, but look at them now, with kids of their own."

Ineke smiled as she sat quietly in her private thoughts while knitting away on her latest project.

On the third day of the reunion, Tim's family needed to leave and head back to Stacey's family farm. As they packed up from the campout, I held on to Sadie just as long as I could. We got lots of hugs and kisses, and a few tears from Paige, Chloe, and Tyson before they headed to the car. We were all trying to be brave, none of us wanted to part. Little Tyson ran back three times to hug and hold me tight.

"Tyson, it won't be as long this time. Opa and I are going to be with you in China for over two weeks at Christmastime. That's just a few months away. And then when we say goodbye, it will only be a few more months when you will be coming home to stay! I promise, we will have so much fun when we see you again, and I will talk to you on the computer as often as Mommy and Daddy will let us. I will miss you so much, but we will be ok. Right, Tyson?" I said to him through our tears. Tyson just nodded his head up and down as I walked him to the car for the last time.

Mark and I did not stop waiving until we could no longer see their borrowed car. A couple of my sisters came to comfort me. "I can only imagine what you are going through Mar. It was hard enough for us to watch, and they aren't even our grandchildren," Sue said.

My consolation was knowing I would see them in December, just four months away. "We will be ok. Right, Tyson?" I reminded myself.

The second week in December 2013, Mark and I packed our bags and hopped on a jet for a 14-hour flight to Shanghai. Tim and his personal driver were there to meet us at the airport. We arrived in the late evening, after the children had all gone to bed. After a little snack and a glass of wine, we were all ready to go to bed as well.

The following morning around 0700, we both heard little whispers outside our bedroom door. "Mark, they're here. Get ready!" I quietly said to him.

"Mom, Dad, are you awake?" Tim whispered to us behind the door.

"Yep, we're awake now!" Mark replied. Before he could even finish his sentence, the door opened to the sound of hoots and hollers of three small children, and a nine-month-old little girl hanging on tight around her Daddy's neck, not quite sure what to make of the commotion in the room.

What a perfect greeting. Just what I had hoped for this morning. Paige, Chloe, and Tyson jumped onto the bed and began snuggling with their Opa and Oma.

"Come on Sadie, its ok! It's Oma and Opa!" the twins announced. Sadie was placed on the floor, and she crawled to the frame of the bed and stood up. Still checking us out, she slowly inched her way over to Opa's side of the bed, the braver she got.

Before too long, we had all four of these grandkids either snuggling with us, or jumping on the bed. Like I said. What a perfect greeting!

*

When Mark and I married in 1973, there was no way to imagine where we would be, and what we would be doing when we hit the anniversary milestones throughout our marriage.

Our 10 year anniversary was shared with our three small boys at the Inn at the Spanish Head on the Oregon coast, where we spent our weekend honeymoon. Our 25th (silver) wedding anniversary in Pasco was my wedding do-over, and our first group cruise. Our 30th was spent in Hawaii. Our 35th was celebrated with our trip to Rome, Mediterranean cruise, and Holland. Our 40th wedding anniversary, well, was in Shanghai, China. Never in my wildest dreams did I ever imagine that. Dare I say it again? *I did not see that one coming.*

What a journey and education Tim, Stacey, and the kids were having in this exotic and very culturally diverse land. It was a grand adventure sharing a small piece of their time in the midst of it all.

My life would have been profoundly different had my parents not crossed the Atlantic Ocean with us so many years ago. I never would have thought to cross the entire Pacific Ocean to a place so unlike any other I have been, were it not for having children blessed with a similar spirit of adventure as their Opa and their Mom had.

At this new stage of our lives, what other leaps of faith will my family encourage Mark and me to take that will stretch us to learn and grow? Hmm? I will have to explore that, after I finish this leap of faith first, and publish this book.

2014-2016

I'm sure my family and friends got tired of hearing me say, "I'm almost done with the book!" They may have stopped believing that there really was a book. Maybe I've been a little nervous to let go of something that I have held on to so tightly and for so long.

Most of the memoir was written over the last three years. I've missed many self-imposed deadlines, but there was always a good reason. I was still busy with family, purchasing and managing my rental pool of homes, staying as healthy as I could, dealing with an unexpected health crisis Mark suffered, nurturing new friendships, and spending more time finding out what God wants for me.

I spend time praying for my family and friends, and for the future of my family's adopted country, the United States of America. This is still the best country in the world to live in true freedom! I hope and pray it continues for generations to follow.

*

My siblings and my children will each get a copy of everything I have written. If these many pages are just for them, it was all worth it. If there is a wider audience, I will be honored for them to read it too.

Simply put, "Long Shall You Live," is a testament to the love and sacrifices made by Mienus and Suze on behalf of all of us. The dark and dangerous years they survived were made possible for a greater purpose, and were guided by the hand of God's saving grace for His glory. There is no room for any of us to feel survivor's guilt, but only a survivor's peace and joy.

Important Dates:

- April 13, 1945, Liberation of Buchenwald causes General Patton to witness the atrocities

- April 13, 1956, The Mienus and Suze van Lith family land in the United States of America.

- April 13, 1966, Dominicus Marinus van Lith Jr. is born into the family. The Mienus van Lith name will follow another generation, and another.

- April 13, 2011, Marja Henderson wins the HAL contest and suffers a second heart attack, 55 years to the day after arriving in New York City as a child.

Endings

How do I end a story that keeps on living, with so much more that could be said on so many different levels? The threads within this book have weaved into a story quite different from what I had originally envisioned. How do I end this?

Silly me! Even this had to be given to me. It arrived in a dream one morning. I was sure of the message and the messenger. There are two short endings. You are free to close the book after the first ending if you want, but I hope you are open to the second ending too.

Long shall you live, in Peace!

Marja (van Lith) Henderson

Dear Dad and Mom,

Mark and I went on three cruises in the last twelve months. We're starting to live like you did during your early retirement years. Last summer, I finally got Mark to go to Alaska with me and it was one of our favorite cruises. Alaska was even more beautiful than I remembered it, when your five daughters got you back into cruising after Papa died. Our favorite excursion was a trip in a floatplane that took us though the mountains and into some beautiful fjords where we landed on the water and looked at all the beauty around us. It was spectacular. We had a sobering moment two weeks later though, when nine passengers on the exact same ship, same itinerary, and very same excursion crashed into a mountain, killing everyone on board. I was pretty pensive that day, just thinking that what had happened to those people could have happened to us. I wrote about my guardian angel in this memoir. This felt like one of those moments of protection again.

In early December of 2015, we went on another warm weather cruise back to the Caribbean. The first half was great, but then I slipped on a wet deck and fell on my face and broke my nose and smashed my lips. It was not pretty. You should have seen the size of my black eye. It went half way down the left side of my face, and the other eye wasn't much better. Very impressive. Oh, and my upper lip, let's just say I looked like a duck! Thank God for make-up. Seriously, thank Him!

Then, in May 2016, Mark and I flew back to Rome, stayed at the Maryknoll Mission again for three nights, went to the Vatican twice, and had an audience with Pope Francis. It was an intimate encounter, just me, Mark, and about 12,000 other pilgrims from around the world. That was meant to be funny.

Then we boarded the *MS Oosterdam* and spent twelve days in the Western Mediterranean. It was awesome. Now, having cruised the Eastern and Western Mediterranean, I can check them off my bucket list. Oh, Dad, you don't know about a bucket list. It's from a movie by the same title that came out after you passed away. It's a list of things you want to try and do before you, how shall I say, "Kick the bucket!" Another attempt at humor, but you get it. I can check Africa off the list now too. We spent a few hours in Spanish Morocco, on the continent of Africa during this trip. Now I can check off having been to: North America, Asia, Europe, and Africa. What does that leave me? Let's see, Antarctica, South America, and Australia. I've still got time!

Now you are both caught up with what's been going on in my life. You don't have to write back though, I know that there is no possible way for you to describe what you are experiencing right now, and I'm not ready for it yet. I still need to wait longer before I hope to share it with you both.

I already know that you no longer have *faith,* because you don't need it, nor *hope,* because you are living it. You have nothing left but *love,* to embrace it, because that is all there is left. Your wait is over.

We miss you Dad and Mom. You are never far from any of your children, and now the next generation will get to know you in a much more intimate way when they read this book.

I pray that I have told your story with as much accuracy as I possibly could. You are remembered with love and pride by your descendants. Now it will be up to the younger generation to "Never forget this! Never again!" And God willing, I have hope that your words may still have an impact on the lives of whoever else might read this.

I hope you like the title of the book. Who knew that such a simple song would have such an important message to share? Right? This has been one of the most extraordinary journeys of my life. What a privilege.

Lang zal ze leven, lang zal ze leven, lang zal ze leven in de Gloria, in de Gloria, in de Gloria. Hieperdepiep, hoera!

Second Ending

Dear God,

Here we are, Lord. It feels right that we should spend these three hours together again. It's Good Friday today, but it feels very different from the one we shared on April 22, 2011. I can't believe that it's been nearly five years since you answered my prayer in such a profound way. You gave me hope, and a new direction. You provided me with a new patron saint, St. Francis de Sales to guide me. Later that same year, after blessing me with such a wonderful return to Holland, you healed me from my emotional turmoil and put me on the path of physical healing. I love what you have done. I was reduced to clay, and you, the potter, remolded me into a better person.

Five years was a long time to wait for this memoir to be finished. I felt bad when each of my self-imposed deadlines slipped away. "I should have been done by now," so I thought. What was I worried about? What was I thinking? You never put me on a timeline. On the contrary. You gave me plenty of time.

You told me to "write what you know." Writing helped me to see how you loved and protected Dad and Mom. You helped me recognize that same love and protection you've always had for me too. Every generation needs to experience that love, and embrace it through everything good that life brings, and especially hold tight to it through the trials that causes us to question it. I hope you allow this story to prevent us from making the same mistakes that were made in the past. Help us to seek peace in your love.

This was never about what I wanted to say. I thought I knew what my call was about. I was only partially right. The story about Mienus and Suze needed to be told. They were too humble to write it themselves. Then you guided my hands to incorporate some of my extraordinary life experiences. I began to see the threads in the story weaving an even greater meaning behind "Long Shall You Live." It's not only about how long we live, but *that* we lived, *how* we lived, and *what* or more accurately *who* we are living for.

Jesus, what does an ordinary person from Pasco, Washington have to say that might be important to anyone else? Help me to be satisfied even if just one person recognizes themselves as a second generation survivor, and finds some peace and understanding. If just one other person who has experienced horrible trauma, similar to that of Mienus and Suze, choose Option C. If just one person is moved to explore and write about their roots, I'd be honored. If just one person is grieving a sick or elderly parent, I hope they don't feel so alone. If sharing my health crisis prevents just one other person from a similar experience, that would be awesome.

And just for fun, I hope that someone who has never cruised before, after reading this book, decides to have some fun. Bon voyage! I'm always ready to go again.

Having held onto this part of my life for so long, I am almost afraid to let go. I don't want to leave anything out that you wanted me to include. I trust you Lord to take my gift, and use it for your greater glory.

This is the last written page of "Long Shall You Live." I love you Lord.

Your humble daughter,

Marja

The End?

To meet the family and see more pictures from the story, visit
www.longshallyoulive. com

Mother's Memorial 2010

Marja meets Joke on the cruise

Blarney Sisters!

Return to Holland

Bruggeman Bakery

Vlaardingen Courthouse

Cousin Reunion 2011

Geuzen   Memorial

Christmas 2016

Citations

Campert, Jan. Translated by Marja Henderson. *Het lied de Achttien Dodden*. 1943. Vlaardingen, Netherlands. Poem.

Cochrun, Anne. *After all these years*. By Jim Brickman. S.n., 2009, Song.

FactMonster.com. "The Statue of Liberty Poem." Homework Help, Dictionary, Encyclopedia, and Online Almanac. Accessed June 21, 2017. https://www.factmonster.com/us/speeches-documents/statue-liberty-poem.

Goossens, Reuben. "The Three Dutch "Victory" Ships." SS Zuiderkruis, Groote Beer, Waterman. Accessed June 21, 2017. http://www.ssmaritime.com/DutchVictoryTrio-1.htm.

History.com. "The Holocaust." History.com. 2009. Accessed June 21, 2017. http://www.history.com/topics/world-war-ii/the-holocaust.

Houghton Mifflin Harcourt Publishing. "The American Heritage Dictionary entry: holocaust." American Heritage Dictionary Entry: holocaust. Accessed June 21, 2017. https://ahdictionary.com/word/search.html?q=holocaust&submit.x=0&submit.y=0.

Karnaat, Klaas, Dr. "The Shock of the Unknown—Vlaardingen during the crisis occupation and liberation 1936-1947." Translated by Gert Helvey and Marja Henderson. Nieuwe Uitgevers BV / European Library.

Kluger, Jeffrey. "Genetic Scars of the Holocaust: Children Suffer Too." Time. September 09, 2010. Accessed June 26, 2017. http://content.time.com/time/health/article/0,8599,2016824,00.html.

Merriam-Webster.com. "Emigrate." Accessed June 21, 2017. https://www.merriam-webster.com/dictionary/emigrate.

Merriam-Webster.com. "Holocaust." Accessed June 21, 2017. https://www.merriam-webster.com/dictionary/holocaust.

Murrow, Edward R. "Buchenwald: Report from Edward R. Murrow." April 16, 1945. Accessed June 21, 2017. http://www.jewishvirtuallibrary.org/report-from-edward-r-murrow-on-buchenwald.

Niemöller, Martin. "First They Came." Holocaust Memorial Day Trust. Accessed June 21, 2017. http://hmd.org.uk/resources/poetry/first-they-came-pastor-martin-niemoller.

Paape, Harry. De Geuzen. S.l.: "Vereeniging ter bevordering des belangen des Boekhandels," 1965.

Rodriguez, Tori. "Descendants of Holocaust Survivors Have Altered Stress Hormones." Scientific American. Accessed June 26, 2017. https://www.scientificamerican.com/article/descendants-of-holocaust-survivors-have-altered-stress-hormones/.

Schlebaum, Pieter. "Geuzen Resistance." Go2War2.nl - Geuzen Resistance. April 25, 2013. Accessed June 21, 2017. http://www.go2war2.nl/artikel/2899/Geuzen-Resistance.htm?page=2.

Schouten, Hugo. Hugo's Groote Beer page. Accessed June 21, 2017. http://members.ozemail.com.au/~dutch/beer.html.

Song of Buchenwald. Translated by Marja Henderson. "Buchenwald-Lied". Accessed June 21, 2017. http://www.almissa.com/pave_matulic/himnabuchenwalda_.htm.

The Free Dictionary. "Freedom." Accessed June 22, 2017. http://www.thefreedictionary.com/freedom.

Wikipedia. "Ellis Island." June 17, 2017. Accessed June 21, 2017. https://en.wikipedia.org/wiki/Ellis_Island.

Wikipedia. "Grand Central Terminal." June 21, 2017. Accessed June 22, 2017. https://en.wikipedia.org/wiki/Grand_Central_Terminal.

YourDictionary.com. "Emigrate." Accessed June 22, 2017. http://www.yourdictionary.com/emigrate.